Transformational Approaches to Systolic Design

PARALLEL AND DISTRIBUTED COMPUTING SERIES

Series editors: Chris Jesshope, University of Surrey,
Guildford,
UK
Sartaj Sahni, University of Florida
Gainesville,
USA

Parallel and distributed computing has matured over the last two decades, developing from a rather specialized field concerning only a few manufacturers and users, to one in which even the bedrock of the computer industry, the silicon manufacturers, have been developing products to support it. During this period the emphasis has moved away from the pipelined vector computer to massively parallel MIMD computers using powerful microprocessors which themselves adopt the same pipeline techniques as the former supercomputers. Be assured though that this area of computing will not remain static. As always the development of software systems is less mature than that of the underlying hardware. Also the development of networks and communications will aid the convergence of the parallel and distributed computing communities. The goal of this series therefore is to focus the past and future development of this area of computing by publishing a range of books which cover the mature work as course texts and the developing areas as advanced or research texts. The series will cover all aspects of this area including, but not limited to, the enabling technologies, architecture, software systems, applications and formal methods.

1. Parallel Lisp Systems
   C.K. Yuen, with contributions from M.D. Feng, W.F. Wong and J.J. Yee
2. Transformational Approaches to Systolic Design
   Edited by G.M. Megson

Transformational Approaches to Systolic Design

Edited by G.M. Megson

CHAPMAN & HALL

London · Glasgow · New York · Tokyo · Melbourne · Madras

Published by Chapman & Hall, 2–6 Boundary Row, London SE1 8HN, UK

Chapman & Hall, 2–6 Boundary Row, London SE1 8HN, UK

Blackie Academic & Professional, Wester Cleddens Road, Bishopbriggs, Glasgow G64 2NZ, UK

Chapman & Hall Inc., One Penn Plaza, 41st Floor, New York NY 10119, USA

Chapman & Hall Japan, Thomson Publishing Japan, Hirakawacho Nemoto Building, 6F, 1-7-11 Hirakawa-cho, Chiyoda-ku, Tokyo 102, Japan

Chapman & Hall Australia, Thomas Nelson Australia, 102 Dodds Street, South Melbourne, Victoria 3205, Australia

Chapman & Hall India, R. Seshadri, 32 Second Main Road, CIT East, Madras 600 035, India

First edition 1994

© 1994 G.M. Megson

Commissioned by Technical Communications (Publishing) Ltd

Printed in Great Britain by Richard Clays Ltd, St Ives PLC, Bungay, Suffolk

ISBN 0 412 44830 0

Contents

List of Contributors   ix

Preface   xiii

Chapter 1: Systematic synthesis of processor arrays from uniform
recurrence equations   1
K. N. Ganapathy and B. W. Wah
1.1   Introduction   1
1.2   Parameter method: special case   4
1.3   General parameter method   15
1.4   Final remarks   32
     Acknowledgements   33
     References   33

Chapter 2: Topological transformation of systolic systems   34
K. Culik II and S. Yu
2.1   Introduction   34
2.2   Computation diagrams and network algorithms   38
2.3   Systolic networks and systolic conversion   42
2.4   Simulation between computation networks   46
2.5   Applications   47
     References   51
     Bibliography   52

Chapter 3: Processor-time minimal systolic arrays   53
P. R. Cappello
3.1   Introduction   53
3.2   A processor-time-minimal systolic array for a 2D mesh   57
3.3   A processor-time-minimal systolic array for a 3D mesh   58
3.4   Extant work   72
3.5   Conclusion   72
     References   73
     Bibliography   75

Chapter 4: Systematic pipelining of processor arrays   77
      W. Luk
4.1   Introduction   77
4.2   Notation   77
4.3   Pipelining strategies   82
4.4   Examples   90
4.5   Concluding remarks   95
      Acknowledgements   97
      References   97

Chapter 5: Clocks, retimings and transformations of synchronous
      concurrent algorithms   99
      K. M. Hobley and J. V. Tucker
5.1   Introduction   99
5.2   Clocks and retimings   101
5.3   Synchronous concurrent algorithms and their relation
      to hardware design   115
5.4   Classification of non-unit delays   121
5.5   Synchronous concurrent algorithms with local clocks   124
      Acknowledgements   130
      References   131

Chapter 6: Array compiler design for VLSI/WSI systems   133
      J. S. N. Jean and S. Y. Kung
6.1   Introduction   133
6.2   Basic techniques in array compilers   136
6.3   An implementation example: VACS   145
6.4   Future extensions of VACS   153
6.5   Conclusion   156
      Acknowledgements   156
      References   156

Chapter 7: DECOMP – A program for mapping DSP algorithms
      onto systolic arrays   159
      U. Vehlies
7.1   Introduction   159
7.2   Decomposing algorithms into building blocks   161
7.3   The DECOMP compiler and its language   164
7.4   The internal data structure   167
7.5   Projecting DGs onto SFGs   168
7.6   Adaptation of the input data sequences   170
7.7   Extraction of building blocks and netlists   171
7.8   Implementation notes and results   173
7.9   Conclusion   176

Acknowledgement   176
References   177

Chapter 8: Adapting a sequential algorithm for a systolic design   179
C. Lengauer and J. Xue
8.1   Introduction   179
8.2   The method   180
8.3   The application   182
8.4   The specification   183
8.5   The source program   184
8.6   Towards a systolic implementation   185
8.7   Adaptation of the source program   187
8.8   Independence   195
8.9   The systolic array   196
8.10   Conclusions   199
Acknowledgements   201
References   201

Chapter 9: Systolic algorithm design environments (SADEs)   205
G. M. Megson and D. Comish
9.1   Introduction   205
9.2   Basic concepts   206
9.3   SADE and DTAGS   209
9.4   Examples   218
9.5   Design principles   233
9.6   Conclusions   238
Acknowledgement   239
References   239

Chapter 10: From architecture to algorithm – a formal approach   242
N. Ling and M. A. Bayoumi
10.1   Introduction   242
10.2   Formal approaches to systolic design: related work   244
10.3   Systolic temporal arithmetic (STA): a formalism for systolic
       design   246
10.4   Specification of systolic design: a formal approach   250
10.5   Verification of systolic design: a formal approach   255
10.6   VSTA: a Prolog-based formal verifier for systolic design   262
10.7   Correctness of a 2D systolic design: a formal approach   265
10.8   Correctness of a triangular systolic design: a formal approach 267
10.9   Correctness of a bidirectional systolic design: a formal
       approach   268
10.10 Conclusion   270
Acknowledgements   271

Appendix 10.A Syntax of STA   271
Appendix 10.B A brief presentation of the semantics of STA 274
Appendix 10.C Specification of matrix-matrix multiplication
                     systolic array input to VSTA   277
Appendix 10.D VSTA proof output for matrix-matrix
                     multiplication systolic array   281
Appendix 10.E Formal specification and verification of LU
                     decomposition systolic array   284
References   291

Epilogue   295

Index   297

List of contributors

M. A. Bayoumi
Center for Advanced Computer Studies
University of Southwestern Louisiana
Lafayette
LA 70504
USA

P. R. Cappello
Department Computer Science
University of California
Santa Barbara
CA 93106
USA

D. Comish
Computing Laboratory
University of Newcastle-upon-Tyne
Claremont Tower, Claremont Rd
Newcastle-upon-Tyne
NE1 7RU
UK

K. Culik II
Department of Computer Science
University of South Carolina
Columbia
SC 29208
USA

K. N. Ganapathy
Center for Reliable and High Performance Computing
Coordinated Science Laboratory
MC228 1101 W. Springfield Avenue
Urbana, Illinois
USA

K. M. Hobley
Programming Research Group
Oxford University Computing Laboratory
Oxford
OX1 3QD
UK

J. S. N. Jean
Department of Computer Science and Engineering
Wright State University
Dayton
Ohio 45435
USA

S. Y. Kung
Department of Electrical Engineering
Princeton University
Princeton
NJ 08544
USA

C. Lengauer
Laboratory for Foundations of Computer Science
Department of Computer Science
University of Edinburgh
Edinburgh EH9 3SZ
UK

N. Ling
Computer Engineering Department
Santa Clara University
Santa Clara
CA 95053
USA

W. Luk
Programming Research Group,
Oxford University Computing Laboratory
11 Keble Road
Oxford
OX1 3QD
UK

G. M. Megson
Computing Laboratory
University of Newcastle-upon-Tyne
Claremont Tower, Claremont Rd
Newcastle-upon-Tyne
NE1 7RU
UK

J. V. Tucker
Department of Mathematics and Computer Science
University College of Swansea
Swansea
SA2 8PP
UK

U. Vehlies
Laboratorium für Informationtechnologie
University of Hannover
Schneiderberg 32
3000 Hannover 1
Germany

B. W. Wah
Center for Reliable and High Performance Computing
Coordinated Science Laboratory
MC228 1101 W. Springfield Avenue
Urbana, Illinois
USA

J. Xue
Laboratory for Foundations of Computer Science
Department of Computer Science
University of Edinburgh
Edinburgh EH9 3SZ
UK

S. Yu
Department of Computer Science
University of Western Ontario
London
Ontario
Canada
N6A 5B7

Preface

In the last decade the rapid development of VLSI computing techniques
has had a significant impact on the development of novel computer
architectures. One class of architectures, the so-called systolic arrays, have
gained popularity because of their ability to exploit massive parallelism
and pipelining to produce high performance. Informally a systolic system
can be envisaged as an array of synchronized processors (or cells) which
process data in parallel by passing it from cell to cell in a regular rhythmic
pattern. Systolic arrays have been designed for a wide variety of problems
from signal processing, numerical problems, pattern recognition, database
and dictionary machines, graph algorithms and automata to name a few.
With the evolution of synthesis techniques to systematically derive
alternative designs the systolic approach has developed into an established
design paradigm.

In the systolic paradigm every algorithm requires a specialized systolic
design in which communication data streams, cell definitions, and input-
output are customized. Consequently the terms *algorithm* and *array* are
often synonymous and designs are often referred to as algorithmically
specialized. Where high throughput and real-time performance is required
for an algorithm such devices have been shown to be both fast and cost
effective. The early arrays were designed using the 'seat-of-the-pants'
method, an *ad hoc* process where a designer sits down with a pen and a
piece of paper and tries various draft data flows until one that works is
found. This early approach was criticized as a 'black art' and it was clear
that if systolic design was to develop new more systematic methods based
on an underlying mathematical theory of design were required. Since
approximately 1984 there has been a concerted movement towards such a
theoretical framework based on dependence manipulation and the association of geometry with computation through the mapping of loop programs
and recurrences into lattice space. These important developments have
utilized concepts from source to source program transformation methods,
signal flow graphs in control engineering, and the formulation of loop
computations as uniform, affine, and more recently linear recurrence
equations. They have been shown to be effective for a wide class of
algorithms including many important applications. In particular the
systematic re-timing of data dependency graphs to remove broadcasting
and non-local connections occupies a place of particular importance. The
theoretical framework has also allowed considerable progress in extending
the range of problems considered. Much more complicated 'hybrid'
designs are now possible which rely on more sophisticated cells than first

envisaged in the original 'pure' concepts of the systolic model. The idea of 'soft' systolic or programmable algorithms which describe the abstract model of computation and are mapped onto existing parallel architectures with restricted topologies are also gaining importance.

Currently considerable effort is being expended in the direction of computer aided design (CAD) tools and systolic compilers to support synthesis procedures. It is hoped that such tools will make the acceptance and utilization of systolic techniques more widespread than at present. The articles in this text provide an overview of current directions in systolic algorithm design using transformational synthesis methods. For simplicity the contributions are arranged into three loose categories which can be listed as follows. Chapters 1–3 explore the theoretical framework of systolic design methods and their extension at the level of data dependency manipulation. Chapters 4 and 5 concentrate on re-timing methods at the array and cell level, while Chapters 6–10 address the issue of compiler and CAD tools to support the design process. The text is aimed primarily at senior undergraduates and junior postgraduates of computing science and computer engineering. Although it can be used as a starting place for more accomplished researchers.

1

Systematic Synthesis of Processor Arrays from Uniform Recurrence Equations

Kumar N. Ganapathy and Benjamin W. Wah

1.1 Introduction

The rapid growth of technology in the last decade has had a great impact on the evolution of computer architectures. High performance specialized computer systems, called systolic arrays, are used to meet application-specific requirements. Systolic arrays have been recognized as excellent candidates for high performance parallel computing (Kung, 1982). The fundamental concept behind a systolic architecture is that the Von-Neumann bottleneck is greatly alleviated by repeated use of fetched data items in a physically distributed array of processing elements. The flow of data through the array at clock beat is rhythmic and regular, like the pumping of a heart and hence the name systolic. The regularity of the arrays lead to cheap and dense VLSI implementations, which implies high-performance and low overhead cost. Systolic arrays fit naturally into the concept of a hardware library (Heller, 1985), where functional units are in relation to the host computer as subroutines from a software library are to a production code.

Initial designs of systolic arrays were *ad hoc* and relied heavily on designer's skill and intuition. Since every algorithm needs a specialized systolic design customized to its communication patterns, a systematic technique for generating systolic arrays from the algorithm description is necessary. Hence, a great deal of effort has been devoted by numerous researchers to generate the systolic arrays in a systematic fashion. An overview of the different methods can be found in (Fortes *et al.*, 1988).

1.1.1 Algorithm representation: recurrences

In mapping algorithms to processor arrays, the representation of the algorithm is often in the form of a recurrence equation. Recurrences have long been used to express a large body of computations (Karp *et al.*, 1967;

Rajopadhye, 1986). Informally, a recurrence equation depicts the dependencies between points in the domain over which it is evaluated. Mathematically, a recurrence equation over an N-dimensional domain D is defined as an equation of the form,

$$Z(p) = \phi [Z(q_1), Z(q_2), \ldots, Z(q_m)] + \psi(p) \qquad (1.1)$$

where p, $q_i \in D$, for $i = 1, \ldots, m$, ϕ is a single-valued function strictly dependent on each of its arguments, and ψ represents the input. Based on the nature of the dependencies, recurrences can be classified as uniform, linear or nonlinear.

A recurrence equation is called a uniform recurrence equation if $q_i = p + d_i$, for $i = 1, \ldots, m$, where d_i are constant N-dimensional vectors independent of p or q. Matrix multiplication of two matrices, A and B, is an example of uniform recurrence and is represented as,

$$C(i, j, k) = C(i, j, k-1) + A(i, k).B(k, j) \qquad (1.2)$$

Here, $p = (i, j, k)$, $q_1 = (i, j, k-1)$, $d_1 = (0, 0, -1)$.

A recurrence equation is said to be linear if $q_i = A_i\, p + b_i$, where A_i is a constant $N \times N$ matrix and b_i is a constant N-dimensional vector. Finding the transitive closure of a matrix C is example of a linear recurrence equation and is stated as,

$$C(i, j, k) = C(i, j, k-1) + C(i, k, k-1) \times C(k, j, k-1) \qquad (1.3)$$

where $+$ is boolean OR operation; $\times$ is boolean AND operation. In the above recurrence,

$$q_1 = [i\ \ j\ \ k-1] = \begin{bmatrix} 1 & 0 & 0 \\ 0 & 1 & 0 \\ 0 & 0 & 1 \end{bmatrix} \begin{bmatrix} i \\ j \\ k \end{bmatrix} + \begin{bmatrix} 0 \\ 0 \\ -1 \end{bmatrix} \qquad (1.4)$$

$$q_2 = [i\ \ k\ \ k-1] = \begin{bmatrix} 1 & 0 & 0 \\ 0 & 0 & 1 \\ 0 & 0 & 1 \end{bmatrix} \begin{bmatrix} i \\ j \\ k \end{bmatrix} + \begin{bmatrix} 0 \\ 0 \\ -1 \end{bmatrix} \qquad (1.5)$$

$$q_3 = [k\ j\ k-1] = \begin{bmatrix} 0 & 0 & 1 \\ 0 & 1 & 0 \\ 0 & 0 & 1 \end{bmatrix} \begin{bmatrix} i \\ j \\ k \end{bmatrix} + \begin{bmatrix} 0 \\ 0 \\ -1 \end{bmatrix} \qquad (1.6)$$

A recurrence equation is said to be nonlinear if $q_i = \chi(p)$ for some nonlinear function χ. The formulation of a knapsack problem (Karp and Held, 1967) is an example of a nonlinear recurrence equation.

$$f(0, 0) = 0 \qquad (1.7)$$

$$f(k, w) = \min_{j \in \{j_1\}} \{f(j, w - a_k)\} \qquad (1.8)$$

where $j_1 = (j : j < k)$ and $(j, w - a_k)$ corresponds to an equivalence class.

1.1.2 Systematic methods

Most of the methods for synthesizing systolic structures consider only a system of uniform recurrence equations. The work done by Moldovan and Fortes (Moldovan and Fortes, 1986; Moldovan, 1982) laid the foundation for a number systematic methods of array synthesis from uniform recurrences.

Dependency method
In the method due to Moldovan and Fortes, called in this chapter the dependency method, the algorithm (A) is represented as a 5-tuple (J^n, C, D, X, Y). J^n is a finite n-dimensional index set of A, C is the set of triples which represent the set of computations performed, D is the set of dependencies, X is the set of input variables and Y is the set of output variables. A feasible design is obtained by a linear transformation, represented as an $n \times n$ matrix T ($\in Z^{n \times n}$), of the index space. Thus,

$$T = [\pi S]^t \qquad (1.9)$$

where π is $1 \times n$ schedule vector and S is the processor allocation matrix. For any index point $\hat{j}$, S_j denotes the processor at which the index point executes and π_j is the time of execution at that processor. Constraints are imposed on matrix T to ensure valid execution of the algorithm.

The design of a systolic array is then equivalent to determining the N^2 parameters of the transformation matrix, T. This is an integer programming problem in N^2 variables and solution methods are of exponential complexity. Hence, the allocation matrix S is chosen and the schedule π which minimizes the total execution time for that choice of S is found. The resulting designs are therefore 'optimal' up to the choice of S.

In case of uniform recurrences, the dependencies are homogeneous, in the sense that the collection of dependence vectors emanating from each point are translates of one another. This means that the dependence status at one point is the same as any other in the domain (denoted by D). Therefore, once a transformation matrix T is chosen, the time between execution of points $\hat{j}_1$ and $\hat{j}_2$ where $\hat{j}_1 = \hat{j}_2 + d$ is equal to $\pi.d$ which is a constant independent of $\hat{j}_1$ or $\hat{j}_2$. Thus the computation would be periodic along the dependence direction d, which is a chain of index points $\hat{j}_1, \hat{j}_2,$ $\ldots, \hat{j}_k$, where $\hat{j}_{i+1} = \hat{j}_i + d$. Similarly, the distance in the processor space between the execution locations of points $\hat{j}_1$ and $\hat{j}_2$ is a constant equal to $S.d$. Therefore, for uniform recurrences, the coefficients of matrix T are chosen to have a periodic execution along any dependence direction. This indicates that the search space for determining T can be restricted to those that yield periodic execution profiles. This intuition is succinctly embodied in the parameter method (see below) to devise an efficient strategy that systematically yields optimal systolic designs.

In this chapter, a parameter-based approach, called the **parameter method**, to synthesize systolic structures for uniform recurrences is presented. In the parameter method (Li and Wah, 1985) the operation of the target systolic array is represented by a minimal set of parameters. These parameters capture exactly the function of the systolic array which executes the uniform recurrence. This is in contrast to the dependency method which in principle can also be applied to non-uniform recurrences. The number of parameters are often smaller than N^2 (the number of elements in the T matrix). The design objectives like the execution time or the number of processors in the array, can be easily represented in terms of the parameters. The optimal target array can then be found by a systematic enumeration over a polynomial search space.

The organization of the chapter is broadly as follows. The next section describes a special (simpler) case of the parameter method for generating 2-dimensional arrays from 3-dimensional recurrences. Section 1.3 presents a generalization of the simple parameter scheme and discusses the issues involved in searching for the optimal design. Examples are provided in both sections 1.2 and 1.3 to illustrate the techniques described. The final section concludes with remarks on future work possible.

1.2 Parameter method: special case

In this section, a simpler case of the parameter method, proposed originally by Li and Wah (1985), is described to bring out the ideas clearly.

The structure of the uniform recurrence considered, for the computation of a 2-dimensional output Z from 2-dimensional inputs X and Y, is

$$Z^k_{i,j} = \phi[Z^{k-\delta}_{i,j}, x_{i,k}, y_{k,j}] \qquad (1.10)$$

where ϕ is a single valued function (to be executed in each processing element or PE). The recurrence is termed forward if $\delta = 1$ and backward if $\delta = -1$. $x_{i,k}$ and $y_{k,j}$ are linear functions (called **subscript access functions** or **indexing functions**) which define the indices of 2-dimensional inputs X and Y in the k step or iteration of the recurrence. In the following, the coefficients of i, j, k in $x_{i,k}$ and $y_{k,j}$ are assumed to be 1 or -1. The case of the coefficients greater than one is given later. Linear indexing functions such as $x_{i,k}$ can be represented by constant coefficient matrices. For example if i_1, i_2 are the indices of X then $x_{i,k}$ could be given by the matrix in the following equation.

$$\begin{bmatrix} i_1 \\ i_2 \end{bmatrix} = \begin{bmatrix} 1 & 0 & 1 \\ 1 & 0 & -1 \end{bmatrix} \begin{bmatrix} i \\ j \\ k \end{bmatrix} \qquad (1.11)$$

Another form of recurrence considered is a 2-dimensional recurrence computing a 1-dimensional output from 1-dimensional inputs X and a, given as

$$Z_i^k = \phi[y_i^{k-1}, x_{i,k}, a_k] \tag{1.12}$$

Most of the description in this section will be in reference to the 3-dimensional recurrence in (1.10). The case of 2-dimensional recurrence is almost similar to the 3-dimensional case.

The goal of the parameter method is to generate a 2-dimensional (resp. 1-D) systolic array to solve problems represented as 3-dimensional (resp. 2-D) recurrences. In order to see the significance of the particular forms of recurrence chosen above, a number of examples of the same general form are presented below.

1.2.1 Examples

1. **FIR filtering** can be considered as a matrix-vector multiplication of an upper-triangular Toeplitz band matrix of bandwidth m with a vector of size n.

$$y_i^0 = 0 \qquad\qquad 1 \leqslant i \leqslant n$$
$$y_i^k = y_i^k + a_k x_{i+k-1}, \quad 1 \leqslant i \leqslant n, 1 \leqslant k \leqslant m \tag{1.13}$$
$$x_j = 0 \text{ for } j > n$$

2. **Discrete Fourier transform** (DFT) is a matrix-vector multiplication in which the matrix has $\omega = \exp 2\pi\sqrt{-1}/n$, the nth root of unity.

$$y_i^0 = 0 \qquad\qquad 0 \leqslant i \leqslant n-1$$
$$y_i^k = y_i^{k-1}\omega^i + x_{n-k} \quad 1 \leqslant k \leqslant n, \;\; 0 \leqslant i \leqslant n-1 \tag{1.14}$$

3. **Polynomial multiplication** of two degree-n polynomials.

$$c_i^0 = 0 \qquad\qquad 0 \leqslant i \leqslant 2n-2$$
$$c_i^k = c_i^{k-1} + a_{k-1}b_{i-k+1} \quad 0 \leqslant i \leqslant 2n-2, \; 1 \leqslant k \leqslant n \tag{1.15}$$
$$b_j = 0 \text{ for } j < 0 \text{ or } j \geqslant n$$

4. **Deconvolution** expressed in recurrence form with a temporary variable z_i

$$z_i^0 = y_i \qquad\qquad 1 \leqslant i \leqslant n$$
$$z_i^k = z_i^{k-1} - a_{m-k+1}x_{i+m-k} \quad 1 \leqslant k \leqslant m-1, 1 \leqslant i \leqslant n$$
$$x_j = 0 \text{ for } j > n \tag{1.16}$$
$$x_i = \frac{z_i^{m-1}}{a_i} \qquad\qquad 1 \leqslant i \leqslant n$$

5. **Two-dimensional matrix multiplication** of two $n \times n$ matrices A and B.

$$c_{i,j}^0 = 0 \qquad\qquad 1 \leqslant i, j \leqslant n$$
$$c_{i,j}^k = c_{i,j}^{k-1} + a_{i,k}b_{k,j} \qquad 1 \leqslant i, j, k \leqslant n \qquad (1.17)$$

6. **Triangular matrix inversion:** matrix inversion of an upper triangular matrix U to $V = U^{-1}$ by a temporary variable $w_{i,j}$

$$w_{i,j}^{i+1} = 0 \qquad\qquad 1 \leqslant i < j \leqslant n$$
$$w_{i,j}^k = w_{i,j}^{k+1} - u_{i,k}v_{k,j} \quad 1 \leqslant i < k \leqslant j \leqslant n$$
$$v_{i,j} = \frac{w_{i,j}^{i+1}}{u_{i,i}} \qquad\qquad 1 \leqslant i < j \leqslant n \qquad (1.18)$$
$$v_{i,i} = \frac{1}{u_{i,i}} \qquad\qquad 1 \leqslant i \leqslant n$$

7. **Two-dimensional tuple comparison:** given two 2-dimensional matrices A and B, determining if the ith row of A is identical to the jth row of B.

$$c_{i,j}^0 = TRUE \qquad\qquad 1 \leqslant i,j \leqslant n$$
$$c_{i,j}^k = c_{i,j}^{k-1} \wedge (a_{i,k} = b_{j,k}) \qquad 1 \leqslant i,j,k \leqslant n \qquad (1.19)$$

The first four in the above list are 2-dimensional recurrences while the others are 3-dimensional.

1.2.2 Pipelining

Consider the 3-dimensional recurrence in (1.10). The subscript access functions of X and y involve only two of the three index variables i, j, k. Therefore, the same input data token $X(x_{i,k})$ is used at all the index points (i, j, k), for all j. If the number of values j can take in the domain of the recurrence is n_j, the input data token must be circulated to all the n_j computation points. We assume that broadcasting of an input token is not allowed and that no input token is duplicated and sent into the array. Therefore, the input data token has to be pipelined through the n_j computation points which use the data. For our case of uniform recurrence, the input $X(x_{i,k})$ flows along the increasing or decreasing j index. For example, if we assume increasing j then,

$$X(x_{i,j,k}) = X(x_{i,j-1,k}) \qquad (1.20)$$

Similarly, the other input y is pipelined to flow along the increasing or decreasing i index as its indexing function does not involve i.

Thus for the recurrence in (1.10) we introduce two extra dependencies $(0, +1, 0)$ for variable X and $(+1, 0, 0)$ for y and the recurrence becomes,

$$X(x_{i,j,k}) = X(x_{i,j-1,k}) \tag{1.21}$$

$$Y(y_{i,j,k}) = Y(y_{i-1,j,k}) \tag{1.22}$$

$$Z_{i,j}^k = \phi\,[Z_{i,j}^{k-1},\, X(x_{i,j,k}),\, Y(y_{i,j,k})] \tag{1.23}$$

1.2.3 Parameters

The crux of the parameter method is the characterization of the behaviour, correctness and performance of the systolic array by a set of parameters. To understand the parameter method we must see the rationale behind the choice of the parameters. Earlier we noted that when a uniform recurrence is executed on a systolic array the computation is periodic and equally-spaced along any dependence direction. Thus, we can associate a period with the computation along every dependence direction. In addition, since the computation is equally-spaced, a data token moves the same distance between consecutive computations. Hence the speed of the data remains constant along the dependence direction and is chosen as a parameter. Once the velocity is fixed the relative distance between two data tokens of the same variable remains unchanged throughout the entire computation. Therefore, it parameterizes the data distribution during the execution of the recurrence on the array.

Parameter 1: periods
For the uniform recurrence given above, there are three dependence directions associated with each variable, Z, X, Y. So there are three periods of computation, one along each direction. They are defined as follows.

Suppose the time at which a computation is performed is defined by the function τ_c, and the time at which an input is accessed for a particular computation is τ_a, the period of i and j for 2-dimensional outputs are defined as

$$t_i = \tau_c(Z_{i+1,j}^k) - \tau_c(Z_{i,j}^k) \tag{1.24}$$

$$t_j = \tau_c(Z_{i,j+1}^k) - \tau_c(Z_{i,j}^k) \tag{1.25}$$

The period of **iterative computation** (k) for 2-dimensional outputs is defined as

$$t_k = \tau_c(Z_{i,j}^{k+1}) - \tau_c(Z_{i,j}^k) \tag{1.26}$$

Since the recurrence is assumed to be in backward form, t_k is always positive. In computing $Z_{i,j}$, data items of X indexed by $x_{i,k}$ and $x_{i,k+1}$ are accessed successively, as is the case with $y_{k,j}$ and $y_{k+1,j}$. So we could define periods of X, Y with respect to k as,

$$t_{kx} = \tau_a(x_{i,k+1}) - \tau_a(x_{i,k}) \tag{1.27}$$

$$t_{ky} = \tau_a(y_{k+1,j}) - \tau_a(y_{k,j}) \qquad (1.28)$$

t_{kx} and t_{ky} may be negative depending on the order of access defined in subscript-access functions. Since the data needed in the computation of $Z_{i,j}^{k+1}$ after the computation of $Z_{i,j}^{k}$ must be assembled in time t_k, it must be that

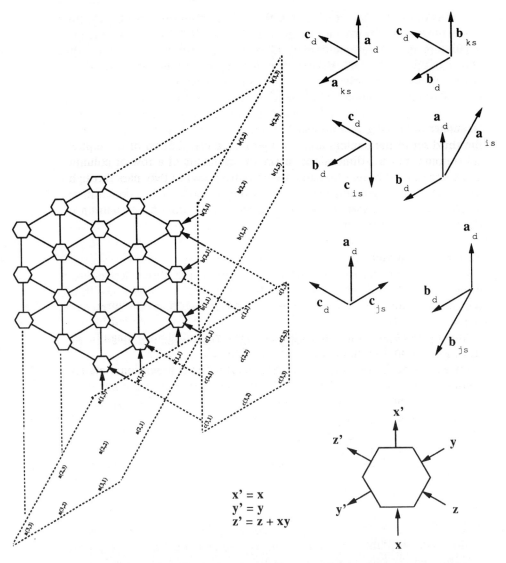

Figure 1.1 Two-dimensional systolic array for multiplying two 3×3 2-dimensional matrices. Also included are the vector equations and a single PE.

$$t_k = |t_{kx}| = |t_{ky}| \qquad (1.29)$$

Note that the absolute value of the periods must be greater than or equal to 1 since there is no broadcasting of data.

Parameter 2: velocity
Each variable has its own velocity along its dependence direction. Velocity of a datum x is defined as the directional distance passed during a clock cycle and is denoted as x_d. Since PEs are at unit distance from their neighbours, and buffers (if present) must be equally spaced between PEs, the magnitude of the velocity must be a rational number of the form i/j where i, j are integers and $i \leq j$ (to prevent broadcasting). This implies that in j clock cycles, x propagates through i PEs and $j - i$ buffers.

Parameter 3: spacing or data distribution
The third set of parameters are spacing or data distribution of the inputs and outputs. For a 2-dimensional array the elements of a row or column are arranged in a straight line and are equally spaced as they pass through the systolic array, and their relative positions are iteration independent. Other forms of data spacing are not considered here. Suppose i and j are row and column indices respectively, the row displacement of X is defined as the directional distance between $x_{i,j}$ and $x_{i+1,j}$ and is denoted by $\mathbf{x}_{is}$. Similarly, the column displacement of X ($\mathbf{x}_{ks}$) is defined as the directional distance between $x_{i,j}$ and $x_{i,j+1}$. If X is 1-dimensional then the item displacement of $X(\mathbf{x}_s)$ is defined as the directional distance between x_i and x_{i+1}. Since data are spaced equally along the row or column the displacements are independent of i or j. Note that the data distribution parameters are defined in a subscript-increasing direction with magnitudes which are rational numbers due to pipelining.

For example, Fig. 1.1 shows the systolic array for 2-dimensional matrix multiplication. The array A referenced through indices i and k has data distribution vectors defined by $\mathbf{a}_{is}$ and $\mathbf{a}_{ks}$. Similarly, array B has $\mathbf{b}_{ks}$ and $\mathbf{b}_{js}$. The periods are t_k, t_i, t_j are all equal to 1.

1.2.4 Constraint equations

There are a total of twelve parameters defined for 3-dimensional uniform recurrence in (1.10), of which three are velocities of data flow, x_d, y_d, z_d, six are data spacings, $\mathbf{x}_{is}$, $\mathbf{x}_{ks}$, $\mathbf{y}_{ks}$, $\mathbf{y}_{js}$, $\mathbf{z}_{is}$, $\mathbf{z}_{js}$ and three are periods, t_i, t_j, t_k. For 1-dimensional problems only eight parameters x_d, a_d, z_d, x_s, a_s, z_s, t_k, t_i exist. These parameters cannot be chosen arbitrarily and are related by constraint equations to ensure correctness of the resulting design. The performance of the design (like the completion time or number of PEs) can be expressed in terms of the parameters, which can be chosen to optimize the performance objective.

The following theorem states the relationships among these parameters for the correctness of the target systolic design.

Theorem 1
Suppose the two-dimensional recurrence in (1.10) is implemented in a systolic array, then the velocities, data spacings and periods must satisfy the following vector equations:

$$t_k \mathbf{z}_d = \mathbf{x}_{ks} + t_k \mathbf{x}_d \tag{1.30}$$

$$t_k \mathbf{z}_d = \mathbf{y}_{ks} + t_k \mathbf{y}_d \tag{1.31}$$

$$t_i \mathbf{y}_d = \mathbf{x}_{is} + t_i \mathbf{x}_d \tag{1.32}$$

$$t_i \mathbf{y}_d = \mathbf{z}_{is} + t_i \mathbf{z}_d \tag{1.33}$$

$$t_j \mathbf{x}_d = \mathbf{y}_{js} + t_j \mathbf{y}_d \tag{1.34}$$

$$t_j \mathbf{x}_d = \mathbf{z}_{js} + t_j \mathbf{z}_d \tag{1.35}$$

For 1-dimensional problems, only the first four of the above equations are necessary.

The proof of this theorem can be obtained as a special case of the proof for the general recurrence given later in section 1.3.

1.2.5 Design methodology

The design of the optimal systolic array can be formulated as an optimization problem. The constraints of the optimization provided by Theorem 1 show the fundamental space-time relationships that govern the correctness of the design. The objective function to be optimized is expressed in terms of the parameters and problem size and the design problem is formulated as follows:

$$\text{Minimize} \quad \#\text{PE} \times T^2 \quad \text{or} \quad \#\text{PE} \times T \quad \text{or} \quad \#\text{PE} \quad \text{or} \quad T$$

subject to constraints in (1.30)–(1.35). Additional constraints on the optimization are

$$\tfrac{1}{t_{j\max}} \leq |\mathbf{x}_d| \leq 1 \text{ or } |\mathbf{x}_d| = 0 \tag{1.36}$$

$$\tfrac{1}{t_{i\max}} \leq |\mathbf{y}_d| \leq 1 \text{ or } |\mathbf{y}_d| = 0 \tag{1.37}$$

$$\tfrac{1}{t_{k\max}} \leq |\mathbf{z}_d| \leq 1 \text{ or } |\mathbf{z}_d| = 0 \tag{1.38}$$

$$1 \leq |t_k| \leq t_{k\max} ; 1 \leq |t_i| \leq t_{i\max} ; 1 \leq |t_j| \leq t_{j\max} \tag{1.39}$$

$$|t_k|\,|\mathbf{z}_d| = k_1 \leq t_{k\max} ; |t_i|\,|\mathbf{y}_d| = k_2 \leq t_{i\max} ; |t_j|\,|\mathbf{x}_d| = k_3 \leq t_{j\max} \tag{1.40}$$

$$|\mathbf{x}_{is}|, |\mathbf{x}_{ks}|, |\mathbf{y}_{ks}|, |\mathbf{y}_{js}|, |\mathbf{z}_{is}|, |\mathbf{z}_{js}| \neq 0 \tag{1.41}$$

$t_{i\max}$, $t_{j\max}$, $t_{k\max}$ are the maximum values of the periods that have to be considered in the optimization. These bounds can be derived by requiring the completion time $T \leqslant T_{serial}$. Then by using the minimum value of 1 for two of the three periods in the inequality, the bound on the third period can be obtained.

k_1, k_2, k_3 are integers representing the distance travelled between computations. Since a computation must be performed in PEs which are at integer locations, the distance traversed must be integral. The upper bounds on k_1, k_2, k_3 are t_{kmax}, t_{imax}, t_{jmax}, respectively, because the maximum permissible values of speeds are 1. Velocities smaller than the lower bound need not be considered as there is a more efficient way of computing the recurrence in a single PE. The other constraints follow directly from the definitions. The velocities and spacings are 2-dimensional (resp. 1-dimensional) vectors for 3-dimensional (resp. 2-dimensional) recurrences.

In our recurrence equation, as there are only three variables the data flow has to be in one, two or three independent directions. When data flows in two independent directions, without loss of generality they can be assumed to be orthogonal (90°) to each other. In the case of three independent directions of data flow, again without loss of generality they can be assumed to be 120° to each other.

Since the magnitudes of the velocities and periods are chosen from a finite set, the search space for the parameters is bounded from above. There are $O(t_{kmax}^2)$ possible combinations of t_k and k_1. Similarly for t_i and $|\mathbf{y}_d|$, t_j and $|\mathbf{x}_d|$, there are $O(t_{imax}^2)$, $O(t^2_{jmax})$ combinations of values, respectively. Therefore, the optimization problem has a finite search space of complexity $O(t_{kmax}^2 t_{jmax}^2 t_{imax}^2)$.

There are two ways to further reduce this complexity. First, instead of requiring that $T \leqslant T_{serial}$, the requirement that $T \leqslant O(T_{serial}/\#PE)$ may be used to reduce the upper bounds on the periods. Secondly, the constraint equations for correctness of the design are independent of problem size. Therefore, to reduce the search complexity, an optimal design for a smaller problem can be found and used to extend to a larger version of the same problem. However, the scheme will not lead to an optimal solution for the larger problem in general. This is because the objective function increases monotonically with problem size and the fact that the objective function is better at a given problem size does not imply that this design is better at a different problem size.

1.2.6 Enumeration procedure

The optimal solution to the design problem can be found by a systematic enumeration over the space of parameters. The procedure for minimizing the completion time T (which is usually a linear function of the periods) is as follows.

1. Compute the upper bounds on periods t_{kmax}, t_{jmax}, t_{imax}.
2. Select values of periods t_i, t_j, t_k that minimize the completion time.
3. Choose $k_1 = k_2 = k_3 = 1$ and evaluate the velocities.
4. Solve for the six unknown spacing parameters from the constraint equations.
5. If no feasible solution is found, increment one of k_1, k_2, k_3 and repeat step 4.
6. If a feasible solution has still not been found, find another set of periods which increase the completion time by the minimum possible amount. Go to step 3.

Clearly the first feasible solution will also be the optimal one in terms of the completion time.

To minimize $\#PE.T^2$, it is necessary to know the lower bound on the $\#PE$. The lower bound on $\#PE$ for 2-dimensional ($n \times n$) inputs can be 1 (both inputs are serial), n (one input is serial and the other has n streams of data flow) or n^2 (both inputs have n streams of data flow). The number of streams of data flow of a matrix X is the number of distinct parallel lines that must be drawn in the direction of the data flow so that each element is in exactly one stream. It is easy to show that serial inputs do not lead to feasible solutions. and the lower bound is n^2. To determine the design with minimum $PE.T^2$ product, the procedure for minimizing completion time is used to get a feasible design. Suppose the feasible design requires P_1 PEs and T_1 time. Then any design with $T_2 \geqslant \sqrt{P_1}.T_1/n$ will not lead to a better solution and hence can be eliminated from consideration. The search is then continued to find better solutions with completion times between T_1 and T_2.

Thus, by systematically enumerating and reducing the search space that is a polynomial in the size of the problem, the optimal design can be found very efficiently.

The basic steps in the design process are listed below.

1. Write the recurrence equation for the problem to be solved.
2. Write the objective function based on the design requirements in terms of the parameters and problem size.
3. Write the constraint equations for correct systolic processing and the constraints on the values of the parameters.
4. Find the parameter values that minimize the objective function and satisfy the constraints by enumerating over the limited search space.
5. Design the basic cell for the systolic array and find a possible interconnection of the cells and buffer assignment from the parameters. Eliminate cells that do not perform any useful computation.

In the following section, two examples are provided to illustrate the application of the parameter method. The first one is matrix multiplication which is a 3-dimensional recurrence. Following it is an example of deconvolution which is a 2-dimensional recurrence with feedback.

1.2.7 Examples

Two-dimensional matrix multiplication
The recurrence equation for the multiplication of two 2-dimensional matrices each of size $n \times n$ is given in (1.17). The computation time, which is the objective function in this example, is related to the parameters as follows.

Lemma 1
The computation time T for $n \times n$ matrix multiplication is

$$1 + (n - 1)(t_k + |t_i| + |t_j|)$$

Proof: The critical path in the execution is the computation of $c_{n,n}$. It takes $(n-1)\ |t_i|$ steps to start the computation of $c_{n,1}$ after the start of the computation of $c_{1,1}$. Further $(n-1)\ |t_j|$ steps are needed to start the computation of $c_{n,n}$ from the start of $c_{n,1}$. Additional $(n-1)t_k + 1$ steps are needed to complete the computation of $c_{n,n}$. Thus the total time needed is $1 + (n - 1)(t_k + |t_i| + |t_j|)$. ■

The completion time is minimized when the periods are as small as possible. The search is started with $t_k = t_j = t_i = 1$ on all combinations of data flows. For this example, when data flows are in three different directions (120° to each other without loss of generality) and the periods are $t_k = t_j = t_i = 1$, a feasible solution is obtained that satisfies all the constraint equations. Since the search progressively uncovers solutions with increasing completion time, the first feasible solution is also optimal. The final VLSI structure, basic cell design and solution vectors obtained are shown in Fig. 1.1 for $n = 3$. The completion time for general n is $3n - 2$ with $[3n(n - 1) + 1]$ PEs. This is the fastest 2-dimensional systolic array for matrix multiplication as the lower bound on time from the dependence graph is $3n - 2$.

On the other hand, if $\#PE \times T^2$ is to be minimized, the search has to be continued to find all the feasible designs with completion time less than $\sqrt{19 \times 7^2 / 3^2} = 10.2$. It turns out that in the optimal solution, the output matrix is stationary, with periods $t_k = t_i = t_j = 1$. The design uses n^2 PEs and the completion time is $4n - 2$ units with $3n - 2$ units of computation time and n units of drain time.

Note that the recurrence for 2-dimensional tuple comparison (1.19) is identical to that for matrix multiplication except for the operations performed in the PEs. Hence the systolic array for matrix multiplication could be applied in this case. In fact, matrix multiplication is an instance

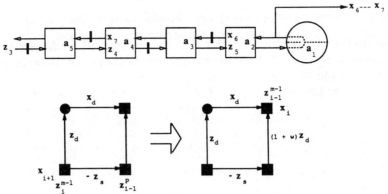

Figure 1.2 Systolic array for deconvolution for $n=5$, $m=4$ after 6 clock beats.

of a class of algorithms called 3-D cube graph algorithms (Kung, 1988) whose dependence graph is in the form of a 3-dimensional cube. Other examples of this class are L-U decomposition, triangular matrix inversion, 3-pass transitive closure (Guibas *et al.*, 1979) and 2-dimensional tuple comparison. The systolic array for matrix multiplication, with appropriate modifications to the PE design, can be applied to other members in this class also.

Deconvolution
This example illustrates the design of systolic array for recurrences with feedback. When outputs are routed back to the array in the form of feedbacks the direction of data flows has to be changed. The correctness of feedbacks is hard to express in constraint equations because the format of feedback depends on the way outputs are generated. A possible method is to treat the feedbacks as a separate independent input and design the systolic array in the usual way. After a good design is obtained the feedbacks are checked to determine if they are generated before they are fed back. The process is repeated until a correct design is found.

In the discussion so far, the processing times in the PEs are assumed to be identical. This implies the periods of data flow are independent of the PE along the direction of the flow. However in some applications, different operations may be performed in PEs along a direction of data flow. In the deconvolution example considered, the last operation is a division, which may be a bottleneck of data flow. The recurrence for deconvolution shows that the x_is are fed back into the pipeline for future computations. Let the delay of a PE performing division be w and the delay of other PEs be 1. The last iteration of computing Z_i followed by the division of Z_i to obtain x_i takes $w + 1$ units of time. Hence, the period t_i of input χ is given as

$$|t_i| = w + 1 \tag{1.42}$$

In this particular example, the fact that the inputs and feedbacks are one-dimensional lets us write down the relationships of data flows formally. For the following discussion refer to Fig. 1.2.

Let PE A be the one where the last iteration of Z_i, Z_i^{m-1} is computed using x_{i+1} before being sent to the division unit (PE D). The token Z_{i-1} exists in PE B in its pth iteration ($p < m - 1$) as Z_{i-1}^p. In $(w + 1)$ units of time, Z_i^{m-1} is sent to PE D, converted to x_i, and sent to PE C for the computation of Z_{i-1}^{m-1}. In that time, the token Z_{i-1}^p arrives at PE C after completing $(m - 1)$ iterations. Hence, a constraint equation can be written as

$$\mathbf{z}_d + \mathbf{x}_d = -\mathbf{z}_s + (w + 1)\mathbf{z}_d \rightarrow \mathbf{x}_d = w\mathbf{z}_d - \mathbf{z}_s \tag{1.43}$$

Equations (1.43) must be included in the optimization with the other constraint equations applicable to 2-dimensional recurrences. Note that X is a 1-dimensional vector with one spatial-distribution parameter $\mathbf{x}_s$, although the subscript access function depends on i and k.

A possible solution is

$$w = 2, \ t_k = \frac{-3}{2}, \ t_i = 3, \tag{1.44}$$

$$|\mathbf{a}_d| = 0, \ |\mathbf{z}_d| = \tfrac{2}{3}, \ |\mathbf{x}_d| = \tfrac{2}{3} \tag{1.45}$$

$$|\mathbf{a}_s| = -1, \ |\mathbf{z}_s| = 2, \ |\mathbf{x}_s| = -2 \tag{1.46}$$

However the problem with this solution is the feedback cannot be generated at the right time from Z. The following values for the parameters yields a solution that minimizes completion time

$$T = (m - 1 + w)t_k + (n - 1) |t_i|$$

The values are

$$t_i = -3, \ t_k = \frac{-3}{2} \tag{1.47}$$

$$|\mathbf{z}_d| = \tfrac{2}{3} \tag{1.48}$$

$$|\mathbf{z}_s| = 2 \tag{1.49}$$

$$|\mathbf{x}_d| = \tfrac{-2}{3} \tag{1.50}$$

$$|\mathbf{x}_s| = -2 \tag{1.51}$$

Figure 1.2 shows the systolic array for $m = 4$, $n = 5$ with a feasible assignment of buffers. Note that the velocities represent average over three cycles.

1.3 General parameter method

In this section, extension of the parameter method to synthesize systolic arrays for N-dimensional recurrences is presented. The general form of N-dimensional recurrence considered is

$$Z(I) = \phi[Z(I - d_1), Z(I - d_2), \ldots,$$
$$Z(I - d_q)] + \psi[X_1 (\hat{x}_1(I)), \ldots, X_r(\hat{x}_r(I))] \qquad (1.52)$$

where I denotes a point (N-dimensional vector) in the domain of the recurrence, d_i, $1 \le i \le q$ are the dependence vectors associated with any point in the domain (uniform recurrence) and $X_j(\hat{x}_j(I))$, $1 \le j \le r$ is the jth input that is needed in the computation of the function Z. $\hat{x}_j(I)$ is the linear subscript access (indexing) function for the array indices of input X_j. So in the specific recurrence considered earlier, $N = 3$, $M = 2$, $r = 2$, $q = 1$. Note that without loss of generality the dependence vectors d_i can be taken to be distinct.

As in section 1.2.2, if the subscript access function of input X_j does not involve a particular index variable i_l, then each input token of input X_j is used at all index points which differ along the index i_l. Thus the input element has to be pipelined through the set of index points used. If a subscript access function is such that an input token (element) is used at only one point in the domain then it does not make sense to talk of data flows for that input. That token is used in one computation only and is not needed any more. Hence it could be preloaded and stays in the PE it is going to be used in, for the duration of the computation.

Therefore, a dependence vector is associated with each input which then fixes the sequence of PEs that a token, belonging to that input, has to visit. Thus, r dependencies may have to be introduced to pipeline the flow of the inputs between the computation points.

As an illustration for the discussion on the general parameter method the following recurrence will be used as a running example. This example is used only for illustrating the terminology and the equations derived. The example for which an array is given is the matrix multiplication example considered in section 1.2.

Example
A 3-dimensional recurrence with $N = 3$, $q = 3$, $r = 2$.

$$Z(i, j, k) = Z(i, j, k-1) + Z(i, j-2, k) +$$
$$Z(i-3, j-1, k) + X (j, k)y(k, i) \qquad (1.53)$$

where Z, X, y are 2-dimensional $n \times n$ matrices. The index space is a 3-dimensional cube of size $n \times n \times n$ if $k = 1, 2, \ldots n$.

The indexing functions for the inputs are

$$\hat{x} = \begin{bmatrix} 0 & 1 & 0 \\ 0 & 0 & 1 \end{bmatrix} \qquad (1.54)$$

$$\hat{y} = \begin{bmatrix} 0 & 0 & 1 \\ 1 & 0 & 0 \end{bmatrix} \qquad (1.55)$$

$\hat{x}(I)$ and $\hat{y}(I)$ gives the indices for the inputs X and y respectively.
The dependence vectors are collected into a matrix as follows:

$$D = \begin{bmatrix} 0 & 0 & 3 & 1 & 0 \\ 0 & 2 & 1 & 0 & 1 \\ 1 & 0 & 0 & 0 & 0 \end{bmatrix} \tag{1.56}$$

$$Z\ Z\ Z\ X\ y \tag{1.57}$$

Pipelining leads to dependencies $(1, 0, 0)$ and $(0, 1, 0)$ for variables X and y respectively.

$$\hat{x}(i, j, k) = \hat{x}(i-1, j, k) \tag{1.58}$$
$$\hat{y}(i, j, k) = \hat{y}(i, j-1, k) \tag{1.59}$$

∎

Next we present an informal discussion on why the parameter set considered in section 1.2 needs to be augmented for the case of general recurrence. After the inputs have been pipelined, there are $q + r$ dependence directions for the given recurrence in the domain. We need to have a different velocity for data motion along each dependence direction. Suppose for contradiction we let the velocity of recurrence variable Z be the same along directions d_1 and d_2, then in the computation of $Z(I)$ at PE A (illustrated in Fig. 1.3), $Z(I - d_1)\ Z(I - d_2)$ are needed

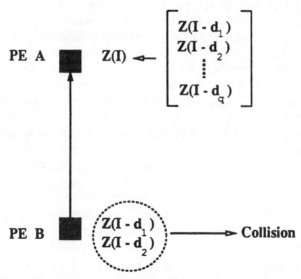

Figure 1.3 Demonstrates the need for different velocities along different dependence directions. If the velocities of $Z(I\text{-}d_1)$ and $Z(I\text{-}d_2)$ are the same, collision occurs in PE B.

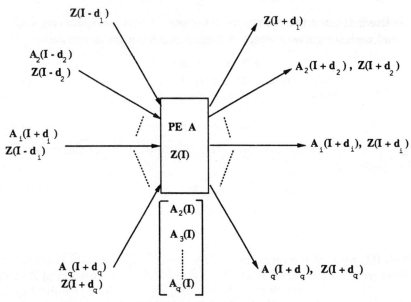

Figure 1.4 A single PE computing the recurrence in the general parameter method.

at the same processor A. Since their velocities are the same they must have travelled together and must have been generated at the same time at processor B. This violates our **fundamental** assumption that no two computations can be mapped to the same processor at the same time.

Since the velocities are different along each dependence direction, the data distribution or spacing has to be different for variable Z in each direction. In addition a different period of computation has to be associated with each dependence direction to avoid computational conflicts. Thus for each dependence direction there is a velocity of data flow, period of computation and distribution parameters for the data flowing in that direction.

From the structure of the recurrence given in (1.52), the value $Z(I)$ is computed at point I ($\in$ *domain*) by combining q other values $Z(I - d_i)$, $(1 \leqslant i \leqslant q)$ generated at other points in the domain. Similarly the value $Z(I)$ is used at q other points (called consumer points), $Z(I + d_i)$, $1 \leqslant i \leqslant q$. There are three ways of sending this value of $Z(I)$ to the points where it is used (Fig. 1.4).

1. **Full replication:** q copies of $Z(I)$ are sent to the q points which need it.
2. **Full propagation:** Only one copy of $Z(I)$ exists and this copy is sequenced through its q consumer points. Thus these q consumers can be thought of as being on a chain of size q.

3. **Mixed:** $k(<q)$ copies of $Z(I)$ are made at PE P, where $Z(I)$ is generated and each copy is sequenced through a subset of the q consumer points. Thus multiple smaller chains of size less than q are formed.

Note that the way in which $Z(I)$ is sent to its consumers could change the structure of the target systolic array significantly. In this discussion only the case of **full replication** is considered.

Since we need to have a different set of parameters (velocity, spacing and period) along each dependence direction, the recurrence is rewritten in the following manner to explicitly bring this out and simplify the reasoning about the recurrence

$$Z(I) = \phi[Z(I - d_1), A_2(I - d_2), A_3(I - d_3), \ldots ,$$
$$A_q(I - d_q)] + \psi[X_1(\hat{x}_1(I)), \ldots , X_r(\hat{x}_r(I))] \qquad (1.60)$$
$$A_i(I) = Z(I), \quad i = 2, \ldots , q \qquad (1.61)$$

With this form of the recurrence each dependence direction is associated with exactly one variable. Each of the A_i indicate the movement of Z along the direction d_i. Note that the rewritten form is functionally identical to the original recurrence in terms of the computations performed. The rewritten form is, however, conceptually simpler to deal with. The elements of each of the variables move periodically between computations with constant velocity. Thus the distance between the elements of that variable remains constant and the data distribution can be captured by a set of spacing parameters.

Example
The rewritten form of the recurrence is

$$Z(i, j, k) = Z(i, j, k) + A_2(i, j-2, k) + A_3(i-3, j-1, k)$$
$$+ X(\hat{x}(i, j, k))\mathcal{Y}(\hat{y}(i, j, k)) \qquad (1.62)$$
$$A_2(i, j, k) = Z(i, j, k) \qquad (1.63)$$
$$A_3(i, j, k) = Z(i, j, k) \qquad (1.64)$$

Each dependency is now associated with one variable. ■

1.3.1 Constraint equations

For the general form of recurrence the parameter set is as below. For ease of notation the variables $\{Z, A_i, X_j\}$ are ordered so that

$$\text{the } i\text{th variable refers to} \begin{cases} Z & \text{if } i = 1 \\ A_i & \text{if } i = 2, 3, \ldots , q \\ X_{i-q} & \text{if } i = q + 1, q + 2, \ldots , q + r \end{cases}$$

For each $i \in (1, 2, \ldots , q+r)$, $t_i = \tau_c(Z(I)) - \tau_c(Z(I - d_i))$ is the period between the computations of variable i in the ordering defined above.

$\tau_c(Z(I))$ is the time at which computation $Z(I)$ is executed on the array. V_i is the velocity of flow of the token of the ith variable in the direction d_i. For instance, variable i moves along direction d_i through the points (called a dependence chain of i) in the domain of the recurrence as follows:

$$\ldots \; Z(I - 2d_i) \rightarrow Z(I - d_i) \rightarrow Z(I) \rightarrow Z(I + d_i) \rightarrow Z(I + 2d_i) \;\ldots$$

The spacing or data distribution parameters are denoted by S_i^d, and defined as the directional distance between the elements of variable i along direction $\mathbf{d}$, i.e. between elements $X_i(\hat{x}_i(I - d))$ and $X_i(\hat{x}_i(I))$. The number of the spacing parameters will be clear once the constraint equations are given. Note that the magnitude of all velocities $|V_i| \leqslant 1$ since broadcasting is not permitted.

Example

Z is the 1st variable, A_2 is the 2nd variable, A_3 is the 3rd variable, X is the 4th variable and y is the 5th variable in the ordering defined above. The parameters t_1, t_2, t_3, t_4, t_5 are the periods, $\mathbf{V}_1$, $\mathbf{V}_2$, $\mathbf{V}_3$, $\mathbf{V}_4$, $\mathbf{V}_5$ are the velocities.

$$t_1 = \tau_c(Z(i, j, k)) - \tau_c(Z(i, j, k-1)) \tag{1.65}$$

$$t_2 = \tau_c(Z(i, j, k)) - \tau_c(Z(i, j-2, k)) \tag{1.66}$$

$$t_3 = \tau_c(Z(i, j, k)) - \tau_c(Z(i-3, j-1, k)) \tag{1.67}$$

$$t_4 = \tau_c(Z(i, j, k)) = \tau_c(Z(i-1, j, k)) \tag{1.68}$$

$$t_5 = \tau_c(Z(i, j, k)) = \tau_c(Z(i, j-1, k)) \tag{1.69}$$

■

Theorem 2

The parameters, velocities, spacings and periods must satisfy the following constraint equations for correct systolic processing of the general recurrence.

$$\begin{aligned}
\mathbf{V}_i t_i &= \mathbf{V}_j t_i + S_j^{d_i - d_j} \quad 1 \leqslant i \leqslant q+r, \; 1 \leqslant j \leqslant q, \; j \neq i \\
&= \mathbf{V}_j t_i + S_j^{d_i} \qquad 1 \leqslant i \leqslant q+r, \; q+1 \leqslant j \leqslant q+r, j \neq i
\end{aligned} \tag{1.70}$$

Proof: Consider the computation of Z at the index point $I \in D$ (domain). Let the PE where it is computed be denoted by A. To compute Z all the $q+r$ variables are needed at A at the same time. For simplicity consider the movement of the 1st variable $Z(I - d_1)$ to PE A. Let B denote the PE where it was generated. In the time $Z(I - d_1)$ moves from PE B to PE A, the other $q+r-1$ variables must move from their respective locations to PE A. Consider the movement of one such variable j, where $1 \leqslant j \leqslant q+r$.

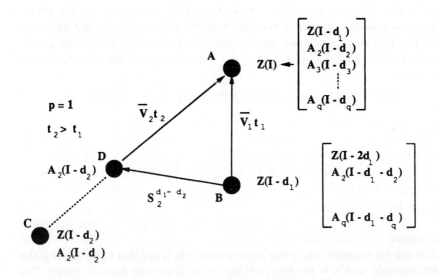

Figure 1.5 General parameter method: Data movement between variables 1 and 2. The dashed line indicates the movement in the past, i.e., $A_2(I-d_2)$ has been generated.

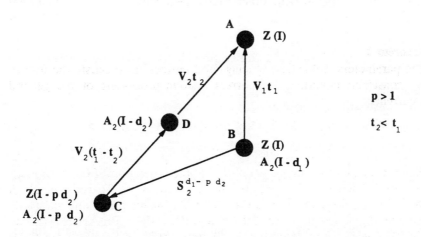

Figure 1.6 Data movement between variables 1 and 2 for $p > 1$. The token $A_2(I-pd_2)$ becomes $A_2(I-d_2)$ as it travels towards PE A.

Case 1: $1 \leqslant j \leqslant q$

Without loss of generality, consider the motion of the 2nd variable (A_2). Since $Z(I - d_1)$ was generated at PE B, $A_2(I - d_1)$ resides at PE B. When $Z(I - d_1)$ is generated, $A_2(I - d_2)$ might not exist in the array. In general, let $A_2(I - pd_2)$ ($p \geqslant 1$) be the latest value generated along the dependence chain passing through $Z(I)$. Therefore, if $t_2 > t_1$ then $p > 1$; otherwise $p = 1$.

Case 1A: $p = 1$

This is depicted in Fig. 1.5. $S_2^{d_1-d_2}$ denotes the distance between $A_2(I - d_1)$ and $A_2(I - d_2)$. Therefore by vector composition we get (1.70).

Case 1B: $p > 1$

As depicted in Fig.1.6, the distance between $A_2(I - d_1)$ and $A_2(I - pd_2)$ is now given by $S_2^{d_1-pd_2}$. Hence it appears that we need to know the value of p or how far the computation of A_2 has proceeded along the computation chain. But the crucial idea is that the token or element of the variable A_2 which is now called $A_2(I - pd_2)$ will eventually go through $p - 1$ computations along direction d_2 and be called $A_2(I - d_2)$. Thus $A_2(I - pd_2)$ for all p is the **same** element, or token, of the data stream A_2. This can be visualized as a register (data element) propagating through the array and having different values at different times in the execution. The apparent difficulty was because the register was referred to by the value it contained and this value kept changing through the execution. There-fore, irrespective of the value of p, we can say that the token which will be called $A_2(I - d_2)$ in future, is at a distance $S_2^{d_1-d_2}$ from PE B which has $A_2(I - d_1)$ at the present time. Thus again by vector composition the theorem is proved.

Case 2: $q+1 \leqslant i \leqslant q+r$

Arguments similar to case 1 can be provided to prove the theorem.   ∎

Example

The constraint equations are

$$\mathbf{V}_1 t_1 = \mathbf{V}_2 t_1 + S_2^{(0,\,-2,\,1)} \tag{1.71}$$

$$= \mathbf{V}_3 t_1 + S_3^{(-3,\,0,\,1)} \tag{1.72}$$

$$= \mathbf{V}_4 t_1 + S_4^{(0,\,0,\,1)} \tag{1.73}$$

$$= \mathbf{V}_5 t_1 + S_5^{(0,\,0,\,1)} \tag{1.74}$$

Similarly, there are sixteen additional equations for the 2nd, 3rd, 4th and 5th variables. There are four spacing parameters with each variable. For the 2nd variable, $S_2^{(0,\,-2,\,1)}$, $S_2^{(3,\,-2,\,0)}$, $S_2^{(1,\,-2,\,0)}$, $S_2^{(0,\,-1,\,0)}$ are the spacings and $S_2^{(0,\,-2,\,1)}$ is the directional distance from $A_2(i, j, k-1)$ and $A_2(i, j-2, k)$ and so on.

1.3.2 Generating lower dimensional arrays

In the previous subsection, the theorem provided constraint equations based on recurrence being mapped without any idea of the dimension of the target systolic array. The key observation is that the systolic constraint equations are vector equations. So if the target systolic array is M-dimensional the velocity and spacing parameters are M-dimensional too. Hence, the constraint equations are solved in M-dimensions to get M-dimensional solutions.

To determine the number of parameters to be chosen, let us do a count of the number of equations available and the number of parameters defined. For each one of the $(q + r)$ variables, there is a constraint equation relating its movement to the movement of other $(q + r - 1)$ variables. Hence there are $(q + r)(q + r - 1)$ vector equations. For each variable there is total of $(q + r - 1)$ spacing parameters, each of which appears in the equations relating its movement to every one of the other $(q + r - 1)$ variables. In addition each variable has a velocity and period of computation. Thus there are $(q + r + 1)$ parameters for each variable, and $(q + r)(q + r + 1)$ parameters in total. The number of parameters exceeds the number of equations by $2(q + r)$ and therefore $2(q + r)$ of the parameters have to be chosen. The remaining $(q + r)(q + r - 1)$ parameters can be determined from the $(q + r)(q + r - 1)$ constraint equations.

To decide which of the $2(q + r)$ parameters have to be chosen, we look at how the performance of the design such as total execution time T or number of PEs (#PE) is related to the parameters. The performance of the design is usually a function of the periods and velocities only. Hence, a strategy could be to choose the $2(q + r)$ periods and velocities to optimize a performance criterion and then determine the other $(q + r)(q + r - 1)$ spacing parameters from the constraint equations. It should be pointed out that any objective that is expressible in terms of the parameters defined, can be used in the optimization instead of completion time or the #PE in the design. However, the enumeration procedure might have to be modified appropriately if the objective function is not monotonically increasing with the parameters such as periods or velocities.

Example

There are 5 variables and each variable has 1 period, 1 velocity and 4 spacings. So the total number of parameters is 30. Each variable has 4 vector equations and so the total number of equations is 20. So 10 of the 30 parameters are chosen and the remaining 20 parameters are determined from the equations. We can choose the 5 velocities and 5 periods to optimize completion time, or the number of PEs in the array.   ∎

The goal is to generate an M-dimensional array for the N-dimensional recurrence where M is in the range $(1, 2, 3, \ldots, N-1)$. (For $M \geqslant N$ we have a PE at each computation point in the N-dimensional domain and there is no need for any synthesis.) In order to obtain a clear understanding, consider the cases for different values of M, q, r. The discussion below is with respect to any arbitrary input j. Let the dimension of the input Matrix be H. Let the size of the input matrix be $(L_1 \times L_2 \times \ldots \times L_H)$.

Since the dimension of the input Matrix is H, the position of every element can be described by a basis of size H, i.e. H linearly independent vectors. But since the target array is M-dimensional the matrix is fed as an M-dimensional array. A total of $(q + r - 1)$ spacing parameters are obtained from the constraint equations for systolic processing. It is possible that these spacings are such that two elements of the input matrix are sent into the matrix together into the same PE and travel together throughout the execution (since they have the same velocity). This is called a **data conflict** as two data tokens are in the same physical location at all times.

Data conflicts are not permissible within the framework, as extra control bits that travel with the two elements are necessary to determine which of the two inputs is to be used in the computation. Therefore, if we are concerned only with pure systolic arrays without explicit control bits, then no two data tokens must travel together into any PE in the array. The following lemma (Lemma 2) expresses this notion mathematically.

Let G be the minimum of H and $(q + r - 1)$. If $H < (q + r - 1)$ only H of the spacings are necessary. The additional $(q + r - 1) - H$ spacing parameters must be checked to ascertain that they do not conflict with the H chosen parameters. If $H > (q + r - 1)$ then the remaining $(q + r - 1) - H$ spacings can be chosen arbitrarily. Therefore, there are at least G spacing parameters obtained from constraint equations. Let $S^1, S^2, \ldots, S^G$ be the G spacing parameters, each of which is M-dimensional. Let S be a $G \times M$ matrix which is given by $S = [S^1, S^2, \ldots, S^G]^T$ where T refers to the transpose of the matrix. Let α, β, γ be vectors with G integer elements.

Lemma 2
Data conflicts occur in the input matrix iff $\alpha S = 0$, $\alpha \neq 0$, where $\alpha_i \in [-(L_i - 1), \ldots, (L_i + 1)]$, $\forall i$ such that $1 \leqslant i \leqslant G$.

Proof: Data conflicts

$$\Leftrightarrow \beta S = \gamma S, \beta \neq \gamma \text{ and } 1 \leqslant \gamma_i, \beta_i \leqslant L_i$$
$$\Leftrightarrow (\beta - \gamma)S = 0$$
$$\alpha S = 0, \alpha = \beta - \gamma, \alpha_i \in [-(L_i-1), \ldots, (L_i+1)], \alpha \neq 0 \qquad \blacksquare$$

It is instructive to see how the lemma applies to the simplified recurrence case described in section 1.2. In the simplistic case, $H = 2$, $M = 2$, $N = 3$, $q + r - 1 = 2$. From the structure of the constraint equations it can be seen that if the data flow is in two or three independent directions, the 2-dimensional spacing parameters will lay along two independent directions and hence be linearly independent. Thus, the lemma is automatically satisfied irrespective of the size of the matrix and there are no data conflicts.

Example

The dimensions of X, Y, and Z matrices are 2 and their sizes are all $n \times n$. The constraint equations result in 4 spacing parameters to describe 2-dimensional matrices. So 2 of the 4 spacing parameters are dependent on the other two. In this example for input X with the indexing function $\hat{x}$ let the 4 spacing parameters be S_4^1, S_4^2, S_4^3, S_4^4, which describe the distance from $\{(X(i, j) \rightarrow X(i, j+1)), (X(i, j) \rightarrow X(i+2, j)), (X(i, j) \rightarrow X(i+1, j)),$ $(X(i, j) \rightarrow X(i+1, j))\}$ respectively. So S_4^3 should be equal to S_4^4 and S_4^2 should be twice S_4^3. These additional constraints have to be introduced to have consistent spacing parameters.

If the array sought is 1-dimensional then the spacing parameters are all one dimensional scalars. So S_4^1, S_4^3 are the two independent spacings for input X. Therefore according to the lemma, data conflicts occur in input X if and only if

$$[\alpha_1 \alpha_2] \begin{bmatrix} S_4^1 \\ S_4^3 \end{bmatrix} = 0 \tag{1.75}$$

where $-(n-1) \leqslant \alpha_1, \alpha_2 \leqslant (n-1)$ and $\alpha_1, \alpha_2 \neq 0$.

1.3.3 Enumeration procedure

As done earlier, we define $k_i = t_i V_i$, $1 \leqslant i \leqslant q + r - 1$ as the distance traversed by the elements of variable i between two computations.

Additional constraints on the optimization are that the magnitude of the velocities are less than unity and none of the spacing parameters can be zero. These are similar to those given for the simplified 3-dimensional recurrence in section 1.2.5 and are not repeated here.

The completion time T is a function (usually linear) of the periods of the variables. The upper bounds for the periods are computed in a similar manner to that outlined in section 1.2.5. Let t_{imax} denote the upper bound for period t_i. If the upper bounds are computed naively then t_{imax} is of the order of sequential execution time T_{serial}, which is polynomial in the size of the problem. The procedure is as follows:

1. Compute the upper bounds t_{imax}, $1 \leqslant i \leqslant (q + r - 1)$.
2. Choose values of periods to minimize T.
3. Choose the distances k_i as unity and compute the velocities.
4. Solve for the spacing parameters from the constraint equations.

5. Check for data conflicts from the spacing parameters (Lemma 2).
6. If no feasible solution is found, increment one of k_i and repeat steps 4 and 5 until no k_i can be increased.
7. If there is still no feasible solution, find another set of periods which increase the completion time by the lowest possible value. Go to step 3.

The complexity of the search procedure is polynomial in t_{imax}, $1 \leqslant i \leqslant q+r$. Thus by a systematic enumeration of the limited search space the optimal design can be found very efficiently.

The next section describes the example of matrix multiplication to illustrate the general parameter method. This example was chosen because it represents an important class of algorithms, and deriving optimal arrays for it would be a significant step. The target array sought is linear in this case ($M = 1$, $N = 3$).

1.3.4 Example: 3-dimensional cube graph algorithms

These are algorithms with dependence graphs as a 3-dimensional cube. They have $[(1, 0, 0)^T, (0, 1, 0)^T, (0, 0, 1)^T]$ as their dependence vectors. Matrix multiplication is the popular example in this class. In this subsection, a 1-dimensional array (as opposed to the 2-D array) for matrix multiplication is presented.

The recurrence equation for matrix multiplication before pipelining is

$$Z_{i,j}^k = Z_{i,j}^{k-1} + x_{i,k}y_{k,j} \tag{1.76}$$

Hence, $N = 3$, $q = 1$, $r = 2$ and $M = 1$ since a linear array is sought. Let the size of the matrix be $L \times L$.

There are 3 variables, 6 constraint equations and a total of 12 parameters. The parameters and constraint equations are as described in section 1.2 in equations (1.30)–(1.35). The vector equations result in two distinct spacing parameters for each variable X, Y and Z. Thus there are no data conflicts if the target array is 2-dimensional. If the target array is linear (1-dimensional) then the two spacings of each variable have to satisfy Lemma 2. For this example the conditions for data conflicts can be refined as follows.

Consider one of the variables, say X. The spacings parameters of X are x_{is} and x_{ks} (they are written as scalars since the array is linear).

Lemma 3
Data conflicts occur in input X if and only if,

$$\left| \frac{x_{is}}{m} \right| < L, \quad \text{and} \quad \left| \frac{x_{ks}}{m} \right| < L \tag{1.77}$$

where $m = GCD(x_{is}, x_{ks})$ and $GCD(a, b)$ is the greatest common divisor of a and b.

Proof: ($\Leftarrow$) Since m is the $GCD(x_{is}, x_{ks})$, $x_{is} = m.\alpha_2$ and $x_{ks} = m.\alpha_1$, where α_2, α_1 (which denote the product of the rest of the divisors) are integral. Therefore,

$$\frac{x_{is}}{\alpha_2} = \frac{x_{ks}}{\alpha_1} , \text{ where } |\alpha_1|, |\alpha_2| < L \tag{1.78}$$

$$\Rightarrow [\; \alpha_1 \alpha_2' \;] \begin{bmatrix} x_{is} \\ x_{ks} \end{bmatrix} = 0, \text{ where } \alpha_2' = -\alpha_2, |\alpha_1| , |\alpha_2| < L \tag{1.79}$$

$\Rightarrow$ Data conflicts in X

($\Rightarrow$)

Data conflicts in X $\Rightarrow x_{is}\alpha_1 = x_{ks}\alpha_2$ (1.80)

$$\Rightarrow \frac{x_{is}}{\alpha_2} = \frac{x_{ks}}{\alpha_1} \tag{1.81}$$

where $\alpha_1, \alpha_2 \in \{-(L-1), \ldots , (L-1)\}$ and $GCD(\alpha_1, \alpha_2) = 1$ (if not scale α_1 and α_2 by their GCD).

Note that if x_{is}/α_2 is not integral, then x_{js} will not be integral. Therefore, x_{is}/α_2, x_{ks}/α_1 are both integral and must be equal to their GCD.

$$\frac{x_{is}}{\alpha_2} = \frac{x_{ks}}{\alpha_1} = m \tag{1.82}$$

$$\Rightarrow \alpha_2 = \frac{x_{is}}{m} \text{ and } \alpha_1 = \frac{x_{ks}}{m} \tag{1.83}$$

$$\Rightarrow \left|\frac{x_{is}}{m}\right| < L, \text{ and } \left|\frac{x_{ks}}{m}\right| < L \tag{1.84}$$

∎

The following lemma relates the #PE needed in the linear array to the distance parameters k_1, k_2, k_3 which are as defined in section 1.2.5.

Lemma 4
The #PE needed to execute an $L \times L$ matrix multiplication on a linear array is $(L - 1)(k_1 + k_2 + k_3) + 1$.

Proof: Since all velocities are in 1-dimension (linear array) two of the three velocities should be in the same direction. Without loss of generality assume that the two velocities are to the right (refer to Fig. 1.7 for the proof). Assume that k_1 and k_2 are the displacements which correspond to the velocities flowing to the right. Since the constraint equations are symmetric in Z, Y, X no generality is lost here. Let A be the PE where the computation indexed by (0, 0, 0) occurs. Therefore the computation (0,

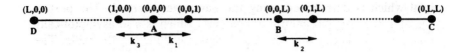

Figure 1.7 PE Allocation when Z and y flow to the right and X moves to the left.

$0, L)$ is executed at a PE B, which is at a distance of $(L - 1)k_1$ from A. Similarly, the computation $(0, L, L)$ is executed at PE C which is $(L - 1)k_2$ PEs to the right of B. Now the computation $(L, 0, 0)$ is at a distance of $(L - 1)k_3$ in PE D to the left of PE A (since k_3 corresponds to the left moving variable X). All other computations in the domain are executed by PEs between C and D. Therefore the total number of PEs required are $(L - 1) (k_1 + k_2 + k_3) + 1$. ∎

Table 1.1 shows the optimal linear designs found by the enumeration procedure when the objective is to minimize completion time. LK is the linear array design proposed by Lee and Kedem (1988). Their approach is similar to the dependency method outlined in section 1.1. The schedule vector is $(1, 2, n-1)$ and the PE allocation matrix (vector in the case of a linear array) is $(1, 1, -1)$ for $n \times n$ matrices. But the above transformation is only **asymptotically** optimal (for large n). But using the parameter method the optimal design at every n can be determined very

Table 1.1 Matrix multiplication: Optimal linear array synthesis for completion time T (Dev. refers to the deviation from the optimal)

Size	Optimal Design								LK	H1
(N)	Periods			Distances					Design	Design
	t_k	t_i	t_j	k_1	k_2	k_3	T	#PE	Dev.	Dev.
3	1	2	2	1	1	1	11	7	0.00%	0.00%
4	1	2	3	1	1	1	19	10	0.00%	0.00%
5	1	2	3	1	1	2	25	17	16.00%	0.00%
10	2	3	4	1	1	3	82	46	32.93%	0.00%
17	3	3	5	1	2	4	177	113	72.32%	9.04%
25	3	4	6	2	7	1	313	193	107.35%	23.00%
40	3	4	9	2	1	8	625	430	162.24%	49.94%
50	4	5	8	3	2	7	834	589	205.64%	70.54%
100	6	7	10	5	4	9	2278	1783	343.33%	134.72%

efficiently. Table 1.1 shows the deviation of the LK design from the optimal which is determined using the parameter method. The performance of a heuristic parametric design (H1) which is also asymptotically optimal but does better than the LK design is included in the table. The parameter set for this design is

$$\{(t_k,\ t_i,\ t_j) = (1,\ 2,\ \lceil \tfrac{L+1}{2} \rceil) \quad \text{and} \quad (k_1,\ k_2,\ k_3) = (1,\ 1,\ \lceil \tfrac{L+1}{2} \rceil - 1)\}$$

The spacing parameters can be uniquely determined from the constraint equations and are not given. The linear array together with the data flows for $L = 4$ is depicted in Fig. 1.8.

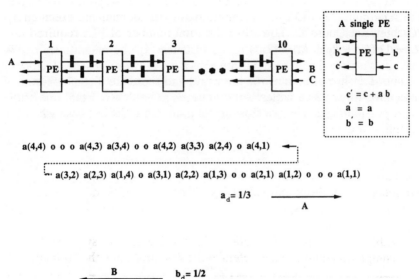

Figure 1.8 Linear array for multiplying two 4×4 matrices. The array is optimal, for completion time, #PEs and $\#PE.T^2$ product.

If the objective is to minimize the number of PEs required in the linear array then the following lemma characterizes the optimal design.

Lemma 5
The set of parameters $\{(t_k, t_i, t_j) = (1, 2, L-1)$ and $(k_1, k_2, k_3) = (1, 1, 1)\}$ results in a linear array with the minimum number of PEs.

Proof: The parameters k_1, k_2 and k_3 are defined as

$$k_1 = |t_k|\,|\mathbf{z}_d| \tag{1.85}$$

$$k_2 = |t_i|\,|\mathbf{y}_d| \tag{1.86}$$

$$k_3 = |t_j|\,|\mathbf{x}_d| \tag{1.87}$$

Therefore $k_i \geq 1$ and from Lemma 2, the values $k_1 = k_2 = k_3 = 1$ gives the minimum #PE ($3L - 2$). So to prove the lemma, the above given parameter set must be shown to be feasible.

For given values of periods t_i and distances k_i, the magnitudes of the velocities are fixed (can be determined as k_i/t_i). However, each velocity can be in one of two directions (linear array) and there are 8 combinations of data flows for the 3 variables. All that needs to be shown is that one of the eight possibilities leads to a feasible solution. Consider the case when the velocities are

$$\mathbf{z}_d = 1, \; \mathbf{y}_d = \frac{1}{2}, \; \mathbf{x}_d = \frac{-1}{L-1} \tag{1.88}$$

where the negative sign refers to the flow along the negative x-axis (assuming the array is along the x-axis).

The spacing parameters can be then be determined from the constraint equations as follows:

$$\mathbf{x}_{is} = t_i(\mathbf{y}_d - \mathbf{x}_d) = \frac{L+1}{L-1} \tag{1.89}$$

$$\mathbf{x}_{ks} = t_k(\mathbf{z}_d - \mathbf{x}_d) = \frac{L}{L-1} \tag{1.90}$$

$$\mathbf{y}_{ks} = t_k(\mathbf{z}_d - \mathbf{y}_d) = \frac{1}{2} \tag{1.91}$$

$$\mathbf{y}_{js} = t_j(\mathbf{x}_d - \mathbf{y}_d) = \frac{-(L+1)}{2} \tag{1.92}$$

$$\mathbf{z}_{is} = t_i(\mathbf{y}_d - \mathbf{z}_d) = -1 \tag{1.93}$$

$$\mathbf{z}_{js} = t_j(\mathbf{x}_d - \mathbf{z}_d) = -L \tag{1.94}$$

To determine if there are data conflicts, Lemma 3 can be applied to the spacings of each of the variables X, Y and Z. Consider the case of input X. Since the denominators in the fractions of $\mathbf{x}_{is}$ and $\mathbf{x}_{ks}$ are identical, only the numerators need to be considered. Since the $GCD(L,L+1) = 1$,

$$\frac{L}{GCD(L,\,L+1)} \geq L \quad \text{and} \quad \frac{L+1}{GCD(L,\,L+1)} \geq L.$$

Therefore, by Lemma 3 X is conflict-free. Similarly, for Y and Z since

$GCD(1, L+1)$ and $GCD(1, L)$ are 1 and hence they are conflict-free too. So all the inputs are conflict-free and the parameter set is feasible.   ∎

The above lemma gives a closed form expression for the parameters if the number of PEs is to be minimized in the linear array to solve matrix multiplication (and other 3-D cube algorithms). Figure 1.8 shows the array for $L = 4$. Thus the design is optimal both in terms of the number of PEs and the completion time. But for $N > 4$ (Table 1.1), the designs for optimal completion time do not minimize the #PE.

If the objective is to design an array with minimum $\#PE.T^2$ product, then the parameters of the optimal design could be, in general, different from those for optimal completion time and #PE. The search strategy for minimizing $\#PE.T^2$ is to first find a design which minimizes the completion time. Let T_{min} and P_1 be the completion time and #PE of the design. Then, a design is searched for using the search space (which is polynomial in L, the size of the problem) – a design that minimizes the $PE.T^2$ product with completion time between

$$T_{min} \quad \text{and} \quad \frac{T_{min}\sqrt{P_1}}{\sqrt{3L-2}}$$

For $N = 4$, since the array in Fig. 1.8 minimizes both the completion time and #PE, it also minimizes the $\#PE.T^2$ product (or any objective in the form of $\#PE^m.T^n$, $m, n \geqslant 1$).

1.4 Final remarks

Hardware implementations of algorithms have a tremendous impact on real-time applications where speed is of utmost importance. Systematic techniques of generating these hardware arrays are crucial for the design of large systems involving a number of these arrays, which can be visualized as hardware libraries accessible from a general purpose host computer.

In this chapter, a systematic parameter-based approach to generate systolic architectures for problems expressible as uniform recurrences has been described. Table 1.2 contrasts the parameter method with the dependency method. Lower dimensional arrays to solve the recurrence can be generated optimally using the parameter-based approach. However, the size of the target array is a function of the size of the index space defined by the recurrence. This leads to a different array for every problem size which is not desirable from a cost and reusability perspective. There are schemes available to partition and map the recurrence into smaller arrays (Moldovan and Fortes, 1986) but these are not optimal. Hence, a number of issues in partitioning of algorithms and mapping them to arrays with fixed I/O or PEs are still to be explored.

The recurrences considered by researchers so far have been mostly uniform ones. It will be of significant interest and value to have systematic techniques to transform non-uniform recurrences (which can be used to represent a number of important problems in optimization) into hardware arrays.

Table 1.2 Comparison of the parameter method with the dependency method

	GPM	DM	
		I	II
Type of recurrence	Uniform	Uniform	Uniform
Algorithm – Capability	N-dim $\rightarrow M$-dim $(M \leqslant N - 1)$	$N \rightarrow N - 1$ dim.	N-dim $\rightarrow M$-dim $(M \leqslant N - 1)$
– Complexity	Polynomial in the size of the problem and the parameters chosen	Integer linear programming to determine the matrix. Hence could be exponential in the worst case	
Solution Character- istics	The target array has uniform data flows and does not require extra control bits to govern the data flows. So simple and modularly expandable design	Solution generated might have irregular data flows. The method only generates the mapping and not the implementation. So control bits might have to be added to achieve the required data movement increasing the complexity of the design	
	Able to generate optimal solutions with respect to time, PE count or any objective function expressible in terms of the parameters	Only heuristic solutions due to high complexity (for instance the S matrix is heuristically chosen and π vector is then found)	

GPM – General Parameter Method
DM I – Dependency method orginally proposed by Moldovan
DM II – Dependency method extended by Lee and Kedem/Fortes to handle lower dimensional arrays

Acknowledgements

Research supported by National Science Foundation, grant MIP 88-10584 and Joint Services Electronics Program contract N00014-90-J-1270.

References

Fortes, J. A. B., Fu, K.-S., and Wah, B. W., 1988, Systematic design approaches for algorithmically specified systolic arrays, in *Computer Architecture: Concepts and Systems* (ed. V. M. Milutinovic), North Holland, 454–94.

Guibas, L. J., Kung, H. T., and Thompson, C. D., 1979, Direct VLSI implementation of combinatorial algorithms, in *Proceedings of CALTECH Conference on VLSI*, 509–25.

Heller, D., 1985, Partitioning big matrices for small systolic arrays, in *VLSI and modern signal processing* (eds S. Y. Kung, H. J. Whitehouse, and T. Kailath), Prentice Hall, 185–99.

Karp, R. M., and Held, M., 1967, Finite state processes and dynamic programming, *SIAM Journal of Applied Mathematics*, **15**; 693–718.

Karp, R. M., Miller, R. E., and Winograd, S., 1967, The organization of computations for uniform recurrences, *Journal of the ACM*, **14**; 563–90.

Kung, H. T., 1982, Why systolic architectures? *IEEE Computer*, **15**; 37–46.

Kung, S. Y., 1988, *VLSI Processor Arrays*, Prentice Hall.

Lee, P.-Z., and Kedem, Z. M., 1988, Synthesizing linear array algorithms from nested FOR loop algorithms, *IEEE Trans. Comput.*, **C-37**(12); 1578–97.

Li, G.-J., and Wah, B. W., 1985, The design of optimal systolic arrays, *IEEE Trans. Comput.*, **C-34**(1); 66–77.

Moldovan, D. I., 1982, On the analysis and synthesis of VLSI algorithms, *IEEE Trans. Comput.*, **C-31**(11); 1121–6.

Moldovan, D. I., and Fortes, J. A. B., 1986, Partitioning and mapping algorithms into fixed size systolic arrays, *IEEE Trans. Comput.*, **C-35**(1); 1–12.

Rajopadhye, S. V., 1986, Synthesis, optimization and verification of systolic architectures, PhD thesis, University of Utah, Salt Lake City, Utah.

2

Topological Transformation of Systolic Systems

Karel Culik II and Sheng Yu

2.1 Introduction

Informally, systolic systems are arrays of synchronized processors which process data in parallel by passing them from one processor to neighbouring ones in a regular rhythmic pattern. In a systolic system, there are only a few different types of processors arranged in a regular pattern.

Systolic architecture and algorithms were introduced by Kung and Leiserson in the late 1970s (Kung, 1982). However, cellular automata, iterative arrays, etc., which have been studied for many years (Cole, 1969; Smith, 1972; Kosaraju, 1975; Dyer, 1980; Umeo *et al.*, 1982; Culik and Yu, 1984; Ibarra *et al.*, 1985), are actually special types of systolic systems in which all communications between processors are of one unit delay and all processors are finite-state machines. The study of cellular automata was initiated by von Neumann in the late 1950s.

Systolic networks for a wide variety of problems have been designed. Systolic networks, sometimes, have also been called systolic algorithms. In this chapter, we will make a clear distinction between these two notions. Our main goal is to give a relatively general method for the design of systolic networks and for the conversion of one network into an equivalent one with a different underlying structure. In practice the design of a systolic network solving a certain problem usually starts without a precise description of the problem and the design is an interactive process producing both the desired systolic network as well as a more precise specification of the given problem. Here we need to start with a precisely described problem to be implemented.

Informally, a systolic algorithm is a collection of diagrams, one for each input size, that describe the locality, timing, and directions of data flows on certain processes (nodes) and the functions performed by the processes (nodes) for solving a certain problem. Each of the diagrams is an **acyclic directed graph** in which the nodes with in-degree (out-degree) zero are mapped to the inputs (outputs) of the algorithm and are called input (output) nodes. The nodes that are neither input nodes nor output nodes are called internal nodes. All nodes except input nodes are labelled by basic functions. The diagrams are independent of input values although they are dependent on the size of the input.

A systolic network is a directed, possibly cyclic, graph with each node being a processor. If we draw a space-time diagram, which we call unrolling, of a computation on a systolic network for each legal input size and omit the actual computed values, then we get a systolic algorithm which is implemented by the systolic network. On the other hand if we replace each internal node of a systolic algorithm by a processor that implements the function labelling the node, we obtain a systolic network which trivially implements the systolic algorithm. We say that this implementation is trivial because each processor of the underlying digraph is used once at most. In order to design more efficient systolic networks, we may 'roll' the given systolic algorithm so that many nodes with the same label (function) can be implemented by a single processor. This is the essence of what later we call topological transformation.

Two systolic networks N_1 and N_2 (finite or infinite) that produce the same output for the same input are naturally considered equivalent. However, this notion of equivalence does not tell us the computation structures of the algorithms and, therefore, is hardly helpful in the design of systolic networks. We introduce a stronger notion of equivalence which we call **topological equivalence**. Two networks N_1 and N_2 are topologically equivalent if they implement (unroll into) the same systolic algorithm. Besides the notion of equivalence, we will later also make precise what is meant by systolic network N_1 simulating systolic network N_2.

We start with a simple example which, we hope, will intuitively explain the notion of topological equivalence and the technique of topological transformation. Our task in this example is to design, as well as to prove the correctness of, a distributed sorting systolic network with a unidirectional ring architecture. We assume that all processors (microcomputers) are identical, in particular, each processor can store the same number of records. We first consider the well known odd-even transportation sorting method for $2n$ records (Knuth, 1973) which, presented as a systolic algorithm for $n = 4$, is partially (first 4 levels) shown in Fig. 2.1. For any $n > 1$ each of $2n$ input nodes gets a (sorted) pair of records. There are $2n - 1$ rows of internal nodes with alternately $n - 1$ and n nodes in each row and finally one row of n output nodes. All the internal and output nodes are of in-degree two and all are labelled by a function that takes a pair of records one from each input and sorts them, i.e. computes an ordered pair with the left component smaller than or equal to the right component. All the input nodes and the internal nodes are of out-degree two with the left (right) output taking the left (right) component of the sorted pair. Eventually, the records when reaching the output nodes are sorted in ascending order from left to right, one pair in each node.

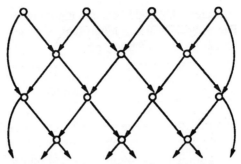

Figure 2.1 Systolic sorting algorithm.

As the second step we assume that the inputs are pairs of ordered multisets rather than pairs of single records. We replace the operation of sorting two elements (records) by the merging of two ordered multisets and the operation of splitting a pair into left and right components by the splitting of an ordered multiset into two equal parts (Knuth, 1973). Hence, with these modifications Fig. 2.1 also shows a systolic algorithm for the multiset sorting problem (for 4 multisets). Now, we observe that the diagram in Fig. 2.1 can be transformed into that in Fig. 2.2 by replacing each curved edge by a pair of dotted edges with a newly added intermediate node for the two curved edges on each level. Now, we label all newly added nodes by the function that forms a sequence of elements by simply concatenating the multisets coming from left and right and then splitting them again so that these new nodes are really just resending their input to their output.

We observe that (except for the insertion of the new nodes) the diagrams in Figs 2.1 and 2.2 are representing the same systolic algorithm. Indeed, the internal nodes in Fig. 2.2 are cyclically shifted by one in each

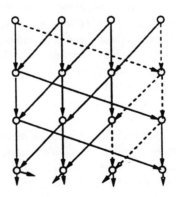

Figure 2.2 Modified systolic sorting algorithm.

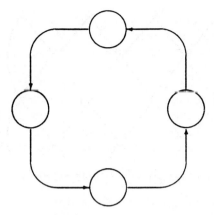

Figure 2.3 One-way ring.

row. So, after n steps the output nodes correctly match the output nodes in Fig. 2.1. Hence, we have shown that Fig. 2.2 with the above described labelling functions gives a correct systolic algorithm for distributed sorting. Finally, we observe that the diagram in Fig. 2.2 can be rolled into (implemented by) the unidirectional (one-way) ring of identical four processors shown in Fig. 2.3 (n processors for $2n$ multisets) providing we can label all the internal and output nodes in Fig. 2.2 by the same function. This can be achieved by using the **fence** symbol which is originally stored at the end of the nth (last) multiset and during the sorting is sent at the half speed from right to left through the ring. Each processor of the ring then executes the same function.

Each processor sends the 'left half' of a multiset, i.e. the k smallest elements (or all of them if there are fewer than k), to the left neighbour and merges the remaining elements with those coming from the right neighbour. The only exception is that no sorting is done across the fence. The fence is sent at 'half speed' through the processors, i.e. it is in the 'middle' of the $(n-t)$th processor at time $2t+1$ and that processor is 'inactive'. After $2n$ steps the 'fence' returns to its original position and the sorting is completed as shown in the following example of three processors, each containing four numbers. The bar represents the fence.

$$
\begin{array}{llll\ llll\ llll}
3 & 4 & 6 & 8 & 1 & 3 & 5 & 6 & 1 & 4 & 6 & 9| \\
1 & 3 & 6 & 8 & 1 & 4 & 5 & 6 & 6 & 9| & 3 & 4 \\
1 & 4 & 6 & 8 & 5 & 6 & 6 & 9| & 1 & 3 & 3 & 4 \\
5 & 6 & 6 & 8 & 6 & 9| & 1 & 3 & 1 & 3 & 4 & 4 \\
6 & 6 & 8 & 9| & 1 & 1 & 3 & 3 & 4 & 4 & 5 & 6 \\
8 & 9| & 1 & 1 & 3 & 3 & 4 & 4 & 5 & 6 & 6 & 6 \\
1 & 1 & 3 & 3 & 4 & 4 & 5 & 6 & 6 & 6 & 8 & 9|
\end{array}
$$

Note that if some processor is not 'full', i.e. contains less than $2n$ elements, it still sends n elements to the left, which means that it pretends that it contains additional dummy elements considered larger than all the others, and therefore these dummies are always retained.

Note that in Fig. 2.3 we omit a loop at each processor of the systolic ring since each loop can be implemented by a processor's local memory.

In an actual implementation of this sorting network the two tasks of merging the two sorted files and communicating one half-file to the left were done simultaneously and took about the same time.

2.2 Computation diagrams and network algorithms

In designing an algorithm for a systolic network, we need to draw diagrams to specify the locality, timing, and direction of required data flow on processors as well as the functions performed by certain processors at certain computation times. We call those diagrams **computation diagrams**. For a given problem, a collection of computation diagrams that cover all the possible input of the problem is called a **network algorithm**.

Formally, a computation diagram (CD) S is a structure $S = (V, E, Q, \Delta, g)$, where (V, E) is an ordered acyclic digraph, Q is a set of states (finite or infinite), Δ is a finite set of functions in $\{Q^k \rightarrow Q \mid k \geq 0\}$, and $g : V \Rightarrow \Delta$ is a map which associates with each node in V a function in Δ. For each $v \in V$, let $In(v)$ and $Out(v)$ denote the ordered sets $\{u \mid u \rightarrow v \in E\}$ and $\{w \mid v \rightarrow w \in E\}$, respectively. We call the cardinalities of $In(v)$ and $Out(v)$ the in-degree and out-degree of v, respectively. We are only interested in the CDs that have bounded in-degrees and out-degrees. Therefore, the in-degrees and out-degrees of all nodes in the CDs of a network algorithm are always assumed bounded in this chapter. We use V_i, $i \geq 0$, to denote the set $\{v \mid In(v) = i\}$, which is the set of all nodes in V that have an in-degree i.

In the above definition, each node is assigned a function and the state of the node is the function of the states of the nodes which have an edge directed to the node. Each output of a node is the state of the node. Therefore, all outputs of the same node are the same. Alternatively, we can use a model, as we have used in the example in the previous section, where each output of a node is a function of its inputs. However, the two models are equivalent and one can easily be transformed to another. Although the latter may be more realistic in some cases, we adopt the former for convenience and simplicity.

A computation c on a CD $S = (V, E, Q, \Delta, g)$ is a map $V \rightarrow Q$ such that for each $v \in V$ with $In(v) = (v_1, \ldots v_k)$, for some $k > 0$ and $v_1, \ldots v_k \in V$, we have

$$c(v) = g(v)(c(v_1), \ldots, c(v_k)).$$

Note that $g(v) \in \Delta$ is the function associated with v. The above condition implies that in every computation the state of a node v in $V - V_0$ is uniquely determined by the states of the nodes in $In(v)$ and the function $g(v)$, while the nodes in V_0 are not bounded by this condition. We call the nodes in V_0 the input nodes of the CD.

Let $S = (V, E, Q, \Delta, g)$ be a CD and c a computation on S. Then c is uniquely determined by the restriction of c to V_0. In other words, given a function $c_0 : V_0 \rightarrow Q$, there is at most one computation $c : V \rightarrow Q$ such that c is an extension of c_0.

Let $A_1 = (V_1, E_1, Q_1, \Delta_1, g_1)$ and $A_2 = (V_2, E_2, Q_2, \Delta_2, g_2)$ be two computation diagrams. A_1 and A_2 are said to be **isomorphic** if the following conditions hold:

1. The two underlying digraphs (V_1, E_1) and (V_2, E_2) are isomorphic under a bijection $\tau_V : V_1 \rightarrow V_2$.
2. There exist bijections $\tau_Q : Q_1 \rightarrow Q_2$ and $\tau_\Delta : \Delta_1 \rightarrow \Delta_2$ such that $f(a_1, \ldots, a_k) = a$ for $f \in \Delta_1$ and $a_1, \ldots, a_k, a \in Q_1$ iff $\tau_\Delta(f)$ $(\tau_Q(a_1), \ldots, \tau_Q(a_k)) = \tau_Q(a)$.
3. $g_1(v) = f$, $v \in V_1$ and $f \in \Delta_1$, iff $g_2(\tau_V(v)) = \tau_\Delta(f)$.

It is obvious that if two CDs A_1 and A_2 are isomorphic, then they perform the same computations, i.e. there is a computation c on A_1 iff there is a computation $\tau_Q(c)$ on A_2.

Formally, a network algorithm for a given problem is a collection of computation diagrams such that:

1. all inputs of the same length have the same computation diagram;
2. computation diagrams for shorter inputs can be extended to computation diagrams for longer inputs; and
3. the collection of computation diagrams for all inputs is described by a finite set of rules.

In other words, a network algorithm is a schema of computation diagrams for solving a given problem.

Two network algorithms A_1 and A_2 are equivalent if, for any input of the given problem, the computation diagrams of A_1 and A_2 for the input are isomorphic.

Note that we are defining network algorithms in terms of computation diagrams rather than specific computation networks, for which we will give a formal definition subsequently. A network algorithm may not be associated to only one network. Each algorithm may be associated with many networks with different underlying structures. We say that a network algorithm may have many implementations.

A computation network (CN) is a structure $N = (V, E, Q, \Delta, g, d, t^{(0)})$ where (V, E, Q, Δ, g) is a computation diagram except that the underlying digraph (V, E) can be cyclic, $d : E \rightarrow Z$ is a delay function for the edges which shows the number of steps needed for a symbol (state information) to travel from a node to a neighbouring node, and $t^{(0)} : V \to Z$ is an initiation function which tells when a computation begins at each node in V.

For a network $N = (V, E, Q, \Delta, g, d, t^{(0)})$, we now define $\hat{V}$, $\hat{E}$ and $\hat{g}$, respectively, which will be used subsequently in defining the unrolling of N.

$\hat{V}$ is a subset of $V \times Z$ such that:

1. for each $v \in V$, $< v, t^{(0)}(v) >$ is in $\hat{V}$;
2. for each $v \in V_0$, $< v, t >$ is in $\hat{V}$ for all $t > t^{(0)}(v)$;
3. with $In(v) = (u_1, \ldots, u_k)$, $k \geq 1$,
   and $d_1 = d(u_1, v), \ldots, d_k = d(u_k, v)$,
   then $< v, t >$ is in $\hat{V}$, for some $t > t^{(0)}(v)$,
   if $< u_1, t - d_1 >, \ldots, < u_k, t - d_k >$ are all in $\hat{V}$.

$\hat{E}$ is a subset of $\hat{V} \times \hat{V}$ such that $< v_1, t_1 > \to < v_2, t_2 >$ is in $\hat{E}$, for $< v_1, t_1 >, <v_2, t_2 > \in \hat{V}$, iff $v_1 \to v_2 \in E$ and $t_2 - t_1 = d(v_1 \to v_2)$.

$\hat{g} : \hat{V} \to \Delta$ is an extension of g such that $\hat{g}(<v, t>) = g(v)$.

We say that the initiation function $t^{(0)}$ of N is **properly defined** if the symbols from the in-coming edges of each node always arrive at the node synchronously, i.e. for any node $v \in V$ and $t \in Z$, if $u_i, u_j \in In(v)$ and $u_i \to v \neq u_j \to v$, then

$$< u_i, t - d(u_i \to v) > \in \hat{V} \text{ iff } < u_j, t - d(u_j \to v) > \in \hat{V}$$

Let $N = (V, E, Q, \Delta, g, d, t^{(0)})$ be a CD and $\hat{V}$, $\hat{E}$ and $\hat{g}$ are defined as above. Clearly, $\hat{N} = (\hat{V}, \hat{E}, Q, \Delta, \hat{g})$ is a computation diagram. We call $\hat{N}$ the **unrolling** of N if $t^{(0)}$ is properly defined.

Note that there is no explicit timing information in the unrolling of a network. The timing information of a network is embedded into the underlying graph of its unrolling.

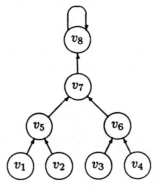

Figure 2.4 T: a systolic tree with feed-back.

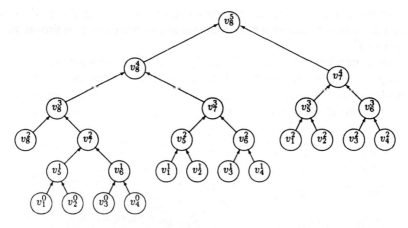

Figure 2.5 The 6-step unrolling of network T.

A computation on a CN N is defined to be a computation on the unrolling of N.

By an implementation of a network algorithm A on a CN N, we mean an embedding of the computation diagrams of A onto the unrolling of N. Naturally, if the unrollings of CN N_1 and CN N_2 are isomorphic, a network algorithm can be implemented on N_1 iff it can be implemented on N_2.

Let $N = (V, E, Q, \Delta, g, d, t^{(0)})$ be a CN and $\hat{N}$ the unrolling of N. Then we call the restriction of $\hat{N}$ to $V \times \{t \in Z \mid t \leqslant k\}$, for some $k \in Z$, the k-step unrolling of N.

Example

A systolic tree T with feed-back (Culik and Jürgensen, 1989) is shown in Fig. 2.4. Every internal node represents a processor that performs the same associative operation, say multiplication. We will show that by feeding $4n$ numbers $a_1, \ldots, a_{4n}$ at the input nodes four at a time:

$$(a_1, a_2, a_3, a_4), (a_5, a_6, a_7, a_8), \ldots$$

in consecutive steps, we can compute the product $a_1 a_2 \ldots a_{4n}$. If the number of inputs is not divisible by 4 we can fill it by ones. The structure of a 6-step unrolling of network T is shown in Fig. 2.5. In this figure the node v_i^j corresponds to the processor v_i of tree T at time j. It is clear that this computational diagram is a correct one for computing the product providing that the left-most node with in-degree zero, corresponding to the looping node in T_1 at time 2, is assigned the value 1. Network T with k leaves ($k = 4$ in Fig. 2.4) will compute the product approximately in $n/k + \log k$ steps.

Two computation networks N_1 and N_2 are (topologically) **equivalent** iff their unrollings are isomorphic. Equivalently, we say that N_1 and N_2 are (topologically) equivalent iff for any integer $t \geq 0$ the t-step unrollings of N_1 and N_2 are isomorphic.

Topological equivalence is a strong notion of equivalence which requires that two networks not only perform the same function, but also have the same internal computation structure. To illustrate the applications of the above definitions, we give a simple alternative proof for the retiming lemma which was first introduced and proved by Leiserson and Saxe (1981). We will introduce a weaker notion of equivalence, i.e. topological simulation, in a later section.

Lemma 1 (retiming)

Let $N = (V, E, Q, \Delta, g, d, t^{(0)})$ be a computation network and $l : V \to Z$ a function, called a lag function. Define $d_l : V \to Z$ by

$$d_l(u, v) = d(u, v) - l(u) + l(v)$$

for each $e = u \to v \in E$ and $t_l^{(0)} : V \to Z$ by

$$t_l^{(0)}(v) = t^{(0)}(v) + l(v)$$

Consider the computation network $N_l = (V_l, E_l, Q, \Delta, g, d_l, t_l^{(0)})$ where $V_l = V$ and $E_l = E$. If the unrolling of N exists, then the unrolling of N_l exists and the following statements hold.

1. The unrollings of N and N_l are isomorphic.
2. If $c : \hat{V} \to Q$ is a computation of N, then $c_l : \hat{V}_l \to Q$, defined by $c_l(v, t) = c(v, t-l(v))$, is a computation on N_l.
3. N and N_l are (topologically) equivalent.

Proof: Statements 2 and 3 are straightforward consequences of statement 1. So, it suffices to prove statement 1. Let τ_V be a mapping $V \times Z \to V_l \times Z$ defined by $\tau_V(v, t) = (v, t+l(v))$ for $v \in V$ and $t \geq t^{(0)}(v)$. It is easy to show by the definition of unrollings that (v, t) is in $\hat{V}$ iff $(v, t + l(v))$ is in $\hat{V}_l$, i.e. τ_V is a bijection, and that $(\hat{V}, \hat{E})$ and $(V_l, \hat{E}_l)$ are isomorphic under the bijection τ_V. Define τ_Δ and τ_Q to be identity functions. Therefore, the unrollings of N and N_l, i.e. $\hat{N}$ and $\hat{N}_l$, are isomorphic. ∎

From now on, we use the notation N_l to denote the resulting CN obtained by retiming the computation network N with the lag-function l.

2.3 Systolic networks and systolic conversion

First we observe that in general there might not exist any computation on a CN. This may happen on networks with zero or negative delays. Following (Leiserson and Saxe, 1981), we call a CN

$N = (V, E, Q, \Delta, g, d, t^{(0)})$ a semisystolic CN if $d(u, v) \geq 0$ for all $u \rightarrow v \in E$. It is systolic if $d(u, v) > 0$ for all $u \rightarrow v \in E$.

The following two theorems are generalizations of systolic conversion theorem from (Leiserson and Saxe, 1981). They give the necessary and sufficient conditions for the existence of a lag function l which by using the retiming lemma converts a computation network to an equivalent semisystolic (systolic) network.

Given a CN $N = (V, E, Q, \Delta, g, d, t^{(0)})$ we extend the definition of d such that if a path $p = e_1 \ldots e_t$ then $d(p) = d(e_1) + \ldots + d(e_t)$. We define $\bar{d} : V \times V \rightarrow Z \cup \{-\infty, \infty\}$ by $\bar{d}(u, v) = inf\{d(p) \mid p$ is path from u to $v\}$ for all u, v in V. Note that $inf(0) = \infty$, i.e., if there is no path from u to v then $\bar{d}(u, v) = \infty$. By the definition of $\bar{d}$, it is clear that $\bar{d}(u, v) = -\infty$ for $u, v \in V$ if u and v are in a negative loop. Note that d and $\bar{d}$ coincide on all $u \rightarrow v \in E$.

Theorem 1 (semisystolic conversion)
Let $N = (V, E, Q, \Delta, g, d, t^{(0)})$ be a CN. Then there exists a lag function $l : V \rightarrow Z$ such that CN N_l is semisystolic iff

$$\bar{d}(u, v) > -\infty \text{ for all } u, v \in V \tag{2.1}$$

Proof: Assume (2.1) holds. Then the following properties of $\bar{d}$ are clearly true:

1. $\bar{d}(u, v) + \bar{d}(v, w) \geq \bar{d}(u, w)$ for all u, v, w in V;
2. $\bar{d}(u, u) \geq 0$ for each u in V; and
3. $\bar{d}(u, v) + \bar{d}(v, u) \geq 0$ for all u, v in V.

Now we show that there exists a lag function $l : V \rightarrow Z$ such that $d_l(u, v) \geq 0$ for each $u \rightarrow v \in E$, where d_l is defined by $d_l(u, v) = d(u, v) - l(u) + l(v)$. Let U be a maximal subset of V on which there exists a lag function $l : U \rightarrow Z$ such that

$$\bar{d}(u, v) - l(u) + l(v) \geq 0 \text{ and } \bar{d}(v, u) - l(v) + l(u) \geq 0 \tag{2.2}$$

hold for all u, v in U. If $U = V$ then N_l is a semisystolic CN and, therefore, the theorem holds. We now assume that $U \neq V$. Consider $w \in V - U$. We first show that

$$l(u) + \bar{d}(w, u) \geq l(v) - \bar{d}(v, w), \text{ for all } u, v \text{ in } U \tag{2.3}$$

This is true because

$$l(u) + \bar{d}(w, u) - l(v) + \bar{d}(v, w) \geq \bar{d}(v, u) - l(v) + l(u)$$

by applying statement 1 and (2.2) where

$$\bar{d}(v, u) - l(v) + l(u) \geq 0$$

Expression (2.3) implies that there exists a value $l(w)$ such that

$l(v) + \bar{d}(w, v) \geq l(w) \geq l(v) - \bar{d}(v, w)$, holds for all $v \in U$.

Then we have $\bar{d}(w, v) - l(w) + l(v) \geq 0$ and $\bar{d}(v, w) - l(v) + l(w)$, which contradicts the fact that U is a maximum subset of V for which (2.2) holds. Thus, $U = V$ and l can be defined on the whole V. Define N_l with the delay function d_l defined by $d_l(u, v) = d(u, v) - l(u) + l(v)$ for $u \to v \in E$. By the retiming lemma, N and N_l are equivalent. Since

$$d_l(u, v) = d(u,v) - l(u) + l(v) \geq \bar{d}_l(u, v) - l(u) + l(v) \geq 0$$

for all $u \to v$ in E, N_l is semisystolic.

To prove the converse, assume that there exists a lag function l such that N_l is semisystolic. Then $\bar{d}_l(u, v) \geq 0$ for all $u, v \in V_l$. Note that $\bar{d}_l(u, v) = \bar{d}(u, v) - l(u) + l(v)$. So, $\bar{d}(u, v) \geq l(u) - l(v) > -\infty$. ∎

For a CN with a finite number of nodes, the above proof has actually given an algorithm that transforms the CN into an equivalent semisystolic CN. The algorithm can be described as follows.

1. Choose a node u in V arbitrarily and define $l(u) = 0$ and $U = \{u\}$.
2. Choose a node $v \in V - U$ and assign to $l(v)$ an integer value between $\min\{l(u) + \bar{d}(w, u) \mid u \in U\}$ and $\max\{l(u) - \bar{d}(u, w) \mid u \in U\}$.
3. Let $U = U \cup \{v\}$. If $U \neq V$ then go back to step 2.

Given a CN $N = (V, E, Q, \Delta, g, d, t^{(0)})$, we define $[N + k]$, $k \in Z$, to be a CN $(V, E, Q, \Delta, g, [d + k], t^{(0)})$ where $[d + k]$ is defined by $[d + k](e) = d(e) + k$ for all $e \in E$. More generally, we define $[f(N)] = (V, E, Q, \Delta, g, [f(d)], t^{(0)})$ for any function $f : Z \to Z$, where $[f(d)]$ is defined by $[f(d)](e) = f(d(e))$ for all $e \in E$. Then it is clear what we mean by, e.g. $[kN]$, $[N - 1]$, etc.

Clearly, N is systolic iff $N - 1$ is semisystolic.

Theorem 2 (systolic conversion)
Let $N = (V, E, Q, \Delta, g, d, t^{(0)})$ be a CN. There exists a lag function $l : V \to Z$ such that $N_l = (V, E, Q, \Delta, g, d_l, t_l^{(0)})$ is systolic iff for all $u, v \in V$

$$inf\{d(p) - |p| \mid p \text{ is a path from } u \text{ to } v\} > -\infty, \qquad (2.4)$$

where $|p|$ denotes the number of edges in p.

Proof: We have already noted that there exists a lag function l such that N_l is systolic iff $[N_l - 1]$ is semisystolic. Clearly $[N_l - 1] = [N - 1]_l$. By Theorem 1 there is a lag function l such that $[N - 1]_l$ is semisystolic iff $\bar{d}_{[N-1]} > -\infty$ for all u, v in V (i.e. $V_{[N-1]}$). Since $\bar{d}(u, v) = inf\{d(p) \mid p$ is a path from u to $v\}$, it is clear that $\bar{d}_{[N-1]}(u, v) = inf\{d(p) - |p| \mid p$ is a path from u to $v\}$. Thus, the theorem holds. ∎

The following corollaries can be immediately derived from the above theorem.

Corollary 1
Let N be a semisystolic CN in which paths of zero delays are bounded in the number of edges by an integer $b > 0$. Then there exists an integer k, $0 < k \leqslant b + 1$, and a lag function $l : V \to Z$ such that $[kN]_l$ is systolic.

Proof: Let p be an arbitrary path from u to v. Then $d(p) \geqslant \lceil |p| / (b + 1) \rceil$ where $|p|$ is the number of edges in p. Choose $k = b + 1$. Then we have $d_{[kN]}(p) = k * d(p) \geqslant |p|$. Therefore, $d_{[kN]}(p) - |p| \geqslant 0$ for any path p between u and v. By Theorem 2, $[kN]$ is convertible to a systolic system.   ∎

Corollary 2
Let $N = (V, E, Q, \Delta, g, d, t^{(0)})$ be a finite semisystolic CN. Then there exists an integer $k > 0$ and a lag function $l : V \to Z$ such that $[kN]_l$ is systolic iff there are no cycles of zero delay in N.

Proof: Since N is finite and has no cycles of zero delay, there is a bound for paths of zero delay.   ∎

Example 1
The infinite CN N given by the diagram in Fig. 2.6 is a semisystolic CN. This network can be transformed into a systolic CN by retiming with a lag function l defined by $l(u_i) = i$ for $i \geqslant 0$. The resulting CN is shown in Fig. 2.7.

Example 2
The infinite semisystolic CN M given by the diagram in Fig. 2.8 does not satisfy (2.4) of Theorem 2, but $[2M]$ does. $[2M]$ can be interpreted as M

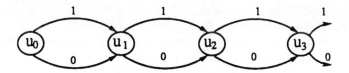

Figure 2.6 A semisystolic CN.

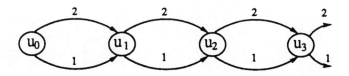

Figure 2.7 A resulting systolic CN by retiming.

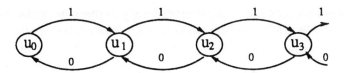

Figure 2.8 The semisystolic CN M.

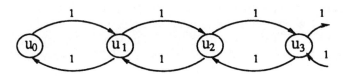

Figure 2.9 $[2M]_l$.

running twice as slowly. Define a lag function $l : V \to Z$ by $l(u_i) = -i$ for $i \geqslant 0$. Then $[2M]_l$ is a systolic CN which is shown in Fig. 2.9.

2.4 Simulation between computation networks

In section 2 we have defined the topological equivalence of CNs. However, the notion of topological equivalence does not cover the cases where a network follows basically the computation pattern of another network but in a different pace and locality, and the cases where a processor in one network is functioning as several processors in another network or vice versa, etc. In this section, we introduce the notion of topological simulation, which is a notion weaker than topological equivalence and can be used to describe the aforementioned cases.

Let $S_1 = (V_1, E_1, Q_1, \Delta_1, g_1)$ and $S_2 = (V_2, E_2, Q_2, \Delta_2, g_2)$ be two computation diagrams. We say that S_2 (topologically) simulates S_1 if

1. there is a function $\rho_V : V_1 \to V_2$ such that there is a path $p_1 : u \to v$ in S_1, for $u, v \in V_1$, iff there is a path $p_2 : \rho_V(u) \to \rho_V(v)$ in S_2;
2. there is a mapping $\rho_Q : Q_2 \times V_1 \to Q_1$ such that for any computation c_1 on S_1 there is a computation c_2 on S_2 for which

$$c_1(v) = \rho_Q(c_2(\rho_V(v)), v)$$

for all v in V_1.

Informally speaking, CD S_2 (topologically) simulates CD S_1 if the topological structure of S_1 can be embedded into S_2 and the value of each node of S_1 in a computation can be recovered from the corresponding computation of S_2.

Let N_1 and N_2 be two computation networks. We say that N_2 simulates N_1 if the unrolling of N_2 simulates N_1.

If CN N_2 simulates CN N_1 and a network algorithm A_1 is implemented on N_1 to solve a given problem, then we can easily transform A_1 to a network algorithm A_2 implemented on N_2 to solve the same problem. We call this transformation of network algorithms a topological transformation.

2.5 Applications

The technique of topological transformations is a tool that can be used to design or transform network algorithms. It can also be used to prove the equivalence of certain parallel computation models. In the following, we give three examples which demonstrate the use of our tools. Many other applications are interesting as well. For example, matrix computation algorithms on systolic systems of certain types (Kung and Leiserson, 1979; Kramer and van Leuwen, 1983) can be transformed to algorithms on systolic systems of different types using the tools of topological transformation. In particular, the bidirectional array (or toroid) can be simulated by a unidirectional toroid.

Example 1

First we show that a two-dimensional iterative array (2D IA) with global control can be simulated by a 2D IA without global control. A 2D IA with global control, A, is shown in Fig. 2.10, where edges without arrows are bidirectional edges and all unlabelled edges are assumed to have a label 1. A is a semisystolic CN. Obviously, A can be simulated by $[2A]$ and $[2A]$ can be retimed into a systolic CN B shown in Fig. 2.11. Again, B can be simulated by C, shown in Fig. 2.12, which is a 2D IA without global control.

Next we show that a one-way linear array and a trellis network are

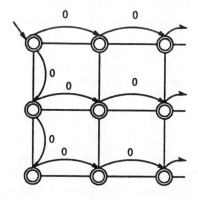

Figure 2.10 A 2D iterative array with global control.

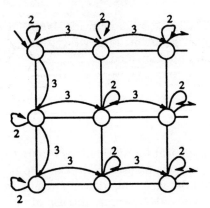

Figure 2.11 Network *B*.

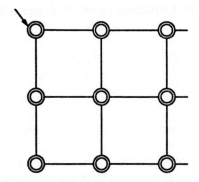

Figure 2.12 A 2D iterative array.

topologically equivalent. For more details and a theoretical application of this fact see (Culik and Choffrut, 1984).

Example 2
A one-way cellular automaton (OCA) is shown in Fig. 2.13 and the trellis network with 5 levels in Fig. 2.14(b). Note that each processor of a trellis is used only once, therefore a trellis is isomorphic to its unrolling. The

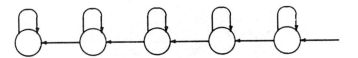

Figure 2.13 An OCA.

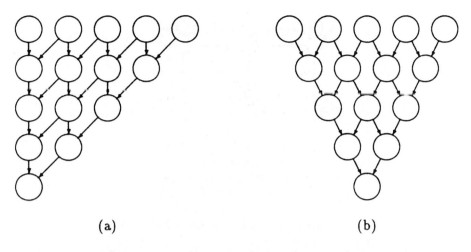

(a)   (b)

Figure 2.14 Unrollings of an OCA and a trellis.

5-step unrolling of the OCA is shown in Fig. 2.14(a). Obviously, the t-step unrolling of a real-time OCA and a real-time trellis are isomorphic for each $t \geqslant 0$. Therefore, real-time OCAs and real-time trellises are topologically equivalent.

Example 3

The last example, in more practical terms, shows that every program for linear array with parallel input, i.e. one input line in every processor, can be mechanically translated into an equivalent program for linear array with one serial input line at the left-most processor. Theoretically the linear

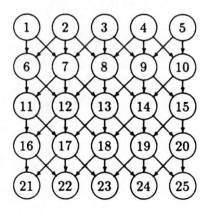

Figure 2.15 Computations on a CA.

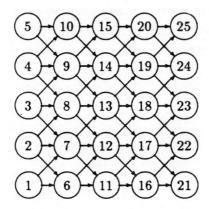

Figure 2.16 Computation on an iterative array.

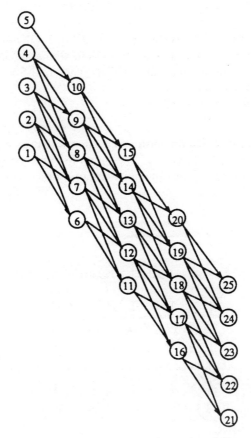

Figure 2.17 Computation on the retimed linear array.

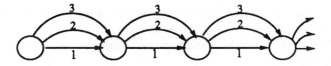

Figure 2.18 The retimed linear array.

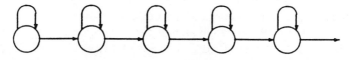

Figure 2.19 One-way linear array.

array of finite automata with parallel input is called a cellular automaton and the one with serial input an iterative array.

The simulation of (two-way) cellular automata (CA) by iterative arrays (IA) has been studied in (Umeo *et al.*, 1982), where the simulation takes $6n - 2$ steps. Using the systolic conversion theorem to improve the algorithm, the simulation time can be reduced to $3n - 1$. Here we show that it can be done in $2n - 1$ steps. Figure 2.15 shows an unrolling of a real-time CA. To transform it into one with sequential input we turn it anticlockwise through a right angle. It becomes the CD shown in Fig. 2.16, which is not even an unrolling of a semisystolic CN. Further by shifting every next column two steps down, we get the CD shown in Fig. 2.17, which is the unrolling of the CN shown in Fig. 2.18, and this CN can be simulated by the one-way linear array shown in Fig. 2.19. By using the systolic conversion theorem, the collecting of a result of any cell at any step can be converted to the collecting at the first cell at the same step. So, our result is obtained.

References

Cole, S. N., 1969, Real-time computation by n-dimensional iterative arrays of finite-state machines, *IEEE Trans. Comput.*, **C-18**, 349–65.

Culik II, K. and Choffrut, C., 1984, On real-time cellular automata and trellis automata, *Acta Informatica*, **21**, 393–407.

Culik II, K. and Jürgensen, H., 1985, Programmable finite automata, *Int. J. Computer Math.*, **14**, 259–75.

Culik II, K. and Yu, S., 1984, Iterative tree automata, *Theoret. Comput. Sci.*, **32**, 227–47.

Dyer, C. R., 1980, One-way bounded cellular automata, *Inform. and Control*, **44**, 261–81.

Ibarra, O. H., Palis, M. A. and Kim, S. M., 1985, Some results concerning linear iterative (systolic) arrays, *J. of Parallel and Distributed Computing*, **2**, 182–218.

Knuth, D. E., 1973, *The Art of Computer Programming*, vol 3, Addison-Wesley, Reading.

Kosaraju, S. R., 1975, Speed of recognition of context-free languages by array automata, *SIAM J. Comput.*, **4**, 331–40.

Kramer, M. R. and van Leuwen, J., 1983, Systolic computation and VLSI, Foundations of Computer Science IV, Part 1, In *Algorithms and Complexity* (eds DeBakker and van Leuwen), 75–103.

Kung, H. T., 1982, Why systolic architecture? *Computer*, **15**, 37–46.

Kung, H. T. and Leiserson, C. E., 1979, Systolic arrays (for VLSI), *SIAM Proc. Sparse Matrix* (eds I. S. Duff and G. W. Stewart), 256–82.

Leiserson, C. E. and Saxe, J. B., 1981, Optimizing synchronous systems, *Proc. 22nd Ann. Symp. on Foundations of Comp. Sci.*, Nashville, Tennessee, 23–36.

Smith III, A. R., 1972, Real-time language recognition by one-dimensional cellular automata, *J. of Computer and System Science*, **6**, 233–53.

Umeo, H., Morita, K. and Sugata, K., 1982, Deterministic one-way real-time cellular automata and its related problems, *Inform. Proc. Letters*, **14**, 158–61.

Bibliography

Culik II, K., and Fris, I., 1985, Topological transformation as a tool in the design of systolic networks, *SIAM J. Comput.*, **37**, 183–216.

Culik II, K., Gruska, J. and Salomaa, A., 1984, Systolic trellis automata, Part I, *Int. J. Computer Math.*, **15**, 195–212.

Culik II, K., Gruska, J. and Salomaa, A., 1984, Systolic trellis automata, Part II, *Int. J. Computer Math.*, **16**, 3–22.

Culik II, K., Pachl, J. and Yu, S., 1989, On the limit sets of cellular automata, *SIAM J. Computing*, **18**, 831–42.

Culik II, K. and Yu, S., 1985, Translation of systolic algorithms between systems of different topology, *Proc. IEEE Int. Conf. on Parallel Processing*, 756–63.

Culik II, K. and Yu, S., 1987, Fault-tolerant schemes for some systolic systems, *Int. J. Computer Math.*, **22**, 13–42.

Ibarra, O. H., Palis, M. A. and Kim, S. M., 1984, Design systolic algorithms using sequential machines, *Proc. 25th Ann. Symp. on Foundation of Comp. Sci.*, Singer Island, Florida 46–55.

Mead, C. A. and Conway, L., 1980, *Introduction to VLSI*, Addison-Wesley, Reading.

Ullman, J. D., 1984, *Computational Aspects of VLSI*, Computer Science Press, New York.

3

Processor-Time
Minimal Systolic Arrays

Peter Cappello

3.1 Introduction

In this chapter, we investigate realizations of systolic algorithms that maximally exploit the parallelism in the algorithm, using a minimum of processors. With regard to the representation of the algorithms under consideration, we adopt the point of view expressed by Papadimitriou and Ullman (1987).

> We model the computational problem to be solved as a directed acyclic graph (DAG), with nodes corresponding to computed values, and arcs denoting dependencies (i.e. the children of a node are the values used to compute the node). **Naturally, in most cases this DAG is part of the algorithm design sought, but it seems reasonable, at least at this point, to consider the DAG fixed and given.** [emphasis added]

Such DAGs can be extracted automatically from, for example, uniform recurrent equations (Quinton, 1984), a system of uniform recurrence equations (Karp *et al.*, 1967), regular iterative arrays (Rao, 1985; Jagadish *et al.*, 1987), a system of linear recurrence equations (Rajopadhye *et al.*, 1986; Rajopadhye and Fujimoto, 1987; Dongen and Quinton 1988), as well as the computational model used by Moldovan and Fortes (Moldovan, 1982; Fortes, 1983; Moldovan, 1983; Fortes and Moldovan, 1985).

The **time** to compute a DAG is determined when we assign a schedule to the nodes subject to the constraints that:

- a node can be computed only when its children have been computed at previous time steps;
- no processor can compute two different nodes during the same time step.

Definition
A multiprocessor schedule for a DAG is **time-minimal** when the number

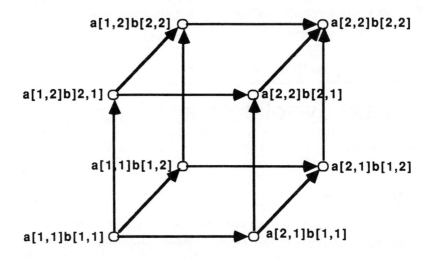

Figure 3.1   A 2 × 2 × 2 mesh representing 2 × 2 matrix product.

of steps in the schedule equals the number of nodes in a longest directed path in the DAG.

Time-minimality is a **machine-independent** measure of a DAG's **maximum parallelism**.

Starting with Kung and Leiserson's (1979) seminal paper, there has been a steady stream of successful research on systolic arrays, especially for computing a matrix product. Kung and Leiserson were the first to present a systolic array for banded matrix product (Kung and Leiserson, 1979). This soon was followed by Weiser and Davis's (1981) systolic array that uses one third as many time steps. This was followed by S-Y Kung's time-minimal design for full matrix product completing in $3n-2$ time steps, for $n \times n$ matrices, using n^2 processors.

All these systolic arrays share two things:

First, they all use the same dependence DAG, a 3D mesh[1]. An illustration of this DAG, for the product of 2 × 2 matrices A and B, is given in Fig. 3.1.

Second, they all map this 3D mesh into processor-time with a transformation of the indices that is linear. That is, if we are given the computation

$$\text{for } 1 \le i,\, j \le n \text{ do } \{c(i,\, j) \leftarrow \sum_{k=1}^{n} a(i,\, k) \cdot b(k,\, j)\}$$

---

[1]The dependence DAG associated with banded matrix product is a subgraph of the 3D mesh.

then each term of the summation – each inner product step – corresponds to an index vector, $[i \; j \; k]^T$. The **time step** and **processor location** of each of these inner-product steps is given by:

$$\begin{bmatrix} time \\ space_1 \\ space_2 \end{bmatrix} - A \begin{bmatrix} i \\ j \\ k \end{bmatrix}$$

for some matrix $A \in Z^{3 \times 3}$. The resultant systolic arrays thus are all 2-dimensional. Fig. 3.2 illustrates a map that produces a time-minimal systolic array using n^2 processors. Inspection reveals that both rules for a valid schedule are satisfied. For this illustration,

$$A = \begin{bmatrix} 1 & 1 & 1 \\ 1 & 0 & 0 \\ 0 & 1 & 0 \end{bmatrix}$$

As the figure illustrates, the DAG's spatial projection is a 2×2 processor array.

Linear maps of iterative dependence DAGs, such as the one illustrated in Fig. 3.2, have been researched intensely. Such maps are implicit in the research of Johnsson and Cohen (Johnsson *et al.*, 1981; Johnsson and Cohen, 1981), Weiser and Davis (1981), and Ramakrishnan, Fussell, and Silberschatz (Ramakrishnan *et al.*, 1986). Linear maps are explicit in the research of Moldovan (1982, 1983), Cappello and Steiglitz (1984), Quinton (1984, 1987), Gachet *et al.* (1986), Huang and Lengauer (1987), and Lengauer (1989). Such investigations are surveyed by Fortes, Fu, and Wah (Fortes *et al.*, 1988), and Quinton (1988). Work on enumerating, or otherwise exploring, the various linear maps associated with an iterative dependence DAG has been reported by Moldovan (1987), Miranker and Winkler (1984), Danielsson (1984), Moldovan and Fortes (1985), Rao (1985), Delosme and Ipsen (1986), Rajopadhye *et al.* (Rajopadhye *et al.*, 1986; Rajopadhye and Fujimoto, 1987), and Lee and Kedem (1988).

There has been a great deal of work on optimizing systolic arrays. The work pursued by Li and Wah (1985), Fortes and Parisi-Presicce (1984), Rao (1985), Delosme and Ipsen (1985), Chen (1986, 1988), Lee and Kedem (1988), Shang and Fortes (1988), and most recently by Wong and Delosme (1989a,b), all contribute to methods for optimizing systolic arrays. These efforts constrain the processor-time mapping to be a linear or affine transformation of the problem's index set. The first reason that this constraint is used is because it yields systolic arrays that are both intuitively appealing and practical to implement. The question nonetheless arises as to whether relaxing the linearity constraint results in an even more efficient use of time and space. This question leads to the second reason that extant optimization efforts constrain the processor-time mapping to be linear or affine: the general problem of precedence

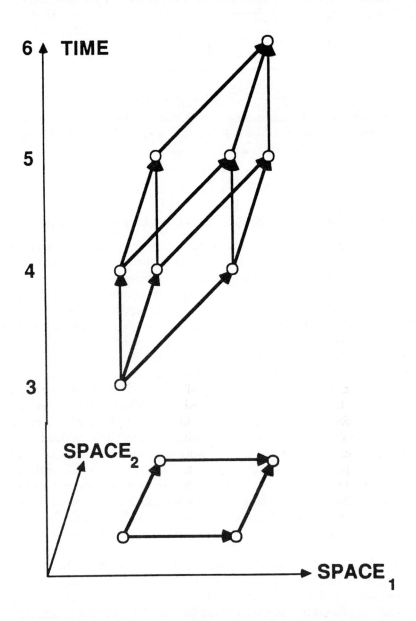

Figure 3.2 A spacetime embedding of the matrix product DAG. This
embedding constitutes a systolic array for computing 2×2 matrix
product (in general, $n \times n$ matrix product), using 4 time steps
(in general, $3n - 2$ steps), and 4 processors (in general, n^2 processors).

constrained scheduling onto a set of processors is NP-complete (see Garey and Johnson, 1979 for references to a variety of such problems). While the problem of computing an optimal schedule for an arbitrary DAG is NP-complete, we can often solve this problem for fundamental or canonical dependence DAGs.

Definition
A multiprocessor schedule for a DAG is **processor-time-minimal** when it uses as few processors as any time-minimal schedule for the DAG.

Although only one of many performance measures, processor-time-minimality is useful because it measures the **minimum processors** needed [sufficient] to extract the **maximum parallelism** from a DAG. Being machine-independent, it is a more fundamental measure than those that depend on a particular machine or architecture.

3.2 A processor-time-minimal systolic array for a 2D mesh

We now illustrate a processor-time-minimal array for a simple problem: a triangular system of linear equations. In this problem, the size parameter is n; the parameterized time-minimal schedule is $2n-1$; we will see that the parameterized processor-time-minimal systolic array uses $\lceil n/2 \rceil$ processing elements.

Figure 3.3(a) depicts a DAG of processes for solving a triangular system of linear equations by forward substitution. Cappello and Laub (1988) note that the processor-time map, depicted in Fig. 3.3(b), is processor-time-minimal.

Why is this map processor-time-minimal? Let us focus on the time steps in which all three processors are used (which we refer to as the **processor-maximal** time steps). They are time steps 6, 7, and 8. In order to reduce the number of processors, during the processor-maximal time steps the nodes scheduled for some processor must be rescheduled onto the other two processors. Two processors suffice, for example, if the nodes named (1,5), (1,6) and (2,6) can be rescheduled from processor 2 onto processors 0 and 1. These nodes are in a longest directed path in the DAG. This means that none can be rescheduled for earlier completion without violating a dependence. Neither can they be scheduled for later completion without either violating a dependence, or extending the overall completion time, violating time-minimality. In fact, in this DAG, every node is on some longest directed path, and hence can be rescheduled onto neither an earlier nor a later time step. In particular, the nodes scheduled for the processor-maximal time steps cannot be rescheduled onto different time steps. The number of processors therefore cannot be reduced: the map is processor-time-minimal. Also, in order for the dependence DAG of Fig. 3.3(a) to be mapped to a processor-time-minimal systolic array, the map must be nonlinear.

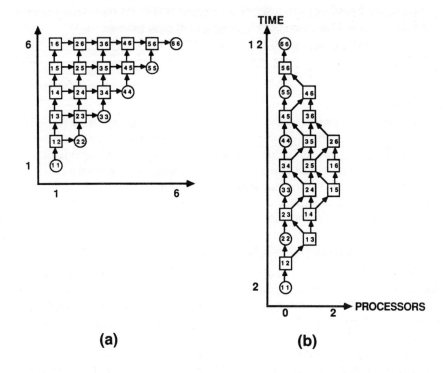

(a)   **(b)**

Figure 3.3(a) A process DAG for solving a triangular system of 6 linear equations by forward substitution. (b) A processor-time-minimal mapping of the DAG of (a).

An experienced systolic array engineer can usually devise by inspection a processor-time-minimal systolic array, given a 2D systolic algorithm. Automating this synthesis problem however is a topic of current research.

3.3 A processor-time-minimal systolic array for a 3D mesh

Synthesizing a processor-time-minimal schedule for 3D algorithms is apparently more difficult. We illustrate the synthesis problem on the standard dependence DAG for systolic matrix product: the $n \times n \times n$ mesh. Beyond matrix product, Ibarra and Palis (1987) point out that the 3D mesh is the dependence DAG of a variety of recurrences over three variables (e.g. finding the longest common subsequence among three strings). Other computations include LU factorization, a 3-pass transitive closure (Guibas *et al.*, 1979), matrix triangulation, matrix inversion, and

2-dimensional tuple comparison (Li and Wah, 1985). The cube-shaped 3D mesh (i.e. the $n \times n \times n$ mesh) can be defined as follows.

$G_{n \times n \times n} = (N, A)$, where

- $N = \{(i, j, k) \mid 1 \leqslant i, j, k \leqslant n\}$.
- $A = \{[(i, j, k)), (i', j' k')] \mid$ where exactly one of the following conditions holds

    1. $i' = i + 1$
    2. $j' = j + 1$
    3. $k' = k + 1$

    for $1 \leqslant i, j, k \leqslant n\}$.

Time-minimal schedule: $3n - 2$ steps. It is clear that the longest directed path in this DAG has $3n - 2$ nodes.

3.3.1 The processor-time lower bound

Definition
Let $G = (N, A)$ be a DAG. We label each node $v \in N$ with number:

- i, when v is the ith node in some longest directed path;
- 0, otherwise.

This labelling partitions N. We refer to each non-zero equivalence class as a **concurrent** set of nodes.

Using this definition, we state a simple but useful theorem.

Theorem 1
Let $G = (N, A)$ be a DAG, $Q \subseteq N$ be a concurrent set of nodes, and P be the number of processors implementing a time-minimal schedule. Then $|Q| \leqslant P$.

Proof: This follows immediately from the rules for multiprocessor schedules.   ■

The $n \times n \times n$ mesh DAG contains a concurrent set of size $\lceil (3/4)n^2 \rceil$. This is argued as follows. Each node in this DAG is on some longest path. Figure 3.4 depicts a $6 \times 6 \times 6$ mesh. Each node is labelled with its time step in a time-minimal schedule. By inspection, we can see that time step 8 is processor-maximal. In general, this is the midpoint of the computation: time step $\lceil (3n - 2)/2 \rceil$. The ceiling notation is used in case n is odd. Since the DAG of Fig. 3.4 contains 27 nodes labelled with time step 8, according to Theorem 1, we need at least 27 processors to complete this computation DAG in 16 time steps. A general expression for the number of processors needed for the midpoint time step depends on whether n is even or odd:

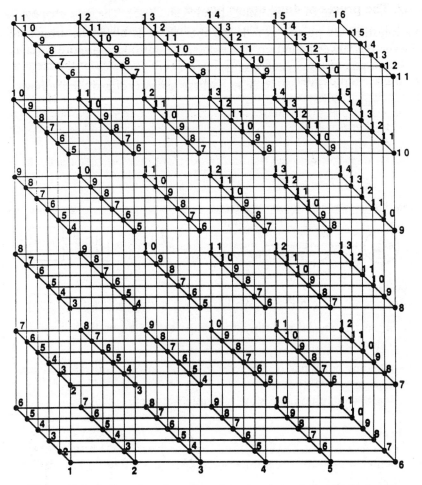

Figure 3.4 A 6 × 6 × 6 mesh, where each node is labelled with its time step in a time-minimal schedule. A processor-maximal time step is 8.

$$\text{even } n: \sum_{i=\frac{n}{2}+1}^{n} i \; + \sum_{i=\frac{n}{2}}^{n-1} i = \frac{3n^2}{4}$$

$$\text{odd } n: \sum_{i=\lceil\frac{n}{2}\rceil}^{n} i + \sum_{i=\lceil\frac{n}{2}\rceil}^{n-1} i = \left\lceil \frac{3n^2}{4} \right\rceil$$

Thus, according to Theorem 1, we need at least $\lceil (3/4)n^2 \rceil$ processors to complete this computation DAG in $3n-2$ time steps.

3.3.2 The processor-time upper bound

The question we pursue now is whether there is a systolic array that achieves this lower bound on processors. We introduce a more succinct representation of the 3D mesh. All the nodes in a column of the mesh in Fig. 3.4 are represented by a single node in Fig. 3.5. The nodes in Fig. 3.5 are labelled with an interval of time steps. These are the time steps used by the n nodes in the column represented. For example, the node in Fig. 3.5 representing column (1, 1) of Fig. 3.4 is labelled with the time step interval [1 6].

The strategy for mapping the set of nodes onto the processor array is as

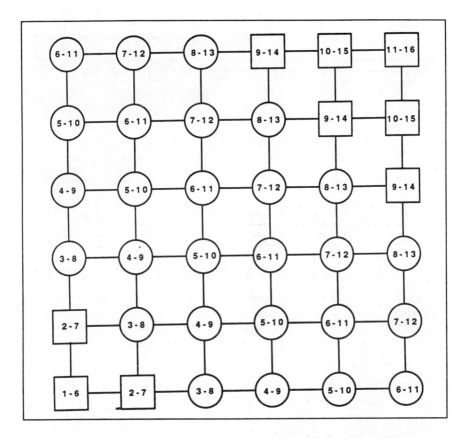

Figure 3.5 A partial mapping of columns onto the 27 processors. Each node in the figure is labelled with the interval of time steps used by the nodes in the column it represents. Columns containing a node assigned to time step 8 are represented by a disk; others are represented by a square.

follows. There is a processor for every node labelled with time step 8 in
Fig. 3.4. A distinct processor is assigned to each vertical column of nodes
(Fig. 3.4) that contains a node labelled with time step 8 (in general, every
column with a node labelled with time step $\lceil(3n - 2)/2\rceil$). These
processors correspond to the circular nodes in Fig. 3.5. The processor
array developed so far (i.e. the array of circular nodes in Fig. 3.5) is
shaped hexagonally. As can be seen from the figure, the perimeter of the
array has 3 pairs of parallel boundaries.

To complete the mapping, we need to assign the 9 remaining (square)
columns in Fig. 3.5 (in general, $\lfloor(1/4)n^2\rfloor$ columns) to processors. Figure

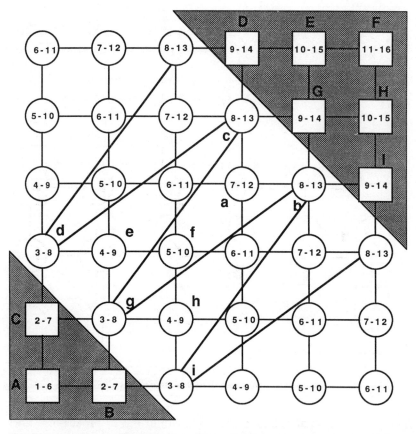

Figure 3.6 The complete assignment of columns to processors. Virtual
processors with upper-case names are assigned to processors with
corresponding lower-case names. The resulting connectivity between
boundary processors is indicated.

3.6 presents such a completion. In the figure, these columns are labelled A, B, C, D, E, F, G, H, and I; their assigned processors are labelled correspondingly (in lower case). Thus there are 9 processors that have 2 columns assigned to them. When a processor is assigned two columns, its first column finishes execution **just before** its second column begins execution (i.e., scheduling constraints are met). The connectivity implied by this mapping requires, for example, that the processor named d must communicate directly to the processor named c. In general, these boundary processors communicate directly with the processors on the opposite (parallel) boundary. To bring these directly communicating boundary processors into proximity, we map the hexagonally shaped array

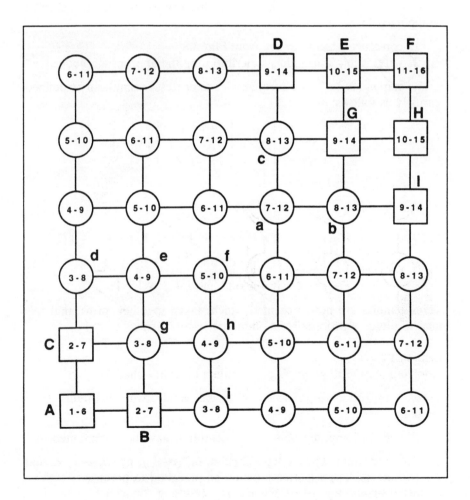

Figure 3.7 The systolic array before wrapping.

onto the surface of a cylinder. One simply wraps the $n \times n$ mesh of Fig. 3.7 (where each node represents a column of processes) so that each node with an upper case label is superimposed onto the node with the corresponding lower case label. In this way, each column of processes maps onto a processor.

This processor-time map generalizes to any even n. To visualize this map:

1. construct a transparency from Fig. 3.7;
2. wrap it into a cylinder, superimposing the appropriate nodes.

The cylindrical wrapping is the same when n is odd, except that the boundary connectivity is skewed slightly. This connectivity is illustrated, for $n = 5$, in Fig. 3.8. An especially useful way to visualize this skewed wrapping is to:

1. construct a transparency from Fig. 3.8;
2. wrap it into a cylinder, superimposing the appropriate nodes.

The map $m : N \rightarrow Z^3$ (i.e., from nodes to processor-time) can be defined formally as follows:

$$\begin{bmatrix} time \\ space_1 \\ space_2 \end{bmatrix} = \begin{bmatrix} t(i, j, k) \\ s_1(i, j, k) \\ s_2(i, j, k) \end{bmatrix}, \text{ where}$$

$t(i, j, k) = i + j + k - 2$

$s_1(i, j) = (i + j - \lceil \frac{n}{2} \rceil - 1) \bmod n$

$$s_2(i, j) = \begin{cases} i - j, & \text{if } n \text{ is even or } \lceil \frac{n}{2} \rceil + 1 \leqslant i + j \leqslant \lceil \frac{3n}{2} \rceil. \\ i - j + 1 & \text{if } n \text{ is odd and } \lceil \frac{n}{2} \rceil + 1 > i + j \\ i - j - 1 & \text{if } n \text{ is odd and } i + j > \lceil \frac{3n}{2} \rceil. \end{cases}$$

Three lemmas are now presented which, taken together, prove that this map results in a processor-time-minimal systolic array.

Lemma 1
Applying map m to graph $G_{n \times n \times n}$ results in a valid schedule.

Proof: In order for a schedule to be valid, two constraints must be met:

1.   A node is computed only after its children have been computed.

   The node (i, j, k) may have 3 children: $(i-1, j, k)$, $(i, j-1, k)$ and $(i, j, k-1)$. The schedule honours all precedences because
   $t(i, j, k) = i + j + k - 2 > i + j + k - 3$
   $= t(i-1, j, k) = t(i, j-1, k) = t(i, j, k-1)$.

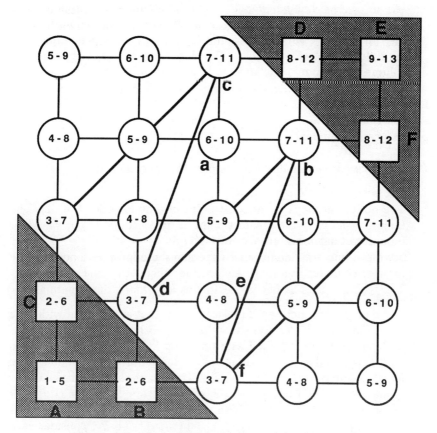

Figure 3.8 The cylindrical connectivity for n = 5.

2. No processor computes two different nodes during the same time step:

Since the spatial components of the map (i.e., s_1 and s_2) do not depend on k, a processor is the image of all of a k-column or none of it. The n nodes in column (i, j) are executed at n different time steps, depending on the node's k value. The only case we need consider, then, is when a processor is the image of more than one column. Let column (i_1, j_1) and column (i_2, j_2) both be mapped to the same processor. Then

$$(i_1 + j_1 - \lceil \tfrac{n}{2} \rceil - 1) \bmod n = (i_2 + j_2 - \lceil \tfrac{n}{2} \rceil - 1) \bmod n.$$

That is, $|(i_1 + j_1) - (i_2 + j_2)| = n$. Let us assume, without loss of generality, that $i_1 + j_1 + n = i_2 + j_2$. Then column (i_1, j_1) finishes at time step $t(i_1, j_1, n) = i_1 + j_1 + n - 2$ and column (i_2, j_2) starts at time step $t(i_2, j_2, 1) = i_1 + j_1 + n - 1$. When two columns are mapped to the same processor, their scheduling thus does not overlap. (Columns that map to the same processor cannot have index sums that differ by a multiple of n greater than 1; the difference between the smallest column index sum, 1+1, and the largest, $n+n$, is less than $2n$.)   ■

Lemma 2
Applying map m to graph $G_{n \times n \times n}$ results in a multi-processor that is processor-time-minimal.

Proof: Spacetime-minimality decomposes into two claims:

1. The schedule is time-minimal.
    The node that maps to the least point in time is node $(1, 1, 1)$. The node that maps to the greatest point in time is node (n, n, n). Their time coordinates are respectively $t(1, 1, 1) = 1$ and $t(n, n, n) = 3n - 2$. Since the number of time steps used, $3n - 2$, equals the number of nodes in a longest path, the schedule is time-minimal.
2. The schedule uses as few processors as any that is time-minimal.

    We know that there are $\lceil (3/4)n^2 \rceil$ nodes that are labelled with time step $\lceil (3n - 2)/2 \rceil$. We now show that every column of nodes that does not contain a node labelled with time step $\lceil (3n - 2)/2 \rceil$ is mapped to a processor that is also the image of a column that **does** contain a node labelled with time step $\lceil (3n - 2)/2 \rceil$. This enables us to place an upper bound of $\lceil (3/4)n^2 \rceil$ on the number of processors. If column (i, j) does not contain a node labelled with time step $\lceil (3n - 2)/2 \rceil$, then either $t(i, j, n) < \lceil (3n - 2)/2 \rceil$ or $t(i, j, 1) > \lceil (3n - 2)/2 \rceil$. We consider each of these cases:

    Case $t(i, j, n) < \lceil (3n-2)/2 \rceil$: This case decomposes into two, depending on whether n is even or odd:

    even n: We will show that:

    (a) column (i, j) maps to the same processor as column $(i + (\frac{n}{2}), j + (\frac{n}{2}))$;
    (b) column $(i + (\frac{n}{2}), j + (\frac{n}{2}))$ contains a node with time label $\lceil (3n - 2)/2 \rceil$.

    This is sufficient because it means that column (i, j) maps to one of at most $\lceil (3/4)n^2 \rceil$ processors.

    First, we show part (a) by substituting directly into the definition of s_1 and s_2, the spatial components of the map.

$$s_1(i, j) = (i + j - \lceil \tfrac{n}{2} \rceil - 1) \bmod n$$
$$= (i + \tfrac{n}{2} + j + \tfrac{n}{2} - \lceil \tfrac{n}{2} \rceil - 1) \bmod n$$

$$= s_1(i + \tfrac{n}{2}, j + \tfrac{n}{2})$$

$$s_2(i, j) = i - j = i + \tfrac{n}{2} - j - \tfrac{n}{2} = s_2(i + \tfrac{n}{2}, j + \tfrac{n}{2})$$

We now show part (b): column $(i + (n/2), j + (n/2))$ must contain a node whose time step is $\lceil(3n - 2)/2\rceil$.
That is, if $t(i, j, n) < \lceil(3n - 2)/2\rceil$, then

$$t(i + \tfrac{n}{2}, j + \tfrac{n}{2}), 1) \leqslant \left\lceil\tfrac{3n-2}{2}\right\rceil \leqslant t(i + \tfrac{n}{2}, j + \tfrac{n}{2}, n)$$

The first inequality is established as follows.
Since $t(i, j, n) < \lceil(3n - 2)/2\rceil$, we have $i + j \leqslant n/2$. Therefore,

$$t(i+\tfrac{n}{2}, j+\tfrac{n}{2}, 1) = i + j + n - 1 \leqslant \left\lceil\tfrac{3n-2}{2}\right\rceil$$

For the second inequality,

$$\left\lceil\tfrac{3n-2}{2}\right\rceil \leqslant t(i + \tfrac{n}{2}, j + \tfrac{n}{2}, n)$$
$$= i + \tfrac{n}{2} + j + \tfrac{n}{2} + n - 2 \Longleftrightarrow$$
$$1 \leqslant i + j + \tfrac{n}{2}$$

odd n: We will show that:

(a) column (i, j) maps to the same processor as column $(i + \lceil\tfrac{n}{2}\rceil, j + \lfloor\tfrac{n}{2}\rfloor)$;
(b) column $(i + \lceil\tfrac{n}{2}\rceil, j + \lfloor\tfrac{n}{2}\rfloor)$ contains a node with time label $\lceil(3n - 2)/2\rceil$.

This is sufficient because it means that column (i, j) maps to a processor that was already allocated (see (a) above).

First, we show part (a) by substituting directly into the definition of s_1 and s_2, the spatial components of the map.

$$s_1(i, j) \;=\; (i + j - \lceil\tfrac{n}{2}\rceil - 1) \bmod n$$
$$= (i + \lceil\tfrac{n}{2}\rceil + j + \lceil\tfrac{n}{2}\rceil - \lceil\tfrac{n}{2}\rceil - 1) \bmod n$$
$$= s_1(i + \lceil\tfrac{n}{2}\rceil, j + \lfloor\tfrac{n}{2}\rfloor)$$

To use the definition of s_2, we first establish that $i + j < \lceil n/2\rceil + 1$.
This follows from the inequality $t(i, j, n) < \lceil(3n - 2)/2\rceil$. Therefore, $s_2(i, j) = i - j + 1$. On the other hand,

$$\lceil\tfrac{n}{2}\rceil + 1 \leqslant i + \lceil\tfrac{n}{2}\rceil + j + \lfloor\tfrac{n}{2}\rfloor \leqslant \lceil\tfrac{3n}{2}\rceil.$$

The first inequality is clear; the second inequality holds since when $t(i, j, n) < \lceil(3n - 2)/2\rceil$, we have that $i + j \leqslant \lceil n/2\rceil$. Therefore,

$$s_2(i + \lceil\tfrac{n}{2}\rceil, j + \lfloor\tfrac{n}{2}\rfloor) = i + \lceil\tfrac{n}{2}\rceil - j - \lfloor\tfrac{n}{2}\rfloor = i - j + 1$$

Summarily,

$$s_2(i, j) = i - j + 1 = i + \lceil\tfrac{n}{2}\rceil - j - \lfloor\tfrac{n}{2}\rfloor = s_2(i + \lceil\tfrac{n}{2}\rceil, j + \lfloor\tfrac{n}{2}\rfloor)$$

We now show part (b): column $(i + \lceil n/2 \rceil, j + \lfloor n/2 \rfloor)$ must contain a node with time label $\lceil (3n - 2)/2 \rceil$.

That is, if $t(i, j, n) < \lceil (3n - 2)/2 \rceil$, then

$$\left[t(i + \lceil \tfrac{n}{2} \rceil, j + \lfloor \tfrac{n}{2} \rfloor, 1) \leq \lceil \tfrac{3n-2}{2} \rceil \leq t(i + \lceil \tfrac{n}{2} \rceil, j + \lfloor \tfrac{n}{2} \rfloor, n) \right]$$

For the first inequality, since $t(i, j, n) < \lceil (3n - 2)/2 \rceil$, we have that $i + j \leq \lceil n/2 \rceil$. Therefore,

$$t(i + \lceil \tfrac{n}{2} \rceil, j + \lfloor \tfrac{n}{2} \rfloor, 1) = i + j + n - 1 \leq \lceil \tfrac{3n-2}{2} \rceil$$

For the second inequality,

$$\begin{aligned} \lceil \tfrac{3n-2}{2} \rceil \ &\leq \ t(i + \lceil \tfrac{n}{2} \rceil, j + \lfloor \tfrac{n}{2} \rfloor, n) \\ &= \ i + \lceil \tfrac{n}{2} \rceil + j + \lfloor \tfrac{n}{2} \rfloor + n - 2 \Longleftrightarrow \\ 1 \leq \ &i + j + \lfloor \tfrac{n}{2} \rfloor \end{aligned}$$

Case $t(i, j, 1) > \lceil (3n - 2)/2 \rceil$: The details of this case are handled similarly. ∎

We now show that the multi-processor schedule defined by m results in a systolic array.

Lemma 3
Applying map m to graph $G_{n \times n \times n}$ results in a systolic array.

Proof: We show that communication is local in both time and space. Direct communication is represented by arcs in the graph.

Time: Communication in time is local; if (u, v) is an arc in the mesh DAG, then $t(u) = t(v) - 1$.

Space: There are three types of arcs: i, j, and k arcs (refer to the definition of the arc set of the mesh DAG). Let there be an arc directed from node $v = (i, j, k)$ to node $v' = (i', j', k')$. We may assume that this is either an i arc or a j arc: $i' = i + 1$, or $j' = j + 1$, but not both. (Recall that if two nodes differ only in coordinate k, then they are mapped to the same processor.) For these two cases, we now show that the spatial components of the processor-time map, s_1 and s_2, preserve locality.

$i' = i + 1$: The difference in their first coordinate,

$$s_1(v') - s_1(v) =$$

$$(i' + j - \lceil \tfrac{n}{2} \rceil - 1) \bmod n - (i + j - \lceil \tfrac{n}{2} \rceil - 1) \bmod n =$$

$$(i' - i) \bmod n = 1$$

The difference in their second coordinate clearly is 1 when n is even. When n is odd, the map into the second coordinate, s_2, decomposes into three cases, depending into which interval the sum $i + j$ falls:

- $\lceil \frac{n}{2} \rceil + 1 > i + j$;
- $\lceil \frac{n}{2} \rceil + 1 \leqslant i + j \leqslant \lceil \frac{3n}{2} \rceil$;
- $i + j > \lceil \frac{3n}{2} \rceil$.

When n is odd, the difference in the nodes' second coordinate depends on whether both $i + j$ and $i' + j$ fall into the same interval (in which case their difference is 1), or they fall into different intervals (in which case the difference in the nodes' second coordinate is 0):

$$s_2(i', j') - s_2(i, j) = \begin{cases} 1 \text{ if } n \text{ is even or} \\ \quad \text{if } \lceil \frac{n}{2} \rceil + 1 \leqslant i' + j, i + j \leqslant \lceil \frac{3n}{2} \rceil \text{ or} \\ \quad \text{if } \lceil \frac{n}{2} \rceil + 1 > i' + j, i + j \text{ or} \\ \quad \text{if } i' + j, i + j > \lceil \frac{3n}{2} \rceil \\ 0 \text{ otherwise} \end{cases}$$

$j' = j + 1$: This case is similar to the one above. The difference in the nodes' first coordinate,

$$s_1(v') - s_1(v) =$$

$$(i + j' - \lceil \tfrac{n}{2} \rceil - 1) \bmod n - (i + j' - \lceil \tfrac{n}{2} \rceil - 1) \bmod n =$$

$$(j' - j) \bmod n = 1$$

The difference in the nodes' second coordinate,

$$s_2(i', j') - s_2(i, j) = \begin{cases} 1 \text{ if } n \text{ is even or} \\ \quad \text{if } \lceil \frac{n}{2} \rceil + 1 \leqslant i + j', i + j \leqslant \lceil \frac{3n}{2} \rceil \text{ or} \\ \quad \text{if } \lceil \frac{n}{2} \rceil + 1 > i + j', i + j \text{ or} \\ \quad \text{if } i + j', i + j > \lceil \frac{3n}{2} \rceil \\ -2 \text{ otherwise} \end{cases}$$

In Fig. 3.8, the skewed wrap around connections (for odd n) correspond to the analysis above: an arc that wraps around also drops down 2 rows (i.e. the difference in rows between the destination of the arc and the source of the arc is -2).

From Lemmas 1–3, we have the following:

Theorem 2

Applying the map m to graph $G_{n \times n \times n}$ results in a processor-time-minimal systolic array.

3.3.3 Array layout

In the cylindrical processor-time-minimal array, these left [bottom] processors form a line that is inscribed on the surface of the cylinder. For these processors, the input schedule is given by the rule: $a(i, j)$ and $b(j, i)$ are input during step $i + j - 1$. The output (i.e. the product matrix) is held in place by the processors. Cylindrically connected meshes are directly implementable in current PCB technology. They are also easy to embed in more densely connected systems (e.g. in a hypercube, using a suitable grey code).

There is however a simple way to embed this cylinder in the Euclidean plane: fold it along the line drawn in Fig. 3.9, resulting in a trapeziodally shaped array. When n is even, the trapezoid encompasses exactly

$$\frac{n}{2}(n - 1) + \frac{n}{2}(\frac{n}{2} + 1) = \frac{3n^2}{4}$$

processors. When n is odd, this fold results in an array that is similar (Fig. 3.10). Connectivity differences occur along the right boundary processors. When n is even and $n/2$ is odd, there is another natural way to embed the hexagonally shaped, cylindrically connected mesh in the Euclidean plane.

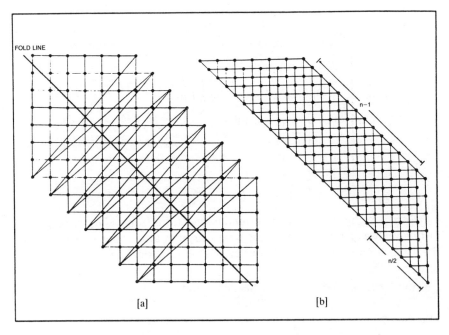

FOLD LINE

[a]   [b]

Figure 3.9 The hexagonally shaped cylindrically connected 2D mesh, for $n=14$. (a) Before folding. (b) After folding.

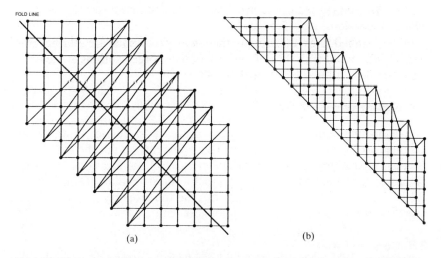

Figure 3.10 The hexagonally shaped cylindrically connected 2D mesh, for $n=13$. (a) Before folding. (b) After folding.

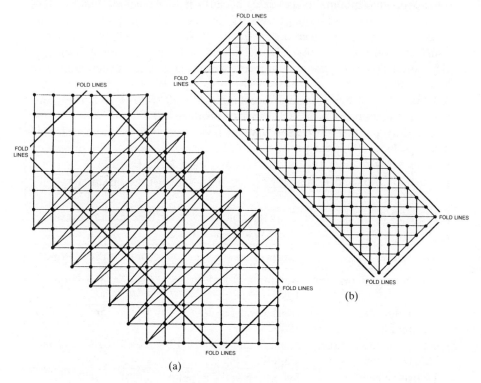

Figure 3.11 The hexagonally shaped 2D mesh, for $n=14$. (a) Before folding. (b) After folding.

As Fig. 3.11 makes plain, the array can be folded into a rectangular array whose dimensions are $n/2 \times 3n/2$.

In the embeddings illustrated, the $3n^2/4$ processors are placed compactly, and routed with short wires. All of these organizations are feasible, for example, on the CHiP (Snyder, 1982).

3.4 Extant work

Processor-time-minimal systolic arrays are easy to devise, in an *ad hoc* manner, for 2D systolic algorithms. This apparently is not the case for 3D systolic algorithms. There have been several publications regarding processor-time-minimal systolic arrays for fundamental 3D algorithms. Each of the algorithms listed in Table 3.1 has the property that, in its DAG representation, every node is on a longest path.

3.5 Conclusion

A definition was introduced for a processor-time-minimal multiprocessor schedule of a DAG. Although only one of many performance measures, processor-time-minimality is useful because it is a machine-independent measure of the minimum processors needed [sufficient] to extract the maximum parallelism from a dependence DAG. This definition was first illustrated on the triangular 2D mesh, and then on the cubical 3D mesh. This latter DAG is fundamental, representing several important computations, including matrix product. The presented bounds are not merely asymptotic, they are precise. For example, the $20 \times 20 \times 20$ dependence mesh for computing a 20×20 matrix product requires at least 58 time steps. Any parallel processor that achieves this time-minimal schedule needs at least 300 inner-product step processing elements. The presented systolic array realizes this processor-time lower bound.

Each of the algorithms, for which a processor-time-minimal systolic

Table 3.1 Some 3D algorithms for which processor-time-minimal systolic arrays are known

Algorithm	Citation	Time	Processors
Algebraic path problem	Benaini and Robert, 1990	$5n-2$	$n^2/3 + O(n)$
Gauss–Jordan elimination	Louka and Tchuente, 1989	$4n$	$5n^2/18 + O(n)$
Gaussian elimination	Benaini and Robert, 1990	$3n-1$	$n^2/4 + O(n)$
Matrix product	Capello, 1989	$3n-2$	$\lceil 3n^2/4 \rceil$
Transitive closure	Scheiman and Cappello, 1990	$5n-4$	$\lceil n^2/3 \rceil$

array has been devised, has the property that every node in its dependence DAG is on a longest path. This graph property greatly simplifies the analysis and synthesis of processor-time-minimal systolic arrays.

Investigating fundamental algorithms with respect to processor-time-minimality contributes to our basic understanding of the limits and potential of systolic arrays.

References

Benaini A., and Robert, Y., 1990, Spacetime-minimal systolic arrays for gaussian elimination and the algebraic path problem, in *Proc. Int. Conf. on Application Specific Array Processors*, IEEE Computer Society, Princeton, 746–57.

Cappello, P. R., and Laub, A. J., 1988, Systolic computation of multivariable frequency response, *IEEE Trans. Autom. Control*, **33**(6), 550.

Cappello, P. R., and Steiglitz, K., 1984, Unifying VLSI array design with linear transformations of space-time, in *Advances in Computing Research*, vol. 2: *VLSI theory*, JAI Press, Inc., Greenwich, CT, 23–65.

Chen, M. C., 1986, A design methodology for synthesizing parallel algorithms and architectures, *J. Parallel Distrib. Comput.*, Dec. 461–91.

Chen, M. C., 1988, The generation of a class of multipliers: synthesizing highly parallel algorithms in VLSI, *IEEE Trans. Computers*, **C-37**(3), 329–38.

Danielsson, P. E., 1984, Serial/parallel convolvers, *IEEE Trans. Computers*, **C-33**(7), 652–67.

Delosme, J. M., and Ipsen, I. C. F., 1985, An illustration of a methodology for the construction of efficient systolic architectures in VLSI, in *Proc. 2nd Int. Symp. on VLSI Technology, Systems and Applications*, Taipei, 268–73.

Delosme, J. M., and Ipsen, I. C. F., 1986, Systolic array synthesis: computability and time cones, Technical Report Yale/DCS/RR-474, Yale.

van Dongen, V., and Quinton, P., 1988, Uniformization of linear recurrence equations: a step towards the automatic synthesis of systolic arrays, in *Proc. Int. Conf. on Systolic Arrays*, San Diego, IEEE Computer Society, 473–82.

Fortes, J. A. B., 1983, Algorithm transformations for parallel processing and VLSI architecture design. PhD thesis, University of Southern California, Los Angeles.

Fortes, J. A. B., and Moldovan, D. I., 1985, Parallelism detection and algorithm transformation techniques useful for VLSI architecture design, *J. Parallel Distrib. Comput*, **2**, 277–301.

Fortes, J. A. B., and Parisi-Presicce, F., 1984, Optimal linear schedules for the parallel execution of algorithms, in *Int. Conf. on Parallel Processing*, 322–8.

Gachet, P., Jouannault, B., and Quinton, P., 1986, Synthesizing systolic arrays using DIASTOL, in *Proc. Int. Workshop on Systolic Arrays*, (eds W. Moore, A. McCabe, and R. Urquhart), University of Oxford, Adam Hilger, 25–36.

Garey, M. R., and Johnson, D. S., 1979, *Computers and Intractability: A Guide to the Theory of NP-Completeness*. W. H. Freeman, San Francisco, CA.

Guibas, L. J., Kung, H.-T., and Thompson, C. D., 1979, Direct VLSI implementation of combinatorial algorithms, in *Proc. Caltech Conf. on VLSI*, 509–25.

Huang, C.-H., and Lengauer, C., 1987, The derivation of systolic implementations of programs, *Acta Informatica*, **24**, 595–632.

Ibarra, O. H., and Palis, M., 1987, VLSI algorithms for solving recurrence equations and applications, *IEEE Trans. Acoust., Speech, and Signal Processing*, **ASSP-35**(7), 1046–64.

Jagadish, H. V., Rao, S. K., and Kailath, T., 1987, Multi-processor architectures for iterative algorithms. *Proc. IEEE*, September.

Li, G. J., and Wah, B. W., 1985, The design of optimal systolic algorithms, *IEEE Trans. Computers*, **C-34**(1), 66–77.

Lennart Johnsson, S., and Cohen, D., 1981, A mathematical approach to modeling the flow of data and control in computational networks, in *VLSI Systems and Computations*, (eds H. T. Kung, R. Sproull, and G. Steele), Computer Science Press, Rockville, MD 213–25.

Lennart Johnsson, S., Weiser, U., Cohen, D., and Davis, A. L., 1981, Towards a formal treatment of VLSI arrays, in *2nd Caltech Conf. on VLSI*, 375–98.

Karp, R. M., Miller, R. E., and Winograd S., 1967, The organization of computations for uniform recurrence equations, *J. ACM*, **14**, 563–90.

Kung, H.-T., and Leiserson, C. E., 1979, Systolic arrays (for VLSI), in *Sparse Matrix Proceedings 1978* (eds I. S. Duff and G. W. Stewart), SIAM, 256–82.

Lee, P., and Kedem, Z. M., 1988, Synthesizing linear array algorithms from nested FOR loop algorithms, *IEEE Trans. Comput.*, **37**(12), 1578–98.

Lengauer, C., 1989, Towards systolizing compilations: an overview, in *Proc. Conf. Parallel Architectures and Languages Europe (PARLE '89)*, Springer-Verlag.

Miranker, W. L., and Winkler, A., 1984, Spacetime representations of computational structures, *Computing*, **32**, 93–114.

Moldovan, D. I., 1982, On the analysis and synthesis of VLSI algorithms, *IEEE Trans. Comput.*, **C-31**, 1121–6.

Moldovan, D. I., 1983, On the design of algorithms for VLSI systolic arrays, *Proc. IEEE*, **71**(1), 113–20.

Moldovan, D. I., 1987, ADVIS: a software package for the design of systolic arrays, *IEEE Trans. Computer-Aided Design*, **CAD-6**(1), 33–40.

Papadimitriou, C. H., and Ullman, J. D., 1987, A communication-time tradeoff, *SIAM J. Comput.*, **16**(4), 639–46.

Quinton, P., 1984, Automatic synthesis of systolic arrays from uniform recurrent equations, in *Proc. 11th Ann. Symp. on Computer Architecture*, 208–14.

Quinton, P., 1987, *The Systematic Design of Systolic Arrays*, Princeton University Press, 229–60.

Quinton, P., 1988, Mapping recurrences on parallel architectures, in *Supercomputer Design: Hardware & Software,* Int. Supercomputing Inst. Inc., 1–8.

Rajopadhye, S. V., and Fujimoto, R. M., 1987, Systolic array synthesis by static analysis of program dependencies, in *Parallel architectures and languages, Europe, Lecture Notes in Computer Science*, **258** (eds J. W. DeBakker, A. J. Nijman, and P. C. Treleaven), Springer-Verlag, 295–310.

Rajopadhye, S. V., Purushothaman, S., and Fujimoto R. M., 1986, On synthesizing systolic arrays from recurrence equations with linear dependencies. in *Foundations of Software Technology and Theoretical Computer Science, Lecture Notes in Computer Science*, **241:** (ed. K. V. Nori), Springer-Verlag, 485–503.

Ramakrishnan, I. V., Fussell, D. S., and Silberschatz, A., 1986, Mapping homogeneous graphs on linear arrays, *IEEE Trans. Comput.*, **C-35**(3), 189–209.

Rao, S. K., 1985, *Regular iterative algorithms and their implementation on processor arrays*. PhD thesis, Stanford University.

Shang, W., and Fortes, J. A. B., 1988, Time optimal linear schedules for algorithms with uniform dependencies, in *Int. Conf. on Systolic Arrays*, San Diego, CA, 393–402.

Snyder, L., 1982, Introduction to the configurable highly parallel computer. *Computer*, **15**(1), 47–56.

Weiser, U., and Davis, A. L., 1981, A wavefront notation tool for VLSI array design, in *VLSI Systems and Computations*, (eds H. T. Kung, R. Sproull, and G. Steele), Computer Science Press, Rockville, MD, 226–34.

Wong, Y., and Delosme, J.-M., 1989a, Optimization of computation time for systolic arrays, Dept. of Computer Sci. RR-651, Yale Univ.

Wong, Y., and Delosme, J.-M., 1989b, Optimization of processor count for systolic arrays, Dept. of Computer Sci. RR-697, Yale Univ.

Bibliography

Cappello, P., 1992, A processor-time-minimal systolic array for cubical mesh algorithms. *IEEE Trans. Parallel and Distributed Systems*, **3** (1), 4–14.

Cappello P.R., 1989, A spacetime-minimal systolic array for matrix product, in *Systolic Array Processors*, (eds John V. McCanny, John McWhirter, and Earl E. Swartzlander Jr.), Prentice-Hall, Killarney, Ireland, 347–56.

Fortes, J. A. B., Fu, K. S., and Wah, B. W., 1988, Systematic design approaches for algorithmically specified systolic arrays, in *Computer Architecture: Concepts and Systems*, (ed. Veljko M. Milutinović), North-Holland, Elsevier Science Publishing Co., New York, ch. 11, 454–94.

Louka, B., and Tchuente, M., 1989, An optimal solution for Gauss-Jordon elimination on 2D systolic arrays, in *Systolic Array Processors,* (eds John V. McCanny, John McWhirter, and Earl E. Swartzlander Jr.), Prentice-Hall, Killarney, Ireland, 264–74.

Scheiman, C., and Cappello, P. R., 1990, A processor-time minimal systolic array for transitive closure, in *Proc. Int. Conf. on Application Specific Array Processors*, IEEE Computer Society, Princeton, 19–31.

4

Systematic Pipelining of Processor Arrays

Wayne Luk

4.1 Introduction

Pipelining is an effective technique for improving the speed of digital systems by parallelism. The aim is to partition a circuit into stages so that in each stage a new calculation can proceed once the previous one is completed. In synchronous systems, successive circuit stages can be isolated from one another by placing latches between them. If possible effects of clock skew are ignored, then pipelining results in reducing the clock cycle from the propagation delay through the entire circuit to the delay through a single stage.

This chapter examines a framework for systematically developing pipelined designs consisting of an array of processors. There are two components in this framework: a notation based on simple mathematics, and a repertoire of techniques for transforming expressions written in that notation. The notation is intended for capturing designs precisely and succinctly. The transformations relate associated designs by mathematical reasoning to provide a basis for documenting design commitments, for reusing design efforts, and for assessing design trade-offs.

An intention of this chapter is to extend previous work on pipelining homogeneous arrays (Luk and Jones, 1988; Sheeran, 1988) to cover the pipelining of heterogeneous arrays; the method will be illustrated by developing designs for recursive filtering and for matrix multiplication.

4.2 Notation

The formalism we use is based on Jones and Sheeran's (1990) relational framework, and the author's heterogeneous combinators (Luk, 1990). In this chapter we will introduce only those definitions and concepts which are relevant to our discussion.

4.2.1 Describing and composing designs

There are two ways of specifying the behaviour of a design: at the object

level and at the relation level. At the object level, a component's
behaviour will be described by a predicate of the form $a \; R \; b$ where R is
a binary relation on a and b, the domain and range of R, represent
interface signals. Given that the behaviour of a composite circuit is
obtained by combining the behaviour of its components by logical
conjunction, $\wedge$, and that internal signals not directly observable to the
outside world are 'hidden' by existential quantification, $\exists$, we can define
relational composition as follows:

$$a(Q \; ; \; R)b \equiv \exists \; c. \; (a \; Q \; c) \wedge (c \; R \; b)$$

Relational composition enables the behaviour of a component to be
specified at the relation level, namely in the form $x \; ; \; R \; ; \; y$ where x, y are
constant relations that generate the domain and range signals for R. To
simplify the notation, such constant relations are given the same name as
the values that they produce: that is, $a \; x \; b \equiv a = b = x$. Hence a circuit
for computing squares or square roots can be specified either at the object
level as $x \; \mathrm{Sqr} \; x^2$, or at the relation level as $x; \; \mathrm{Sqr} \; ; \; x^2$. Since relation level
descriptions facilitate both algebraic transformations and the analysis of
circuit behaviour by non-standard interpretation techniques (Luk, 1990b),
they will be used in preference to object level descriptions.

Objects in our notation are either atoms (such as numbers or relations)
or tuples of objects: for instance the object $\langle 0, \langle 1, 2 \rangle \rangle$ is a two-tuple
containing the number 0 and the tuple $\langle 1, 2 \rangle$. A tuple is an ordered
collection of elements, with the empty tuple denoted by $\langle \rangle$. Given that x
is a tuple, $\#x$ represents the number of elements in it, and x_i (where
$0 \leqslant i < \#x$) is its ith element. If x is a tuple of tuples, then $x_{i,j} = (x_i)_j$.

Parallel composition of designs operating independently on components
of tuples of signals is defined using square brackets as follows:

$$\langle a_i \mid 0 \leqslant i < N \rangle \; [R_i \mid 0 \leqslant i < N] \; \langle b_i \mid 0 \leqslant i < N \rangle \equiv$$
$$\forall i : 0 \leqslant i < N . a_i \; R_i \; b_i$$

The right-hand side can be read as 'for all values of i in the range 0 to $N-1$,
a_i is related by R_i to b_i'. Circuits with multiple inputs or outputs can be
specified at the relation level using parallel composition. For example, we
can describe an adder by $[x, y] \; ; \; \mathrm{Add} \; ; \; x + y$.

Other useful definitions include relational converse, given by $x \; ; \; R^{-1}$;
$y = y \; ; \; R; \; x$, and the identity relation, given by $x \; ; \; Id \; ; \; x$. Frequently-used
expressions involving these entities are abbreviated below:

fst $R = [R, \mathrm{Id}]$	(applies R to the first component of a two-tuple),
snd $R = [\mathrm{Id}, R]$	(applies R to the second component of a two-tuple),
$R \backslash P = \; P^{-1} \; ; \; R \; ; \; P$	(conjugation of R by P),
$R \backslash\backslash \; [P, Q] = [Q^{-1}, P^{-1}] \; ; \; R \; ; \; [P, Q]$	(conjugation of R by $[P,Q]$).

A relation that relates two-tuples can be used to represent circuits with different interface configurations. For example, given that $[a, b]$; R ; $[c, d]$, the four interface connections a, b, c and d may be all vertical or all horizontal, or there may be one connection on each side of the circuit such that a, b, c and d correspond respectively to the connection for the western, the northern, the southern and the eastern side. The configuration of signal positions will be determined by the environment in which the circuit is placed.

4.2.2 Representing array structures

Combinators are higher-order functions that capture common patterns of computation as parametrized expressions. We have already seen several examples of combinators such as relational composition, parallel composition and conjugation. Given that R is a tuple of relations each of which may be different from one another, and that $\#R = \#x = \#y = N$, common array structures can be described by the following combinators (Figs 4.1–4.3):

$$a \ (\, \stackrel{\circ}{9} R) \ b \equiv \exists s.(s_0 = a) \wedge (s_N = b) \wedge \forall i : 0 \leqslant i < N . \ s_i \ R_i \ s_{i+1}$$
(chain)

$$\langle a, x \rangle (\!\!+\!\!\!+\!R) \ \langle y, b \rangle$$

$$\equiv \exists s.(s_0 = a) \wedge (s_N = b) \wedge \forall i : 0 \leqslant i < N. \ \langle s_i, x_i \rangle \ R_i \ \langle y_i, s_{i+1} \rangle \quad \text{(row)}$$

$$\langle x, a \rangle \ (\ddagger R) \ \langle b, y \rangle$$

$$\equiv \exists s. \ (s_0 = b) \wedge (s_N = a) \wedge \forall i : 0 \leqslant i < N .$$
$$\langle x_i, s_{i+1} \rangle \ R_i \ \langle s_i, y_i \rangle \quad \text{(column)}$$

One can check that $\ddagger \langle R_i \mid 0 \leqslant i < N \rangle = (\!\!+\!\!\!+\!\langle R_i^{-1} \mid 0 \leqslant i < N \rangle)^{-1}$, so any theorem for row can readily be converted for column.

Given $\Psi \in \{\, \stackrel{\circ}{9} \, , \ +\!\!\!+ \, , \ \ddagger \}$ and $0 \leqslant N \leqslant \#R$, we shall adopt the abbreviation

$$\mathop{\Psi}_{i<N} R_i = \Psi \ \langle R_i \mid 0 \leqslant i < N \rangle$$

so that, if R is an M-tuple of N-tuples, then a rectangular grid of heterogeneous components can be described by the following combinator:

$$\mathop{+\!\!\!+}_{i,j<M,N} R_{i,j} = \mathop{\ddagger}_{i<M} (\mathop{+\!\!\!+}_{j<N} R_{i,j})$$

Despite their simplicity, these combinators can be used to represent a wide range of array structures including triangular-shaped (Luk, 1990a) and hexagonally-connected (Luk and Jones, 1988) circuits. Sometimes it is

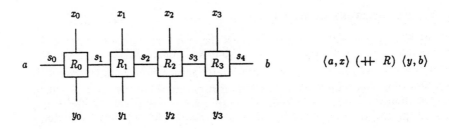

Figure 4.1 A chain (#R = 4).

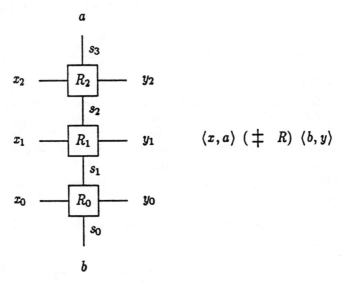

Figure 4.2 A row (#R = #x = #y = 4).

Figure 4.3 A column (#R = #x = #y = 3).

convenient to specialize them for describing arrays of identical components. If R does not depend on i, homogeneous networks can be
represented by

$$R^N = \overset{\circ}{\underset{i<N}{\circ}} R \qquad \text{(homogenous chain)} \qquad (4.1)$$

$$\text{map}_N\, R = [R \mid 0 \leqslant i < N] \qquad \text{(map)} \qquad (4.2)$$

$$\Delta_N\, R = [R^i \mid 0 \leqslant i < N] \qquad \text{(triangle)} \qquad (4.3)$$

$$\bar{\Delta}_N\, R = [R^{N-i-1} \mid 0 \leqslant i < N] \quad \text{(reverse triangle)} \qquad (4.4)$$

$$\text{row}_N R = \underset{i<N}{++} R \qquad \text{(homogenous row)} \qquad (4.5)$$

$$\text{col}_N\, R = \underset{i<N}{\ddagger} R \qquad \text{(homogenous column)} \qquad (4.6)$$

The subscripts associated with these combinators correspond to the size of the arrays, often omitted when they can be deduced from context. Prefix combinators have a higher precedence than infix ones and the conjugation combinators have a lower precedence than all other infix combinators except relational composition, so map $P \setminus\setminus Q ; R = ((\text{map } P) \setminus\setminus Q) ; R$. As we shall see later, the combinators Δ and $\bar{\Delta}$ are particularly useful for describing the skewing circuitry often associated with pipelined designs.

4.2.3 Dealing with state

We use streams – infinite tuples with the innermost subscript representing time – to describe and to reason about systems with sequential elements (Jones and Sheeran, 1990). A stream relation relates a single stream in its domain to a single stream in its range. Signal generators need to be redefined to produce streams, $a \times b \equiv \forall t.\, a_t = b_t = x_t$. The universal quantification ($\forall$) is assumed to range over the set of time subscripts T, which is usually taken to be the set of integers and is often left implicit. Definitions of combinators, except for relational composition and chain, also need to be revised so that they take stream relations as arguments and deliver stream relations as results. For instance, given that every element of the streams x and y is an N-tuple (that is, for all t, $\#x_t = \#y_t = N$), parallel composition becomes

$$\langle x_t \mid t \in T \rangle\, [R_i \mid 0 \leqslant i < N]\, \langle y_t \mid t \in T \rangle \equiv$$
$$\forall i : 0 \leqslant i < N.\ \langle x_{t,i} \mid t \in T \rangle\, R_i\, \langle y_{t,i} \mid t \in T \rangle$$

and similar alterations can be made to the other combinators.

By describing everything at the relation level one can avoid explicit time subscripts in expressions; for instance, a stream adder can be defined by $[x,y]$; Add ; $x + y$ where $+$ is elementwise addition: given that x, y and z are streams, $z = x + y \equiv \forall t.\, z_t = x_t + y_t$.

A delay $\mathcal{D}$ is defined by $x \mathcal{D} y = \forall t.y_t = x_{t-1}$. Those xs with $t < 0$ can be regarded as undefined values or values defined by initialization. An **anti-delay** $\mathcal{D}^{-1}$ is such that $\mathcal{D} ; \mathcal{D}^{-1} = \mathcal{D}^{-1} ; \mathcal{D} = \text{Id}$. A latch is modelled by a delay with data flowing from domain to range, or by an anti-delay with data flowing from range to domain. From its definition $\mathcal{D}$ can be used on all types of signals, so that for example $\mathcal{D}$; map R = map $\mathcal{D}$; map R = map $(\mathcal{D}$; $R)$.

We shall use the symbols ─▷─ and ▽ to represent delays for horizontal and vertical dataflows respectively, so for instance $\mathcal{D}^5$ can be pictured as

$$─▷─ ─▷─ ─▷─ ─▷─ ─▷─$$

Similarly ─◁─ and △ represent anti-delays for horizontal and vertical dataflows.

4.3 Pipelining strategies

In this section our notation will be used to develop methods for pipelining based on two techniques: retiming and slowdown.

4.3.1 Retiming

Retiming (Sheeran, 1988; Leiserson and Saxe, 1983) is a method for pipelining a circuit by introducing and relocating latches. It can be applied to circuits containing no primitives which possess a measure of absolute time. For such circuits, simultaneously delaying every domain signal and anti-delaying every range signal will not alter the behaviour (Fig. 4.4): $R = \mathcal{D}$; R ; $\mathcal{D}^{-1} = R \setminus \mathcal{D}^{-1}$. Circuits with this property are known as **timeless** (Jones and Sheeran, 1990). It is the only precondition required for retiming to be applicable.

The first observation is that delays and anti-delays are timeless, since $\mathcal{D}$ = $\mathcal{D} \setminus \mathcal{D}^{-1}$ and $\mathcal{D}^{-1} = \mathcal{D}^{-1} \setminus \mathcal{D}^{-1}$. Combinational circuits are also timeless as shown in the following calculation (comments and justifications are enclosed by curly brackets):

$$x(R \setminus \mathcal{D}^{-1})y$$

$\equiv$ {by definition of relational composition}

$$\exists u, v. (x \, \mathcal{D} \, u) \wedge (u \, R \, v) \wedge (v \, \mathcal{D}^{-1} \, y)$$

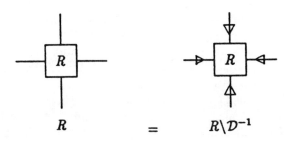

Figure 4.4 Basis for retiming.

$\equiv$ {by definition of $\mathcal{D}$
and since R combinational, let $u\ R\ v \equiv \forall t.\ u_t\ cR\ v_t$}

$\exists u, v.\ \forall t.\ (u_t = x_{t-1}) \wedge (u_t\ cR\ v_t) \wedge (v_t = y_{t-1})$

$\equiv$ {eliminating u and v}

$\forall t.x_{t-1}cRy_{t-1}$

$\equiv$ {since $(\forall t.x_{t-1}\ cR\ y_{t-1}) \equiv (\forall t.\ x_t\ cR\ y_t)$}

$x\ R\ y$

It is easy to show that relational composition preserves timelessness:

$(Q\ ;\ R)\backslash \mathcal{D}^{-1}$

$=$ {since $\mathcal{D}^{-1}\ ;\ \mathcal{D} = \mathrm{Id}$}

$(\mathcal{D}\ ;\ Q\ ;\ \mathcal{D}^{-1})\ ;\ (\mathcal{D}\ ;\ R\ ;\ \mathcal{D}^{-1})$

$=$ {since Q, R timeless}

$Q\ ;\ R$

and similar results can be derived for other combinators – for example, $[Q, R]\backslash \mathcal{D}^{-1} = [Q, R]$, and $(\mathbin{+\!\!+} R)\backslash \mathcal{D}^{-1} = \mathbin{+\!\!+} R$.

Next, we present theorems which can be used to pipeline timeless circuits. The simplest examples of these are theorems for distributing delays through arrays of processors and for gathering anti-delays to the edges, and they are particularly useful for pipelining arrays of components which have all domain signals as inputs and all range signals as outputs. We shall explain later how to deal with circuits with counter-flowing data.

First of all, let us look at chains. The following theorem states that one can distribute delays within a chain so long as the same number of anti-delays are placed at the edge of the chain (Fig. 4.5):

$$\mathop{\overset{\circ}{\raisebox{0.2em}{$,$}}}_{i<N} R_i = \mathop{\overset{\circ}{\raisebox{0.2em}{$,$}}}_{i<N} (R_i\ ;\ \mathcal{D})\ ;\ \mathcal{D}^{-N} \tag{4.7}$$

This theorem can be proved by induction on N, using the lemma $R_i = R_i\backslash \mathcal{D}^N$. Because of the duality of delays and anti-delays, it remains valid if all delays are changed to anti-delays and vice versa. Other

$$\mathop{\overset{\circ}{\raisebox{0.2em}{$,$}}}_{i<N} R_i \quad = \quad \mathop{\overset{\circ}{\raisebox{0.2em}{$,$}}}_{i<N} (R_i\ ;\ \mathcal{D})\ ;\ \mathcal{D}^{-N}$$

Figure 4.5 A theorem for retiming a chain ($N = 3$).

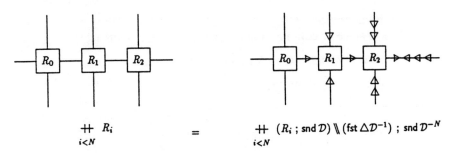

$$\underset{i<N}{+\!\!+} \ R_i \qquad = \qquad \underset{i<N}{+\!\!+} \ (R_i \ ; \ \text{snd} \ \mathcal{D}) \ \backslash\!\backslash \ (\text{fst} \ \Delta\mathcal{D}^{-1}) \ ; \ \text{snd} \ \mathcal{D}^{-N}$$

Figure 4.6 A theorem for retiming a row ($N = 3$).

variations of this theorem are possible, such as placing some of the anti-delays to the left of the chain; the only constraint is that the total number of anti-delays must be the same as that of delays.

The corresponding theorem for row is similar to that for chain, except that triangles of delays and anti-delays are needed to skew and de-skew the vertical signals (Fig. 4.6):

$$\underset{i<N}{+\!\!+} R_i = \underset{i<N}{+\!\!+} (R_i \ ; \ \text{snd} \ \mathcal{D}) \ \backslash\!\backslash \ (\text{fst} \ \Delta\mathcal{D}^{-1}) \ ; \ \text{snd} \ \mathcal{D}^{-N} \qquad (4.8)$$

From this, one can derive a theorem for pipelining columns,

$$\underset{i<N}{\text{±}} R_i = \underset{i<N}{\text{±}} (R_i \ ; \ \text{fst} \ \mathcal{D}) \ \backslash\!\backslash \ (\text{snd} \ \bar{\Delta}\mathcal{D}^{-1}) \ ; \ \text{fst} \ \mathcal{D}^{-N} \qquad (4.9)$$

and (4.8) and (4.9) can be combined to give a theorem for pipelining rectangular arrays (Fig. 4.7),

$$\underset{i,j<M,N}{+\!\!+} R_{i,j} = \underset{i,j<M,N}{+\!\!+} (R_{i,j} \ ; \ \mathcal{D}) \ \backslash\!\backslash \ [\Delta\mathcal{D}, \ \bar{\Delta}\mathcal{D}]^{-1} \ ; \ [\mathcal{D}^{-M}, \ \mathcal{D}^{-N}] \qquad (4.10)$$

Theorems like these can also be used for refining word-level circuit representations to bit-level implementations (Jones and Sheeran, 1991).

4.3.2 Design implications of retiming theorems

Both latency (the number of clock cycles elapsed before the first output appears) and data skewing information may be extracted from retiming theorems. As an example, consider a row of N identical circuits R, each of which has inputs in its domain and outputs in its range. The relevant retiming theorem can be derived from (4.8):

$$\text{row}_N \ R = \text{snd} \ \Delta\mathcal{D} \ ; \ \text{row}_N(R \ ; \ \text{snd} \ \mathcal{D}) \ ; \ [\Delta\mathcal{D}^{-1}, \ \mathcal{D}^{-N}] \qquad (4.11)$$

Composing both sides of (4.11) with $\mathcal{D}^N$ yields

$$\text{row}_N R \ ; \ \mathcal{D}^N = \text{snd} \ \Delta\mathcal{D} \ ; \ \text{row}_N(R \ ; \ \text{snd} \ \mathcal{D}); \ \text{fst} \ (\mathcal{D} \ ; \ \bar{\Delta}\mathcal{D})$$

since $\Delta_N\mathcal{D} \ ; \ \bar{\Delta}_N\mathcal{D} = \mathcal{D}^{N-1}$. This shows that the retimed array row

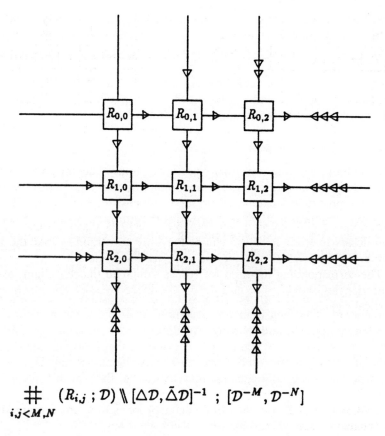

$$\mathop{\#}_{i,j<M,N} (R_{i,j} ; \mathcal{D}) \, \backslash\!\backslash\, [\Delta\mathcal{D}, \bar{\Delta}\mathcal{D}]^{-1} \;;\; [\mathcal{D}^{-M}, \mathcal{D}^{-N}]$$

Figure 4.7 A pipelined rectangular array, with skewing delays at the boundary ($M = N = 3$).

(R ; snd $\mathcal{D}$) has its latency extended by N clock cycles, and requires data skews represented by $\Delta\mathcal{D}$ and $\mathcal{D}$; $\bar{\Delta}\mathcal{D}$ for the appropriate domain and range signals respectively.

Delays and anti-delays, together with combinators like Δ, provide a simple means of characterizing the boundary conditions – the latency and data-skews – for pipelined circuits. When subsystems are put together, data-skews between adjacent circuits should be matched to minimize the number of latches required for skewing. Moreover, given the number of each type of component together with their area and power consumption, one can compute a lower bound of the area and power consumption of a composite circuit. This kind of calculation can also be formalized in our framework (Luk, 1990b).

For systems with counter-flowing data streams, introducing a delay latches the data-flow in one direction but creates predictors in the opposite direction. A predictor is a non-implementable element, since it outputs values before inputing them; it is a delay with data flowing from range to domain or an anti-delay with data flowing from domain to range. Predictors at the edges of an array can always be cancelled by composing them with latches. Predictors within the array can be cancelled by using components with enough latches on the corresponding connections. This will be illustrated by an example in section 4.4.

4.3.3 Graphical method

The retiming theorems essentially perform a house-keeping role: if delays are added to a circuit, then the same number of anti-delays must be added at the appropriate locations to preserve the circuit's behaviour. There is a simple graphical method that provides the intuition behind the concise equations. This method relies on using contours to enclose particular parts of the system. At each intersection of a contour with a wire, we introduce a delay on the wire if the intersection falls on the domain (the west or north side) of the enclosed component, and an anti-delay if the intersection falls on the range (the south or east side) of the enclosed component. The idea is to use a contour to identify the locations of a specific component and its converse; different contours can be employed for different types of components. A retiming theorem thus corresponds to a family of contours on the circuit diagram. Contours can also intersect with one another, although this may make the diagram difficult to read (Fig. 4.8).

Similar graphical methods have been proposed by other researchers; examples include the 'cut theorem' (Kung and Lam, 1984) and the 'cut-set' retiming procedure (Kung, 1988). They can be applied to any circuit, not just regular ones. We emphasize in our graphical construction that the retiming contours should be **closed** curves to maintain correct sequencing for all input and output signals. For a circuit with three or more dimensions, the contours become surfaces or hypersurfaces.

Pictures complement textual descriptions by providing a means of visualizing the retiming transformations. They may also provide inspiration for novel retiming strategies. Algebraic theorems, on the other hand,

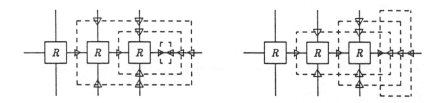

Figure 4.8 Alternative contours for retiming a row of components.

are applicable to entire families of circuits, and are more tractable for formal manipulations.

4.3.4 Controlling pipelining

Although pipelining can increase the throughput of a system, it may also increase its latency and the amount of area and power for latches, both within the array and at its periphery for data-skewing. A recent study (Hatamian and Cash, 1987) shows that the area overhead for pipelining in fabricated designs can be as much as 60–70%. Moreover the increase in throughput may not be linear with respect to the number of pipelined stages, because the speed of the processor array may, for instance, be limited by the available input-output bandwidth or by clock skew or the settling delay of registers.

It is therefore essential to be able to incorporate the appropriate amount of pipelining. For processor arrays this can be achieved by grouping the components into clusters before placing latches between the clusters. The size of the clusters then determines the degree of pipelining: the larger the number of components in the cluster, the lower the degree of pipelining, which in general will result in a slower design with a smaller area and latency.

To synthesize expressions that denote designs with variable degrees of pipelining, we first use **clustering theorems** to express the target array as an array of clusters of components; we then distribute latches between clusters using retiming theorems.

It is obvious how to cluster a chain; just express it as a chain of chains:

$$\overset{\circ}{\underset{i<NK}{\Omega}} R_i = \overset{\circ}{\underset{i<N}{\Omega}} \left(\overset{\circ}{\underset{j<K}{\Omega}} R_{iK+j} \right) \tag{4.12}$$

To cluster rows, we need the relation $Group_N$ to relate an MN-tuple to an N-tuple of M-tuples,

$$[x_i| \ 0 \leqslant i < MN]; \ Group_N; \ [[x_{Mi+j}| \ 0 \leqslant j < M] \ | \ 0 \leqslant i < N]$$

$Group_N$ formats the vertical signals to match the structure required by a row of rows,

$$\underset{i<NK}{+\!\!+} R_i = \underset{i<N}{+\!\!+} \left(\underset{j<K}{+\!\!+} R_{iK+j} \right) \backslash\backslash \ \text{fst} \ Group_N^{-1} \tag{4.13}$$

A similar theorem can be derived for rectangular arrays,

$$\underset{ij<MP, NQ}{\#} R_{i,j} = \underset{ij<M, N}{\#} \left(\underset{u, v<P, Q}{\#} R_{iP+u, \ jQ+v} \right) \backslash\backslash \ [Group_N^{-1}, \ Group_M^{-1}] \tag{4.14}$$

We can now combine the above clustering theorems with the retiming theorems presented earlier to give theorems for controlling pipelining:

$$\overset{\circ}{\underset{i<NK}{\S}} R_i = \overset{\circ}{\underset{i<N}{\S}} \left(\overset{\circ}{\underset{j<K}{\S}} R_{iK+j} ; \mathcal{D} \right); \mathcal{D}^{-N} \tag{4.15}$$

$$\underset{i<N}{+\!\!\!+} \left(\underset{j<K}{+\!\!\!+} R_{iK+j} \right) = \underset{i<N}{+\!\!\!+} \left(\underset{j<K}{+\!\!\!+} R_{iK+j} ; \text{snd } \mathcal{D} \right) \backslash\backslash \text{ (fst } \Delta \mathcal{D}^{-1}) ;$$
$$\text{snd } \mathcal{D}^{-N} \tag{4.16}$$

$$\underset{i,j<M,N}{+\!\!\!+} \left(\underset{u,v<P,Q}{+\!\!\!+} R_{iP+u,\ jQ+v} \right) = \underset{i,j<M,N}{+\!\!\!+} \left(\underset{u,v<P,Q}{+\!\!\!+} R_{iP+ujQ+v} ; \mathcal{D} \right)$$
$$[\Delta\mathcal{D}, \tilde{\Delta}\mathcal{D}]^{-1} ; [\mathcal{D}^{-M}, \mathcal{D}^{-N}] \tag{4.17}$$

An instance of (4.16) is shown in Fig. 4.9. The above transformations, while straightforward, may not always lead to the most efficient implementations; an example of such inefficiency and its remedy will be presented in section 4.4.

4.3.5 Slowdown

A technique related to retiming is slowdown (Jones and Sheeran, 1990; Leiserson and Saxe, 1983). Sometimes extra delays or anti-delays are needed to fully pipeline a circuit. They may be introduced by making an n-slow system, replacing every delay in the circuit by n delays in series, and similarly for anti-delays. However, instead of getting output at every cycle, output should be sampled every n cycles. Hence the definition of $\text{slow}_n R$, the n-slow version of R, should satisfy

$$\text{ev}_n ; R = \text{slow}_n R ; \text{ev}_n \tag{4.18}$$

where ev_n, pronounced 'every nth', involves a range stream consisting of every nth element of its domain stream: $\langle \cdots, x_0, x_1, x_2, \cdots \rangle \text{ ev}_3 \langle \cdots, x_0, x_3, x_6, x_9, \cdots \rangle$. ev_n can be defined by

$$x \text{ ev}_n y \equiv \forall t. y_t = x_{nt} \tag{4.19}$$

ev_n shares with $\mathcal{D}$ the property that it can be applied to streams of any structure. For example, $\text{ev}_n ; [Q, R] = [\text{ev}_n, \text{ev}_n] ; [Q, R]$. However, while $\text{ev}_n^{-1}; \text{ev}_n = \text{Id}$, it is the case that $x(\text{ev}_n ; \text{ev}_n^{-1}) y \equiv \forall t. y_{nt} = x_{nt}$. That is, only every nth element of x and of y are required to be equal.

We shall define slow_n by $\text{slow}_n R = R \quad \text{ev}_n^{-1}$, since this satisfies (4.18). A

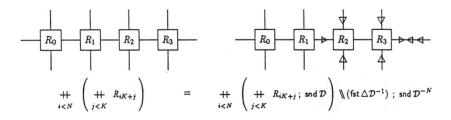

$$\underset{i<N}{+\!\!\!+} \left(\underset{j<K}{+\!\!\!+} R_{iK+j} \right) \quad = \quad \underset{i<N}{+\!\!\!+} \left(\underset{j<K}{+\!\!\!+} R_{iK+j} ; \text{snd } D \right) \backslash\backslash (\text{fst } \Delta \mathcal{D}^{-1}) ; \text{snd } \mathcal{D}^{-N}$$

Figure 4.9 A theorem for retiming a row with clustering ($N = K = 2$).

combinational circuit cR can be used to implement $slow_n$ cR, since x ($slow_n$ cR) $y \equiv x$ cR y. $\mathcal{D}^n$ and $\mathcal{D}^{-n}$ can be used to implement $slow_n$ $\mathcal{D}$ and $slow_n$ $\mathcal{D}^{-1}$, since

$$x(slow_n \ \mathcal{D}) \ y \Leftarrow x \ \mathcal{D}^n \ y$$

$$x \ (slow_n \ \mathcal{D}^{-1}) \ y \Leftarrow x \ \mathcal{D}^{-n} \ y$$

$slow_n$ can be shown to distribute through our collection of combinators; for instance,

$$slow_n \ (Q \ ; R)$$

= {by definition of $slow_n$}

$$ev_n \ ; (Q; R) \ ; ev_n^{-1}$$

= {since $ev_n^{-1} \ ; ev_n = Id$}

$$ev_n \ ; Q \ ; ev_n^{-1} \ ; ev_n \ ; R \ ; ev_n^{-1}$$

= {by definition of $slow_n$}

$$slow_n \ Q \ ; slow_n \ R$$

The implementation of slowdown will be discussed in section 4.5. For now just note that our definition of $slow_n$ does not commit the implementation to perform the same caclulation in all n interleaved computations; any mechanism that devotes at least one of the n computations to the required calculation is adequate. Implementations that perform the same calculation in all interleaved computations can be concisely described by an alternative definition of $slow_n$ (Sheeran, 1988).

4.3.6 Summary

Let us summarize how the transformations discussed in this section can be used in a coherent manner for pipelining array architectures. First of all, given the required speed of the array and the propagation delay of the components, one can work out the optimal degree of pipelining. This determines the size of clusters, the formation of which is governed by clustering theorems. Next, from the dataflow of the array components an appropriate retiming transformation is selected to latch the clusters while avoiding the insertion of predictors which cannot be eliminated. The graphical technique mentioned earlier can be useful here. Sometimes slowdown may help in pipelining networks with counter-flowing data by increasing the number of delays and anti-delays. In other cases it may be better to reverse the direction of signal-flow if, for instance, an associative operation or a broadcasting circuit is involved.

The trade-off of each parametrized pipelined design can then be analysed; for instance the complexity of the boundary conditions may pose a problem for subsequent implementation. The effects of pipelining on latency, area and power consumption should also be studied. It will be useful to capture such effects parametrically (Luk, 1990b), so that one can check quickly to see whether an existing design can be altered to meet new requirements.

4.4 Examples

In this section a number of case studies are presented to illustrate the approach and the techniques introduced.

4.4.1 Recursive filtering

Given input x and coefficients $a_1, \cdots, a_N$ and $b_1, \cdots, b_N$, a recursive filter computes

$$\forall t \, . \, y_t = \sum_{1 \leq i \leq N} a_i \times y_{t-i} + \sum_{1 \leq i \leq N} b_i \times x_{t-i}. \tag{4.20}$$

We shall start with $RF0$, the well-known canonical form implementation (Kung, 1988). $RF0$ is a semi-systolic design; it consists of a heterogeneous chain of N components $F_0 \ldots F_{N-1}$, each of which contains two multipliers and two adders. A wiring cell G on the right-hand boundary provides the feedback and selects the output (Fig. 4.10).

$$RF0 = \overset{\circ}{\underset{i<N}{9}} \, (F_i \, ; \, \text{snd} \, (\text{fst} \mathcal{D}^{-1})) \, ; \, G$$

where F_i and G satisfy

$$[y, \, [u,x]] \, ; \, F_i \, ; \, [y', \, [u, \, x']]$$

where $y' = b_{N-i} \times u + y$

and $x' = a_{N-i} \times u + x$, $[y, \, [x, \, x]] \, ; \, G \, ; \, y$.

Given that 0 represents a constant stream of zeroes and $\perp$ represents a 'don't care' output, the expression

$$[0, \, [\perp, \, x]] \, ; \, RF0 \, ; \, y$$

can be shown to satisfy (4.20). Readers interested in deriving the initial

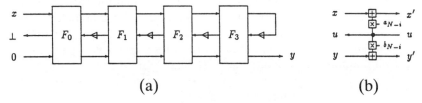

(a)   (b)

Figure 4.10 Design RF0. (a) An array with four components.
(b) Structure of F_i.

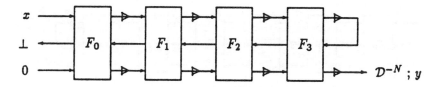

Figure 4.11 Design RF1 ($N=4$).

circuit representation may consult related work (Luk and Jones, 1988; Jones and Sheeran, 1990).

$RF0$ has N latches and a latency of N cycles (all designs in this section have a latency which is the same as the number of latches in the array). Its cycle time is restricted by the propagation delay $T_m + NT_a$ where T_m and T_a are respectively the times required by a multiplication and an addition. If we apply the retiming theorem for heterogeneous chain ((4.7) in section 4.3.1), we get

$$RF0 = \overset{\circ}{\underset{i<N}{2}}(F_i \; ; \; \text{snd} \; (\text{fst}\mathcal{D}^{-1}) \; ; \; \mathcal{D}) \; ; \; G \; ; \; \mathcal{D}^{-N}$$
$$= RF1 \; ; \; \mathcal{D}^{-N}$$

where $RF1 = \overset{\circ}{\underset{i<N}{2}}(F_i \; ; \; [\mathcal{D}, \text{snd}\mathcal{D}]) \; ; \; G$

since snd $(\text{fst}\mathcal{D}^{-1}) \; ; \; \mathcal{D} = \text{snd} \; (\text{fst}\mathcal{D}^{-1}) \; ; \; [\mathcal{D}, [\mathcal{D}, \mathcal{D}]] = [\mathcal{D}, \text{snd}\mathcal{D}]$.

Transforming $RF0$ to $RF1$ (see Fig. 4.11) doubles both the number of latches in the array and the circuit latency, although the cycle time is reduced to $NT_p + T_m + T_a$ where T_p represents the time for a signal to propagate through the middle wire of an F_i.

Two other solutions will be given. The first solution uses slowdown: the idea is to double the number of latches on the middle path first, so that retiming can transfer them to the lower and the upper path:

$$\text{slow}_2 \; RF0 = \overset{\circ}{\underset{i<N}{2}}(F_i \; ; \; \text{snd}(\text{fst}\mathcal{D}^{-2})) \; ; \; G$$
$$= \overset{\circ}{\underset{i<N}{2}}(F_i \; ; \; \text{snd}(\text{fst}\mathcal{D}^{-2}) \; ; \; \mathcal{D}) \; ; \; G \; ; \; \mathcal{D}^{-N}$$
$$= RF2 \; ; \; \mathcal{D}^{-N},$$

where $RF2 = \overset{\circ}{\underset{i<N}{2}}(F_i \; ; \; [\mathcal{D}, [\mathcal{D}^{-1}, \mathcal{D}]]) \; ; \; G$.

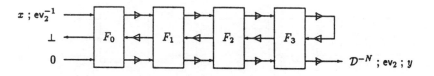

Figure 4.12 Design RF2 ($N=4$).

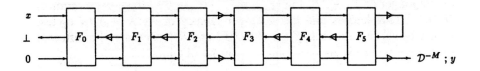

Figure 4.13 Design $RF3$ ($N=6$, $K=3$, $M=2$).

$RF2$ (Fig. 4.12) is a fully-pipelined circuit: its speed is limited by $T_m + T_a$. Remember, however, that since $RF2 = $ slow$_2$ $RF0$; $\mathcal{D}^N$, two computations have to be interleaved and successive elements of a particular computation are only available every other cycle. Also it has tripled the number of latches and the latency of $RF0$.

The second solution consists of grouping the N components of $RF0$ into M clusters, each with K components (hence $M = N/K$). Latches are then inserted between the clusters by retiming.

$$RF0 = \overset{\circ}{\underset{i<M}{\text{\large 5}}}\left(\overset{\circ}{\underset{j<K}{\text{\large 5}}}\ (F_{iK+j}\ ;\ \text{snd}(\text{fst}\mathcal{D}^{-1}))\right)\ ;\ G$$

$$= \overset{\circ}{\underset{i<M}{\text{\large 5}}}\left(\overset{\circ}{\underset{j<K}{\text{\large 5}}}\ (F_{iK+j}\ ;\ \text{snd}(\text{fst}\mathcal{D}^{-1}))\ ;\ \mathcal{D}\right)\ ;\ G\ ;\ \mathcal{D}^{-M}$$

$$= \overset{\circ}{\underset{i<M}{\text{\large 5}}}\left(\overset{\circ}{\underset{j<K-1}{\text{\large 5}}}\ (F_{iK+j}\ ;\ \text{snd}(\text{fst}\mathcal{D}^{-1}))\ ;\ F_{iK+K-1};\ \text{snd}(\text{fst}\mathcal{D}^{-1})\ ;\ \mathcal{D}\right);$$
$$G\ ;\ \mathcal{D}^{-M}$$

$$= RF3\ ;\ \mathcal{D}^{-M}$$

where $RF3 = \overset{\circ}{\underset{i<M}{\text{\large 5}}}\ \left(\overset{\circ}{\underset{j<K-1}{\text{\large 5}}}\ (F_{iK+j}\ ;\ \text{snd}(\text{fst}\mathcal{D}^{-1}))\ ;\ F_{iK+K-1}\ ;\ [\mathcal{D},\ \text{snd}\mathcal{D}]\right)\ ;\ G$.

$RF3$ (Fig. 4.13) has a cycle time of $T_m + KT_a$, and has $N(K+1)/K$ latches in the array. Alternatively, $RF1$ can be grouped into M clusters of K elements each,

$$RF1 = \overset{\circ}{\underset{i<M}{\text{\large 5}}}\ \left(\overset{\circ}{\underset{j<K}{\text{\large 5}}}\ (F_{iK+j}\ ;\ [\mathcal{D},\ \text{snd}\mathcal{D}])\right)\ ;\ G$$

$$= RF4\ ;\ \mathcal{D}^{M}$$

where $RF4 = \overset{\circ}{\underset{i<M}{\text{\large 5}}}\ \left(\overset{\circ}{\underset{j<K-1}{\text{\large 5}}}\ (F_{iK+j}\ ;\ [\mathcal{D},\ \text{snd}\mathcal{D}])\ ;\ F_{iK+K-1}\ ;\ \text{snd}(\text{fst}\mathcal{D}^{-1})\right)\ ;\ G$.

In comparison with $RF3$, $RF4$ (Fig. 4.14) has a shorter cycle time given

Figure 4.14 Design $RF4$ ($N=6$, $K=3$, $M=2$).

by the longer of $T_m + 2T_a$ and $(K - 1)T_p + T_m + T_a$. However, it requires $N(2K - 1)/K$ latches and has a longer latency of $N(2K - 1)/K$ cycles. Hence by varying the cluster size K in $RF3$ and $RF4$, designs with different trade-offs in speed, area and latency can be obtained.

4.4.2 Matrix multiplication

Given $M \times N$ coefficients $B_{i,j}$ and input stream $A_{t,i}$ where $0 \leqslant i < M$ and $0 \leqslant j < N$, a matrix multiplier computes the output stream $C_{t,j}$ such that

$$\forall t, j : 0 \leqslant j < N. \; C_{t, j} = \sum_{0 \leqslant i < M} A_{t, i} \times B_{i,j}.$$

Let $a = A_t$ and $c = C_t$, so that $c_j = \sum_{0 \leqslant i < M} a_i \times B_{i,j}$. It can be shown that the expression $[a,[0 \mid 0 \leqslant i < N]] \; ; \; MM \; ; \; [c, a]$, where

$$MM = \mathop{\#\#}_{i, j < M, N} Mult \; B_{i,j} \quad \text{and}$$

$$[p, x] \; ; \; Mult \; B_{i,j} \; ; \; [(p \times B_{i,j} + x), p],$$

satisfies this definition of c (Fig. 4.15).

Since MM is in the form of a rectangular array, we can use (4.14) and (4.17) to pipeline it. Suppose we decide to form clusters of K by K cells. Given that T_a is the delay of the horizontal output of cell $Mult$ and T_c is the delay of its vertical output, then the resulting pipelined array MM' has

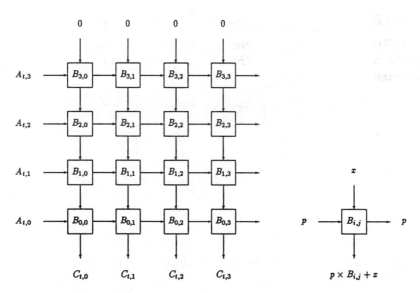

Figure 4.15 An array for matrix multiplication.

a cycle time of $(K-1)T_a + KT_c$ and a latency of $(M + N - K)/K$ cycles. There are $2MN/K$ latches in MM' and $(M(M - K) + N(N - K))/2K$ latches for skewing, since we only need to skew the a input and the c output.

An alternative strategy for pipelining MM involves a new combinator *gtrail* (for **generalized trail**), which takes three arguments. The first argument of *gtrail* consists of a tuple of tuples that describes the triangular array above the trailing diagonal, which is arranged as rows with increasing number of elements. The first element of the tuple of tuples is always an empty tuple, since for a one-by-one *gtrail* array there will not be any components other than the single element on the trailing diagonal. The middle argument of *gtrail* consists of a tuple describing the components on the trailing diagonal. The third argument of *gtrail* describes the triangular array below the trailing diagonal, but this time it is arranged as columns with an increasing number of elements. As an example, the arguments for *gtrail* in Fig. 4.16 are

$$P = \langle\langle\rangle, \langle P_{1,0}\rangle, \langle P_{2,0}, P_{2,1}\rangle\rangle$$

$$Q = \langle Q_0, Q_1, Q_2\rangle$$

$$R = \langle\langle\rangle, \langle R_{1,0}\rangle, \langle R_{2,0}, R_{2,1}\rangle\rangle$$

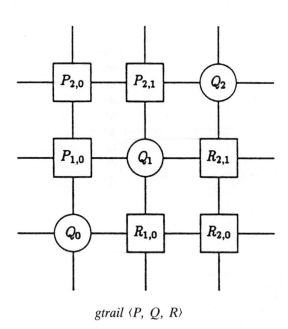

gtrail $\langle P, Q, R\rangle$

Figure 4.16 A trailing array.

The recursive definition of a similar combinator can be found in (Luk, 1990).

To pipeline a rectangular array using *gtrail*, we first form clusters of square arrays by applying (4.14). The square arrays can then be expressed as a trailing array using (4.21):

$$\underset{i,\,j<N,\,N}{\#} R_{i,j} = gtrail \,\langle\!\langle\!\langle R_{i,\,j} \mid 0 \leqslant j < i\rangle \mid 0 \leqslant i < N\rangle$$
$$\langle R_{i,i} \mid 0 \leqslant i < N \rangle, \langle\!\langle R_{i,j} \mid 0 \leqslant i < j\rangle \mid 0 \leqslant j \leqslant N\rangle\!\rangle\!\rangle \qquad (4.21)$$

The final step is to apply (4.22) which states that, given $\forall i, j : 0 \leqslant i < M, 0 \leqslant j < N.\#P_{i,j} = \#Q_{i,j} = \#R_{i,j} = K,$

$$\underset{i,\,j<M,\,N}{\#} (gtrail \,\langle P_{i,j}, Q_{i,j}, R_{i,j}\rangle) \qquad (4.22)$$
$$= \underset{i,\,j<M,\,N}{\#} (gtrail \,\langle P_{i,j}, Q'_{i,\,j}, R_{i,\,j}\rangle) \,\backslash\!\backslash\, [\Delta\mathcal{D}, \bar{\Delta}\mathcal{D}]^{-1} \,;\, [\mathcal{D}^{-M}, \mathcal{D}^{-N}]$$

where $\forall k : 0 \leqslant k < K, Q'_{i,\,j,\,k} = Q_{i,\,j,\,k}\,;\,\mathcal{D}.$

Equation (4.22) corresponds to pipelining 'through' the clusters by latching the square arrays along their trailing diagonals (Fig. 4.17). Usually this entails a more even distribution of latches, providing better performance. If we apply this transformation to *MM* with a cluster size of K, then given that $T_c < T_a$ the resulting array will have a cycle time of only KT_c. The number of latches and the latency of this design are the same as those of *MM'*.

4.5 Concluding remarks

Our work provides a method for representing a range of designs with different performance trade-offs by a single parametrized expression. Theorems for transforming such expressions have also been presented. Such theorems contribute to a mathematical basis for developing array architectures in a rigorous manner, and at the same time serve as documentation of design decisions. The application of these theorems is straightforward: it mainly involves substitution of equal expressions, and can be guided by the graphical interpretation of retiming theorems. Moreover, our pipelining procedure is applicable to arrays of any size provided that they are expressed in the required form, and the resulting designs often preserve the regularity of the original circuit.

To facilitate the assessment of alternative pipelining strategies, the design implications of retiming theorems have been examined in section 4.3.2, and the use of quantitative measures, such as clock speed and latency, to compare designs has been demonstrated in section 4.4. These techniques can be formalized and automated (Luk, 1990b). However, since it has been assumed that the cycle time decreases linearly with the degree of pipelining, the clock speed for highly-pipelined arrays may be over-estimated when clock skew as well as propagation delay and settling time of registers become significant. The percentage increase in area and

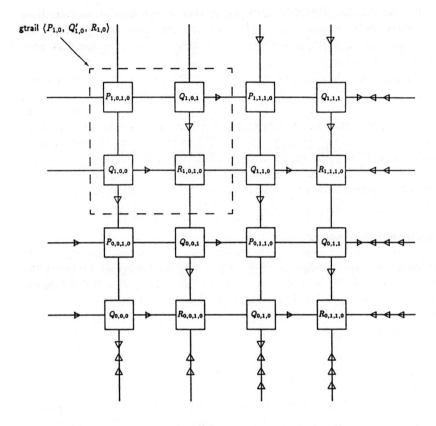

gtrail $\langle P_{1,0},\ Q'_{1,0},\ R_{1,0}\rangle$

$$\underset{i,j<M,N}{\#}\ (\text{gtrail}\ \langle P_{i,j},\ Q'_{i,j},\ R_{i,j}\rangle)\,\backslash\!\backslash\,[\Delta\mathcal{D},\tilde{\Delta}\mathcal{D}]^{-1}\ ;\ [\mathcal{D}^{-M},\mathcal{D}^{-N}]$$

Figure 4.17 Pipeline 'through' the clusters $(M{=}N{=}K{=}2)$.

power consumption for adopting a higher degree of pipelining depends on the ratio of area and power for a latch to that for a computational element; for instance one would expect circuits with dynamic latches to feature a smaller increase than circuits with static latches. There will be an increase in area and power for clock drivers as well.

If necessary the array can be partitioned first so that the array size is a multiple of the cluster size; for instance, given $0 \leqslant M < K$,

$$R^{NK+M} = R^M\ ;\ \mathcal{D}\ ;\ (R^K\ ;\ \mathcal{D})^N\ ;\ \mathcal{D}^{-(N+1)}.$$

Since the speed of a partially-pipelined array is restricted by the slowest stage, the clusters should be grouped in such a way that all clusters have the same propagation delay. The clusters can also be optimized individually, by further pipelining or by other means, as long as each preserves its behaviour.

Throughout it has been assumed that all latches are driven by a single clock. For useful work to be performed on every cycle, n distinct computations should be interleaved in an n-slow array. In technologies such as nMOS or CMOS, one can drive successive stages of latches by alternate phases of a two-phase clock; this can be modelled by interleaving two identical computations. Hence these circuits can still be described and reasoned about by our method. We only need to ensure that in the implementation successive stages of latches are being activated by alternate clock phases (Luk and Brown, 1990).

Acknowledgements

Thanks to Michael Jampel, Geraint Jones and Mary Sheeran for providing useful suggestions, and to the UK Alvey Programme, the Croucher Foundation and Rank Xerox UK Limited for their support.

References

Hatamian, M., and Cash, G. L., 1987, Parallel bit-level pipelined VLSI designs for high-speed signal processing, *Proc. IEEE*, **75**(9), 1192–202.

Jones, G., and Sheeran, M., 1990, Circuit design in Ruby, in *Formal Methods for VLSI Design* (ed. J. Staunstrup), North-Holland, 13–70.

Jones, G., and Sheeran, M., 1991, Relations and refinement in circuit design, in *Proc. Third Refinement Workshop* (eds C. C. Morgan and J. C. P. Woodcock), Springer–Verlag, 133–52.

Kung, S. Y., 1988, *VLSI Array Processors*, Prentice-Hall, New Jersey.

Kung, H. T., and Lam, M. S., 1984, Wafer-scale integration and two-level pipelined implementations of systolic arrays, *J. Parallel and Distributed Computing*, **1**, 32–63.

Leiserson, C. E., and Saxe, J. B., 1983, Optimizing synchronous circuitry by retiming, in *Third Caltech Conf. on VLSI* (ed. R. Bryant) Computer Science Press, Rockville Maryland, 87–116.

Luk, W., 1990a, Specifying and developing regular heterogeneous designs, in *Formal VLSI Specification and Synthesis* (ed. L. Claesen), North-Holland, 391–409.

Luk, W., 1990b, Analysing parametrized designs by non-standard interpretation, in *Proc. Int. Conf. on Application-specific Array Processors* (eds S. Y. Kung *et al.*), IEEE Computer Society Press, 133–44.

Luk, W., and Brown, G., 1990, A systolic LRU processor and its top-down development, *Science of Computer Programming*, **15**, 217–33.

Luk, W., and Jones, G., 1988, From specification to parametrised architectures, in *The Fusion of Hardware Design and Verification* (ed. G. Milne), North-Holland, 267–88.

Sheeran, M., 1988, Retiming and slowdown in Ruby, in *The Fusion of Hardware Design and Verification* (ed. G. Milne), North-Holland, 289–308.

5

Clocks, Retimings and Transformations of Synchronous Concurrent Algorithms

K. M. Hobley and J. V. Tucker

5.1 Introduction

We consider transformations, called retimings, of clocks modelling discrete time, and their use in the analysis of timing properties and the transformation of synchronous concurrent algorithms and architectures. We use algebraic methods to formalise the clocks and synchronous concurrent systems.

5.1.1 Overview

A **clock** is an algebra that consists of a set $T = \{0,1,2, \ldots \}$ of natural numbers, modelling discrete time cycles, constant 0 and operation $t + 1$. If R and T are clocks then a **retiming** of T to R is a transformation $\lambda: T \to R$, satisfying some simple conditions, that models the idea that $\lambda(t)$ is the time cycle on R that corresponds with time cycle t in T. In particular, T is thought to be faster or at a lower level of abstraction than R. Let $Ret(T, R)$ be the set of all retimings.

Retimings were introduced in Harman and Tucker (1987) and developed as a formal tool for the requirements capture and the specification of digital systems (see also Harman and Tucker (1988), Harman (1989) and Hobley (1990)).

First we will examine approximation properties of retimings by means of a metric space topology on $Ret(T, R)$. Special attention will be paid to the set $LR(T, R)$ of **linear retimings** which are retimings of the form $\lambda(t) = \lfloor \alpha t + \beta \rfloor$ for α, β real numbers and $0 < \alpha \leq 1$ and $0 \leq \beta < 1$. We will characterize and approximate linear retimings in various ways (Envelope Lemma 4, Rational Approximation Lemma 12).

We show that although $LR(T, R)$ cannot be used to approximate

Ret(*T*, *R*), the set *ALR*(*T*, *R*) of **almost linear retimings** can be used to approximate *Ret*(*T*, *R*) (Density Lemma 14).

In the second part of the paper we consider timing properties of synchronous concurrent algorithms.

A **synchronous concurrent algorithm** consists of a network of modules, computing in parallel, communicating data along channels, and synchronized by a global clock. Many types of algorithms and architectures are examples of synchronous concurrent algorithms. First, conventional digital hardware are made from components which are synchronous concurrent algorithms. Further, many new specialized models of computation possess the essential features of synchronous concurrent algorithms, including: systolic arrays, neural nets, cellular automata, deterministic data flow and coupled map lattice dynamical systems. A mathematical theory of synchronous concurrent algorithms that applies to these forms of computing systems has been developed from universal algebra and computability theory, see Thompson and Tucker (1991) and Tucker (1991) and the references cited there.

In our first model we shall assume that in any given computation, a module may select any value previously computed by its neighbours (i.e. those modules from which it receives an input channel); for such a network we must introduce delay maps to determine times. This property relaxes the usual **unit delay hypothesis** for synchronous concurrent algorithms, in which each module receives the values computed by its neighbours at the previous clock cycle. We will formalize synchronous concurrent algorithms with these non-unit delays using equations and we shall discuss some implementations of one particular class of non-unit delays, called the **constant delays**.

We then further generalize our notion of a synchronous concurrent algorithm to allow a **local clock** to be associated with each module, and formalize these algebraically. For such a network we must introduce **synchronization maps** to relate and control these clocks.

Both models are generalizations of synchronous concurrent algorithms with unit delay and are both deterministic parallel models of computation. Our formalizations are algebraic in form, and are intimately connected with the algebraic specification methods for abstract data types. It is possible to recant systematically the material of this paper in the theory of algebraic specifications and in the languages of its software tools. For a case study of a unit delay synchronous concurrent algorithm see Eker, Stavridou, and Tucker (1991).

5.1.2 Context

The mathematical ideas of this paper are a contribution to the development of a general mathematical theory of hardware, based on synchronous concurrent algorithms. The theory is intended to be abstract and therefore independent of specific types of (i) hardware systems, (ii) hardware description languages, and (iii) specification and verification tools. Many of the case studies that have shaped the theory have been systolic systems – see, for example, Thompson (1987) for unit delay, and Hobley (1990) for non-unit delay, systolic examples. The aim of the theory is simply to establish the fundamental scientific structure of a wide variety of hardware systems (including cellular automata, neural networks and so on) and hence to unify their special theories (where these exist).

The current state of the theoretical foundations of hardware is surveyed in McEvoy and Tucker (1990). A noteworthy general approach to the study of systolic systems with non-unit delays is Abdulla (1990) and Abdulla (1991).

5.1.3 Preliminaries

We recommend Meinke and Tucker (1992) and Tucker and Zucker (1988) for relevant basic material on algebras and models of computation over algebras. We recommend Ehrig and Mahr (1985) and Wirsing (1990) for basic material on algebraic specifications. For the algebraic specification of hardware see Goguen (1989) and Goguen (1990).

Throughout this paper we shall use the symbols $\mathbf{N}$, $\mathbf{Z}$, $\mathbf{Q}$, $\mathbf{R}$ and $\mathbf{N}_k$ to represent the sets of **naturals**, **integers**, **rationals**, **reals** and the set of natural numbers $\{1, \ldots, k\}$ respectively.

5.2 Clocks and retimings

5.2.1 Basic concepts

We define a clock to be an algebra $T = (T, 0, t + 1)$ consisting of a set $T = \{0, 1, 2, \ldots\}$ of time cycles, constant 0 for the first cycle, and operation $t+1$ to represent 'tick'. Clearly with this definition all clocks are isomorphic as algebras.

Let $T = (T, 0, t + 1)$ and $R = (R, 0, r + 1)$ be two clocks. We say that R is at a **higher level of abstraction** than T if each clock cycle of R corresponds with one or more clock cycles of T. We can formalize this by means of a function $\lambda : T \to R$, such that for any $t \in T$ the time on clock R is $\lambda(t)$.

Definition 1

We say that $\lambda : T \to R$ is a **retiming** from T to R if:

(i) $\lambda(0) = 0$;

(ii) λ is **surjective**, i.e. for all $r \in R$ there exists a $t \in T$ such that $\lambda(t) = r$; and

(iii) λ is **monotonic**, i.e. for all $t, t' \in T$, if $t \leq t'$ then $\lambda(t) \leq \lambda(t')$.

We shall denote the set of retimings from T into R by $Ret(T, R)$.

We shall define four functions which we will find useful later.

Definition 2
Let $\lambda \in Ret(T, R)$ be a retiming. The **immersion** of λ is given by $\bar{\lambda} : R \rightarrow T$ defined by the following function:

$$\bar{\lambda}(r) = (\text{least } t \in T)(\lambda(t) = r) \tag{5.1}$$

with the intended meaning that since one clock cycle of R corresponds to one or more clock cycles of T, given any time $r \in R$, $\bar{\lambda}$ selects the first time $t \in T$ for which $\lambda(t) = r$. Thus $\bar{\lambda}$ acts as the right inverse of λ, formally $\lambda\bar{\lambda}(r) = r$.

However, since $\bar{\lambda}$ is not necessarily the left inverse of λ we find it useful to make the following definition.

Definition 3
Let $\lambda \in Ret(T, R)$ be a retiming. The **start** of the current R clock cycle in which t lies is given by

start: $T \rightarrow T$ defined by the following function
$$\text{start}(t) = \bar{\lambda}\lambda(t) \tag{5.2}$$

An analogous function that selects the last T time which corresponds to the same R time, associated with any time $t \in T$, is provided by the following definition.

Definition 4
Let $\lambda \in Ret(T, R)$ be a retiming. The **end** of the current R clock cycle in which t lies is given by

end: $T \rightarrow T$ defined by the following function
$$\text{end}(t) = \bar{\lambda}(\lambda(t)+1)-1 \tag{5.3}$$

Finally, since we will often require a minimum number of T clock cycles to correspond to any given R clock time we make the following definition.

Definition 5
Let $\lambda \in Ret(T, R)$ be a retiming. The **length** of retiming is given by $l : R \rightarrow N$ defined by the following function:

$$l(r) = \bar{\lambda}(r+1) - \bar{\lambda}(r) \tag{5.4}$$

Notice that $l(\lambda(t)) = \text{end}(t) - \text{start}(t)+1$.

Lemma 1
$Ret(T, R)$ is uncountable.

Proof: If we consider any retiming $\lambda: T \rightarrow R$ then clearly λ may be uniquely determined by the infinite sequence $l(0), l(1), l(2), \ldots$ of its cycle lengths. In this way we can see a 1–1 correspondence between the set $Ret(T, R)$ and the set $[\mathbf{N} \rightarrow \mathbf{N} - \{0\}]$. ∎

Recall that the floor function $\lfloor \cdot \rfloor : \mathbf{R} \rightarrow \mathbf{Z}$ is defined for any $r \in \mathbf{R}$ by

$$\lfloor r \rfloor = \max \{n \in \mathbf{Z} : n \leq r\}$$

However, for our discussions we will require the following restriction of this function $\lfloor \cdot \rfloor_N : \mathbf{R} \rightarrow \mathbf{N}$ defined for any $r \in \mathbf{R}$ by

$$\lfloor r \rfloor_N = \max \{0, \lfloor r \rfloor\}$$

We will drop the subscript **N** where this does not lead to confusion.

We now describe three properties which hold for the **floor function**, and which we shall use in our work.

Lemma 2

Let $r, s \in \mathbf{R}$ and $n \in \mathbf{N}$ then the following three properties hold:

$$\lfloor r+n \rfloor_N = \lfloor r \rfloor_N + n \tag{5.5}$$

$$\lfloor r+s \rfloor_N \geq \lfloor r \rfloor_N + \lfloor s \rfloor_N \tag{5.6}$$

$$r < 1 \Rightarrow \lfloor r \rfloor_N = 0 \tag{5.7}$$

∎

Example A

(a) If clock T beats twice as fast as clock R, then they are related by the retiming $\lambda(t) = \lfloor \frac{t}{2} \rfloor$ (Fig. 5.2). We see that $\lambda(2) = \lambda(3) = 1$, $\bar{\lambda}(2) = 4$, start(2) = 2, end(2) = 3 and $l(1) = 4 - 2 = 2$.
(b) If clock T is related to clock R by the retiming $\lambda(t) = \lfloor \sqrt{t} \rfloor$ (Fig. 5.3). We see that $\lambda(5) = \lambda(6) = 2$, $\bar{\lambda}(2) = 4$, start(7) = 4, end(2) = 3 and $l(2) = 9 - 4 = 5$.

Retimings from relations

Let P be a unary relation on T. We imagine some computation being sampled at times defined by P and consider the set $\{t \in T : P(t)\}$.

Let $C_P : T \rightarrow \mathbf{N}$ be defined by the following function
$$C_P(t) = |\{t' \in T : t' \leq t \text{ and } P(t')\}| \tag{5.8}$$

or equivalently,

$$C_p(t) = \begin{cases} 1 & \text{if } t = 0 \text{ and } P(0) \\ 0 & \text{if } t = 0 \text{ and } \neg P(0) \\ C_P(t-1) + 1 & \text{if } t > 0 \text{ and } P(t) \\ C_P(t-1) & \text{if } t > 0 \text{ and } \neg P(t) \end{cases} \tag{5.9}$$

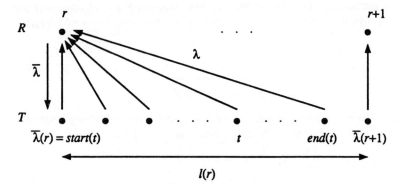

Figure 5.1 Basic structure of a retiming.

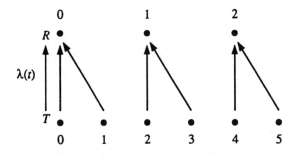

Figure 5.2 The retiming $\lambda\ (t)\ =\ \lfloor t/2 \rfloor$.

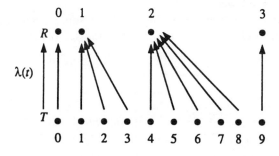

Figure 5.3 The retiming $\lambda\ (t)\ =\ \lfloor \sqrt{t}\ \rfloor$.

So $C_P(t) = r$ if, and only if, at time t the predicate P has been true on r occasions. We can interpret this sampling by P, by introducing a new clock R_P that beats exactly when P holds on T. Formally, we interpret C_P as a map $T \to R_P$. For C_P to be a retiming it is necessary and sufficient that:

(i) $P(0)$ is false;
(ii) $\{t \in T : P(t)\}$ is infinite.

If C_P is a retiming then its start predicate is P and its immersion $\overline{C_P}$ enumerates times on T when P is true.

5.2.2 Results about linear retimings

There are many ways that we might choose to describe a retiming $\lambda : T \to R$. We shall here discuss the class of retimings which can be expressed in terms of the **floor** of a **polynomial** over T.

Let $\mathbf{R}[t]$ be the set of polynomials over the set $\mathbf{R}$ of reals in the indeterminate t. Let $p(t) \in \mathbf{R}[t]$ be of the form

$$a_n t^n + a_{n-1} t^{n-1} + \ldots + a_1 t + a_0$$

thus $p : \mathbf{R} \to \mathbf{R}$.

Consider $P : \mathbf{N} \to \mathbf{N}$ defined by $P(t) = \lfloor p(t) \rfloor_{\mathbf{N}}$; henceforth we drop the subscript $\mathbf{N}$. Let us interpret P as a mapping $P : T \to R$ where T and R are clocks.

Theorem 1
P is a retiming if, and only if,

(i) $a_n = a_{n-1} = \ldots = a_3 = a_2 = 0$,
(ii) $0 < a_1 \leqslant 1$ and
(iii) $a_0 < 1$.

Condition (iii) admits negative a_0, however we will restrict our attentions only to values of $a_0 > 0$ since this leads to a more natural equivalence class for retimings (Uniqueness Corollary).

This result shows that the only retimings that can be expressed as the floor of a polynomial over T are **linear**.

Definition 6
A retiming $\lambda : T \to R$ is linear if there exists $\alpha, \beta \in \mathbf{R}$ with $0 < \alpha < 1$ and $0 \leqslant \beta < 1$ and for all t

$$\lambda(t) = \lfloor \alpha t + \beta \rfloor$$

We define the set of linear retimings to be $LR(T, R)$.

For simplicity we will prove a special case of the theorem when $n = 2$. The proof of the general case is an exercise.

Lemma 3

Let $P : T \to R$ be defined by $P(t) = \lfloor a_2t^2 + a_1t^1 + a_0 \rfloor$ for $a_2, a_1, a_0 \in \mathbf{R}$. P is a retiming if, and only if, $a_2 = 0$, $0 < a_1 \leq 1$ and $a_0 < 1$.

Proof: If we have that $a_2 = 0$, $0 < a_1 \leq 1$ and $a_0 < 1$ then P is such that $P(t) = \lfloor a_1t + a_0 \rfloor$. Clearly we have $P(0) = 0$, that P is monotonic and that P is surjective and hence P is a retiming.

Conversely, let us assume that P is a retiming. Now since P is a retiming we have that it is monotonic, i.e. $P(t+1) \geq P(t)$, and also surjective, i.e. $P(t+1) - P(t) < 1$, hence for all t

$$P(t)+1 \geq P(t+1) \tag{5.10}$$

Furthermore, we have

$$P(0) = 0 \tag{5.11}$$

Let us consider the values of $P(t) = \lfloor a_2t^2 + a_1t + a_0 \rfloor$ and $P(t+1) = \lfloor a_2(t+1)^2 + a_1(t+1) + a_0 \rfloor$ for each $t \in T$.

By (5.10) we have

$$\lfloor a_2t^2 + a_1t + a_0 \rfloor + 1 \geq \lfloor a_2(t+1)^2 + a_1(t+1) + a_0 \rfloor \tag{5.12}$$

or equivalently,

$$\lfloor a_2t^2 + a_1t + a_0 \rfloor + 1 \geq \lfloor a_2t^2 + a_1t + a_0 + (a_2(2 \times t + 1) + a_1) \rfloor$$
$$\geq \lfloor a_2t^2 + a_1t + a_0 \rfloor + \lfloor a_2(2 \times t + 1) + a_1 \rfloor$$

by (5.6). Thus using (5.7), we require

$$a_2(2 \times t + 1) + a_1 < 2$$

Now for this to hold for any t we require $a_2 \leq 0$. In fact $a_2 < 0$ would mean that there is time t such that for all times $t' > t$ we have $P(t') = 0$ and since P is necessarily surjective we have

$$a_2 = 0 \tag{5.13}$$

Hence we require

$$a_1 < 2 \tag{5.14}$$

an inequality which we will strengthen in (5.17).

Now by (5.11) we have

$$P(0) = \lfloor a_0 \rfloor = 0$$

and thus using (5.7).

$$a_0 < 1 \tag{5.15}$$

We now strengthen (5.14) and prove that $a_1 \leq 1$. We prove this by contradiction assuming that $1 < a_1 < 2$, thus there exists a $0 < \delta < 1$ with $a_1 = 1 + \delta$. Now let

$$m = \max \{m' \in \mathbf{N} : m' \times \delta + a_0 < 2\}$$

Setting $t = m$ in (5.12), and using (5.13), gives us

$$\lfloor m + m \times \delta + a_0 \rfloor + 1 \geq \lfloor m + 1 + (m + 1) \times \delta + a_0 \rfloor$$

thus

$$\lfloor m \times \delta + a_0 \rfloor + m + 1 \geq \lfloor (m + 1) \times \delta + a_0 \rfloor + m + 1$$

by (5.5), and thus

$$\lfloor m \times \delta + a_0 \rfloor \geq \lfloor (m + 1) \times \delta + a_0 \rfloor \tag{5.16}$$

By assumption on m we have $m \times \delta + a_0 < 2$ whilst $(m + 1) \times \delta + a_0 \geq 2$ and hence (5.16) is equivalent to

$$1 \geq 2$$

an obvious contradiction, and so

$$a_1 \leq 1 \tag{5.17}$$

Finally since $P(t)$ is surjective we obviously require

$$a_1 < 0 \tag{5.18}$$

We were required to show that $a_2 = 0$, which was done in (5.13), that $0 < a_1 \leq 1$, which was done in (5.17) and (5.18), and finally that $a_0 < 1$, which was done in (5.15). ∎

Observe that, if $\lambda_1(t) = \lfloor t + \frac{1}{2} \rfloor$ and $\lambda_2(t) = \lfloor t + \frac{1}{3} \rfloor$, then for all t we have $\lambda_1(t) = \lambda_2(t)$, but that if $\lambda_1(t) = \lfloor \frac{1}{3}t + \frac{1}{5} \rfloor$ and $\lambda_2(t) = \lfloor \frac{1}{3}t + \frac{4}{5} \rfloor$, then, for example, $\lambda_1(1) \neq \lambda_2(1)$. Thus we have that the coefficient β which defines a particular linear retiming is not necessarily unique. However we shall show that the coefficient α is unique for each linear retiming.

Definition 7

Let f and g be defined by the following functions:

$$\begin{matrix} f(t) = at + b \\ g(t) = at + b - 1 \end{matrix} \left\{ \begin{matrix} \text{where } 0 < a \leq 1 \\ \text{and } 0 \leq b < 1 \end{matrix} \right.$$

Observe that $g(t) = f(t) - 1$ and that they define two parallel lines.

We say that a k-envelope, with respect to a and b, is the region between these two parallel lines, between $t = 0$ and $t = k$, including those points which lie on the line f but not those that lie on the line g.

We say that E is an envelope, with respect to a and b, if for every $k \in \mathbf{N}$, E is a k-envelope.

We depict a k-envelope as the shaded area in Fig. 5.4.

Lemma 4 (envelope)

Given a function $\lambda : \mathbf{N} \to \mathbf{N}$ then there exists an envelope E enclosing the graph of λ if, and only if, $\lambda \in LR(T, R)$.

Proof: Let us assume that $\lambda : \mathbf{N} \to \mathbf{N}$ and that there is an envelope E which encloses the graph of λ. Let us assume that E is generated by the two lines $f(t) = at + b$ and $g(t) = at + b - 1$. Let us define the linear retiming $\mu(t) = \lfloor at + b \rfloor$. We shall show that for all t, $\lambda(t) = \mu(t)$.

For any t we know that $\lambda(t)$ lies between $f(t)$ and $g(t)$, thus we have that $at+b - 1 < \lambda(t) \leq at+b$. Furthermore, we know that $\mu(t) = \lfloor at + b \rfloor$ is such that $at + b - 1 < \mu(t) \leq at+b$, by the definition of $\lfloor \cdot \rfloor$. Thus since, for any t, there is only one integer value between these two limits we have that $\lambda(t) = \mu(t)$.

Conversely given a linear retiming $\lambda \in LR(T, R)$, say $\lambda(t) = \lfloor \alpha t + \beta \rfloor$ where $0 < \alpha \leq 1$ and $0 \leq \beta < 1$, then obviously each $\lambda(t) = r \in R$, lies either on or below the straight line $r = \alpha t + \beta$ and similarly lies above the straight line $r = \alpha t + \beta - 1$, by the definition of $\lfloor \cdot \rfloor$. Thus the envelope E generated by the two lines $f(t) = \alpha t + \beta$ and $g(t) = \alpha t + \beta - 1$ will enclose the graph of λ. ∎

Corollary (uniqueness)

Consider any two linear retimings $\lambda_1(t) = \lfloor \alpha_1 t + \beta_1 \rfloor$ and $\lambda_2(t) = \lfloor \alpha_2 t + \beta_2 \rfloor$, where the envelope enclosing λ_1 is defined by the two lines $f(t) = at + b$ and $g(t) = at + b - 1$, for some a, b. If we have $\lambda_1 = \lambda_2$ then $\alpha_1 = \alpha_2 = a$ and $b - 1 < \beta_1, \beta_2 \leq b$. ∎

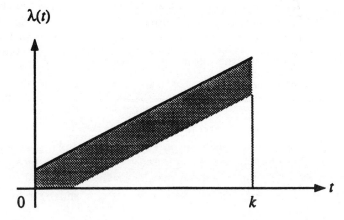

Figure 5.4 A k-envelope on the graph of λ.

Computable retimings

Since $T = R = \{0, 1, \ldots\}$ classical recursion theory can be easily employed to formalize the notion of a computable retiming.

Definition 8

We say $\lambda : T \to R$ is a **computable retiming** if λ considered as a map $\mathbf{N} \to \mathbf{N}$ is a total recursive function.

Thus if λ is computable then the set $\{(t, \lambda(t)) : t \in T\}$ is recursively enumerable. Since there are only countably many computable retimings, most retimings must be non-computable (Lemma 5).

Lemma 5

If λ is a computable retiming then the functions $\bar{\lambda}$, start, end and l are also computable. ∎

It is possible to employ the Envelope Lemma 4 in an algorithm which when applied to a retiming λ identifies whether the retiming λ is **not** a linear retiming. Thus linear retimings are co-recursively enumerable relative to the class of retimings. For reasons of clarity we shall not present this algorithm here.

5.2.3 The topology of retimings

Throughout this section we shall use the following distance function d which makes the space $[T \to R]$, of all functions $T \to R$, into a metric space: (5.19)

$$d(f, g) = \begin{cases} 0 & \text{if } f = g \\ \dfrac{1}{((\text{least } k)(g(k) \neq f(k)) + 1)} & \text{if } f \neq g \end{cases}$$

In fact $[T \to R]$ is a complete metric space. We will discuss the class of retimings $Ret(T, R)$ and linear retimings $LR(T, R)$ as subspaces of $[T \to R]$. Later, in section 5.2.5, we will use this topology to look at approximations to general retimings. We recommend Bourbaki (1966) for an introduction to topological themes.

In investigating these subspaces we will consider whether these subspaces are open, closed and/or dense. To do this we will need the following definitions:

Definition 9

Let B be a metric space with distance function $d : B^2 \to \mathbf{R}$. For any point $a \in B$ and any measure of proximity $\varepsilon \in \mathbf{R}$ with $\varepsilon > 0$ the open ε-ball of a is defined as

$$B_\varepsilon (a) = \{b \in B : d(a, b) < \varepsilon\} \tag{5.20}$$

Definition 10

Let A be a subset of a metric space B.

We say that A is an **open subset** of B if

$$(\forall a \in A)(\exists \varepsilon > 0)(B_\varepsilon(a) \subset A) \qquad (5.21)$$

We say that A is a **closed subset** of B if $B \setminus A$ is an open set of B.

We say A is a **dense subset** of B if each element of B may be approximated arbitrarily closely by an element of A; formally

$$(\forall b \in B)(\forall \varepsilon > 0)(\exists a \in A)(b \in B_\varepsilon(a)) \qquad (5.22)$$

If A is dense in B then there can be no proper subset of B containing A which is closed hence $\bar{A}$, the smallest closed subset of B containing A, is B

$$\bar{A} = B \qquad (5.23)$$

We shall sometimes use this equivalent notion of density.

$$Ret(T, R) \text{ as a subspace of } [T \rightarrow R]$$

Lemma 6

$Ret(T, R)$ is not an open subset of $[T \rightarrow R]$. Moreover $Ret(T, R)$ has an empty interior.

Proof: By (5.21) we are required to show that

$$(\exists \sigma \in Ret(T, R))(\forall \varepsilon > 0)(\exists \lambda \in [T \rightarrow R] \setminus Ret(T, R))(\lambda \in B_\varepsilon(\sigma))$$

Given $\sigma \in Ret(T, R)$ and $\varepsilon > 0$ we choose a $k \in \mathbf{N}$ with $\varepsilon < \frac{1}{k+1}$. Let us define a function $\lambda \in [T \rightarrow R]$, for each $t \in T$, as follows:

$$\lambda(t) = \begin{cases} \sigma(t) & \text{if } t \leq k \\ \lambda(t-1) + 2 & \text{if } t > k \text{ (say)} \end{cases}$$

With this definition λ is clearly not surjective and hence $\lambda \in [T \rightarrow R] \setminus Ret(T, R)$, and further $\lambda \in B_\varepsilon(\sigma)$.   ∎

Lemma 7

$Ret(T, R)$ is not a closed subset of $[T \rightarrow R]$.

Proof: We are required to show that $[T \rightarrow R] \setminus Ret(T, R)$ is **not** open. Thus by (5.21) we are required to show that

$$(\exists \phi \in [T \rightarrow R] \setminus Ret(T, R))(\forall \varepsilon > 0)(\exists \lambda \in Ret(T, R))(\lambda \in B_\varepsilon(\phi))$$

Let us consider $\phi \in [T \rightarrow R]$ defined by $\phi(t) = 0$ for all $t \in T$. Clearly $\phi \in [T \rightarrow R] \setminus Ret(T, R)$.

For any given value $\varepsilon > 0$ we choose a $k \in \mathbf{N}$ with $\varepsilon \frac{1}{k+1}$. Let us define a function $\lambda \in [T \rightarrow R]$, for each $t \in T$ as follows:

$$\lambda(t) = \begin{cases} 0 & \text{if } t \leqslant k \\ \lambda(t-1) + 1 & \text{if } t > k \text{ (say)} \end{cases}$$

With this definition it is easy to see that $\lambda \in Ret(T, R)$, and further that $\lambda \in B_\varepsilon(\phi)$. ∎

Lemma 8

$Ret(T, R)$ is not a dense subset of $[T \to R]$.

Proof: By (5.22) we are required to show that

$$(\exists \lambda \in [T \to R])(\exists \varepsilon > 0)(\forall \sigma \in Ret(T, R))(\lambda \notin B_\varepsilon(\sigma))$$

Let us consider $\lambda \in [T \to R]$ defined by $\lambda(t) = 1$ for all $t \in T$ and let us set $\varepsilon = 1$.

Now since for any $\sigma \in Ret(T, R)$ we have $\sigma(0) = 0$ we clearly have $d(\sigma, \lambda) = 1$ ($\not< 1$) and hence $\lambda \notin B_\varepsilon(\sigma)$. ∎

$$LR(T, R) \text{ as a subspace of } Ret(T, R)$$

Lemma 9

$LR(T, R)$ is not an open subset of $Ret(T, R)$. Moreover $LR(T, R)$ has an empty interior.

Proof: By (5.21) we are required to show that

$$(\exists \lambda \in LR(T, R))(\forall \varepsilon > 0)(\exists \sigma \in Ret(T, R) \setminus LR(T, R))(\sigma \in B_\varepsilon(\lambda))$$

Given $\lambda \in LR(T, R)$ and $\varepsilon > 0$ we choose a k with $\varepsilon < \frac{1}{k+1}$. Let us define a retiming $\sigma \in Ret(T, R)$, for each $t \in T$, as follows:

$$\sigma(t) = \begin{cases} \lambda(t) & \text{if } t \leqslant k \\ \sigma(k) & \text{if } k < t \leqslant l \\ \sigma(t-1) + 1 & \text{if } t > l \end{cases}$$

Where l is chosen as follows:

First, let us suppose we have an envelope E, defined with respect to some a and b, which contains the infinite set of points $(t, \sigma(t))$ for each $t > l$. Notice that, for all $t > l$, we have $\sigma(t) = \sigma(t-1) + 1$ and thus clearly if such an envelope E exists then we require $a = 1$.

Furthermore we require a $0 \leqslant b < 1$ with the property $t + b - 1 < \sigma(t) \leqslant t + b$, for each $t > l$, equivalently $t + b - 1 < \lambda(k) + t - l \leqslant t + b$. Hence we require $0 \leqslant b < 1$ such that $b - 1 < \lambda(k) - l \leqslant b$.

We therefore choose a value for l so that there can be no such b. Let us set $l = \lambda(k) + 1$.

With this definition it is easy to see that $\sigma \in Ret(T, R) \setminus LR(T, R)$ and further $\sigma \in B_\varepsilon(\lambda)$. ∎

Lemma 10
$LR(T, R)$ is a closed subset of $Ret(T, R)$.

Proof: We are required to show that $Ret(T, R) \setminus LR(T, R)$, is open. Thus by equation (5.21) we are required to show

$$(\forall \phi \in Ret(T, R) \setminus LR(T, R))(\exists \varepsilon > 0)(B_\varepsilon(\phi) \subset Ret(T, R) \setminus LR(T, R))$$

Take $\phi \in Ret(T, R) \setminus LR(T, R)$. Using Lemma 4 (the Envelope Lemma) we know that there will be a value k (assumed minimum) for which there is no k-envelope which contains the graph of ϕ. For this value of k we know that the distribution of the points $(0, 0), (1, \phi(1)), \ldots (k, \phi(k))$ is such that there are no values a and b (with $0 < a \leqslant 1$ and $0 \leqslant b < 1$) for which the envelope, defined with respect to a and b, contains these points. Thus if we choose $\varepsilon < \frac{1}{k+1}$ then any retiming $\sigma \in Ret(T, R)$ for which $d(\sigma, \phi) < \varepsilon$ will have the same distribution for its first k points and hence there can be no k-envelope which contains its graph. Thus, any such σ will also be a member of the class $Ret(T, R) \setminus LR(T, R)$. ∎

Lemma 11
$LR(T, R)$ is not a dense subset of $Ret(T, R)$.

Proof: By (5.23) we are required to show that $\overline{LR(T, R)}$ does not equal $Ret(T, R)$. By Lemma 10 we know that $\overline{LR(T, R)} = LR(T, R)$ and obviously $LR(T, R) \neq Ret(T, R)$. ∎

5.2.4 Topology of the class of linear retimings

Let us now consider the metric space of linear retimings further by investigating properties associated with the coefficients α and β which define a linear retiming (Definition 6). We consider the following three classes of coefficients:

(i) α and β are irrational;
(ii) $\alpha = \frac{p}{q}$ and $\beta = \frac{r}{s}$ are taken from the set $\mathbf{Q} \setminus \mathbf{N}$; and
(iii) $\alpha = \frac{1}{k_1}$ and $\beta = \frac{1}{k_2}$ with $k_1, k_2 \in \mathbf{N}$.

Lemma 12 (rational approximation)
The set of linear retimings $\{\lambda_2(t) = \lfloor \frac{p}{q}t + \frac{r}{s} \rfloor : \frac{p}{q}, \frac{r}{s} \in \mathbf{Q} \setminus \mathbf{N}\}$ is dense in the set of linear retimings $\{\lambda_1(t) = \lfloor \alpha t + \beta \rfloor : \alpha, \beta \in \mathbf{R}\}$.

Proof: We need to show that for any such $\lambda_1(t) = \lfloor \alpha t + \beta \rfloor$ and for any choice of $\varepsilon > 0$ there exists such a $\lambda_2(t) = \lfloor \frac{p}{q}t + \frac{r}{s} \rfloor$ with the condition that $d(\lambda_1, \lambda_2) < \varepsilon$, i.e. $\lambda_1 \in B_\varepsilon(\lambda_2)$.

Given $\lambda_1(t) = \lfloor \alpha t + \beta \rfloor$ and $\varepsilon > 0$ we choose a k with $\varepsilon < \frac{1}{k+1}$. Next we need a record of the closest that $\alpha t + \beta$ gets to, from **below**, an integer value as t ranges over $\{1, \ldots, k\}$ and so we set $\delta = (\text{least } l \neq 0)((\forall t \in \{1, \ldots, k\})(l = |\alpha t + \beta - \lceil \alpha t + \beta \rceil|))$.

Next we need to set a range within which to choose our coefficients such that the retiming derived from these coefficients will not exceed $\lceil \alpha t + \beta \rceil$ (for non-integer values of $\alpha t + \beta$) for each $t \in \{1, \ldots, k\}$. We require a $\gamma \in \mathbf{R}$ so that the error γ multiplied by the maximum time k is still less than half δ (the closest that $\alpha t + \beta$ gets to an integer value). Thus we choose a $\gamma < \frac{\delta}{2k}$.

Finally we choose $\frac{p}{q} \in \mathbf{Q}$ such that $\alpha \leq \frac{p}{q}, \leq \alpha + \gamma$ and $\frac{r}{s} \in \mathbf{Q}$ such that $\beta \leq \frac{r}{s} \leq \beta + \gamma$. Notice that we will always be able to choose suitable values of $\frac{p}{q}$ and $\frac{r}{s}$ since the rationals are dense in the reals.

Setting $\lambda_2(t) = \lfloor \frac{p}{q} t + \frac{r}{s} \rfloor$ yields a suitable approximation to λ_1. ∎

Remark The condition $\beta \leq \frac{r}{s} \leq \beta + \gamma$ is far too strong but will suffice for the proof.

Lemma 13

The set of linear retimings

$$\{\lambda_2(t) = \lfloor \tfrac{1}{k_1} t + \tfrac{1}{k_2} \rfloor : k_1, k_2 \in \mathbf{N}\}$$

is not dense in the set of linear retimings

$$\{\lambda_1(t) = \lfloor \tfrac{p}{q} t + \tfrac{r}{s} \rfloor : \tfrac{p}{q}, \tfrac{r}{s} \in \mathbf{Q} \setminus \mathbf{N}\}$$

Proof: We have to show that for some $\lambda_1(t) = \lfloor \frac{p}{q} t + \frac{r}{s} \rfloor$ and for some $\varepsilon > 0$ there is no $\lambda_2(t) = \lfloor \frac{1}{k_1} t + \frac{1}{k_2} \rfloor$ for which $d(\lambda_1, \lambda_2) < \varepsilon$, i.e. there is no such λ_2 with $\lambda_1 \in B_\varepsilon(\lambda_2)$. In fact this condition holds for any choice of λ_1.

First, notice that for any two values $0 \leq a, b < 1$ we have

$$a + 1 > b \tag{5.24}$$

Now given $\lambda_1(t) = \lfloor \frac{p}{q} t + \frac{r}{s} \rfloor$ we consider the pair $n_1, n_2 \in \mathbf{N}$ defined by $n_1 = (\text{least } n)(\frac{1}{n} < \frac{p}{q})$ and $n_2 = (\text{max } n)(\frac{1}{n} > \frac{p}{q})$.

Let us define $\delta_1 = \frac{p}{q} - \frac{1}{n_1}$ and $\delta_2 = \frac{1}{n_2} - \frac{p}{q}$. We now consider each of the two values.

Case 1: $\delta_1 = \frac{p}{q} - \frac{1}{n_1}$

Since $\delta_1 \neq 0$ we may define $m = (\text{least } l)(l \times \delta_1 > 2)$. For this value of m we have

$$m \times \tfrac{p}{q} - m \times \tfrac{1}{n_1} = m \times (\tfrac{p}{q} - \tfrac{1}{n_1}) > 2$$

or equivalently

$$m \times \tfrac{p}{q} > m \times \tfrac{1}{n_1} + 2 \tag{5.25}$$

Now by substituting (5.24), with $a = \frac{r}{s}$ and $b = \frac{1}{k}$ (any $k \neq 1 \in \mathbf{N}$), in (5.25) we see that

$$m \times \tfrac{p}{q} + \tfrac{r}{s} + 1 > m \times \tfrac{1}{n_1} + \tfrac{1}{k} + 2$$

or equivalently

$$m \times \frac{p}{q} + \frac{r}{s} > m \times \frac{1}{n_1} + \frac{1}{k} + 1$$

Clearly choosing an $\varepsilon_1 < \frac{1}{m+1}$ we have $\lambda_1 \notin B_\varepsilon(\lambda_2)$, for any choice of $\lambda_2(t) = \lfloor \frac{1}{k_1} t + \frac{1}{k_2} \rfloor$ with $\frac{1}{k_1} < \frac{p}{q}$.

Case 2: $\delta_2 = \frac{1}{n_2} - \frac{p}{q}$

Since $\delta_2 \neq 0$ we may define $m = $ (least l)($l \times \delta_2 > 2$). For this value of m we have

$$m \times \frac{1}{n_2} - m \times \frac{p}{q} = m \times (\frac{1}{n_2} - \frac{p}{q}) > 2$$

or equivalently

$$m \times \frac{1}{n_2} > m \times \frac{p}{q} + 2 \tag{5.26}$$

Now by substituting (5.24), with $a = \frac{1}{k}$ and $b = \frac{r}{s}$ (some $k \neq 1 \in \mathbf{N}$), in (5.26) we see that

$$m \times \frac{1}{n_2} + \frac{1}{k} + 1 > m \times \frac{p}{q} + \frac{r}{s} + 2$$

or equivalently

$$m \times \frac{1}{n_2} + \frac{1}{k} > m \times \frac{p}{q} + \frac{r}{s} + 1$$

Clearly choosing an $\varepsilon_2 < \frac{1}{m+1}$ we have $\lambda_1 \notin B_\varepsilon(\lambda_2)$, for any choice of $\lambda_2(t) = \lfloor \frac{1}{k_1} t + \frac{1}{k_2} \rfloor$ with $\frac{1}{k_1} > \frac{p}{q}$.

Thus if we set $\varepsilon = \min \{\varepsilon_1, \varepsilon_2\}$ then we have $\lambda_1 \notin \mathbf{B}_\varepsilon(\lambda_2)$, for any choice of $\lambda_2(t) = \lfloor \frac{1}{k_1} t + \frac{1}{k_2} \rfloor$. ∎

5.2.5 Approximation of retimings by almost linear retimings

In the last section we showed that the class of linear retimings, where the parameters α and β are chosen from the set of rational numbers, are dense in the class of linear retimings (Rational Approximation Lemma 12). We also showed that the class of linear retimings $LR(T, R)$ are not dense in the class of general retimings $Ret(T, R)$ and so we must look harder to find an approximating set of functions for a general retiming.

We now present a class of functions that we call **almost-linear** retimings which we claim are dense in the class of retimings. This class of almost-linear retimings is defined as follows:

Definition 11

A retiming is a k-almost-linear retiming if for all $t > k$ we have $\lambda(t) = \lambda(t - 1) + 1$. A retiming is said to be an almost-linear retiming if there exist some k for which it is a k-almost-linear retiming. We shall denote the set of almost-linear retimings from T into R by $ALR(T, R)$.

Obviously we can replace the definition $\lambda(t) = \lambda(t - 1) + 1$ with any other inherently linear behaviour. Furthermore it is obvious that the class of 0-almost-linear retimings is a proper subset of the class of linear retimings.

We can now phrase our claim in the following theorem:

Lemma 14 (density)
$ALR(T, R)$ is dense in $Ret(T, R)$. That is, for any retiming $\lambda \in Ret(T, R)$, and for any desired approximation $\varepsilon > 0$, there exists an almost-linear retiming $\sigma \in ALR(T, R)$, such that $\lambda \in B_\varepsilon(\sigma)$

$$(\forall \lambda \in Ret(T, R))(\forall \varepsilon > 0)(\exists \sigma \in ALR(T, R))(\lambda \in B_\varepsilon(\sigma))$$

Proof: For any $\varepsilon > 0$ we choose a k such that $\varepsilon > \frac{1}{k+1}$. For such a k we generate a k-almost-linear retiming σ for which

$$\sigma(t) = \begin{cases} \lambda(t) & \text{if } t \leq k \\ \sigma(t-1) + 1 & \text{if } t > k \text{ (say)} \end{cases}$$

With this definition it is easy to se that $\sigma \in ALR(T, R)$, and further $\lambda \in B_\varepsilon(\sigma)$. ∎

Example B
Let us consider a 9-almost-linear retiming σ defined as follows:

$\sigma(0) = 0$
$\sigma(1) = \sigma(2) = \sigma(3) = 1$
$\sigma(4) = \sigma(5) = \sigma(6) = \sigma(7) = \sigma(8) = 2$
$\sigma(9) = 3$
$\sigma(t) = t - 6$ for all $t > 9$

Now notice that the square root retiming of examples A, $\lambda(t) = \lfloor \sqrt{t} \rfloor$, can be approximated to an accuracy of $\varepsilon = \frac{1}{9}$ by the 9-almost-linear retiming σ defined above, since

$$\sigma(t) = \begin{cases} \lambda(t) & \text{if } t \leq 9 \\ \sigma(t-1) + 1 & \text{if } t > 9 \end{cases}$$

5.3 Synchronous concurrent algorithms and their relation to hardware design

What is a synchronous concurrent algorithm?
A synchronous concurrent algorithm is a parallel algorithm that consists of a network of **modules**, interconnected by **channels**, which communicate and compute in parallel over a data set A. Computation and data flow between modules are synchronized with respect to a clock $T = \{0, 1, 2, \ldots\}$ measuring discrete time. External communication occurs at modules that are connected to **sources** and **sinks**. We first describe these four constituents: modules, channels, sources, sinks. Then

we describe the notation that we will need to fully specify a network and finally, we describe the synchronization of the modules of a network.

Modules A module is an atomic computational device comprising a **store** and a **processor.** The store is capable of holding a single datum from the set A, and the processor is capable of computing a **total** function over the set A. A typical module m is depicted:

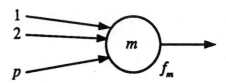

where the arrows are intended to represent the channels by which data is passed between modules.

The function $f_m : A^p \to A$ specifies the behaviour of the module m in the following way.

At a given time cycle we imagine m to be holding a datum from A in its store and some vector $(a_1, \ldots, a_p) \in A^p$ of data to be about to arrive on its input channels (one datum per channel). The module then performs a 'step' that takes up the next time cycle. The step comprises three phases. First the module propagates the value held in its store along its output channel and simultaneously accepts $(a_1, \ldots, a_p)$ from its input channels. Second, the module computes $f_m(a_1, \ldots, a_p)$, and third it stores this value in its store ready for its next step.

Channels Communication between the modules of the network occurs along channels. These channels are unidirectional and have bandwidth one, which is to say that they can only transmit a single datum $a \in A$ (and not for example a vector $(a_1, \ldots, a_n)$). Notice a module m specified by a function f_m with p arguments has p input channels and one output channel.

We will allow channels to branch finitely as, for example,

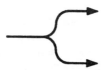

with the intention that the datum transmitted along the original channel is reproduced on both the new channels, although we shall insist that no two channels carrying the same replicated datum shall be input to the same module. However we will not allow channels to merge as, for example,

Delays   For each module m_i and each input channel j for that module we associate a communication delay

$$\delta_{i,j} : T \times [T \to A^n] \times A^k \to T. \tag{5.27}$$

To preclude predictive circuits we shall assume the temporal condition that for any $t \in T$, $\underline{a} \in [T \to A^n]$ and $x \in A^k$ we have

$$\delta_{i,j}\,(t, \underline{a}, x) < t. \tag{5.28}$$

Sources   The sources are where input to the network occurs; we will call any module that is connected to a source an **input module**. A source may have only one output channel (although this may branch so that the source can supply the same input data to several input modules). A typical source is depicted:

Sinks   The sinks are where output from the network occurs; we will call any module that is connected to a sink an **output module**. A sink may have only one input channel. (Notice that since we do not allow channels to merge, this means that any sink is connected to a unique output module.) A typical sink is depicted:

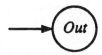

Network specification
In general we suppose that a network N has k modules named $m_1, \ldots , m_k$ specified by functions $f_1, \ldots , f_k$, respectively, with module

m_i having p_i inputs. We say that N has n sources named $In_1, \dots, In_n$ and d output modules named $m_{\eta_1}, \dots, m_{\eta_d}$.

To fully describe the network we will need to describe the connection pattern of the modules and so we introduce the functions γ and β as follows

$$\gamma : \mathbf{N}_k \times \mathbf{N} \to \{S, M\}$$
$$\beta : \mathbf{N}_k \times \mathbf{N} \to \mathbf{N}$$

where $\gamma(i, j)$ indicates whether the jth input to the ith module, m_i, originates from a source or another module and $B(i, j)$ provides the index of that source or module. We require the following three conditions to hold:

1. $(\forall_i)(\forall_j)(\gamma(i, j) = S \Leftrightarrow 1 \leq \beta(i, j) \leq n)$
   with the intended meaning that if the jth input channel of module m_i comes from a source then the index, provided by the β function, is within the range of the source indices.
2. $(\forall_i)(\forall_j)(\gamma(i, j) = M \Leftrightarrow 1 \leq \beta(i, j) \leq k)$
   with the intended meaning that if the jth input channel of module m_i comes from a module then the index, provided by the β function, is within the range of the module indices.
3. $(\forall_i)(\forall_j)(1 \leq i \leq k \wedge 1 \leq j \leq p_i \Leftrightarrow \beta(i, j) \downarrow \wedge \gamma(i, j) \downarrow)$
   with the intended meaning that if i is within the range of the module indices and j is within the range of the input channels to module m_i then both the γ and β functions are defined. This formalizes the architecture or network structure of a synchronous concurrent algorithm.

Synchronization   We can now describe what is 'synchronous' about a synchronous network or algorithm.

Initially we assume that each module m is holding some initial value $x_m \in A$ and that every module starts to perform corresponding steps simultaneously. Suppose that, according to some clock C, the time taken for every module to perform any step is less than or equal to some fixed constant $\tau > 0$. Now since the modules start a step simultaneously with respect to C, they can be made to end the step simultaneously too. Thus the modules of a network can be synchronized. We may normalize τ to unity (that is, take $\tau = 1$) and our 'constant time' hypothesis, after normalization, defines a new **virtual clock** T measuring discrete time $t = 0, 1, 2, \dots$.

5.3.1 Formal tools for specification of these algorithms

In this section we will formalize the synchronous networks of section 5.3 above and show how we can systematically construct functional specifications of the operation of synchronous networks by means of value functions.

Value functions

In order to specify a network's behaviour over time, first notice that the behaviour of the network will be completely specified if we can write down the value held by every module at any time t. Also observe that the value held by any module at any time can be determined from the input to the network, the values initially held by the network's modules, and the current time t.

Let N be a synchronous network over data set A with clock T. If N has $n > 0$ sources then the input to N we represent as a stream $\underline{a} = (\underline{a}_1, \ldots, \underline{a}_n) : T \to A^n$ (with the intention that the ith source supplies $\underline{a}_i(t)$ to the network at time t). Also suppose that N has k modules $m_1, \ldots, m_k$. Then any vector $x = (x_1, \ldots, x_k) \in A^k$ will serve to specify the network's initial values (with the intention that m_i initially holds x_i). Now, the value held by each m_i at a time t can be determined from t, $\underline{a}$ and x, by introducing functions $V_1, \ldots, V_k$ where

$$V_i : T \times [T \to A^n] \times A^k \to A \qquad (5.29)$$

for $i = 1, \ldots, k$; these functions we call the network's value functions. Intentionally, '$V_i(t, \underline{a}, x)$' is read as: 'the value in the ith module at time t given input stream $\underline{a}$ and initial values x'.

We can put $V_1, \ldots, V_k$ together as the coordinates of a function

$$V_N = (V_1, \ldots, V_k) : T \times [T \to A^n] \times A^k \to A^k \qquad (5.30)$$

which we refer to as **the** value function for network N: For each $t \in T$, $\underline{a} : T \to A^n$, and $x \in A^k$, $V_N(t, \underline{a}, x)$ is the vector

$$V_N(t, \underline{a}, x) = (V_1(t, \underline{a}, x), \ldots, V_k(t, \underline{a}, x)) \in A^k$$

that tells us the values held by all the network's modules at time t.

We define V_N by exploiting the single most important consequence of a network's synchronous behaviour: because the network is synchronous, every value in the network at every time is either specified initially, or is specified in terms of the values held at certain previous time cycles.

This fact underwrites the following informal two-stage method which describes how to define V_N.

Value functions for non-unit delay modules   Let N have $n > 0$ sources $In_1, \ldots, In_n$ and $k > 0$ modules $m_1, \ldots, m_k$ and for $i = 1, \ldots, k$ let $p_i > 0$ denote the number of input channels that m_i has from adjacent modules and sources, and let m_i be specified by $f_i : A^{p_i} \to A$. Also let $\underline{a} = (\underline{a}_1, \ldots, \underline{a}_n) : T \to A^n$ and $x = (x_1, \ldots, x_k) \in A^k$.

Stage 1:   To define $V_N(0, \underline{a}, x)$ we must define $V_i(0, \underline{a}, x)$ for $i = 1, \ldots, k$. Since x_i is intentionally the value held by m_i at time $t = 0$, it is appropriate to define, for $i = 1, \ldots, k$,

$$V_i(0, \underline{a}, x) = x_i \qquad (5.31)$$

Stage 2: To define $V_N(t, \underline{a}, x)$ we must define $V_i(t, \underline{a}, x)$ for $i = 1, \ldots, k$. The intention behind a module specification $f_i : A^{p_i} \to A$ is that if $b_1, \ldots, b_{p_i}$ are the values selected by m_i by means of its delay functions, $\delta_{i,1}, \ldots, \delta_{i\,p_i}$, from past or present data transmitted along its input channels then $f_i(b_1, \ldots, b_{p_i})$ is the value held at time t. However, for $j = 1, \ldots, p_i$ the jth input is either supplied by some source, at some previous time $\delta_{i,j}(t, \underline{a}, x)$, (recall our delay hypothesis (5.28) that $\delta_{i,j}(t, \underline{a}, x) < t$,) in which case $b_j = \underline{a}_u(\delta_{i,j}(t, \underline{a}, x))$ for some $u \in [1, n]$, or it is supplied by another module (possibly itself), at some previous time $\delta_{i,j}(t, \underline{a}, x)$ in which case $b_j = V_v(\delta_{i,j}(t, \underline{a}, x), \underline{a}, x)$ for some $v \in [1, k]$. Accordingly we define $V_i(t, \underline{a}, x)$ by

$$V_i(t, \underline{a}, x) = f_i(b_1, \ldots, b_{p_i}) \qquad (5.32)$$

where for $j = 1, \ldots, p_i$,

$$b_j = \begin{cases} \underline{a}_u(\delta_{i,j}(t, \underline{a}, x)) & \text{if the } j\text{th input to } m_i \text{ is from} \\ & \text{source } In_u \\ V_v(\delta_{i,j}(t, \underline{a}, x), \underline{a}, x) & \text{if the } j\text{th input to } m_i \text{ is from} \\ & \text{module } m_v \end{cases} \qquad (5.33)$$

∎

Let us now draw attention to the following three facts.

First, notice that in the case of a module m_i whose inputs come from modules only, say $m_{v(1)}, \ldots, m_{v(p_i)}$, (5.32) becomes

$$V_i(t, \underline{a}, x) = f_i(V_{v(1)}(\delta_{i,1}(t, \underline{a}, x), \underline{a}, x), \ldots,$$
$$V_{v(p_i)}(\delta_{i,p_i}(t, \underline{a}, x), \underline{a}, x)) \qquad (5.34)$$

Secondly, notice how the functional dependencies reflect the wiring between modules.

Finally, notice that (5.31), (5.32) and (5.33) (when written out for $i = 1, \ldots, k$) amount to an effective prescription for calculating the values held in any module at any time t.

Output functions
Notice that a value function V_N tells us the value held by every module in the network, whereas ultimately we are only interested in the values held by output modules (that is, modules that are connected to sinks) since this is where network output appears. We can restrict our attention to just these modules as follows. Let N be a n-source, k-module synchronous network over data set A; then V_N is of the form (see (5.30)):

$$V_N = (V_1, \ldots, V_k) : T \times [T \to A^n] \times A^k \to A^k$$

Now suppose N has m sinks $Out_1, \ldots, Out_m$ and consider a typical sink Out_j. Let the module that supplies Out_j with output data be m_{i_j} (so $i_j \in [1, k]$). Then for a given input stream $\underline{a} : T \to A^n$ and initial values $x \in A^k$, the output sent to Out_j at time t is just $V_{i_j}(t, \underline{a}, x)$.

In order to define a function that tells us the outputs at *all* the sinks at a given time t, we first define $\pi_N : A^k \to A^m$ by

$$\pi_N(a) = (a_{i_1}, \ldots, a_{i_m})$$

for each $a = (a_1, \ldots, a_k) \in A^k$. Given our interpretation of $i_1, \ldots, i_m$ this π_N 'picks out' the values that are sent to the sinks at time t when applied to the vector $V_N(t, \underline{a}, x) \in A^k$. For this reason it is appropriate to define a synchronous network's **output specification** to be the map

$$F_N = (F_1, \ldots, F_m) : T \times [T \to A^n] \times A^k \to A^m$$

defined by

$$F_N(t, \underline{a}, x) = \pi_N(V_N(t, \underline{a}, x)) \tag{5.35}$$

for each $t \in T$, $\underline{a} : T \to A^n$ and $x \in A^k$.

(Notice that an output specification for a synchronous network necessarily depends on initial values since at time $t = 0$ there has been no time for the network to process any input data and so the output at $t = 0$ must be an initially held value.)

Given the time t, input stream $\underline{a}$ and initial values x, the function F_N tells us the vector of output at time t. An alternative idea is to phrase network output as a stream transformer; that is, as a function

$$G_N : [T \to A^n] \times A^k \to [T \to A^m]$$

with the intention that for each input stream $\underline{a} : T \to A$ and initial values $x \in A^k$, the output stream produced by N is $G_N(\underline{a}, x) : T \to A^m$. Such a function is readily definable from F_N. For each $\underline{a} : T \to A$ and $x \in A^k$ we define $G_N(\underline{a}, x) : T \to A^m$ to be the stream defined by

$$G_N(\underline{a}, x)(t) = F_N(t, \underline{a}, x)$$

for each $t \in T$.

5.4 Classification of non-unit delays

In this section we shall present some classes of delay functions which are of practical interest. We discuss two of these classes in greater detail; those of the **unit delay** functions and **constant delay** functions.

For the unit delay case we show how the restriction of our architectures to this class of delay functions greatly simplifies our formalization procedure.

For the class of constant delay functions we present an implementation technique consistent with our model of synchronous concurrent algorithms. This technique comes under the general technique which we term **static buffering**.

5.4.1 Delay constraints

Here we shall discuss the classes of delay functions which result from imposing certain constraints upon the non-unit delays of a synchronous concurrent algorithm. This is by no means a complete list of constraints but does include some of those that commonly occur in architectures.

Case 1:   Unit Delay $\delta_{i,j}(t, \underline{a}, x) = t - 1$.

In this case we are assuming that all modules compute upon data received from its neighbours at the previous clock cycle. Many examples have such a formalization.

Case 2:   Bounded Delay $\delta_{i,j}(t, \underline{a}, x) \in \{t - d_{i,j}, \ldots, t - 1\}$.

Here we restrict the range of the delay function $\delta_{i,j}(t, \underline{a}, x)$ to only times within a fixed period prior to t. Such bounded computation places an upper bound on the memory required by such a system, namely

$$\sum_{i=1}^{k} \sum_{j=1}^{p_i} d_{i,j}$$

Case 3:   Constant Delay $\delta_{i,j}(t, \underline{a}, x) = t \dot{-} d_{i,j}$

Here we assume that all computation is used in order. More formally, we assume the delays $\delta_{i,j}$ are surjective and monotonic. We arc using $\dot{-}$ (ambiguously $-$) to represent restricted subtraction, defined by $a \dot{-} b = \max \{0, a-b\}$.

Notice that Case 3, the constant delay, is a generalization of Case 1, the unit delay.

Let us now consider a synchronous concurrent algorithm with unit delay computation. We shall then return to the synchronous concurrent algorithm with non-unit delay computation for which the delay functions are constant delays.

5.4.2 Synchronous concurrent algorithms with 'Unit Delays'

In this case we have $\delta_{i,j}(t, \underline{a}, x) = t - 1$. Many examples taken from hardware literature have unit delay computation and this class of networks has been given careful and thorough consideration, see Thompson (1987), Hobley, Thompson, and Tucker (1988) and Thompson and Tucker (1991).

Considering the work of section 5.3.1 we see that in the case of unit delay computation the value function for a typical internal module m_i, whose inputs come from modules only, say $m_{v(1)}, \ldots, m_{v(p_i)}$ at a non-initial time $t + 1$ is

$$V_i(t + 1, \underline{a}, x) = f_i(V_{v(1)}(t, \underline{a}, x), \ldots, V_{v(p_i)}(t, \underline{a}, x)) \qquad (5.36)$$

We ask the reader to contrast this equation with (5.34) to see how elegant the formalization of a network by the value functions becomes when we place this unit delay restriction upon the modules' communications.

We now return to the constant delay functions and we shall present a method for implementing a synchronous concurrent algorithm with such communication delays. We shall see how our implementation method involves static buffering techniques. We propose to demonstrate that the operational semantics of our network is *not* determined by the equations.

5.4.3 Modelling synchronous concurrent algorithms with 'Constant Delays'

Here we are assuming that for any $i \in \{1, \ldots , k\}$ and any $j \in \{1, \ldots , p_i\}$ we have $\delta_{i,j}(t, \underline{a}, x) = t - d_{i,j}$, for fixed $d_{i,j} \in \mathbf{N}$. In this case the value function for a typical internal module m_i, at a non-initial time t, will be

$$V_i(t, \underline{a}, x) = f_i(V_{\beta(i,1)}(t - d_{i,1}, \underline{a}, x), \ldots , V_{\beta(i,p_i)}(t - d_{i,p_i}, \underline{a}, x)) \quad (5.37)$$

Notice that for such a constant delay algorithm the $\delta_{i,j}$ are independent of both the input stream $\underline{a}$ and the initial values x and so are maps $\delta_{i,j} : T \rightarrow T$.

Channel buffering

The notion behind this method is to introduce fixed length storage into the definition of a channel. Thus we shall require the jth input channel to a module m_i to have $d_{i,j}$ stores taking the form of sequential shift registers.

Let N be a network which has k modules, $m_1, \ldots , m_k$, for which the value function of a typical module m_i, with functionality $f_i : A^{p_i} \rightarrow A$, is given by

$$V_i(0, \underline{a}, x) = x_i$$

$$V_i(t + 1, \underline{a}, x) = f_i(b_1, \ldots , b_{p_i})$$

where for $j = 1, \ldots , p_i$,

$$b_j = \begin{cases} \underline{a}_u(t - d_{i,j}) & \text{if the } j\text{th input to } m_i \text{ is from source } In_u \\ V_v(t - d_{i,j}, \underline{a}, x) & \text{if the } j\text{th input to } m_i \text{ is from module } m_v \end{cases}$$

for fixed constants $d_{i,j}$. Given such a network N we can construct a new network N' with buffering functions associated with each input channel of each module where for each $i \in \{1, \ldots , k\}$, $j \in \{1, \ldots , p_i\}$ and $l \in \{1, \ldots , d_{i,j} - 1\}$ we define the buffering functions, $b^l_{i,j}$, for each $t \in T$ by

$$b^l_{i,j}(0, \underline{a}, x) = x^l_{i,j}$$

and

$$b_{i,j}^{l}(t+1, \underline{a}, x) = \begin{cases} b_{i,j}^{l-1}(t, \underline{a}, x) & \text{if } l \neq 1 \\ V_{\beta(i,j)}(t, \underline{a}, x) & \text{if } l = \wedge \; \gamma(i, j) = M \\ a_{\beta(i,j)}(t) & \text{if } l = 1 \wedge \gamma(i, j) = S \end{cases}$$

and we define the value function for the module m_i, for each $i = 1$, ... , k, by

$$V_i'(t + 1, \underline{a}, x) = f_i(b_{i,1}^{d_{i,1}-1}(t, \underline{a}, x), \ldots, b_{i,p_i}^{d_{i,p_i}-1}(t, \underline{a}, x)) \qquad (5.38)$$

Observe that with this modelling technique we now have unit delay computation between neighbouring modules and buffers.

It is possible to show that the following lemma holds.

Lemma 15
A synchronous concurrent algorithm specified by functions f_i, for each module m_i, and buffer functions $b^1{}_{i,j}, \ldots, b_{i,j}^{d_{i,j}-1}$, for the channel associated with the jth input to module m_i, can be represented by a synchronous concurrent algorithm with the channels replaced by shift registers.   ∎

5.5 Synchronous concurrent algorithms with local clocks

In this section we explore a notion of a synchronous concurrent algorithm in which each module is equipped with its own clock, and for which there are synchronization mappings to connect these clocks. This informal notion seems to be very rich, but here we are content to examine it in relation to the notion of synchronous concurrent algorithms with a global clock. The global synchronization of the local clocks will be formalized by means of retimings from a master clock.

5.5.1 What is a synchronous concurrent algorithm with local clocks?

The informal notion of a synchronous concurrent algorithm with local clocks is similar to that of section 5.3. We shall assume that associated with input stream $\underline{a}_u$ for $u = 1, \ldots, n$ we have a controlling clock C_u and associated with each module m_v, for $v = 1, \ldots, k$, of the network we have a clock R_v.

Connections between modules are again via channels but now we require synchronization maps associated with each channel of the network to relate the clocks belonging to the modules. Thus for each $i = 1, \ldots, k$ and each $j = 1, \ldots, p_i$, if the input to module m_i along its jth channel comes from some source In_u then we require a map

$$\eta_{i,u} : R_i \rightarrow C_u,$$

and if the input to module m_i along its jth channel comes from some module m_v then we require a map

$$\mu_{i,v} : R_i \rightarrow R_v.$$

This situation may be depicted as in Fig. 5.5.

Of course there will be a number of operational models that are consistent with this association of a channel with a synchronization map.

Thus we may formulate the value functions for such architectures by

$$V_i : R_i \times [C_1 \rightarrow A] \times \ldots \times [C_n \rightarrow A] \times A^k \rightarrow A$$

$$V_i(r_i, \underline{a}, x) = f_i(b_1, \ldots, b_{p_i}) \tag{5.39}$$

where $\underline{a} = (\underline{a}_1, \ldots, \underline{a}_n)$ and where for $j = 1, \ldots, p_i$,

$$b_j = \begin{cases} a_{\beta(i,j)} \, (\eta_{i,\beta(i,j)}(r_i)) & \text{if the } j\text{th input to } m_i \text{ is from} \\ & \text{source } In_{\beta(i,j)} \\ V_{\beta(i,j)}(\mu_{i,\beta(i,j)}(r_i), \underline{a}, x) & \text{if the } j\text{th input to } m_i \text{ is} \\ & \text{from module } m_{\beta(i,j)} \end{cases} \tag{5.40}$$

The complexity of these equations is determined by the nature of the synchronization maps $\eta_{i,u}$ and $\mu_{i,v}$.

5.5.2 Master clock

We consider the case when a synchronous concurrent algorithm with local clocks C_u and R_v can be transformed into a synchronous concurrent algorithm with a global clock T. We simply suppose that the local clocks

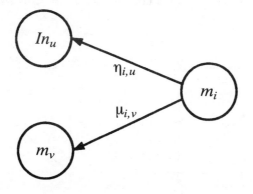

Figure 5.5   Local clocks and scheduling maps.

C_u and R_v and the synchronization maps $\mu_{i,v}$ and $\eta_{i,u}$, between neighbouring modules, can be synchronized by T. We formulate this property as follows:

Definition 12

A family $< C_u, R_v, \eta_{i,u} \mu_{i,u} : i, v \ E \ \{1, \ldots, k\}, u \ E \ \{1, \ldots, n\} >$ of clocks and synchronization maps can be synchronized by a global clock T if there exists a family of retimings $< \gamma_u : T \rightarrow C_u, \lambda_v : T \rightarrow R_v >$ such that the two diagrams of Fig. 5.6 commute i.e.

$$\gamma_u(t) = \eta_{i,u}(\lambda_i(t))$$

and

$$\lambda_i(t) = \mu_{v,i}(\lambda_v(t))$$

We may use the retiming γ_u to schedule the locally controlled input stream $\underline{a}_u$ to produce a new stream $\theta_u(\underline{a}_u)$ controlled by the global clock T, defined by

$$\theta_u : [C_u \rightarrow A] \rightarrow [T \rightarrow A]$$

$$\theta_u(\underline{a}_u)(t) = \underline{a}_u(\gamma_u(t))$$

For notational convenience we define $\theta = (\theta_1, \ldots, \theta_n)$, $\underline{a} = (\underline{a}_1, \ldots, \underline{a}_n)$ and use $\theta(\underline{a})$ to represent $(\theta_1(\underline{a}_1), \ldots, \theta_n(\underline{a}_n))$.

With these definitions we may transform the equations for the synchronous concurrent algorithm with local clocks (see (5.39) and (5.40)) to the following equations for a synchronous concurrent algorithm with master clock T:

$$V_i(\bar{\lambda}_i(r_i), \theta(\underline{a}), x) = f_i(b_1, \ldots, b_{p_i}) \tag{5.41}$$

where for $j = 1, \ldots, p_i$,

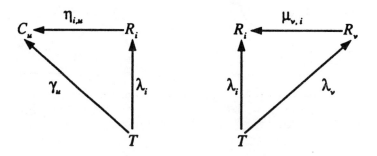

Figure 5.6 Relationships between synchronization maps and retimings.

$$
b_j = \begin{cases}
\theta_{\beta(i,j)}(\underline{a}_{\beta(i,j)})(\gamma_{\beta(i,j)}(\overline{\eta_{i,\beta(i,j)}}(r_i))) & \text{if the } j\text{th input to } m_i \\
& \text{is from source } In_{\beta(i,j)} \\
V_{\beta(i,j)}(\lambda_{\overline{\beta(i,j)}}(\mu_{i,\beta(i,j)}(r_i)),\, \theta(\underline{a}),\, x) & \text{if the } j\text{th input to} \\
& m_i \text{ is from module } m_{\beta(i,j)}
\end{cases}
\tag{5.42}
$$

Thus, if $\overline{\lambda}_i(r_i) = t$, we have that

$$
V_i(t, \theta(\underline{a}), x) = f_i(b_1, \ldots, b_{p_i})
$$

where for $j = 1, \ldots, p_i$,

$$
b_j = \begin{cases}
\theta_{\beta(i,j)}(\underline{a}_{\beta(i,j)})(\text{start}_{\gamma\beta(i,j)}(t)) & \text{if the } j\text{th input to } m_i \text{ is from} \\
& \text{source } In_{\beta(i,j)} \\
V_{\beta(i,j)}(\text{start}_{\lambda_{\beta(i,j)}}(t),\, \theta(\underline{a}),\, x) & \text{if the } j\text{th input to } m_i \text{ is from} \\
& \text{module } m_{\beta(i,j)}
\end{cases}
$$

5.5.3 Sampling synchronous concurrent algorithms

Family of sampling predicates
Let N be an n-source, k-module synchronous concurrent algorithm with global system clock T. Let us consider the operation of each module of N at times determined by a family of predicates $I_1, \ldots, I_n$ for inputs and $P_i, \ldots, P_k$ for modules on T.

Definition 13
A synchronous concurrent algorithm is **determined** by such a family of sampling predicates $I_1, \ldots, I_n$ and $P_1, \ldots, P_k$ if, for any two input streams $\underline{a} = (\underline{a}_1, \ldots, \underline{a}_n)$ and $\underline{a}' = (\underline{a}'_1, \ldots, \underline{a}'_n)$, if they agree on all times satisfying $I_1, \ldots, I_n$ then the values at each module m_i agree at all times satisfying P_i. More formally,

$$
\left((\forall t)(\bigwedge_{i=1}^{i=n} ((I_i(t) \wedge (\underline{a}_i(t) = \underline{a}'_i(t))) \vee \neg I_i(t))) \right)
$$
$$
\Rightarrow \left((\forall t)(\bigwedge_{j=1}^{j=k} ((P_j(t) \wedge (V_j(t, \underline{a}, x) = V_j(t, \underline{a}', x))) \vee \neg P_j(t))) \right)
$$

Sampling predicates for a synchronous concurrent algorithm determined from inputs
Since we know the structure of a synchronous concurrent algorithm from the equations for its value functions we can generate a family of sampling predicates for any given collection of sampling predicates for inputs $I_1, \ldots, I_n$. The idea is to trace out the effect of input data at times defined by $I_1, \ldots, I_n$ on all modules of the synchronous concurrent algorithm by constructing a predicate P_i for module m_i such that

$$
P_i(t) \Leftrightarrow \begin{cases}
\text{the output of module } m_i \text{ at time } t \\
\text{is only dependent on data from} \\
\text{the input streams at time satisfying } I_1, \ldots, I_n
\end{cases}
\tag{5.43}
$$

To make this construction we will require a notion of functional dependence for modules.

Definition 14

We say that $dep(f_i, j)$ holds if the module's function f_i uses its jth argument, for its computations. More formally

$$dep(f_i, j) \Leftrightarrow \begin{cases} (\exists a_1, \ldots, a_{p_i})(\exists x_1, x_2) \\ (f_i(t, a_1, \ldots, a_{j-1}, x_1, a_{j+1}, \ldots, a_{p_i}) \neq \\ f_i(t, a_1, \ldots, a_{j-1}, x_2, a_{j+1}, \ldots, a_{p_i})) \end{cases}$$

Now let us assume that the predicates $P_1, \ldots, P_k$ are initially false, thus for $i = 1, \ldots, k$

$$P_i(0) = \text{false}$$

Then for $t > 0$ and $i = 1, \ldots, k$ we define $P_i(t)$ in terms of the neighbouring modules and sources of module m_i (see (5.33)) as follows:

$$P_i(t) \Leftrightarrow \bigwedge_{j=1}^{j=p_i} \begin{cases} ((dep(f_i, j) \wedge \\ \quad ((\gamma(i, j) = M \wedge P_{\beta(i,j)}(\delta_{i,j}(t, \underline{a}, x))) \vee \\ \quad (\gamma(i, j) = S \wedge I_{\beta(i,j)}(\delta_{i,j}(t, \underline{a}, x)))))) \\ \vee \neg(dep(f_i, j))) \end{cases}$$

Intuitively, $P_i(t)$ holds if, and only if, for any input upon which m_i is functionally dependent at time t, we have that the sampling predicate for those inputs, at those times specified by the channel delay functions, also hold. Equivalently, $P_i(t)$ is false if m_i employs an argument not caught by the sampling predicates.

Definition 15

We say that a network is **input determined** by a family $I_1, \ldots, I_n$ input predicate if it is determined (in the sense of section 5.5.3) by the predicates generated from $I_1, \ldots, I_n$ above.

These notions of determinateness with respect to a family of sampling predicates for modules and inputs arise in considering questions to do with probing the operation of a synchronous concurrent algorithm to determine what input data is significant and what can be considered padding. If data can be partitioned into significant and redundant data we can think of a sub-network of the synchronous concurrent algorithm, defined by time rather than the spatial structure of its architecture. Perhaps it is possible to transform the network to optimize timing conditions or abstract timing conditions to help understand the significant operations of the network.

5.5.4 Transforming a synchronous concurrent algorithm using local clocks

We will consider the reverse situation to that in section 5.5.2 where we implemented local clocks by means of a master clock. Suppose we have an *n*-source, *k*-module synchronous concurrent algorithm, a global clock T, and value function for a typical internal module

$$V_i(t, \underline{a}, x) = f_i(V_{\beta(i,1)}(\delta_{i,1}(t), \underline{a}, x), \ldots, V_{\beta(i,p_i)}(\delta_{i,p_i}(t), \underline{a}, x)) \quad (5.44)$$

Notice that we have assumed that the delay functions are independent of the input data $\underline{a}$ and the initial values x. The reason for this will become clear when we see how such delay functions may be used in the definition of scheduling maps, which are necessarily defined only on times of local clocks.

We propose to introduce local clocks at each module, based on the operational behaviour at that module.

To do this we will examine the operation of the network using a family of sampling predicates.

Let $I_1, \ldots, I_n$ be input sampling predicates on T. Let $P_1, \ldots, P_k$ be the sampling predicates for the k modules of the synchronous concurrent algorithm generated as in section 5.5.3.

Suppose the $I_1, \ldots, I_n$ determine the network in the sense of section 5.5.3. Thus, we are looking at the synchronous concurrent algorithm at times determined by $I_1, \ldots, I_n$ and $P_1, \ldots, P_k$. Do these times define local clocks for the modules?

Recall from section 5.2.1 (Retimings from relations) that any predicate P on T, that satisfies the two conditions

(i) $P(0)$ is false, and
(ii) $\{t \in T : P(t)\}$ is infinite,

can be used to define a clock R_P and retiming $C_P : T \to R_P$ defined by

$$C_P(t) = |\{t' \in T : t' < t \text{ and } P(t')\}|$$

Observe that the start predicate for C_P is P and its immersion $\overline{C_P}$ enumerates time on T when P is true.

Thus if these conditions (i) and (ii) are true of each I_i and each generated P_j then we may define local clocks C_u and R_v and retimings $\gamma_u : T \to C_u$ and $\lambda_v : T \to R_v$. Furthermore, we may use these γ_u to schedule the input stream, $\underline{a}_u$ to produce a new stream $\theta_u(\underline{a}_u)$ defined by

$$\theta_u : [T \to A] \to [C_u \to A]$$
$$\theta_u(\underline{a}_u)(c_u) = \underline{a}_u(\overline{\gamma_u}(c_u))$$

Notice that $\overline{\gamma_u}(c_u)$ selects precisely those times $t \in T$ for which $I_u(t)$ holds, and so $\theta_u(\underline{a}_u)$ carries all and only significant stream data. For notational convenience we define $\theta = (\theta_1, \ldots, \theta_n)$, $\underline{a} = (\underline{a}_1, \ldots, \underline{a}_n)$ and use $\theta(\underline{a})$ to represent $(\theta_1(\underline{a}_1), \ldots, \theta_n(\underline{a}_n))$.

For each $i \in \{1, \ldots, k\}$, each $j \in \{1, \ldots, p_i\}$, and each $r_i \in R_i$ we define module schedule map $\mu_{i,\beta(i,j)} : R_i \rightarrow R_{\beta(i,j)}$ by

$$\mu_{i,\beta(i,j)}(r_i) = \lambda_{\beta(i,j)}(\delta_{i,j}(\overline{\lambda_i}(r_i)))$$

and input schedule map $\eta_{i,\beta(i,j)} : R_i \rightarrow C_{\beta(i,j)}$ by

$$\eta_{i,\beta(i,j)}(r_i) = \gamma_{\beta(i,j)}(\delta_{i,j}(\overline{\lambda_i}(r_i)))$$

With these definitions we may transform the equations for the synchronous concurrent algorithm with global clock T, to the following equations for a synchronous concurrent algorithm with local clocks:

$$V_i(\lambda_i(t), \theta(\underline{a}), x) = f_i(b_1, \ldots, b_{p_i}) \tag{5.45}$$

where for $j = 1, \ldots, p_i$,

$$b_j = \begin{cases} \theta_{\beta(i,j)}(\underline{a}_{\beta(i,j)})(\gamma_{\beta(i,j)}(\delta_{i,j}(t))) & \text{if the } j\text{th input to } m_i \text{ is from} \\ & \text{source } In_{\beta(i,j)} \\ V_{\beta(i,j)}(\lambda_{\beta(i,j)}(\delta_{i,j}(t)), \theta(\underline{a}), x) & \text{if the } j\text{th input to } m_i \\ & \text{is from module } m_{\beta(i,j)} \end{cases} \tag{5.46}$$

Observe that $\overline{\lambda_i}$ enumerates times on T when P_i is true. Thus, it is reasonable to consider those times t for which there is an r_i such that $\overline{\lambda_i}(r_i) = t$, whence

$$V_i(r_i, \theta(\underline{a}), x) = f_i(b_1, \ldots, b_{p_i})$$

where for $j = 1, \ldots, p_i$,

$$b_j = \begin{cases} \theta_{\beta(i,j)}(\underline{a}_{\beta(i,j)})(\eta_{i,\beta(i,j)}(r_i)) & \text{if the } j\text{th input to } m_i \text{ is from} \\ & \text{source } In_{\beta(i,j)} \\ V_{\beta(i,j)}(\mu_{i,\beta(i,j)}(r_i), \theta(\underline{a}), x) & \text{if the } j\text{th input to } m_i \text{ is} \\ & \text{from module } m_{\beta(i,j)} \end{cases}$$

We invite the reader to compare these transformed equations with (5.39) and (5.40). Given this transformation we see that the value function for a typical internal module is:

$$V_i(r_i, \theta(\underline{a}), x) = f_i(V_{\beta(i,1)}(\mu_{i,\beta(i,1)}(r_i), \theta(\underline{a}), x), \ldots, \\ V_{\beta(i,p_i)}(\mu_{i,\beta(i,p_i)}(r_i), \theta(\underline{a}), x)) \tag{5.47}$$

Comparing this with (5.44) we see that we have abstracted out the channel delays $\delta_{i,j}$ by a 'time on a local clock'.

Acknowledgements

This work was partially supported by MRC-SERC-ESRC Grant GR/F 59070 SERC Contract 50/103/91 and SERC Case Award with Mullards

Applications Laboratory, and by SERC/IED Grant GR/F 38839 SERC Contract 4/1/1324.

References

Abdulla, P., 1990, Decision problems in systolic circuit verification, PhD thesis, Department of Computer Systems, Uppsala University.

Abdulla, P., Automatic verification of a class of systolic circuits, *Formal Aspects of Computing*, to appear.

Bourbaki, N., 1966, *General Topology. Part I and Part II*, Addison-Wesley.

Ehrig, H., and Mahr, B., 1985, Fundamentals of algebraic specification I – examples and initial semantics, *EATCS Monograph Series*, **6**, Springer–Verlag, Berlin.

Eker, S. M., Stavridou, V., and Tucker, J. V., 1991, Verification of synchronous concurrent algorithms using OBJ: a case study of the pixel planes architecture, in *Designing Correct Circuits* (eds G. Jones and M. Sheeran), Springer–Verlag, 231–52.

Goguen, J., 1989, OBJ as a theorem prover, with application to hardware verification, in *Current Trends in Hardware Verification and Automated Theorem Proving* (eds V. P. Subramanyan and Graham Birtwhistle), Springer–Verlag, 218–67; also Technical Report SRI-CSL–88–4R2, SRI International, Computer Science Lab, August 1988.

Goguen, J., 1990, Proving and Rewriting, in *Pro., Second Int. Conf. on Algebraic and Logic Programming* (eds Hélène Kirchner and Wolfgang Wechler), Springer–Verlag, 1–24; *Lecture Notes in Computer Science*, **463**.

Harman, N. A., 1989, Formal specifications for digital systems, PhD thesis, School of Computer Studies, University of Leeds.

Harman, N. A., and Tucker, J. V., 1987, Formal specification of a digital correlator, Technical Report 9.87, Centre for Theoretical Computer Science, University of Leeds; also in *Theoretical Foundations of VLSI Design* (eds K. McEvoy and J. V. Tucker), *Cambridge Tracts in Theoretical Computer Science*, **10**, Cambridge University Press, 1990, 161–262.

Harman, N. A., and Tucker, J. V., 1988, Clocks, retimings and the formal specification of a UART, in *The Fusion of Hardware Design and Verification* (ed. G. Milne), North-Holland, 375–96.

Hobley, K. M., 1990, Formal specification and verification of synchronous concurrent algorithms, PhD thesis, School of Computer Studies, University of Leeds.

Hobley, K. M., Thompson, B. C., and Tucker, J. V., 1988, Specification and verification of synchronous concurrent algorithms: a case study of a convolution algorithm, in *The Fusion of Hardware Design and Verification* (ed. G. Milne), North-Holland, 347–74.

McEvoy, K., and Tucker, J. V., 1990, The theoretical foundations of hardware, in *Theoretical Aspects of VLSI Design* (eds. K. McEvoy and J. V. Tucker), Cambridge University Press, 1–62.

Meinke, K., and Tucker, J. V., 1992, Universal algebra, in *Handbook of Logic in Computer Science* (eds S. Abramsky, D. Gabby and T. S. E. Maibaum), Oxford University Press.

Thompson, B. C., 1987, A mathematical theory of synchronous concurrent algorithms, PhD thesis, School of Computer Studies, University of Leeds.

Thompson, B. C., and Tucker, J. V., 1991, Algebraic specification of synchronous concurrent algorithms and architectures, Computer Science Division Research Report CSR–9–91, University College of Swansea.

Tucker, J. V., 1991, Theory of computation and specification over abstract data types and its applications, in *Proc. of the NATO Int. Summer School on Logic, Algebra and Computation, Marktoberdorf, Germany* (ed. F. L. Bauer), Springer-Verlag, 1–39.

Tucker, J. V., and Zucker, J. I., 1988, *Program Correctness over Abstract Data Types with Error-State Semantics*, North-Holland, Amsterdam.

Wirsing, M., 1990, Algebraic specification, in *Handbook of Theoretical Computer Science, Vol B: Formal Models and Semantics* (ed. J. van Leeuwen), 675–788.

6

Array Compiler Design for VLSI/WSI Systems

Jack S. N. Jean and S. Y. Kung

6.1 Introduction

Special-purpose supercomputers with massively concurrent processing by, e.g., systolic/wavefront arrays, have shown a great deal of promise for real-time signal and image processing. Systolic/wavefront arrays, exploiting the regularity inherent in algorithms, are often modular, regular, and therefore suitable for VLSI/WSI implementation. However, it is specially critical to shorten the design turn-around time for the design of these application-specific arrays. So a VLSI computer-aided-design (CAD) tool for the array and system levels (in addition to the processor/layout level) will be very desirable.

When using existing silicon compilers (Denyer, 1986), the designer has to pre-determine the formation and connection of tangible hardware blocks. Therefore, before using the tools, the designer should have his array structure (instead of the algorithm) in mind. An array compiler on the other hand can assist the user to design an 'optimal' array structure, complementing the functions of the silicon compilers. The development of such array compilers can benefit greatly from systematic methodologies of mapping computations onto array structures (Kung, 1988; Moldovan, 1983; Quinton, 1984; Rao, 1985; Shang and Fortes, 1988). Based on such systematic methodologies, some array design tools have been developed. These include SDEF (Engstrom and Cappello, 1988), ADVIS (Moldovan, 1987), DIASTOL (Frison *et al.*, 1986), and SYSTARS (Omizigt, 1988), which are all based on a notion of the dependence graph (DG) as the basic representation of an algorithm. The DG is a directed graph on an indexed grid space, where nodes represent computations of variables and arcs denote data dependency between the nodes. However, the problem domains which may be handled by the above tools are somewhat restrictive. For example, we need to have tools to handle complex DGs for transitive closure (as discussed in section 6.2.1) to provide an effective modification of the DG, as well as to accommodate human interactions whenever needed. The last is essential in deriving an optimal DG.

An Array Compiler System for the design of systolic/wavefront arrays is discussed. A complete array compiler should cover the design in the array level as well as the generation of VLSI layout (Fig. 6.1). The focus of this chapter is on the array level only. The system accepts high-level behaviour inputs in terms of dependence graphs and generates array structures. The system is interactive and graphic-based with several optimality criteria and design tradeoff being evaluated in advance. A

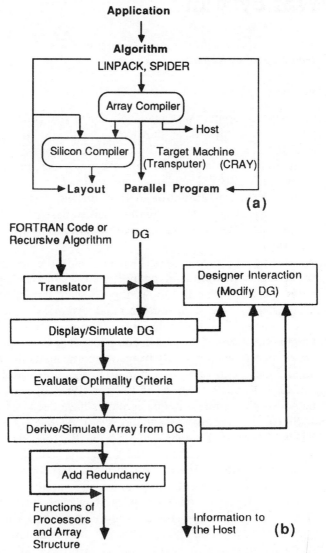

Figure 6.1 (a) An array compiler and (b) the design flow within the array level.

complete system should have included original derivation of DG, DG/SFG transformation, mapping onto arrays, and interfaces with the lower-level compiler and with the host machine. The mapping from an algorithm to array processors can be divided into the following three stages. A design process will in general involve iterations through these stages.

Stage 1: Derivation of dependence graph (DG)
An indexed dependence graph can be considered as a directed graph, $G(V, E)$, where V denotes nodes and E arcs. A node with index i (one-to-one) corresponds to the computation of variables with index i in a single assignment representation of an algorithm. An arc from node i to j denotes a data dependency from an i-indexed variable to a j-indexed variable. A DG can be constructed based on the space-time indices in the recursive algorithm. For example, the DG for the transitive closure problem using the Warshall-Floyd algorithm is shown in Fig. 6.2(a).

For a given problem, the designer first identifies a suitable algorithm and derives a local DG for the algorithm. Since the structure of a DG greatly affects the final array design, if a DG originally derived is unsatisfactory then further modifications should be applied in order to achieve a better DG.

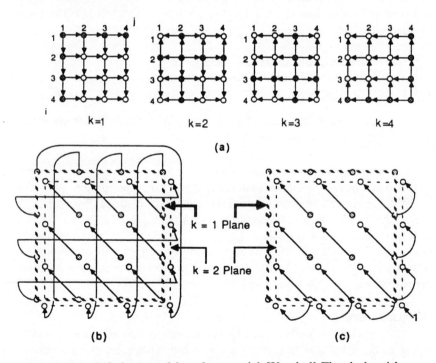

Figure 6.2 DG for transitive closure: (a) Warshall-Floyd algorithm, (b) reindexed, and (c) localized.

Stage 2: SFG structure design

A signal flow graph (SFG) is a directed graph, $[N, A, D(a)]$, in which nodes in N model computations and edges in A, model one-way communications. Each edge, a, has an edge-delay, represented by a non-negative integer weight $D(a)$. The SFG representation derives its power from the fact that the computations are assumed to take zero time. Consequently, all timing information in the system has to be explicitly introduced in the form of delay edges. When an edge is labelled with a capital letter **D** (or 2**D**, . . .), it represents a time delay operator with delay time **D** (or 2**D**, . . .).

In this stage, the nodes of the DG are mapped onto an abstract processor array architecture, which is modelled by an SFG. This mapping involves the assignment of DG nodes to processors and their scheduling in time.

Stage 3: Processor array design

The third stage addresses the issues of implementing the SFG by a processor array. These include the temporal localization of SFGs and finer granularity synthesis to achieve more concurrency. Other issues are to incorporate some redundancy to enhance the fabrication-time yield or the run-time reliability and to partition the problem size to fit into the given smaller array size.

6.2 Basic techniques in array compiler

6.2.1 DG derivation stage

The techniques needed for this stage include generation of (shift-invariant) DG, DG localisation, and DG modification.

Shift-invariant DG

A DG is shift-invariant if the dependence arcs corresponding to **all** nodes in the index space remains unchanged w.r.t. their positions. Formally, this means that if a variable at i_1 depends on a variable at $i_1 - j$, then a variable at i_2 will depend on a variable at $i_2 - j$ in the same manner. Note that the node functions can be different and the border I/O nodes are exempted from such a condition. From the point of view of designing an array processor, only a shift-invariant DG is useful in general.

DG generation

The question of how to develop a DG is not easy to answer. It is much like trying to describe how to invent an algorithm. However, given a general approach to the problem, such as a serial algorithm or a set of recursive equations, there are several steps involved in deriving a DG.

1. Identify the individual primitive computations.
2. Define an index space structure that naturally fits these computations. Associate the intermediate result of each computation with a unique indexed variable, therefore generating the single assignment form. From this, a set of basic (possibly non-local) dependence relations can be determined. This generates the indexed single assignment form.

In (Tseng et al., 1988), a compiler was developed for the CMU Warp machine, which is a programmable systolic array with ring interconnection. The compiler takes a user program and transforms it into a set of programs, each for one of the ten processors. The user program is written in a language, called 'Array Language', which enables the input of some parallelization hints from programmers. The idea of incorporating hints from programmers into high-level descriptions may be key to the DG synthesis problem (at least at this stage).

Localized DG
Global data dependences may imply the need for global communication in the processors. Some algorithms, like the Fast Fourier Transform, require global data dependences. Others, like matrix-vector multiplication, can be written in a locally recursive form in which all dependences are local.

Note that a dependence edge is local if its length is bounded by a fixed constant. A DG is local if all its dependence edges are local.

To localize a DG, several design options can be used if the non-local dependences are of the **broadcast** type, i.e., there is a single data source and multiple data receivers. Since all these receiver nodes are dependent on the source data, this set of receiver nodes constitutes a broadcast contour. Localized data dependences can be derived from the broadcast contour by using a transmittent variable, which propagates data without being modified. Design flexibilities can be obtained by the following techniques to deal with localization.

1. The direction of propagation of the transmittent variable can be very flexible. For example, it may be reversed for the purpose of minimizing the latency or pipeline period.
2. If a chain of dependences represents a series of associative operations, like the chain of partial sums in the matrix-vector example, then the direction of these dependences is very often reversible.
3. Sometimes, if necessary, a given DG may be converted into a more desirable form by reindexing of the nodes. For example, a non-shift-invariant DG may be converted into a shift-invariant form.

Example Warshall–Floyd algorithm for transitive closure problem
A directed graph G can be represented as a tuple $G(V, E)$, where V is the

set of vertices and E is the set of edges in the graph. The graph $G^+(V, E^+)$, which has the same vertex set V as G, but has an edge from v to w if and only if there is a path (length zero or more) from v to w in G, is called the **transitive closure** of G. To compute the transitive closure given the adjacency matrix of a directed graph, there is a famous sequential algorithm, called Warshall–Floyd algorithm (Aho *et al.*, 1974), whose DG is shown in Fig. 6.2(a). Note that the 'source' nodes in the DG move from row (column) k to row (column) $k+1$ from the kth **i-j** plane to the next one. Since the data streams propagated in the **i-j** plane with two opposite directions are transmittent, they can be modifed to propagate in the same direction by the following reindexing:

$$\text{node } (i, j, k) \longrightarrow \text{node } ((i-k)_{\text{MOD } N} + 1, (j-k)_{\text{MOD } N} + 1, k)$$

where N is the number of vertices in the directed graph.

Although the **i-j** plane dependence vectors becomes 'uniform' by reindexing, some spiral links are introduced between adjacent-**k** DG layers. This is shown in Fig. 6.2(b). To localize these spiral links requires a careful inspection of the DG node functions. This leads to two observations: first, the data sent through an $(N-1, N-1, 1)$ spiral link is always one (and is always locally available); and second, the data sent through a $(-1, N-1, 1)$ spiral link is locally available since the data has been locally (and transmittently) propagated first through a $(0, 0, 1)$ link and then through $N-1$ $(0, 1, 0)$ links. The localized DG is shown Fig. 6.2(c). This last modification of the transitive closure DG shows the need of somewhat intelligent decision by the design system so that shorter dependence arcs may be selected within an equivalence class of graphs. Of course, this usually costs some considerable additional CPU time.

Bit-level DG
In some cases, the concurrency/pipelining is to be performed in bit-level. An example is an array with bit-serial multipliers for matrix-vector multiplication. To derive these arrays, the DG node should represent bit-level operations. Note that a bit-level DG is usually with high dimensionality. For example, a four-dimensional bit-level DG can be constructed for matrix-vector multiplication while the corresponding word-level DG is two dimensional.

6.2.2 SFG structure design

The techniques needed for this stage include node assignment and scheduling, multiprojection, and I/O handling.

Node assignment and scheduling
We would like to let each PE execute multiple nodes in the DG and yet achieve maximal parallelism inherent in the DG as well as smooth signal

flow in the array. This requires a mapping from shift-invariant DGs onto arrays with systematic processor assignment and node scheduling, as explained below.

- The processor assignment specifies how nodes in a DG are assigned to the PEs in the array. A **linear assignment (projection)** of a DG is a linear mapping of the nodes of the DG to PEs, in which nodes along a straight line are mapped to a PE. The projection direction is denoted by a vector *d* (see Fig. 6.3(a)).
- The node scheduling specifies the execution time for all the nodes in the DG. The scheduled execution time of a node is represented by a time index (i.e., an integer). A **linear schedule**, denoted by *s*, maps a set of parallel equitemporal hyperplanes to a set of linearly increased time indices, where *s* is the normal vector of the equitemporal hyperplanes (see Fig. 6.3(b)). That is, the time index of a node can be mathematically represented by $s^T i$, where i denotes the index of the node.

In order to obtain a causal SFG design, the projection vector (*d*) and the schedule vector (*s*) have to satisfy two constraints.

1. $s^T e \geq 0$: Here e denotes any edge in the DG. That is, if node i depends on the output of node j, then node j is scheduled no later than node i. The number $s^T e$ denotes the number of delays (**Ds**) on the edge in the array.
2. $s^T d > 0$: The projection vector **d** and the schedule vector **s** cannot be orthogonal to each other. The integer $s^T d$ is equal to the pipelining period of the array (Kung, 1988).

Note that in order to obtain a systolic design, the condition (1) has to be made more restrictive, i.e. $s^T e > 0$.

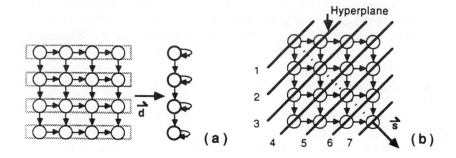

Figure 6.3 Illustration of (a) a linear projection with projection vector **d**, (b) a linear schedule **s** and its hyperplanes.

Multiprojection

In general, it is possible to map an N-dimensional DG directly onto an $(N-k)$-dimensional SFG ($k = 1, 2, .., N - 1$) (Wong and Deslome, 1985). An alternative is to apply the projection method k times and thus reduce the dimension of the array to $N - k$. This scheme is called the multiprojection method.

To simplify the discussion, let us assume that the DG is N-dimensional, the directionally shift-invariant (DSI) (Kung, 1988) subspace is 2-D and is on the ij-plane, and, after one projection (say, in the i direction), the resulting SFG is $(N - 1)$-dimensional. The question is how to further project the SFG to an $(N - 2)$-dimensional SFG? The potential difficulties are, the presence of delay edges in the $(N - 1)$-dimensional SFG and the possibilities of loops or cycles in an SFG, although no loops or cycles can exist in a DG. To handle these problems, an instance graph (at certain time $t = t_0$) is defined as the SFG with all the delay edges removed. According to the SFG schedule, all the nodes in the instance graph are executed simultaneously. An activity instance (at $t = t_0$) can be defined as the nodes represented by the instance graph at t_0. The next activity instance is executed at $t = t_0 + D$.

Recall that a mapping methodology should consist of a projection part and a schedule part.

Projection: Since the assumption of ij DSI subspace implies that the instance graph is itself DSI in the j-direction, the same projection method previously proposed may be applied in the j-direction. The original SFG (with delay edges included) is now projected along the d (i.e., j-direction).

Schedule: The schedule part is somewhat more complicated. Here we assume that there exists a valid SFG schedule vector, s, for the instance graph. (Otherwise, piecewise linear schedule should be used.) To project the $(N-1)$-dimensional instance graph to an $(N-2)$-dimensional graph, it is necessary to create a new type of delay, denoted by τ. The original delay edges with βD is mapped to an edge bearing delay weight $\beta D + s \cdot e\tau$ (Fig. 6.4(b)). Note that the **global** delay D and **local** delay τ are intimately related. In order to guarantee the schedule is feasible, i.e., the assigned PE and all the input data are available at the time when an operation is scheduled for execution, the ratio $\frac{D}{\tau}$ must exceed a certain lower bound. This is discussed below.

To ensure **processor availability**, note that each PE is committed to the tasks of the current instance graph before it can handle tasks of the next activity instance. To guarantee that there is no time overlap between two successive activity instances so that there is no conflict on the use of the processor, the necessary and sufficient condition is:

$$(a)\ D \geqslant \tau + (M - 1)(s \cdot d)\,\tau$$

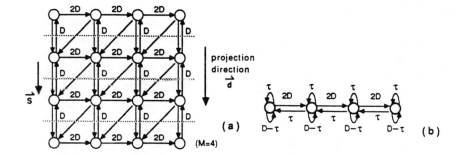

Figure 6.4 (a) The original SFG. (b) The further projected SFG.

For an SFG to be computable, it is necessary that the sum of edge-delays be positive for any loop in the SFG. That is,

$$\text{(b) } \Sigma_i\{\beta_i\, D + (s \cdot e_i)\, \tau\} \geq \tau,$$

where the original SFG edges $\{e_i\}$, each with delay $\beta_i\, D$, are on a loop after the multiprojection. If the SFG satisfies condition (b), then the cut-set retiming (Kung, 1988) can be used to obtain a causal SFG (or a systolic design). That is, the data availability can be assured. Conditions (a) and (b) together are necessary and sufficient to guarantee both the processor and data availability and hence the feasibility of the schedule.

As to the optimality for the multiprojection scheme, an SFG schedule with minimal α should be chosen. In practice, for any commonly used algorithm, an SFG schedule with $\alpha = 1$ may be obtained with almost no exceptions. (This is however not true for a systolic schedule.) In the rare case when the SFG has $\alpha > 1$, it means that the instance graph has some 'pseudo' nodes which were not in the original DG. These pseudo nodes would then be executed in the further projected SFG.

6.2.3 Array realization stage

A good design tool should allow a designer to choose his own array size, array structure, I/O pattern, and granularity. These may be achieved by incorporating the partitioning and the finer granularity synthesis procedure as discussed below.

Finer granularity synthesis

In Stages 1 and 2 of the mapping, the DG node is assumed to be a primitive operation with its computation time as the basic system time unit. Sometimes concurrency may be improved by working with finer time scheduling associated with a finer granularity.

Since the SFG node computations take no time, each SFG node (together with its input/output data) can be refined into a set of zero-time nodes with zero-delayed edges between them. That is, each SFG node can be represented by its 'DG' for the node operation. The scheduling of the (synchronous) fine-grained design may be derived via the following procedure.

1. Decompose each SFG node into several finer operations, $\{O_i\}$, with the respective computation times $\{n_i\}$. All n_i are assumed to be integer.
2. Attach a self-loop to all the finer operations. The number of delay elements on the self-loop is equal to the pipelining period, $\alpha\ (=s^T d)$, of the coarse-grained SFG.
3. Apply cut-set retiming techniques (Kung, 1988) so that the output links of each operation O_i possess at least n_i delay elements.
4. Absorb n_i delays on the output links of O_i, for all i, and replace each operation by a hardware component.

To quantize the speed improvement of the synchronous systems, let γ denote the slow down factor for time-rescaling in the cut-set retiming step. Then $\alpha \times \gamma$ is the new pipelining period. Although the original pipelining period is α, the basic time unit is $\Sigma_i\, n_i$. For the coarse synchronous system, there is one input data out of $\alpha \times (\Sigma_i\, n_i)$ system clocks. However, for the finer synchronous system, there is one input data out of $\alpha \times \gamma$ system clocks. Thus the speed up is

$$\frac{\Sigma_i\, n_i}{\gamma}$$

A convolution example is used to illustrate the procedure. Assume that the computation time of a multiplier is four times of that of an adder. Figure 6.5(a) shows a convolution SFG with $\alpha = 2$. Figure 6.5(b) shows the fine-grained SFG with self-loops attached. Figure 6.5(c) shows the cut-set so that the output links of multipliers possess 4 **D**. Figure 6.5(d) is the resulting array depicting the fine-grained design. Since $\gamma = 2$, the speed up over a coarse grained array is $(4+1)/2 = 5/2$. Note that the functional units, e.g., the adder and the multiplier in Figure 6.5(d), are **not** internally pipelined. A set of registers is required to hold the input data for each functional unit. Furthermore, the self-loops are for control purposes. They indicate when functional units should be enabled. They are not considered as input signal lines.

As another example, we can compare this technique with the two-level pipelining problem as studied in (Kung and Lam, 1984). The problem deals with the internal pipelining of operations within each PE. It is basically a special case with $n_i = 1$, for all i. For this special case, the

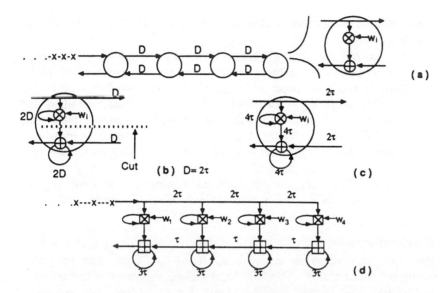

Figure 6.5 Convolution arrays: (a) SFG with $\alpha = 2$, (b) the
fine-grained SFG with self-loops attached, (c) the fine-grained SFG after
the retiming, and (d) the resulting array.

attachment of the self-loop for each primitive operation is not necessary
since the input data sampling rates are the same for all the operations.

Bit-level design
With finer granularity synthesis technique, a bit-level array processor can
be hierarchically derived from a word-level (or even higher-level) DG.
Simply replace each SFG node (higher level) by its lower-level DG
implementation and then apply the finer granularity synthesis technique to
schedule the operations.

Partitioning
The partitioning problem is basically mapping computations of a larger
size problem to a processor array of a smaller size. It is necessary to specify
at what time and in which PE the computation of each DG node takes
place. For a systematic mapping from the DG onto a systolic/wavefront
array, the DG is regularly partitioned into many **blocks**, each consisting of
a cluster of nodes in the DG. There are two categories of methods for
mapping the partitioned DG to an array: the locally sequential globally
parallel (LSGP) method and the locally parallel globally sequential
(LPGS) method.

1. LSGP scheme: In the LSGP scheme, one block is mapped to one PE.
   The number of blocks is equal to the number of PEs in the array.

An optimal scheduling strategy for the LSGP scheme is discussed in (Kung, 1988).

2. LPGS scheme: In the LPGS scheme, the block size is chosen to match the array size, i.e., one block can be mapped to one array. All nodes within one block are processed concurrently, i.e., **locally parallel**. One block after another block of node data are loaded into the array and processed in a sequential manner, i.e., **globally sequential**. Hence the name LPGS. In this scheme, local memory size in the PE can be kept constant, independent of the size of computation. All intermediate data can be stored in certain buffers outside the processor array. Usually, simple FIFO buffers are adequate for storing and recirculating the intermediate data efficiently. For more details, see (Kung, 1988).

Wavefront arrays

The data movements in the systolic arrays are controlled by global timing-reference 'beats'. The burden of having to synchronize the entire computing network will become severe for very-large-scale arrays. A simple solution is to take advantage of the dataflow computing principle which leads to the design of the wavefront arrays. The wavefront array does not employ global synchronization; instead, each PE has its own local clock (self-timed) and exchanges data with neighbouring PEs by asynchronous handshaking, opening up new flexibilities in many design aspects (Kung, 1988).

The wavefront array can be modelled by a data flow graph (DFG), which is a directed graph, $[N, A, D(a), Q(a), \tau(n)]$, in which nodes in N model computation, and arcs in A model asynchronous one-way communication. Each node, n, has an associated non-negative real weight $\tau(n)$ representing its computation time. Each arc, a, is associated with a non-negative integer weight, $D(a)$, representing the number of initial data tokens on the arc, and a positive integer weight, $Q(a)$, representing the (FIFO) queue size of the arc.

The computation sequence of a DFG follows the following firing rule. A node is **enabled** when all input arcs contain tokens and all output arcs contain empty queues. A node **fires** after it has been enabled for its computation time. Whenever a node fires, one input token is taken away from each input arc and each output arc from the node is assigned one more token.

There exist some techniques for transferring an SFG to a DFG under some optimality criteria. A detailed timing analysis of the DFG to minimize queues for the optimal throughput can be found in (Kung, 1988), which is based on the timed Petri net theories. The asynchronous synthesis tool in (Meng *et el.*, 1987), based also on Petri nets, fits well to the wavefront design.

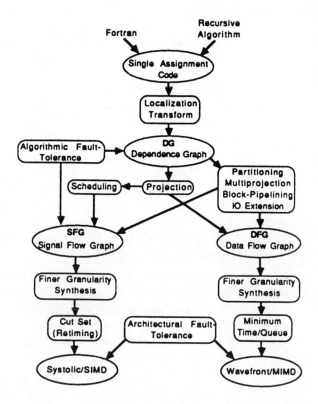

Figure 6.6 CAD packages for the array level design.

Interface with host machine

The same mapping methodology may be adapted for writing a powerful host compiler for a programmable processor array. Knowledges such as special scheduling strategy occurring in this level of design are often valuable for the host software development.

6.3 An implementation example: VACS

A VLSI array compiler accepts high level input, such as recursive algorithms, to ultimately produce VLSI layout as output. In order to facilitate the design of VLSI arrays, a truly user-friendly software tool is desired. Such tools are in our opinion not yet existent and need to be developed. To this end, we have developed a VLSI Array Compiler System (VACS) on a Sun workstation (Sun 3/60C). The current software, though intended to be a CAD tool for designing complete array processors, focuses only on the array level. The interface with the lower level tools is still under development (section 6.4).

6.3.1 Overview of the design tool

Ultimately, different input formats may be accepted by the VACS (Fig. 6.1(b)). It appears very feasible to translate the specific inputs into a DG expression. Some researchers have made very good progress toward this goal (Frison *et al.*, 1986; Chen, 1986; Bu and Deprettere, 1988; Dongen and Quinton, 1989). With the awareness of such development, we have so far focused on using DGs as input in the current VACS. The VACS generates array structures for a variety of algorithms, including those with non-shift-invariant DGs and processors with time-varying functions. Graphic interface, criteria evaluator, and simulation tools are provided to facilitate the design process. A designer can see the DG graphically displayed, modify the DG, simulate the DG, evaluate different optimality criteria, select an 'optimal' design, and evaluate the array. The design flow of the VACS is shown in Fig. 6.1(b).

The VACS, written in C language, is a MENU-based system (Kung and Jean, 1988, 1989) with the following six operation modes:

Demonstration: DGs for several examples have been stored in the system. These include (1) convolution, (2) matrix-vector multiplication, (3) banded matrix-vector multiplication, (4) matrix multiplication, (5) LU decomposition, (6) Gauss–Jordan elimination and (7) transitive closure. A user can choose an example, update it (for later simulation), and then execute a sequence of default operations on it.

Input: The DGs handled by VACS may be non-shift-invariant and may be decomposed into several strictly shift-invariant regions (SSIRs). An SSIR of a DG is a region where not only all the dependence vectors are shift-invariant but also all the node functions are the same. The inputting of such DGs follows a special format as guided by a sequence of questions generated from the VACS.

Graph display: Once a graph (DG or Array) is input (or modified), the structure of the graph (1, 2, or 3-dimensional) and the node operations can be displayed. A graphic display is desirable since a human designer can benefit from the graphical information at all the levels of the design process. A DG display for matrix multiplication is shown in Fig. 6.7(a). In addition, several geometric operations on the graph may be performed, e.g., translation and rotation, to facilitate users' viewing. Furthermore, since a DG projection is equivalent to viewing the DG from a particular angle, a special command is provided that allows the users to 'view' a graph from a specified angle. An example for the matrix multiplication DG with $[1\ 1\ 1]^T$ as the viewing angle is shown in Fig. 6.7(b). Note that the original graph is actually coloured with different colours representing different dependence vectors.

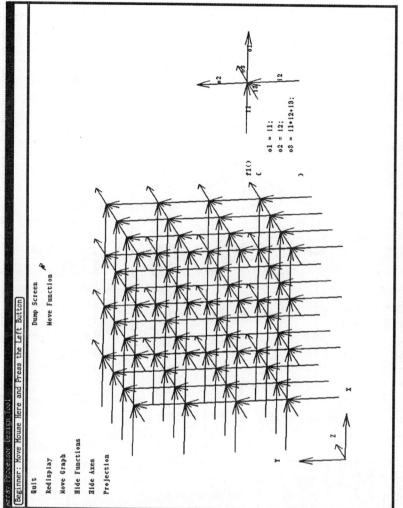

Figure 6.7 Matrix multiplication examples: (a) DG.

Optimality evaluation: To obtain an 'optimal' design, there are two approaches. The first approach is to solve it as an optimization problem (typically, an integer programming problem). For simple criteria, e.g., the pipelining period or the latency, this method works well. However, this method cannot be applied to complicated criteria. For example, the final cost function of the design can be a complicated tradeoff between computation time, pipelining period, number of processors, communication complexity, and I/O patterns. An alternative is to bound the search space and to enumerate different criteria over this search space. The optimal solution can then be chosen according to a combination of these

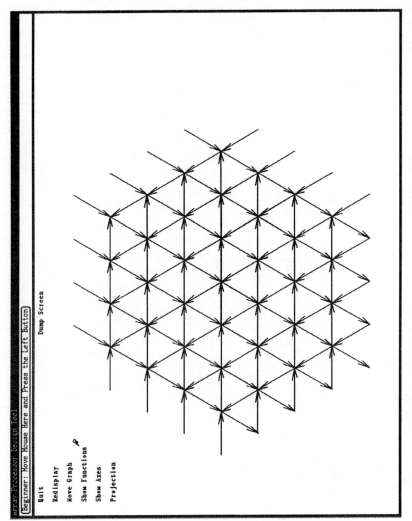

Figure 6.7 (b) DG with [1 1 1]^T as the viewing angle.

criteria. This approach is adopted by the VACS using the following
constraints to restrict the projection vector search space and the scheduling
vector search space.

- A projection vector (p_1, p_2, p_3) is evaluated if it satisfies the following
  two conditions, (1) $|p_1| + |p_2| + |p_3| \leq$ PROJ_MAX, where PROJ_
  MAX is a constant (with 4 as the default value) and (2) the first
  non-zero element of the vector is positive. The second condition is to
  prune away redundant vectors.

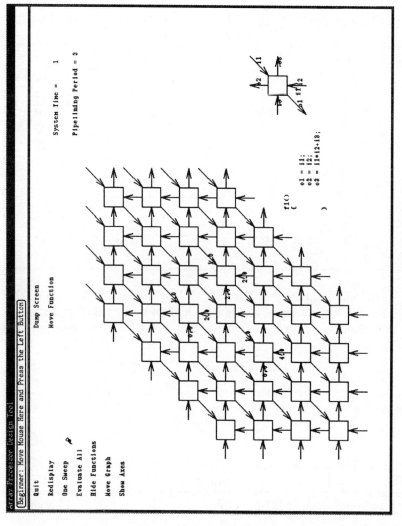

Figure 6.7 (c) an array.

- A scheduling vector (s_1, s_2, s_3) is evaluated if it satisfies the following two conditions, (1) $|s_1| + |s_2| + |s_3| \leq$ SCHE_MAX, where SCHE_MAX is a constant (with 10 as the default value) and (2) it does not violate any data dependences.

The evaluation on different systolic designs for a banded matrix-vector multiplication problem is shown in Table 6.1. Different scheduling and projection vectors are enumerated and evaluated with respect to a set of criteria as discussed before. The results are sorted and displayed so that a user can promptly evaluate the tradeoff between different designs to

Table 6.1 The evaluated optimality results for the original banded matrix-
vector multiplication

Projection Vector	PE No.	Links	Schedule Vector	Latency
1　1	4	2	1　1	13
1　0	7	1	1　2	19
0　1	7	1	2　1	19
1　2	10	3	1　3	25
2　1	10	3	3　1	25
1 −1	13	2	2　3	31
1　3	16	4	1　4	31
3　1	16	4	3　2	31
1 −2	19	3	4　1	31
2 −1	19	3	1　5	37
3 −1	25	4	5　1	37
1 −3	25	4	3　4	43

reach an optimal decision. The column labelled with **links** in the table
indicates the summation of all the edge lengths in the resulting array. For
an m-dimensional array, the length of an edge from $(u_1, u_2, \ldots, u_m)$
to $(v_1, v_2, \ldots, v_m)$ is defined to be

$$|u_1 - v_1| + |u_2 - v_2| + \ldots + |u_m - v_m|$$

Mapping: Mapping is performed when a scheduling vector and a projection vector are specified by a user. The result is an array processor
design.

Table 6.2 The evaluated optimality results for the modified banded matrix-
vector multiplication

Projection Vector	PE No.	Links	Schedule Vector	Latency
1　1	4	2	−1　1	4
1　0	7	1	−2　1	10
0　1	7	1	−1　2	10
1　2	10	3	−3　2	13
2　1	10	3	−2　3	13
1 −1	13	2	−4　3	16
1　3	16	4	−3　4	16
3　1	16	4	−3　1	16
1 −2	19	3	−1　3	16
2 −1	19	3	−5　4	19
3 −1	25	4	−4　5	19
1 −3	25	4	−6　5	22

Table 6.3 All the menu options in VACS (*: not implemented yet,
+: partition and I/O extension not included yet)

DEMONSTRATION	Choose An Example
	Update For New Example
	Mapping Demon
INPUT	Direct Input
	Recursive Input*
	Fortran Loop*
DISPLAY	DG
	SFG
	Systolic Array
	Wavefront Array*
EVALUATE OPTIMALITY+	
MAP+	DG
	SFG
	Systolic Array
	Wavefront Array*
SIMULATE	DG
	SFG
	Systolic Array
	Wavefront Array*
	Update
QUIT	

Simulation: The DG and array can be simulated to protect against any uncertainty introduced during the design process. Furthermore, by checking the snapshots of the array, a human designer can confirm the original design or make necessary modification. A snapshot of a systolic array for the matrix multiplication, with $[1\ 1\ 1]^T$ as both the projection vector and the scheduling vector is shown in Fig. 6.7(c).

To demonstrate the current VACS (and the final VACS), all the MENU options are listed in Table 6.3.

In summary, the mapping method proposed in this chapter can be adopted to design a VLSI or WSI array processor. The current VACS software package focuses only on the array level and many subsystems as well as the interface with lower level tools are yet to be developed. However, when fully developed, the VACS should substantially ease the design of arrays.

6.3.2 Example

Banded matrix-vector multiplication

Let us use one example to illustrate the idea of DG modification, the tradeoff of different optimality criteria, and the graphic display of the tool. The problem is to multiply a band matrix $\mathbf{A}$ of size $N \times N$, with bandwidth P, and a vector $\mathbf{b}$ of size $N \times 1$, i.e., $\mathbf{c} = \mathbf{A}\,\mathbf{b}$. An example with $N = 7$ and $P = 4$ is shown below

$$
\mathbf{A} = \begin{bmatrix}
x & x & 0 & 0 & 0 & 0 & 0 \\
x & x & x & 0 & 0 & 0 & 0 \\
x & x & x & x & 0 & 0 & 0 \\
0 & x & x & x & x & 0 & 0 \\
0 & 0 & x & x & x & x & 0 \\
0 & 0 & 0 & x & x & x & x \\
0 & 0 & 0 & 0 & x & x & x
\end{bmatrix} \quad
\mathbf{b} = \begin{bmatrix}
x \\ x \\ x \\ x \\ x \\ x \\ x
\end{bmatrix}
$$

A DG display for this algorithm is shown in Fig. 6.8(a) (for $P = 4$ case). In most applications, $N \gg P$; therefore, it is uneconomical to use a size N linear array. In order to reduce the size, a diagonal projection direction $d^T = [1\ 1]$ can be adopted to derive an array of size P (as opposed to an array of size N). This point is elucidated by Table 6.1 generated by VACS. For this projection direction, the schedule vector, $[1\ 1]^T$, may be chosen to minimize the computation time. The resulting array has the following parameters:

1. the number of PEs is 4;
2. the latency is 13; and
3. the pipelining period is 2.

DG modification

In the DG shown in Fig. 6.8(a), the dependence vector, $[1\ 0]^T$, is transmittent, i.e., the horizontal data is never modified during the computation. Thus the direction of the horizontal dependence vector may be reversed without affecting the overall computation. This process allows the designer to obtain a DG with a shorter latency, as shown in Fig. 6.8(b). Table 6.2 shows the evaluated optimality results for the modified DG. Apparently, if we want to minimize the number of PEs, the vector $[1\ 1]^T$ should be chosen as the projection vector. If the objective is to minimize the computation time, $[-1,\ 1]^T$ should be chosen as the scheduling vector. However, these two 'optimally' chosen vectors are orthogonal and cannot be used simultaneously. To avoid the conflict, either the projection vector or the scheduling vector has to be changed.

- If we prefer to change the projection vector, then $[1\ 0]^T$ or $[0\ 1]^T$ may be used. The resulting array has the following parameters:

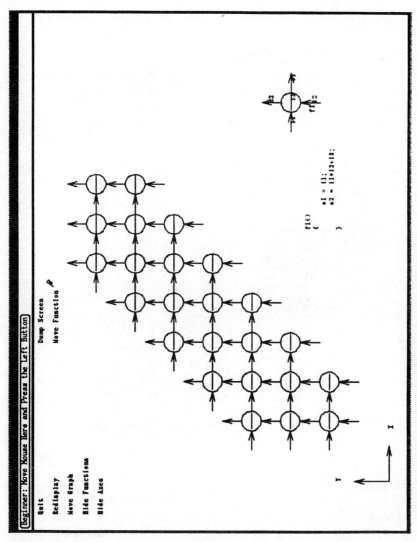

Figure 6.8 (a) DG for banded matrix-vector multiplication;

1. the number of PEs is 7;
2. the latency is 4; and
3. the pipelining period is 1.

- If we decide to alter the scheduling vector, then $[-2\ 1]^T$ or $[-1\ 2]^T$ may be used. The resulting array has the following parameters:

1. the number of PEs is 4;
2. the computation time is 10; and
3. the pipelining period is 1.

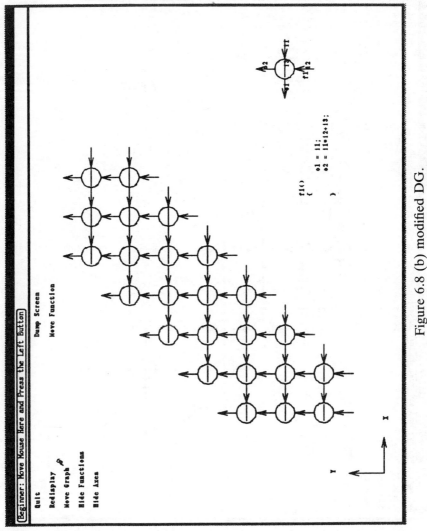

Figure 6.8 (b) modified DG.

The user may choose his own preferred design. Note that the latter design is better than any choice from Table 6.1 in terms of pipelining period and number of PEs. This is an advantage as a result of reversing the dependence vector (see Table 6.2 for comparison).

In addition to the DG modification technique illustrated in the above example, there are several other design options for DG modifications. One option is suitable for a chain of dependences which represents a set of associative operations. For example, the chain of partial sums in the above example is associative (and no other computations are dependent on the intermediate results). In this case, the direction of the dependences may again be reversed without affecting the overall computation.

6.4 Future extensions of VACS

The current VACS focuses on the array level and requires some further extensions to make it complete.

6.4.1 Mapping flexibility

A good design tool should allow a designer to choose his own array size, array structure, I/O pattern, and granularity. These may be achieved by incorporating the partitioning, multiprojection, I/O extension techniques (Kung, 1988), and the finer granularity synthesis procedure. The resulting array compiler should consist of all the software packages shown in Fig. 6.6.

Although VACS allows multiple SSIRs in a DG, the same set of projection vector and scheduling vector is used for all the regions. This represents an unnecessary constraint imposed by the tool. For example, if dependence vectors in different regions are of opposite directions, then no feasible systolic scheduling is possible. However, when different regions are allowed to have different projection (scheduling) vectors, the problem of choosing an optimal array becomes difficult, especially if each DG region can be modified as in the banded matrix-vector multiplication example. In (Hwang and Hu, 1990a, b), the problem, considered as a multi-stage mapping problem, is tackled with a heuristic search algorithm. Some satisfactory results have been demonstrated. A prototype implementation of the algorithm, called MSSM, is built on the top of VACS as an add-in module. The development of MSSM therefore enhances the mapping flexibility of VACS and enlarges its application domain.

6.4.2 Interface with lower level tools

In the broader sense, the array compilation is an extension of the silicon compilation which may be considered as mapping from a higher-level description into VLSI layout. For the development of an array compiler, interface with a commercially available silicon compiler is very desirable in order to obtain the array layout. The effort will involve defining a suitable array description and writing an interface so that the array description can be translated to a form acceptable to the lower-level tool. Furthermore, since the majority of operations for signal and image processing are addition, subtraction, multiplication and division, a library of custom designed cells would be useful.

Interface with LAGER

Currently, we are interfacing VACS with LAGER, software developed at

University of California at Berkeley. According to (LAGER IV, 1989), LAGER, or more specifically LagerIV, is a chip design system that consists of a set of layout generation tools and a set of MOSIS cell libraries. LagerIV can be used to automatically generate the layout for any chip that is constructed using the cell library. A chip designer starts by selecting cells from the cell library to implement the desired chip functions. The designer then defines the chip architecture by drawing a schematic showing the interconnection between the cells. Next, the designer writes a textual description of the schematic using the Structure Description Language (SDL) which is the input language for LagerIV. The designer can then perform the layout generation using the DMoct program. This program is the user interface to LagerIV and it automatically executes various layout generation routines to generate the final chip layout. Final verification of the layout is done by simulating the extracted layout with the switch level simulator (IRSIM) and comparing with the functional THOR simulation.

The current developments include: the definition of a language to describe array processors; the development of the corresponding simulator; and the development of a compiler for the language. Such a language represents an extension to the current array expression used by VACS. The language would allow the description of data type, data width, and various ways of multiplexing data. The output of the compilation can be fed into LAGER to generate chip layout. Various options are to be provided so that a designer can specify implementation restrictions. These include whether multiple-chip design is to be used, whether a synchronous circuit or an asynchronous circuit is to be used, whether bit-serial or bit-parallel component is to be used, and so on.

Automated synthesis tool for asynchronous wavefront arrays
As the VLSI submicron technology advances further, the asynchronous wavefront approach may offer significant improvement over synchronous systolic design in terms of design simplicity, fault-tolerance, and processing speed. There is an increasing need of an automated synthesis tool for asynchronous wavefront arrays. A tool developed by Meng et al. (1987) appears to be very suitable for asynchronous interconnection circuit synthesis (including wavefront arrays), which allows systematic and hazard-free design of asynchronous interconnection circuits such as multiplexers and bus control with least technological constraints and fastest operation. The designers can speedily prototype their systems by the following two steps.

1. The first step involves specifying proper guarded commands (see Dijkstra (1975; Meng et al. (1987) for various interconnection circuits needed in a given system architecture and instruction set. The automated synthesis procedure based on a hardware description language

to systematically translate the given information to the guarded commands is being explored.

2. The second step involves translating from guarded commands to signal transition graphs and then to state diagrams and/or Boolean expressions. An automated synthesis program has been developed (Meng *et al.*, 1987). The program has been successfully used to design a number of signal processing architectures (e.g., DSP processor and VME bus interface).

The comparison between synchronous versus asynchronous designs will play an increasingly important role in the design consideration. When fully developed, the above synthesis tool, together with the existing synchronous tool, will greatly facilitate such comparison.

User-programmable gate arrays
It might be of great interest to consider designing array processors via user-programmable gate arrays. Several drawbacks of traditional (customer-designed or semi-customer-designed) VLSI chip manufacturing impede the popularization of array processors. It usually takes months to manufacture, the manufacturing of a small amount of chips is uneconomical due to the mask (and/or the process) and design changes are time-consuming and costly. A recent progress of VLSI manufacturing is the introduction of user-programmable gate arrays (Freeman, 1988). With the user-programmable interconnection between 1K to 10K gates, such a gate array can be customized (or manufactured) in seconds (and economically). It appears that array processors manufactured on user-programmable gate arrays would require low cost, short manufacturing time, and short design turn-around time if the realization level of the array compiler can be implemented for user-programmable gate arrays. This would make array processors more competitive (in terms of performance over cost ratio) with other architectures.

6.5 Conclusion

The mapping method proposed in this chapter can be adopted to design a VLSI or WSI array processor. A software package, VACS, is developed to ease the design of arrays. The current VACS focuses on the array level and its interface with lower level tools is yet to be developed. The system represents an attempt to establish a prototype for array design tools. It allows us to learn more about the requirements of the complete process of design automation. The same methodology may be adopted for writing a powerful host compiler for a programmable processor array.

Acknowledgements
The research of Jack S. N. Jean was supported by the National Science

Foundation under Grant No. CDA-8911230 and a Research Challenge Grant from Ohio State.

The research of S. Y. Kung was supported in part by the National Science Foundation under Grant MIP-87-14689.

References

Aho, A. V., Hopcraft, J. E., and Ullman, J. D., 1974, *The Design and Analysis of Computer Algorithms*, Reading, MA: Addison-Wesley.

Bu, J. and Deprettere, E. F., 1988, Converting sequential iterative algorithms to recurrent equations for automatic design of systolic arrays, in *Proc. IEEE ICASSP*, 2025–8.

Chen, M. C., 1986, A parallel language and its compilation to multiprocessor machines, *J. Parallel and Distributed Computing*, 3, 461–91.

Denyer, P. B., 1986, System compilers, in *VLSI Signal Processing II*, IEEE Press, 3–13.

Dijkstra, E. W., 1975, Guarded commands, nondeterminacy and formal derivation of programmes, *Communications of the ACM*, **18**(8), 453–7.

Dongen, V. V. and Quinton, P., 1989, Uniformisation of linear recurrence equations: a step toward the automatic synthesis of systolic arrays, in *Proc. of Int. Conf. on Systolic Arrays*, 473–82.

Engstrom, B. R., and Cappello, P. R., 1988, The SDEF systolic programming system, in *Concurrent Computations: Algorithms, Architecture, and Technology*, (eds S. K. Tewksbury, B. W. Dickinson and S. C. Schwartz) Plenum Press, 263–301.

Freeman, R., 1988, User-programmable gate arrays, *IEEE Spectrum*, **25** (13), 32–5.

Frison, P., Gachet, P. and Quinton, P., 1986, Synthesising systolic arrays using DIASTOL, in *VLSI Signal Processing II*, IEEE Press, 93–105.

Hwang Y. T. and Hu, Y. H., 1990a, MSSM: a multi-stage systolic design tool, in *IEEE VLSI Signal Processing IV*, (eds H.S. Moscovitz, K. Yao, and R. Jain) IEEE Press, Piscataway, NJ, 147–56.

Hwang Y. T. and Hu, Y. H., 1990b, Parameterised dependence graph and its applications to multi-stage systolic mapping procedure, in *Proc. of Int. Conf. on Acoustics, Speech, and Signal Processing*, Albuquerque, New Mexico, 1029–32, April.

Kung, S. Y., 1988, *VLSI Array Processors,* Prentice-Hall, Englewood Cliffs.

Kung S. Y. and Jean, S. N., 1988, A VLSI Array Compiler System (VACS) for Array Design, in *Proc. of IEEE Workshop on VLSI Signal Processing*, November, 495–508.

Kung S. Y. and Jean, S. N., 1989, Array compiler design for VLSI/WSI systems, in *Proc. of Int. Conf. on Systolic Arrays*, May, 663–7.

Kung, H. T., and Lam, M. S., 1984, Wafer-scale integration and two-level pipelined implementations of systolic arrays, *J. Parallel and Distributed Computing*, **1**, 32–63.

LagerIV *Silicon Assembly System Manual,* Version 1.3, 1989.

Meng, T. H. Y. Broaderson, R. W. and Messerschmitt, D. G., 1987, Automatic synthesis of asynchronous circuits from high-level specifications, in *IEEE Transactions on CAD* (a previous version is published in *Proc. of ICCAD*, Santa Clara).

Moldovan, D. I., 1983, On the design of algorithms for VLSI systolic arrays, *Proc. IEEE*, January 113–20.

Moldovan, D. I., 1987, ADVIS: a software package for the design of systolic arrays, *IEEE Trans. on Computer-Aided Design*, January 33–40.

Omizigt, E. T. L., 1988, SYSTARS: a CAD tool for the synthesis and analysis of VLSI systolic/wavefront arrays, in *Proc. of Int. Conf. on Systolic Arrays*, San Diego, 383–91.

Quinton, P., 1984, Automatic synthesis of systolic arrays from uniform recurrent equations, in *Proc. of 11th Ann. Symp. on Computer Architecture*, 208–14.

Rao, S. K., 1985, Regular iterative algorithms and their implementations on processor arrays, PhD thesis, Stanford University, California.

Shang, W., and Fortes, J. A. B., 1988, Time optimal linear schedules for algorithms with uniform dependencies, in *Proc. of Int. Conf. on Systolic Arrays*, San Diego, 393–402.

Tseng, P. S., Lam, M., and Kung, H. T., 1988, The domain parallel computation model on Warp, in *Real-Time Signal Processing XI, Proc. of SPIE Symposium*, **977**, Society of Photo-Optical Instrumentation Engineers.

Wong Y. and Delosme. J.-M., 1985, Optimal systolic implementations of n-dimensional recurrences, in *Proc. IEEE ICCD*, 618–21.

7

DECOMP – A Program for Mapping DSP Algorithms onto Systolic Arrays

Uwe Vehlies

7.1 Introduction

By an extensive application of parallel processing and pipelining systolic arrays provide a high computation rate and a high throughput rate (Kung, 1982; Wah and Fortes, 1987). Also design time and design cost are reduced because of their regularity and modularity. They are very suitable for the implementation of computation intensive DSP algorithms of high regularity.

VLSI technology offers a very compact implementation of systolic arrays but even on chip the communication between the processing elements (PEs) is a critical issue. Locally interconnected arrays are of great importance in order to achieve high clock rates. Array implementation on VLSI chips considering localized interconnections is only possible for 1- and 2-dimensional arrays.

In general, many signal processing algorithms have dimensions above two. Therefore, one task of mapping algorithms onto systolic arrays is to reduce the number of dimensions. This mapping also provides a more effective utilization of the PEs. Procedures for mapping algorithms onto systolic arrays have already been published (Kung, 1988; Moldovan, 1983; Rao, 1985; Quinton, 1984).

In the first stage the mapping methodology has to provide a representation of the algorithm by a dependence graph (DG). The derived DG has to satisfy certain structural constraints, e.g. localization. In the second stage a signal flow graph (SFG) can be derived from the DG by a projection method and in the last stage the SFG will be modified to a systolic array by application of a systolization procedure (Kung, 1988).

The mapping process is not unique; several alternative solutions are possible. For this reason it will be necessary to select a systolic array which is optimally adapted to given design constraints such as minimal latency, maximal throughput rate, minimal number of PEs, etc. In order to support the designer, software tools have been developed (Moldovan, 1987; Frison *et al.*, 1986; Engstrom and Capello, 1988; Kung and Jean, 1988; Athavale *et al.*, 1988; Omizigt, 1988), but these tools do not support the complete design process. They are restricted to special design steps or problems and most of the available tools require input descriptions at the DG level. At this level the designer has manually to extract the data dependencies. Further, these tools do not fully support the generation of netlists at the register transfer or gate level which are necessary for a VLSI implementation of the systolic array.

In order to automate the complete process of mapping a wide range of DSP algorithms onto systolic arrays and decomposing the PEs into BBs (building blocks), the CAD-tool DECOMP (DECOMPosition into building blocks) has been developed. It supports the design of systolic arrays considering given design constraints. In the first stage of implementation the DECOMP processes regular-shift invariant algorithms like matrix operations or convolution, and algorithms with a high regularity, for example blockmatching (Komarek and Pirsch, 1989).

The implemented design process starts with a Pascal-like description of an algorithm and given design constraints. From the algorithmic part of the input description DGs are automatically derived. The DGs are projected onto several SFGs and the PEs of a selected SFG are decomposed into BBs such as adders and multipliers. These BBs are generated by the CAD-tool BADGE (Münzner and Pirsch, 1989).

Further, it is not always possible to design systolic arrays which require the input data in the same sequence and on the same number of parallel lines as it is provided by the external source. Another restriction is the limitation of the pincount for the systolic array. Therefore, with the DECOMP circuits for sorting and distributing, the input data, as required by the systolic array, can be generated automatically. These circuits are called RCs (register circuits) because they consist of registers and multiplexers only.

In the last design step the DECOMP extracts the specifications for the BBs. A specification contains information about the word width of the operands, the maximum allowed area, the maximum allowed delay, and so on. The extractor also generates a netlist in the format EDIF-200 at the register transfer level. This netlist represents the BB configuration of the systolic array.

Section 7.2 in this paper characterizes the main steps of the mapping process and introduces the program structure of the DECOMP. In section 7.3 emphasis is given on the compiler that translates the input description into n-dimensional DGs. In section 7.4 the internal data structure representing DGs as well as SFGs is described. Section 7.5 explains the projection of the DGs onto alternative SFGs. In section 7.6 the generation of the RCs is described, and in section 7.7 the decomposition of the PEs is explained. Finally some results and implementation notes are given.

7.2 Decomposing algorithms into building blocks

As proposed in (Kung, 1988) the process of mapping an algorithm onto a systolic array can be divided into the following design stages.

- Algorithm (in a high level language)
- Stage 1: Dependence graph (DG design)
- Stage 2: Signal flow graph (SFG design)
- Stage 3: Systolic array (VLSI array design)

According to these design stages the DECOMP mainly consists of the three program components compiler, mapper, and extractor leading the designer from one design stage to the next. A fourth program component is provided for the adaptation of the input data sequences. The program structure of the DECOMP and the interaction with the user is shown in Fig. 7.1.

The design process starts with an input description of an algorithm in a high level language. The description also contains design constraints on the systolic array. The algorithmic part of the input description is analysed by the compiler and translated into an n-dimensional DG. The design constraints are passed to the data structure without change for use in further design steps.

Most of the existing design programs start with a description at the DG

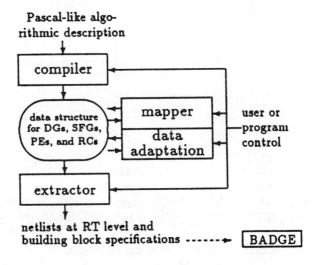

Figure 7.1 The program structure of the DECOMP.

level where the algorithms are given in a localized form with explicitly specified data dependencies. The compiler in the DECOMP automatically generates the data dependencies and localizes broadcast variables from the description in a high level language. A high level language was chosen as input because this has the advantage that the algorithm itself can be developed and verified independently from the design constraints before starting the VLSI implementation.

The mapper projects the n-dimensional DGs onto alternative SFGs with an expansion of two dimensions or less. The projection method is based on the multiprojection scheme as proposed by Kung (1988). Further, in the current state of implementation the mapper allows the projection of similar computation nodes onto the same PEs in the SFG. For the selection of an SFG which is optimal adapted to the given design constraints the resulting SFGs can be compared interactively. For example, design constraints are the number of PEs, the organization of the input and output data sequences, and the number of clock cycles needed for a complete computation of the algorithm.

In the last design step the extractor decomposes the PEs of a selected SFG into BBs which represent the basic operations of the algorithm. As output it generates lists containing the parameters of the required BBs and netlists of the BB configuration at the register transfer level. The BB list is passed to the generator program BADGE which synthesizes the BBs with the elements of a given cell library and produces netlists for them at the gate level. The netlists of the DECOMP and the BADGE together describe the whole systolic array and may serve as input for a simulation or layout generation tool.

The fourth program component, the data adaptation, provides generators for the synthesis of RCs needed to sort, duplicate, and distribute the input data as required by the generated systolic array. These RCs are necessary because it is not always possible to design arrays which required the data input exactly as it is provided by the external source. Also, after a projection the systolic array may require the same input data multiple times at the same input. The generated RCs are represented in the same data structure as the DGs and SFGs, which also allows generation of EDIF netlists for them.

The four program components of DECOMP work on the internal data structure through an interface that allows the addition of new components to the program system easily. In the future, additional components will be implemented for an automatic comparison and selection of the alternative SFGs with regard to the given design constraints. Also the optimization of the generated SFGs may be supported by new program components.

7.3 The DECOMP compiler and its language

The input language of the DECOMP-compiler is a subset of Pascal

Table 7.1 The input language of the DECOMP-compiler

Statements

file access	algorithm
WRITELN	BEGIN
READLN	END
OPEN	IF...THEN
CLOSE	IF...THEN...ELSE
RESET	FOR...:=...TO...DO...
REWRITE	FOR...:=...DOWNTO...DO...
	:=

Declarations

algorithm	design constraints
PROGRAM	DESIGN
CONST	WORD-WIDTH
VAR	MAX-AREA
INTEGER	MAX-DELAY
ARRAY	CLOCK-RATE
TEXT	LATENCY
	NUMBER-OF-PES

Operators

× – */**
MIN MAX ABS
FN....(parl,...,parn)
AND
OR

extended by some declarations for specifying design constraints. A summary of the actually implemented input language is given in Table 7.1.

The input language is specified using a grammar (Aho *et al.*, 1986). Therefore, the language can easily be modified and new statements can be added without changes in the source code of the compiler. A special statement FN_ . . . is provided which introduces user defined operators. In a Pascal-program these operators are defined as **functions** and in the internal data structure they are represented as user defined BBs. DGs for user defined operators can be derived by specific compilations. Thus, more complex algorithms can be processed by application of this statement.

An input description is divided into two parts. One part containing the description of an algorithm and the other part containing design constraints on the systolic array. Using a subset of Pascal as input language has the advantage that the input description can be directly executed with standard Pascal-compilers. During the execution as a Pascal-program the design constraints are enclosed in parentheses to be handled as comments. Thus, the algorithm can be developed in a high level language and simulated before the derivation of a DG.

As an example throughout this paper the algorithm given in Fig. 7.2 is considered. The example is written in single assignment code without explicitly specifying data dependencies. The single assignment code is currently necessary for the correct derivation of the data dependencies. The constant *j* is used to make it possible to easily modify the length of the dimensions. With the IF-condition an additional operator is assigned to all nodes with the index $k = j$ in the DG. Thus, using the IF-condition DGs with different types of nodes can be generated. Also the statement FN_ab is used for the definition of a user defined operator.

From the same input description which is executed as a Pascal-program the DECOMP-compiler derives DGs in two phases. In the first phase it

```
PROGRAM matrix_vector_multiplication_and_FN_ab          {1}
CONST    j = 3;                                          {2}
VAR      b :ARRAY[1..j] OF INTEGER;                      {3}
         a :ARRAY[1..j,1..j] OF INTEGER;                 {4}
         c :ARRAY[1..j,0..j] OF INTEGER;                 {5}
         d :ARRAY[j..j,0..j] OF INTEGER;                 {6}
         i,k :INTEGER;                                   {7}
{FUNCTION FN_ab (x,y :INTEGER) :INTEGER;                 {8}
 BEGIN                                                   {9}
  IF (x < y)                                             {10}
     THEN fn_mincom := x                                 {11}
     ELSE fn_mincom := y                                 {12}
 END;}                                                   {13}
BEGIN                                                    {14}
  FOR k := 1 TO j DO                                     {15}
    BEGIN                                                {16}
      c[k,0]:= 0;                                        {17}
      IF (k = j) THEN d[k,0] := 0;                       {18}
      FOR i := 1 TO j DO                                 {19}
        BEGIN                                            {20}
          c[k,i]:= c[k,i-1] + a[k,i] * b[i]);            {21}
          If (k = j) THEN                                {22}
             d[k,i] := d[k,i-1] + FN_ab(a[k,i],b[i]);    {23}
        END;                                             {24}
      END;                                               {25}
END.                                                     {26}
{DESIGN;                                                 {27}
  NUMBER-OF-PES   j;                                     {28}
  WORD-WIDTH      a[4],b[4],c[4],d[4];                   {29}
  MAX-AREA        25000;                                 {30}
  MAX-DELAY       10;                                    {31}
  LATENCY         40;                                    {32}
  CLOCK-RATE      20;                                    {33}
END.}                                                    {34}
```

Figure 7.2 Example of an input description.

reads the description, performs a lexical and a syntax analysis (Aho *et al.*, 1986) and expands the description into a table which is shown in Fig. 7.3. The table represents the protocol achieved by the execution of the input description as a program. It contains all index points of the algorithm with the variables and operations performed at these index points.

In the second phase the compiler interprets the table and derives a DG. It extracts the number and length of the dimensions for the DG array, the external inputs and outputs, the function of the nodes and the data dependencies between them. The data dependencies can be extracted because in the table all are given with their indices. For example, the variable $C(2\ 1)$ is produced at the index point $(2\ 1)$ and it is used at the index point $(2\ 2)$. Therefore, in the DG it is propagated in the direction $(0\ 1)$ (see Fig. 7.3). If a variable has fewer indices than the number of dimensions it is a broadcast variable which is automatically localized by the compiler. In the example the variable b is transmitted in the direction $(1\ 0)$. If more than one direction for transmitting a broadcast variable is possible the user is asked for a decision. For a more detailed explanation of the compiler see (Vehlies and Crimi, 1991).

Protocol entry	Protocol value		
NODE-LIST	((1) (1 1) (1 2) (1 3) (2) (2 1) (2 2) (2 3) (3) (3 1) (3 2) (3 3))		
ASSIGNMENT-LIST	(C-1-0 C-1-1 C-1-2 C-1-3 C-2-0 C-2-1 C-2-2 C-2-3 C-3-0		
	D-3-0 C-3-1 D-3-1 C-3-2 D-3-2 C-3-3 D-3-3)		
C-1-0	((1)	(C[1 0])	(0))
C-1-1	((1 1)	(C[1 1])	(C[1 0] + A[1 1] * B[1]))
C-1-2	((1 2)	(C[1 2])	(C[1 1] + A[1 2] * B[2]))
C-1-3	((1 3)	(C[1 3])	(C[1 2] + A[1 3] * B[3]))
C-2-0	((2)	(C[2 0])	(0))
C-2-1	((2 1)	(C[2 1])	(C[2 0] + A[2 1] * B[1]))
C-2-2	((2 2)	(C[2 2])	(C[2 1] + A[2 2] * B[2]))
C-2-3	((2 3)	(C[2 3])	(C[2 2] + A[2 3] * B[3]))
C-3-0	((3)	(C[3 0])	(0))
C-3-1	((3 1)	(C[3 1])	(C[3 0] + A[3 1] * B[1]))
C-3-2	((3 2)	(C[3 2])	(C[3 1] + A[3 2] * B[2]))
C-3-3	((3 3)	(C[3 3])	(C[3 2] + A[3 3] * B[3]))
D-3-0	((3)	(D[3 0])	(0))
D-3-1	((3 1)	(D[3 1])	(D[3 0] + FN_ AB(A[3 1],B[1])))
D-3-2	((3 2)	(D[3 2])	(D[3 1] + FN_ AB(A[3 2],B[2])))
D-3-3	((3 3)	(D[3 3])	(D[3 2] + FN_ AB(A[3 3],B[3])))
DESIGN	(matrix_ vector_ multiplication_ and_ FN_ ab)		
WORD-WIDTH	(A[4],B[4],C[4],D[4])		
NUMBER-OF-PES	(3)		
MAX-AREA	(25000)		
MAX-DELAY	(10)		
LATENCY	(40)		
CLOCK-RATE	(20)		

Figure 7.3 Protocol table of the compiler for the example.

7.4 The internal data structure

The DGs derived by the compiler are represented in the same internal data structure as the SFGs. For this reason it will not be exactly distinguished between a DG and an SFG in the following.

An object oriented approach was taken to implement the internal data structure. Every node is represented by an object containing the inputs, outputs, the function of the nodes and the time step at which the node is scheduled for a computation. The DGs are represented by an array which contains the node objects as array elements. The number and length of the array dimensions are adapted to the DGs automatically. Further, the interconnections between the nodes are represented by pointers relative to the array index. Thus relative pointers are the direct representation of the arcs e in the DGs. The considered example leads to the DG shown in Fig. 7.4. This DG has two different types of nodes as shown in Fig. 7.5. The internal representation of the node at the index point (3 2) is shown in Fig. 7.6.

A node in the internal data structure has three slots. The slot :SCHEDULED stores the time step at which a node is scheduled. The slots :INPUTS and :OUTPUTS store lists representing the function of a node as well as the interconnections between them. A list in the slot

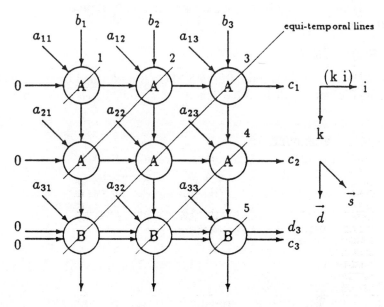

Figure 7.4 The dependence graph for the example.

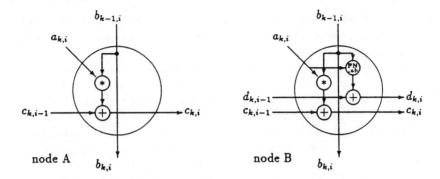

Figure 7.5 The two nodes used for the DG in the example.

:INPUTS contains three elements denoting a signal name, a relative pointer and a value for this signal. The interconnections between the nodes are represented by pointers relative to the array indices. The next node is reached by adding a pointer to the array index of the node. Pointers like a=3−2 denote external inputs or outputs. A list in the slot :OUTPUTS contains five elements denoting a signal name, a relative pointer, a delay for an arc, the function of the output and the word width for the signal. The word width must be specified for the following design steps because the DGs at this design stage are represented at word level.

7.5 Projecting DGs onto SFGs

The projection of DGs onto different SFGs is performed by the mapper. Out of the set of all possible schedules s and all possible projection

```
#S(NODE :SCHEDULED 3
         :INPUTS    ((a a=3-2  value-of-a)
                     (b (-1 0) value-of-b)
                     (c (0 -1) value-of-c)
                     (d (0 -1) value-of-d))
         :OUTPUTS   ((b b=2   0 b 4)
                     (c (0 1) 0 (+ (* a b) c) 9)
                     (d (0 1) 0 (+ (FN_ab a b) d) 9)))
```

Figure 7.6 The internal representation of the DG node at the index point (3 2).

directions d, those are selected which satisfy certain conditions. Each vector s has to fulfil the condition

$$s^T e \geqslant 0 \qquad (7.1)$$

for any arc e in the DG in order to have a valid schedule. This condition ensures the data availability at each node in the created SFG. A valid projection direction d should fold the same type of node into each other. In addition, the condition

$$s^T d > 0 \qquad (7.2)$$

should be valid to ensure processor availability in the created SFG.

In the current state of implementation all possible values for s and d are assumed. Because this results in a large number of allowed projections they can be limited by specifying an upper bound for the components of the vectors s and d. An upper bound of 1, only allows the vectors (1 0), (1 1), and (0 1). Even with these restrictions nine different projections are allowed in 2-dimensional DGs. If none of the projections leads to an SFG which satisfies given constraints the upper bound can be incremented. In the future an optimization technique for reducing the number of projections will be implemented which automatically selects only those projections which are optimal in respect to the given design constraints.

Applying a projection to a DG reduces the number of dimensions by one. Under additional conditions (Kung, 1988) the projection can be applied successively to n-dimensional DGs for projecting them onto SFGs with an expansion of two dimensions or fewer.

For the example discussed in this paper the schedule $s^T = (1\ 1)$ and the projection direction $d^T = (1\ 0)$ as depicted in Fig. 7.4 have been chosen. Figure 7.4 also shows the equitemporal lines for the selected schedule which are orthogonal to the schedule vector. All nodes on an equi-temporal line are active at the same time step.

The chosen projection is allowed because s and d fulfil the conditions (7.1) and (7.2). Also the implemented projection method allows the projection of different nodes into the same PE if the nodes are subtypes of each other. Two nodes are equal if they have the same inputs, outputs, and if the outputs are calculated with the same functions. If a node does not have all outputs (and/or inputs) of another node it is a subtype of it. In the example node A is a subtype of node B (Fig. 7.5). The SFG created with this projection is shown in Fig. 7.7 and the node at the index point (3) of this SFG is shown in Fig. 7.8.

Also, with the implemented projection method, DGs which are not as regular as the example can be projected onto an SFG. For example the same DG without the nodes at the index points (1 1), (1 2), and (2 1) may be projected onto the same SFG except that the data input and output sequences are not the same.

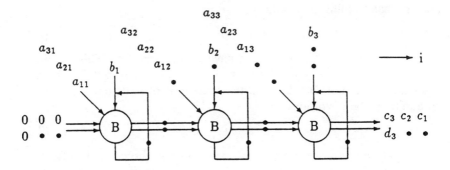

Figure 7.7 The signal flow graph for the considered projection.

In the SFGs multiplexers are required. In the example it must be decided whether the signal b is taken from the external input or from the loop. In the internal representation of the nodes the multiplexers are considered in the inputs of the nodes. The second element of a multiplexed input is a list starting with the keyword MUXIN. The following elements are relative pointers. Further, as shown in Fig. 7.8, a fourth element containing the control information for the selection of the multiplexer input is added to the input.

For deciding which value of the input b will be used, the control information is evaluated using the select input S1, which is also added automatically by performing a projection. For example, if the value of S1 is 1 the external input for b is used.

The sequences of the control information for the select inputs are automatically created by looking at the external input sequences. The input to the node at the index point (3) is ($\bullet\bullet b_2$) and results in the control sequence (0 0 1) for the select input S1 of that node.

An important feature of the DECOMP is a function which, based on the implemented data structure, verifies the created DGs and SFGs. It starts at the external inputs of the graphs and calculates the values of all signals in the graph dependent on the functions of their node outputs. The order of the calculations depends on the relative pointers representing the interconnections, and on the time steps at which the nodes are scheduled. The schedule for the nodes is automatically introduced by another function. The function stops with the calculation of the external outputs of the graph. The start values for the external inputs are taken from the same input data file which is used as input to the Pascal-program of the algorithm. The results obtained at the external outputs of the graph by application of the function can directly be compared to the results obtained by running the Pascal-program.

```
#S(NODE :SCHEDULED 3
    :INPUTS     ((A A=3 value-of-a)
                 (B (MUXIN B=3 (0)) value-of-b
                    (CONTROL (= S_B 1) (= S_B 0)))
                 (S_B S_B=3 value-of-s_b)
                 (C (-1) value-of-c)
                 (D (-1) value-of-d))
    :OUTPUTS    ((B (0) 1 B 4)
                 (C C=3 0 (+ (* A B) C) 9)
                 (D D=3 0 (+ (FN_AB A B) D) 9)))
```

Figure 7.8 The node at the index point (3) of the created SFG.

7.6 Adaptation of the input data sequences

The systolic arrays require the input data with a high clock rate in a specific order at parallel lines. Further, dependent on the algorithm the input data may be required multiple times on the same line. The systolic arrays are designed and optimized according to the given design constraints and the limitations of the pincount. The design process usually leads to arrays which require the input data not in the order as it is provided by the external source. The input data sequences for the systolic array of the example and a possible external source are given in Fig. 7.9.

The data adaptation provides four different types of generators for the synthesis of the RCs. The selection of an appropriate generator is influenced by the quantity of the input data, the number of required repetitions, and the number of necessary delays (Schönfeld *et al.*, 1991). A generator which is optimal in respect to the number of repetitions may not be optimal if a large number of delays between the external sequence and the sequence at the systolic array is required. For example, one generator is provided to generate register chains in the case when a large number of delays is required. Another generator is provided for the generation of rotation elements consisting of one register and one multiplexer. This generator is used if a large number of data items must be duplicated often. For the selection of the appropriate generator, functions are implemented which before synthesizing the RC estimate the number of registers and multiplexers. Because the RCs are stored in the same data structure as the DGs and SFGs, all functions, for example the verification function, can be applied to the RCs.

With this approach it always is possible to generate an RC for the adaptation of a systolic array to an external source independent of the

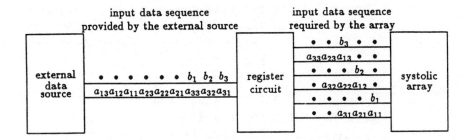

Figure 7.9 Input data sequences for the example.

number of parallel lines and the order of the data sequences. The circuits generated with this approach may not be optimal in every case. However, this concept automates the design of systolic arrays which are adapted to input data sequences as they are provided by external sources.

7.7 Extraction of building blocks and netlists

In the last step of the design process the extractor decomposes the PEs of a selected SFG into BBs. The BBs are specified by their type, the number and the word width of their operands, a maximum area, and a maximum delay. The type of the needed BBs, and the word width of their operands are given by the function and the word width stored in the outputs of the PEs. For the output c of a PE, in the example, an adder and a multiplier both with two operands are required. An example of a BB specification which can be processed by the BADGE is shown in Fig. 7.10. Further, BBs are created for the needed multiplexers and for the registers representing the delays of the arcs.

The word width of the signals must be introduced by the extractor because in the internal data structure the SFGs are represented at word level. Thus, a function is provided which, similar to the verification function, runs through the SFG calculating the word width for every signal dependent on the BB operations and a given number system.

The extractor also provides functions for the specification of a maximum area and a maximum delay for the required BBs. In the input description for an algorithm a maximum area and a maximum delay for the systolic array can be specified. The area is split into all needed BBs dependent upon their type and the word width of their operands. The specified maximum delay for a complete computation is first split into all PEs dependent upon the delay and the direction of their interconnections. Thereby, a global clock for the SFG is calculated. Dependent on this clock and the function of the PE outputs, the maximum delay for the required BBs is calculated.

A list with the required BBs, their parameters and the design constraints on them is passed to the program BADGE which generates the BBs. Also the extractor produces a netlist of the BB configuration at the register transfer level in the format EDIF-200. A netlist for the RCs can also be produced. These netlists together with the netlists returned by the BADGE describe the complete systolic array. The netlists may serve as input for a simulation or layout generation tool.

7.8 Implementation notes and results

The DECOMP is implemented on a μVAX3 and a SUN4 in COMMON LISP. This language was chosen because it offers a very good programming environment for implementing a dynamic data structure and is very suitable for rapid prototyping.

The implemented data structure allows access to the nodes, DGs, and SFGs at every design stage. The data structure is implemented using the COMMON LISP data types structure and list in an object oriented approach. This allows new slots to be easily added into the nodes or to add elements in the input and output descriptions of the nodes

In Table 7.2 some example algorithms are given which have been programmed using the Pascal-like input language and mapped onto several 1- or 2-dimensional systolic arrays by the DECOMP.

The blockmatching algorithm may serve as an example. For simplicity the example was programmed with an upper bound of $n = 3$. Thus, a reference image of 3×3 pixels is searched in an image area of 5×5 pixels. As a result the minimum and the replacement vector are calculated. The

```
REQUIRED-BUILDINGBLOCK
    :TYPE           ADDER
    :BLOCK-FOR-PE   ((PE-3 C))
    :MAX-AREA       2525
    :MAX-DELAY      18
    :WORD-WIDTH-OUT (C 10)
    :WORD-WIDTH-IN  ((IN-0 8) (C 9))
    :NUMBER-OF-OPERANDS 2
    :INPUTS         ((IN-0 0 7)
                    (C 0 8))
    :OUTPUTS        ((C 0 9))
```

Figure 7.10 BB specification for an adder used at the PE with the index (3).

input description shown in Fig. 7.11 is not programmed in strict single assignment code. Also, in the next version of the compiler, single assignment code will not be a necessary requirement.

This input description contains four nested loops with three nested IF-THEN-ELSE-conditions in the inner loop body. The absolute x-y-differences must be calculated at every index point but it is not necessary to calculate the sums and the minimum at every index point. Also the FN_ ... statement is used to introduce a user defined operator. This operator has four input operands and it returns one of the last two operands dependent upon a comparison of the first operators. This user defined operator calculates the replacement vector dependent upon the loop indices.

The DG derived from this description has 4 dimensions and 81 nodes. With the mapper it has been mapped onto different 1-dimensional SFGs by three succeeding projections. One resulting SFG with three PEs, its interconnections, and its required data input sequences is shown in Fig. 7.12.

Two PEs only contain a subtractor, an adder, and a BB for the absolute value. The third PE also contains BBs for the minimum operation and the user defined operator. It also has three loops with different delays for storing intermediate results. In the loop with one delay the variable x_i is stored. In the loop with three delays the variables xx, yy, and x_n are stored and in the loop with nine delays the variables ym, xn, and x_m are

Table 7.2 Selection of algorithms processed by the DECOMP

Processed algorithms	
convolution (2-dimensional)	$y(n) = \sum_{k=0}^{N=1} u(k) * w(n-k)$ $n = 0, 1,..., 2N-2$
matrix-matrix multiplication (3-dimensional)	$c(i, j) = \sum_{k=1}^{N} a(i, k) * b(k, j)$ $i, j = 1, ..., N$
blockmatching (Komarek and Pirsch, 1989) (4-dimensional)	$U = min_{m, n} \sum_{i=1}^{N} \sum_{k=1}^{N} |x_{i, k} - y_{i+m, k+n}|$ $V = (m, n)\|_U$ $n, m = -\dfrac{N}{2}...\dfrac{N}{2}$

```
PROGRAM bma; {blockmatching}                                            {1}
CONST n = 3;                                                            {2}
<...assumed variable declarations...>                                  {3}
{FUNCTION fn_mincom (x,y,lvar,old :INTEGER) :INTEGER;                   {4}
 BEGIN                                                                  {5}
  IF (x < y)                                                            {6}
    THEN fn_mincom := lvar                                             {7}
    ELSE fn_mincom := old                                             {8}
 END;}                                                                  {9}
BEGIN                                                                  {10}
<...assumed input statements...>                                      {11}
 FOR nn := 1 to 3 DO                                                  {12}
  BEGIN                                                               {13}
   IF (nn = 1) THEN                                                   {14}
    BEGIN                                                             {15}
      x_n[0] := 999999; x_m[0] := 999999;                            {16}
      xx[0]  := 0;      yy[0]  := 0;                                 {17}
      xn[0]  := 0;      ym[0]  := 0;                                 {18}
      x_i[0] := 0;      x_k[0] := 0;                                 {19}
    END;                                                             {20}
   FOR m := 1 to 3 DO BEGIN                                          {21}
     FOR i := 1 to n DO BEGIN                                        {22}
       FOR k := 1 to n DO                                            {23}
        IF (k=n) THEN                                                {24}
         IF (k=n) AND (i=n) THEN                                     {25}
          IF (k=n) AND (i=n) AND (m=3) THEN                          {26}
           BEGIN                                                     {27}
            x_k[k]  := x_k[k-1] + abs(x_in[i,k] - y_in[i+nn-2,k+m-2]); {28}
            x_i[i]  := x_i[i-1] + x_k[k];                            {29}
            x_m[m]  := min(x_m[m-1],x_i[i]);                         {30}
            x_n[nn] := min(x_n[nn-1],x_m[m]);                        {31}
            xn[m]   := fn_mincom(x_i[i],x_m[m-1],nn-2,xn[m-1]);      {32}
            ym[m]   := fn_mincom(x_i[i],x_m[m-1],m-2,ym[m-1]);       {33}
            xx[nn]  := fn_mincom(x_m[m],x_n[nn-1],xn[m],xx[nn-1]);   {34}
            yy[nn]  := fn_mincom(x_m[m],x_n[nn-1],ym[m],yy[nn-1]);   {35}
           END ELSE BEGIN                                            {36}
            x_k[k]  := x_k[k-1] + abs(x_in[i,k] - y_in[i+nn-2,k+m-2]); {37}
            x_i[i]  := x_i[i-1] + x_k[k];                            {38}
            x_m[m]  := min(x_m[m-1],x_i[i]);                         {39}
            xn[m]   := fn_mincom(x_i[i],x_m[m-1],nn-2,xn[m-1]);      {40}
            ym[m]   := fn_mincom(x_i[i],x_m[m-1],m-2,ym[m-1]);       {41}
           END ELSE BEGIN                                            {42}
            x_k[k]':= x_k[k-1] + abs(x_in[i,k] - y_in[i+nn-2,k+m-2]); {43}
            x_i[i] := x_i[i-1] + x_k[k];                             {44}
           END ELSE BEGIN                                            {45}
            x_k[k] := x_k[k-1] + abs(x_in[i,k] - y_in[i+nn-2,k+m-2]); {46}
           END; END; END; END;                                      {47}
<...assumed output statements...>                                     {48}
END.                                                                  {49}
<...assumed design constraints...>                                    {50}
```

Figure 7.11 Part of the input description for the blockmatching algorithm.

stored. The variable x_k is propagated from one PE to the next. In Fig. 7.12 the input data sequences required for this systolic array are also shown. The reference image is the input at the left side and the search area is the input at the right side.

The systolic array has been verified by applying the verification function. Thus, for the calculation of the algorithm the created array can be used as well as the Pascal-program. Further, BB specifications and netlists have been extracted and also RCs for the adaptation of the input data to an external source have been generated.

7.9 Conclusion

In this chapter the CAD-tool DECOMP is presented. It maps an algorithm given in a Pascal-like input description onto a systolic array. The program consists of the program components compiler, mapper and extractor which perform the design process from one design stage to the next, and of the program component data adaptation, which generates RCs for the adaptation of the data input sequences.

The algorithms have to be programmed as Pascal-programs which can contain design constraints on the systolic array, too. The compiler derives n-dimensional DGs with automatic generation of the data dependencies. The mapper projects the DGs onto SFGs with an expansion of two dimensions or fewer. This leads to VLSI realizations which have only local

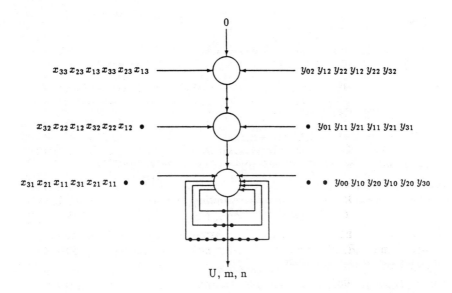

Figure 7.12 A possible SFG for the blockmatching algorithm.

interconnections between the PEs Also nodes which are subtypes of others can be projected into the same PE. The extractor decomposes the PEs of a selected SFG into BBs and extracts netlists at the register transfer level. Further, the DECOMP provides functions for the adaptation of an SFG to given design constraints like maximum computation time, maximum area, and number of PEs.

The functions provided by the DECOMP can be used interactively or can be integrated in an automatic program control. In the current state of implementation the mapping process is automated but the selection of an optimal SFG is performed interactively. Provisions are made to automate the selection, too. It is also planned to implement a graphic output interface.

The currently implemented design process leads to several different solutions. These must be compared to each other interactively. For an automatic comparison controlled by the program and for an automatic design process directed to optimal arrays, heuristics must be considered. However, the presented approach shows that it is possible to decompose an algorithm which is given in a high level language into BBs and further into elements of a cell library at the gate level.

Acknowledgement

This work has been supported by the Fraunhofer Gesellschaft under contract number T/RF33/G0031/G2231.

References

Aho, A. V., Sethi, R., and Ullman, J. D., 1986, *Compilers – Principles, Techniques and Tools*, Addison–Wesley.

Athavale, A., Jàjà, J., and Rowlett, J., 1988, Compiling programs for systolic arrays, *VLSI Signal Processing III* (eds R. W. Brodersen and H. S. Moscovitz), IEEE Press, New York, ch. 46, 509–19.

Engstrom, B. R., and Capello, P. R., 1988, The SDEF systolic programming system, *Concurrent Computations: Algorithms, Architectures and Technology* (ed. S. K. Tewksbury), Plenum Press, 263–301.

Frison, P., Gachet, P., and Quinton, P., 1986, Designing systolic arrays with DIASTOL, *VLSI Signal Processing II* (eds S. Y. Kung, R. E. Owen, and J. G. Nash), IEEE Press, New York, ch. 9, 93–105.

Komarek, T., and Pirsch, P., 1989, Architectures for block matching algorithms, *IEEE Trans. on Circuits and Systems*, **36**(10), 1301–308, October.

Kung, H. T., 1982, Why systolic architectures, *Computer Magazine*, **15**(1), 37–46.

Kung, S. Y., 1988, *VLSI – Array Processors*, Prentice Hall Information and System Sciences Series, Englewood Cliffs, Thomas Kailath edition.

Kung, S. Y., and Jean, S. N., 1988, A VLSI array compiler system (VACS) for array design, *VLSI Signal Processing III* (eds R. W. Brodersen and H. S. Moscovitz), IEEE Press, New York, ch. 45, 495–508.

Moldovan, D. I., 1983, On the design of algorithms for VLSI systolic arrays, *Proc. IEEE*, **71**, 113–20, January.

Moldovan, D. I., 1987, ADVIS: a software package for the design of systolic arrays, *IEEE Trans. on Computer-Aided Design*, **CAD–6**(1), 33–40, January.

Münzner, A., and Pirsch, P., 1989, BADGE – building block adviser and generator, in *Proc. of the Int. Symp. on Circuits and Systems*, **3**, 1887–90, May.

Omizigt, L., 1988, SYSTARS: a CAD tool for the synthesis and analysis of systolic/wavefront arrays, in *Proc. of the International Conference on Systolic Arrays* (eds K. Bromley, S. Y. Kung, and E. Swartzlander) Computer Society Press, 383–92.

Quinton. P., 1984, Automatic synthesis of systolic arrays from uniform recurrent equations, in *Proc. of 11th Symp. on Computer Architectures*, 208–14.

Rao, S. K., 1985, Regular iterative algorithms and their implementation on processor arrays, PhD thesis, Stanford University, October.

Schönfeld, M., Pirsch, P., and Schwiegershausen, M., 1991, Synthesis of intermediate memories needed to handle the data supply of processor arrays, in *Fifth Int. ACM & IEEE Workshop on High-Level Synthesis*, (ed. W. Rosenstiel), 21–8, March.

Vehlies, U., and Crimi. A., 1991, A compiler for generating dependence graphs of DSP-algorithms, *Algorithms and Parallel VLSI Architectures, vol. B, Proceedings* (eds E. F. Deprettere and A. J. Van der Veen), Elsevier, Amsterdam, 319–28.

Wah, B., and Fortes. J. A. B., 1987, Systolic arrays – from concept to implementation, *IEEE Computer*, **20**(7), 12–17.

8

Adapting a Sequential Algorithm for a Systolic Design

Christian Lengauer and Jingling Xue

8.1 Introduction

One appeal of systolic arrays is that they can be derived from a more abstract description that does not specify communication or concurrency. Two choices of such a description are an imperative program or a functional program. Methods exist by which a subclass of such programs – those that contain **uniform recurrences** (Karp *et al.*, 1967; Lamport, 1974) – can be converted mechanically to a systolic array with optimal concurrency, i.e., with the shortest execution time. For introductions according to development methods, we refer to (Quinton, 1984; Rao and Kailath, 1988) in the functional and (Huang and Lengauer, 1987; Lengauer *et al.*, 1991) in the imperative setting.

Many algorithms that one would like to systolize transcend the requirement of uniformity. Efforts are being made to extend mechanical systolic design methods to accept more general recurrence patterns (van Dongen 1989; Quinton and van Dongen, 1989; Rajopadhye, 1989; Rajopadhye and Fujimoto, 1990; Wong and Deslome, 1988 and 1985; Yaacoby and Cappello, 1989). Without such extensions, a manual adaptation of the input to the method is required. One of the more complex problems that has been solved so far is the Algebraic Path Problem. Its solutions were, at first, derived informally (Rote, 1985; Robert and Trystram, 1987); later the derivations were formally retraced and classified, by adapting the source description manually to comply with the requirements of uniform methods, (e.g., Quinton and van Dongen, 1989; Huang and Lengauer, 1989; Kung *et al.*, 1987); then a completely mechanical treatment was achieved (Quinton and van Dongen, 1989; Rajopadhye, 1989); most recently, solutions have been obtained that have both optimal concurrency and a minimal number of processors (Scheiman and Cappello, 1990; Benaini and Robert, 1990) and a method for deriving such solutions has been proposed (Claus *et al.*, 1990).

Here, we take a practical algorithm from an application area, image processing, and subject it to a formal systolic design. The algorithm is phrased imperatively and performs segmentation and border extraction of video images (Burt *et al.*, 1981; Hong *et al.*, 1982; Hong and Rosenfeld, 1984). In its entirety, it is more complex than the algorithms studied previously in systolic design (that we are aware of). It is divided into four consecutive phases. We shall deal only with the first (and simplest) phase and, rather than delving into the details of the subsequent phases, put our development into a wider perspective. A description of the complete problem and its systolic solution can be found elsewhere (Lengauer and Xue, 1991).

Taking a method for uniform recurrences as our systolization tool, the challenge is to adapt the input to satisfy its requirements. We shall distinguish two distinct motivations as we proceed in the development.

Syntactic adaptation: The source program must be brought into a form from which a systolic solution can be derived automatically.

Semantic adaptation: The source program must be modified further such that the desired systolic solution is obtained.

Since we deal with an imperative source program, our adaptations become transformations of sequential programs. We can take traditional algorithms from the literature and test them and the successive stages of their adaptation by implementing them in a conventional language and running them. Or we can prove them and their transformations correct with traditional verification methods for sequential programs. Establishing the correctness of the systolic array is not necessary; it is guaranteed by the correctness of the systolic design method.

8.2 The method

In the past decade, a number of systolic design methods have been developed (Fortes *et al.*, 1988). At least two are completely mechanizable and derive optimal parallelism, i.e., a shortest execution. One expects as input a functional program, i.e., a program in which a variable may be assigned only once (Rao and Kailath, 1988), the other an imperative program, i.e., a program in which a variable may be assigned more than once (Huang and Lengauer, 1984). Both require the program to be uniform in a technical sense (Quinton, 1984; Lengauer, *et al.*, 1991). This section sketches the source and target languages from the imperative viewpoint.

8.2.1 The source description

We accept the following source format:

$$\text{for } x_0 \text{ from } lb_0 \text{ by } st_0 \text{ to } rb_0 \text{ do}$$

$$\text{for } x_1 \text{ from } lb_1 \text{ by } st_1 \text{ to } rb_1 \text{ do}$$
$$\vdots$$
$$\text{for } x_{r-1} \text{ from } lb_{r-1} \text{ by } st_{r-1} \text{ to } rb_{r-1} \text{ do}$$
$$x_0 : x_1 : \cdots : x_{r-1}$$

where $x_0 : x_1 \cdots : x_{r-1}$ is of the form:

$$x_0 : x_1 : \cdots : x_{r-1} :: \text{ if } B_0(x_0,x_1,\cdots,x_{r-1}) \rightarrow S_0$$
$$\text{[] } B_1(x_0,x_1,\cdots,x_{r-1}) \rightarrow S_1$$
$$\vdots$$
$$\text{[] } B_{t-1}(x_0, x_1, \cdots, x_{r-1}) \rightarrow S_{t-1}$$
$$\text{fi}$$

We call $x_0 : x_1 : \cdots : x_{r-1}$ the **basic operation** of the program and refer to its components S_j as **computations**. $B_j \rightarrow S_j$ is called a **guarded command** (Dijkstra, 1976). The bounds lb_i and rb_i are linear or piecewise linear expressions in the loop indices x_0 to x_{i-1} ($0 \leq i < r$) and in additional variables that specify the problem size. The steps st_i are constants. The guards B_j ($0 \leq j < t$) are Boolean expressions. The computations S_j ($0 \leq j < t$) are programs, possibly, with composition, alternation or iteration but without non-local references other than to variables subscripted by the x_i. In a nutshell, they must be uniform recurrences (Karp *et al.*, 1967).

In our source, the computations are phrased imperatively. We have an implementation of the method that accepts an imperative source and have employed it in the systolization of our image processing algorithm. If phrased imperatively, a basic operation must obey the following additional restrictions in order to guarantee the existence of a systolic array (Lengauer *et al.*, 1991):

1. each non-local variable is subscripted by exactly $r - 1$ linear expressions in the loop indices x_0 to x_{i-1} ($0 \leq i < r$); their coefficient matrix is of rank $r - 1$; and
2. non-local variables that agree in name agree in subscripts.

8.2.2 The target description

Both the functional and the imperative method describe a systolic array by two functions. Let **Z** denote the integers, and let O_p be the set of basic operations of the imperative or functional program as follows.

Step: Op $\longrightarrow$ **Z** specifies a temporal distribution of the program's operations. Operations that are mapped to the same step number are performed in parallel.

Place: $O_p \longrightarrow \mathbf{Z}^{r-1}$ specifies a spatial distribution of the program's operations. The dimension of the layout space is one less than the number of arguments of the operations.

The challenge is in the determination of optimal parallelism, i.e., of a step function with the fewest number of steps possible. The methods accomplish this mechanically. After the derivation of *step*, the distribution in time, one chooses a compatible distribution in space by a search. With this choice, one can optimize other aspects of the array, e.g., its throughput, number of processors or channels or storage registers per processor, and so on.

When *step* and *place* are linear functions, we can tell a lot from their definition. To represent an implementable systolic design, step and every dimension of *place* must be linearly independent (Huang and Lengauer *et al.*, 1991); if so, every processor of the array is required to execute at most one operation per step. Other information about the systolic array can also be determined from linear *step* and *place*, notably the flow direction and layout of the data.

Let V be the set of variables of the program.

Flow: $V \longrightarrow Z^{r-1}$ specifies the direction and distance that variables travel at each step. It is defined as follows: if variable v is accessed by distinct basic operations s_0 and s_1 then

$$\text{flow } (v) = (\text{place}(s_1) - \text{place}(s_0)) \, / \, (\text{step}(s_1) - \text{step}(s_0))$$

Flow is only well-defined if the choice of the pair $< s_0, s_1 >$ is immaterial. If necessary, an appropriate scaling of place will make flow (v) an integer vector.

Pattern: $V \longrightarrow Z^{r-1}$ specifies the location of variables in the layout space at the first step. It is defined as follows: if variable v is accessed by basic operation s and fs is the number of the first step then

$$pattern(v) = \text{place}(s) - (\text{step}(s) - fs) \cdot \text{flow } (v)$$

Pattern is only well-defined if the choice of s is immaterial. If flow is well-defined, so is pattern (Huang and Lengauer, 1987).

8.3 The application

Our application is taken from image processing. In the processing of images, the **pyramid** is a useful concept. A pyramid is a hierarchical data structure with rectangular arrays of nodes in a sequence of levels. Image resolution decreases as we move from the bottom level (finest) to the top level (coarsest), as shown in Fig. 8.1. The image to be processed is stored in the base level of the pyramid; each pixel is one node. The values of the nodes can be the grey level, local standard deviation or an edge map, among others. The values of the nodes at higher levels of the pyramid are computed by averaging the values of the nodes, in some neighbourhood, at the level below. The node that is calculated this way is referred to as the **father** of the nodes in the neighbourhood of the lower level, and the nodes

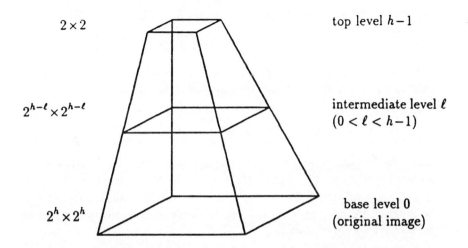

2×2

top level $h-1$

$2^{h-\ell} \times 2^{h-\ell}$

intermediate level ℓ
$(0 < \ell < h-1)$

$2^h \times 2^h$

base level 0
(original image)

Figure 8.1 Structure of a pyramid. The base level contains the original image. The level number is given on the right, the size of each level in pixels on the left.

of that neighbourhood are called the **sons** of the node at the upper level. This averaging process is repeated until values for the nodes at the top level have been determined. The nodes at the base level have no sons, and the nodes at the top level have no fathers.

The algorithm that we have just described is called **pyramid initialization**; it will be the object of our systolization. As we have already pointed out, a pyramid initialized in this way can be used to segment the image into regions of roughly equal nodes, but we shall not get into that here. We need to specify pyramid initialization more formally.

8.4 The specification

Assuming that the original image has $2^h \times 2^h$ pixels, where h is a non-zero natural number, an h-level pyramid, with the levels numbered bottom to top 0 to $h-1$, is initialized by taking the averages of a $2c \times 2c$ area of level $l-1$ to generate a node at level l; the natural non-zero number c is called the **span factor** (Grosky and Jain, 1986), and l ($0 < l < h$) is the level being initialized. The span factor determines the amount of overlapping used in the averaging of the sons; in our case, $c = 2$ results in 50% overlapping.

Let us denote the node at point (i, j) at level l by the triple $[i, j, l]$. If the property that we are interested in is P, initialization is mathematically described as follows (assuming $c = 2$):

$$P([i, j, l]) = \frac{1}{numsons([i, j, l])} \left[\sum_{i'=2i-2}^{2i+1} \sum_{j'=2j-2}^{2j+1} P([i', j', l-1]) \right]$$

$$0 < l < h, 0 \leq i, j < 2^{h-l} \qquad (8.1)$$

The nodes indexed by $[i', j', l-1]$ are the sons of $[i,j,l]$, which is in turn used in determining the values of four nodes located at

$$[i \text{ div } 2, j \text{ div } 2, l + 1], \qquad [i \text{ div } 2, j \text{ div } 2 + 1, l + 1], \qquad (8.2)$$

$$[i \text{ div } 2 + 1, j \text{ div } 2, l + 1], \qquad [i \text{ div } 2 + 1, j \text{ div } 2 + 1, l + 1]$$

where div denotes integer division. These four nodes are the fathers of the node $[i, j, l]$. In (8.1) $numsons([i, j, l])$ is the number of valid sons of $[i, j, l]$ ($numsons([i, j, l]) \leq (2c)^2$); nodes that fall outside the image's boundaries are not considered. Thus, the nodes on the edges of the image have fewer sons and fathers.

8.5 The source program

The following program performs pyramid initialization:

```
for l from 1 to h − 1 do
    for i from 0 to 2^{h-l} − 1 do
        for j from 0 to 2^{h-l} − 1 do
            for i' from 2i − 2 to 2i + 1 do
                for j' from 2j − 2 to 2j + 1 do
                    l : i : j : i' : j'
            l : i : j
```

Index l enumerates the levels of the pyramid, bottom to top; i and j enumerate the nodes at each level; i' and j' enumerate their sons. The operations $l : i : j : i' : j'$ and $l : i : j$ are defined as follows:

$$l : i : j : i' : j' \;::\; node_{i,j,l} := node_{i,j,l} + node_{i',j',l-1}$$
$$l : i : j \;::\; node_{i,j,l} := node_{i,j,l} /16$$

We indicate scoping by indenting: operation $l : i : j : i' : j'$ is the only statement of the loop on j', and $l : i : j$ is the last statement of the loop on j.

The original image is assumed loaded into array elements $node_{i,j,0}$ ($0 \leq i, j < 2^h$) at the start of the computation. The elements of node at higher levels of the pyramid are assumed initialized to zero. The computation of these levels follows the problem description in the previous section, see equation (8.1). We have replaced variable $numsons$ by the constant 16, i.e., $(2c)^2$, disregarding border conditions. We shall later explain why this is legitimate (section 8.9.1).

8.6 Towards a systolic implementation

The methodical way to proceed is to produce a time-optimal systolic execution and choose a suitable processor layout. However, if one has a reasonable idea about the solution space, one might at this point already make a few observations and decisions about what the systolic array ought to look like.

The theory of systolic design tells us that a source program with five nested loops leads to a four-dimensional systolic array. If we choose the obvious processor layout – the one that dedicates one pixel of the image to each processor – the shape of the array will be as in Fig. 8.2. As is often the case with systolic arrays of many dimensions, the use of the individual processors is too infrequent to be efficient. By eliminating dimensions, i.e., by **projecting** the processor layout, we can increase processor utilization and save channels. We pay the price of an increased execution time.

We condense the array by eliminating two dimensions: First the dimension ranging over levels and then the dimension pairing father and son levels. Before applying the second projection, we scale the father level to the size of the son level, which yields the three-dimensional scheme

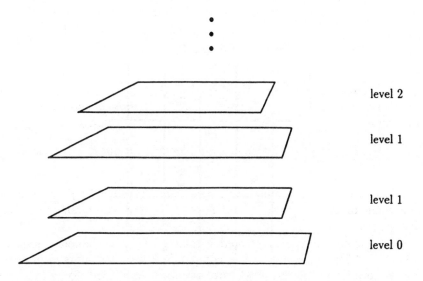

Figure 8.2 Sketch of the four-dimensional systolic array. Two dimensions range over the nodes in one level (drawn in perspective), the third ranges over levels and the fourth (with a constant range) pairs father and son levels.

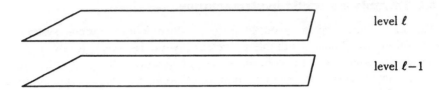

level ℓ

level $\ell-1$

Figure 8.3 Sketch of the three-dimensional systolic array. The missing dimension is the one over levels. That is, the array is for a fixed level l only.

depicted in Fig. 8.3. The two-dimensional systolic array is depicted in Fig. 8.4, viewed from the top.

Thus, the systolic array that we are aiming at consists of $2^h \times 2^h$ processors, one per pixel of the image. That is, each processor corresponds to a node at the base level of the pyramid. Initially, the property values of the image pixels are loaded into the array, each pixel at its respective node. Then the computations that occur at a fixed level of the pyramid are performed systolically and the same systolic array is reused iteratively for successive levels.

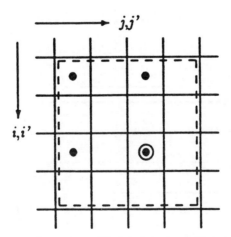

Figure 8.4 Top view of the two-dimensional systolic array. Nodes at level $l - 1$ are depicted as solid boxes, nodes at level l as fat dots. The node at level l that is the father of the 16-son neighbourhood indicated by the dashed box is highlighted with a circle.

At the transition between levels, the node array is reduced: three quarters of the nodes are discarded – the respective processors become inactive; in the rest of the execution, they are only used to pass along data. The remaining active processors are processing the next level. We choose the distribution of active processors such that data communicated at the transition between levels are stationary, i.e., no channels are required for these communications (this choice is reviewed in section 8.10.1). Figure 8.4 shows that, to that end, at each level, the active processors must be evenly distributed throughout the $2^h \times 2^h$ array.

8.7 Adaptation of the source program

We must modify the source program in order to steer our systolic design method towards producing this array.

8.7.1 Fixing the level

To effect a projection, we must eliminate a loop from the program. We eliminate the dimension on levels by dropping the outer loop. We drop also the corresponding argument of the basic statement (it becomes constant):

$$\text{for } i \text{ from } 0 \text{ to } 2^{h-l} - 1 \text{ do}$$
$$\text{for } j \text{ from } 0 \text{ to } 2^{h-l} - 1 \text{ do}$$
$$\text{for } i' \text{ from } 2i - 2 \text{ to } 2i+1 \text{ do}$$
$$\text{for } j' \text{ from } 2j - 2 \text{ to } 2j + 1 \text{ do}$$
$$i : j : i' : j'$$
$$i : j$$

Nothing else has to change, but the systolic solution is now only for one step of the outer loop. The combination of successive steps of that loop is not anymore under the control of the method and must be specified externally. To do so, one must make sure that the output data of one step are available as input data to the next step. This is easiest, if one arranges these data to be stationary (as we do in our array). Otherwise, complicated additional channel patterns may be necessary.

8.7.2 Scaling

At level l, the index space of the sons is of size $2^{h-l+1} \times 2^{h-l+1}$, that of the fathers of size $2^{h-l} \times 2^{h-l}$. Remember our decision to extend the index space of the fathers to that of the sons, doubling the distance between neighbouring fathers. We transform the source program to scale the indices i and j of the father level l by 2 with respect to the son level $l - 1$.

The semantics-preserving transformation for scaling the steps of a loop

$$\text{for } x \text{ from } rb \text{ by } st \text{ to } lb \text{ do } f(x)$$

by a factor *fac* is:

$$\text{for } x_{new} \text{ from } fac \cdot rb \text{ by } fac \cdot st \text{ to } fac \cdot lb \text{ do } f(x_{new}/fac)$$

We must scale the loops on i and j by 2. With simplification, the previous transformation scheme yields:

$$
\begin{aligned}
&\text{for } i \text{ from } 0 \text{ by } 2 \text{ to } 2^{h-l+1} - 2 \text{ do} \\
&\quad \text{for } j \text{ from } 0 \text{ by } 2 \text{ to } 2^{h-l+1} - 2 \text{ do} \\
&\qquad \text{for } i' \text{ from } i - 2 \text{ to } i+1 \text{ do} \\
&\qquad\quad \text{for } j' \text{ from } j - 2 \text{ to } j + 1 \text{ do} \\
&\qquad\qquad (i/2) : (j/2) : i' : j' \\
&\qquad\qquad (i/2) : (j/2)
\end{aligned}
$$

This scales the loop steps; to actually scale the indices of array node, i.e., distribute the fathers over a $2^{h-l+1} \times 2^{h-l+1}$ range, we simply omit the fractions of 2:

$$
\begin{aligned}
&\text{for } i \text{ from } 0 \text{ by } 2 \text{ to } 2^{h-l+1} - 2 \text{ do} \\
&\quad \text{for } j \text{ from } 0 \text{ by } 2 \text{ to } 2^{h-l+1} - 2 \text{ do} \\
&\qquad \text{for } i' \text{ from } i - 2 \text{ to } i+1 \text{ do} \\
&\qquad\quad \text{for } j' \text{ from } j - 2 \text{ to } j + 1 \text{ do} \\
&\qquad\qquad i : j : i' : j' \\
&\quad i : j
\end{aligned}
$$

This does not preserve the semantics of the program, but it does preserve its input-output behaviour with respect to the son level. By induction on levels, the input-output behaviour with respect to the base level (the image) is preserved. Later, we shall stretch the systolic array for level l to size $2^h \times 2^h$ by coding a factor of 2^{l-1} into the place function (section 8.9.1).

We make one more change that is merely stylistic; it does not affect the program's semantics. To match the range of fathers precisely with that of sons, we extend the upper bound of the loops on i and j by 1:

$$
\begin{aligned}
&\text{for } i \text{ from } 0 \text{ to } 2^{h-l+1} - 1 \text{ do} \\
&\quad \text{for } j \text{ from } 0 \text{ by } 2 \text{ to } 2^{h-l+1} - 1 \text{ do} \\
&\qquad \text{for } i' \text{ from } i - 2 \text{ to } i + 1 \text{ do} \\
&\qquad\quad \text{for } j' \text{ from } j - 2 \text{ to } j + 1 \text{ do} \\
&\qquad\qquad i : j : i' : j' \\
&\quad i : j
\end{aligned}
$$

Scaling is one of the ways of transforming an affine to a uniform recurrence (Rajopadhye, 1990) (other ways are reflection, translation, rotation, permutation, and so on). In this sense, it can be viewed as a syntactic adaptation.

8.7.3 Loop elimination

We still have four loops – one too many for a two-dimensional array. This time, we collapse the inner two loops on i' and j', which iterate through the sons, to one. This is a more complex adjustment than dropping the outer loop. We have several choices. Each of the two inner loops has four steps; each step performs one cumulative addition. We can form one loop of 16 steps, or we can enlarge the basic operation to perform more than one cumulative addition.

We choose to let the new basic operation perform not one but four cumulative additions. We rearrange these additions such that each step of the new single loop sums up one quadrant of the 16 sons. We are justified in doing so, because addition is commutative. We make this choice because the notion of a quadrant is central to pyramid initialization: a quadrant is the unit of overlap of neighbourhoods.

The new loop has index k; $k = 0$ selects the lower right quadrant, $k = 1$ the upper right, $k = 2$ the lower left, and $k = 3$ the upper left (Fig. 8.5). To access quadrants correctly, we modify indices i and j by selector functions (in k) to $\bar{\imath}$ and $\bar{\jmath}$:

$$\bar{\imath} = i - 2 \cdot (k \bmod 2)$$
$$\bar{\jmath} = j - 2 \cdot (k \operatorname{div} 2)$$

For each value of k, the basic computation sums one quadrant of the array of 16 sons:

$$i : j : k :: \text{node}_{i,j,l} := \text{node}_{i,j,l} + \text{node}_{\bar{\imath},\bar{\jmath},l-1} + \text{node}_{\bar{\imath},\bar{\jmath}+1,l-1}$$
$$+ \text{node}_{\bar{\imath}+1,\bar{\jmath},l-1} + \text{node}_{\bar{\imath}+1,\bar{\jmath}+1,l-1}$$

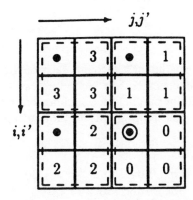

Figure 8.5 A neighbourhood divided into quadrants. Numbers indicate the value of k at which the sons are accumulated. The nodes of each quadrant have identical fathers, e.g., the four fathers in the picture are shared by the nodes of the upper left quadrant ($k=3$).

The three nested loops then look as follows:

$$\text{for } i \text{ from } 0 \text{ by } 2 \text{ to } 2^{h-l+1} - 1 \text{ do}$$
$$\text{for } j \text{ from } 0 \text{ by } 2 \text{ to } 2^{h-l+1} - 1 \text{ do}$$
$$\text{for } k \text{ from } 0 \text{ to } 3 \text{ do}$$
$$i : j : k$$
$$i : j$$

8.7.4 One basic operation

We must make the loop structure conform with the requirements on the source format for a systolic design (section 8.2.1): $i : j$ is the offender. We need to absorb $i : j$ into $i : j : k$. To do this, we extend the range of the inner loop by one step and redefine $i : j : k$ as follows:

$$i : j : k :: \text{if } k < 4 \rightarrow \text{comp}(i, j, k)$$
$$[]\ k = 4 \rightarrow \text{divide}(i, j)$$
$$\text{fi}$$

where comp(i, j, k) is the previous $i : j : k$, and divide(i, j) is the previous $i : j$

$$\text{comp}(i, j, k) :: \text{node}_{i,j,l} := \text{node}_{i,j,l} + \text{node}_{i,j,l-1} + \text{node}_{i,j,+1,l-1}$$
$$+ \text{node}_{i+1,j,l-1} + \text{node}_{i+1,j+1,l-1}$$
$$\text{divide}(i, j) :: \text{node}_{i,j,l} := \text{node}_{i,j,}\,/16$$

Now, the program has only one basic operation :

$$\text{for } i \text{ from } 0 \text{ by } 2 \text{ to } 2^{h-l+1} - 1 \text{ do}$$
$$\text{for } j \text{ from } 0 \text{ by } 2 \text{ to } 2^{h-l+1} - 1 \text{ do}$$
$$\text{for } k \text{ from } 0 \text{ to } 4 \text{ do}$$
$$i : j : k$$

8.7.5 Commutation

Our present program scans linearly through each of the two dimensions of the father level. Conflicts caused by shared accesses of adjacent loop steps reduce the potential for parallelism dramatically. We break the linear progression by moving the loop on k to the outside (again, simply rearranging additions):

$$\text{for } k \text{ from } 0 \text{ to } 4 \text{ do}$$
$$\text{for } i \text{ from } 0 \text{ by } 2 \text{ to } 2^{h-l+1} - 1 \text{ do}$$
$$\text{for } j \text{ from } 0 \text{ by } 2 \text{ to } 2^{h-l+1} - 1 \text{ do}$$
$$i : j : k$$

Commutations are among the most difficult and crucial transformations for an effective systolic design (Huang and Lengauer, 1987; Grosky and Jain, 1986). Source programs, whether imperatively or functionally phrased, tend to overspecify sequencing. This is illustrated most simply with the matrix product: $c = a \times b$. The specification

$$(\forall i, j : 0 < i, j \leqslant n : c_{i,j} = (\Sigma k : 0 < k \leqslant n : a_{i,k} \cdot b_{k,j}))$$

permits cumulative additions in any order (because addition is commutative), but the data dependences in any source program, e.g.,

$$\text{for } i \text{ from 1 to } n \text{ do}$$
$$\text{for } j \text{ from 1 by } n \text{ do}$$
$$\text{for } k \text{ from 1 to } n \text{ do}$$
$$i : j : k$$

whether phrased imperatively, i.e., with basic operation (Huang and Lengauer, 1987)

$$i : j : k :: c_{i,j} := c_{i,j} + a_{i,k} * b_{k,j}$$

(where the $c_{i,j}$ are initialized with zero and the $a_{i,k}$ and $b_{k,j}$ with the input) or functionally, i.e., with basic operation (Quinton and van Dongen, 1989)

$$i : j : k :: a_{i,j,k} = a_{i,j-1,k}$$
$$b_{i,j,k} = b_{i-1,j,k}$$
$$c_{i,j,k} = c_{i,j,k-1} + a_{i,j,k} * b_{i,j,k}$$

(where the $c_{i,j,0}$ are zero and the $a_{i,0,k}$ and $b_{0,j,k}$ hold the input), impose a specific partial order which may adversely affect the outcome of a systolic design. For example, in the case of band matrices, index k should be counted down rather than up (Huang and Lengauer, 1987).

The size of the search space makes the systematic identification of useful commutations a particular challenge which has not been addressed by mechanical systolic design methods so far. A desirable specification would be an unordered source program, as is possible in GAMMA (Banâtre *et al.*, 1988; Banâtre and Mètayer, 1990) in the applicative and Unity (Chandy and Misra, 1988) in the imperative style. But these languages are too general to support an implemented scheme of systolic design. They leave too many implementation choices because they are targetted at a much wider range of architectures than systolic arrays. To support the mechanical development of systolic implementations, we need to address issues in the specification that need not be addressed in GAMMA or Unity programs. One requirement is that a dependence graph (Rao and Kailath, 1988) must be constructable from a specification at that level.

8.7.6 Increasing independence

The crucial property for the infusion of parallelism into programs is independence. The usual independence criterion for systolic design – and the one imposed by the requirement of uniformity on recurrences – is the absence of shared variables. In our program, the computations comp(i, j, k) for each of the four quadrants ($k = 0, 1, 2, 3$) are not independent because they share the target variable node$_{i,j,l}$. This may (and indeed does) reduce the potential for parallelism. We increase the potential for parallelism by giving each quadrant its own target variable $z.k_{i,j,l-1}$. To set the new index k apart from the three indices into the pyramid, we do not subscribe it but attach it by an infix period:

$$\text{comp}(i, j, k) :: z.k_{i,j,l-1} :=$$
$$\text{node}_{i,j,l-1} + \text{node}_{i,j+1,l-1} + \text{node}_{i+1,j,l-1} + \text{node}_{i+1,j+1,l-1}$$

Computation divide(i, j) must then read $z.k$ instead of **node**. Since the read values are now in four separate variables, we must read all four variables and add them:

$$\text{divide}(i, j) :: \text{node}_{i,j,l} := (z.0_{i,j,l-1} + z.1_{i,j,l-1} + z.2_{i,j,l-1} + z.3_{i,j,l-1})/16$$

Now, the computations comp(i, j, k) of different quadrants ($k = 0, 1, 2, 3$) are mutually independent.

8.7.7 Eliminating applications of comp

If a computation is applied to the same arguments more than once, some of these applications can be eliminated. To preserve the semantics of the program, a computation that reads target variables of applications to be eliminated must be changed to read variables of the remaining applications instead. We must be careful when targeting computations for an elimination. A wrong choice can degrade parallelism or increase the cost of communication. At present, no generally successful methods are known.

Computations comp$(i, j, 0)$, comp$(i+2, j, 1)$, comp$(i, j+2, 2)$, and comp$(i+2, j+2, 3)$ all accumulate the same quadrant:

$$z.0_{i,j,l-1} = z.1_{i+2,j,l-1} = z.2_{i,j+2,l-1} = z.3_{i+2,j+2,l-1}$$

We only need to perform one of these computations and can eliminate the other three. We arbitrarily choose one of $z.0$, $z.1$, $z.2$ and $z.3$ – we choose $z.0$ and rename it to z (omitting the constant index). This means that we choose to compute comp$(i, j, 0)$; again, we can omit the constant third argument. In **divide**, we select for each $z.k$ ($k = 0, 1, 2, 3$), when transforming it to z, the indices of the corresponding $z.0$ (by the previous equations). This leaves us with:

$$\text{comp}(i, j) :: z_{i,j,l-1} :=$$
$$\text{node}_{i,j,l-1} + \text{node}_{i,j+1,l-1} + \text{node}_{i+1,j,l-1} + \text{node}_{i+1,j+1,l-1}$$
$$\text{divide}(i, j) :: \text{node}_{i,j,l} := (z_{i,j,l-1} + z_{i,j-2,l-1} + z_{i-2,j,l-1} + z_{i-2,j-2,l-1})/16$$

Note that there is no further need to use the selector functions.

Due to the elimination of three quarters of the computations, the loop on k is now reduced to two steps. The new basic operation is defined as follows:

$$i : j : k :: \text{if } k = 0 \rightarrow \text{comp}(i, j)$$
$$[] \ k = 1 \rightarrow \text{divide}(i, j)$$
$$\text{fi}$$

8.7.8 Decomposing divide

Note that **comp** and **divide** each perform three additions in sequence. Basic operations are atomic; their insides are not subject to a parallelization in systolic design. To increase the possibility of parallelism, we can decompose the sequence of additions into smaller computations which will be applied alternatively in the basic operation and which, therefore, may be subject to a parallelization. Let us first deal with divide this way. We are going to consider comp in the next subsection.

Observe that divide(i, j) and divide$(i+2, j)$ both add $z_{i,j,l-1}$ and $z_{i,j-2,l-1}$. Similarly, divide(i, j) and divide$(i, j+2)$ both add $z_{i,j,l-1}$ and $z_{i-2,j,l-1}$. By breaking divide up, we can save some of these additions. We decompose the sequence of additions in divide(i, j) into a tree that is composed of two different computations:

$$\text{sub-divide}(i, j) :: a_{i,j,l-1} := z_{i,j,l-1} + z_{i,j-2,l-1}$$
$$\text{divide}(i, j) :: \text{node}_{i,j,l-1} := (a_{i,j,l-1} + a_{i-2,j,l-1})/16$$

At one leaf of the tree, the computation sub-divide(i, j), adds $z_{i,j,l-1}$ and $z_{i,j-2,l-1}$ at the other leaf, sub-divide$(i-2, j)$ adds $z_{i-2,j,l-1}$ and $z_{i-2,j-2,l-1}$. Finally, the new divide(i, j) adds the results of sub-divide(i, j) and sub-divide$(i-2, j)$, at the root of the tree. The basic operation $i : j : k$ becomes:

$$i : j : k :: \text{if } k = 0 \rightarrow \text{comp}(i, j)$$
$$[] \ k = 1 \rightarrow \text{sub-divide}(i, j)$$
$$[] \ k = 2 \rightarrow \text{divide}(i, j)$$
$$\text{fi}$$

Note that we have added on step to the loop on k again.

8.7.9 Decomposing comp

Similarly, we may increase parallelism by transforming the sequence of additions in **comp** into a tree of smaller computations:

$$\text{sub-comp}(i, j) :: c_{i,j,l-1} := \text{node}_{i,j,l-1} + \text{node}_{i,j+1,l-1}$$
$$\text{comp}(i, j) :: z_{i,j,l-1} := c_{i,j,l-1} + c_{i+1,j,l-1}$$

The two leaves of the tree apply **sub-comp**, the root applies **comp**. There are twice as many applications of sub-comp as of comp: twice as many as there are nodes at the father level and half as many as there are nodes at the son level.

Incorporating the decomposition of comp correctly into the program requires a rather complex transformation. Since there are more applications of sub-comp than there are father nodes, we must accommodate them at the son level, whose index space is large enough. A regrettable consequence is that the loops on i and j must be converted to range over sons, not fathers. The resulting program is rather complex. We cannot simply eliminate the scaling factor of 2 that we have introduced earlier; that would corrupt the operations comp that are applied only for fathers. Instead, we use the evenness or oddness of i and j and the value of k, in combination, as the program counter. We must decide to which node to attach the two computations sub-comp on which computation comp(i, j) depends. Let us choose nodes $[i, j]$ and $[i+1, j]$; we shall see that this results in a pleasingly regular channel layout. The basic operation $i : j : k$ is then defined as follows:

$$
\begin{aligned}
i : j : k :: \ \text{if} \ & k = 0 && \wedge \ j \ \text{even} \rightarrow \text{sub-comp}(i, j) \\
[] \ & k = 1 \wedge i \ \text{even} \wedge j \ \text{even} \rightarrow \text{comp}(i, j) \\
[] \ & k = 2 \wedge i \ \text{even} \wedge j \ \text{even} \rightarrow \text{sub-divide}(i, j) \\
[] \ & k = 3 \wedge i \ \text{even} \wedge j \ \text{even} \rightarrow \text{divide}(i, j) \\
[] \ & \text{else} \rightarrow \text{skip} \\
& \text{fi}
\end{aligned}
$$

As we mentioned before, i and j now range over sons, i.e., the step specification in the loops disappear:

$$
\begin{aligned}
& \text{for} \ k \ \text{from} \ 0 \ \text{to} \ 3 \ \text{do} \\
& \quad \text{for} \ i \ \text{from} \ 0 \ \text{to} \ 2^{h-l+1} - 1 \ \text{do} \\
& \quad \quad \text{for} \ j \ \text{from} \ 0 \ \text{to} \ 2^{h-l+1} - 1 \ \text{do} \\
& \quad \quad \quad i : j : k
\end{aligned}
$$

The decompositions of divide and comp exploit the associativity of addition to increase the uniformity of data flows; they also reduce the degree of fan-in in the systolic array (Chen 1986). The decomposition of divide also removes broadcasts of variable z (Wong and Deslome, 1988).

8.7.10 Renaming variables

The program contains one more violation of the required source format: variables are referred to with different subscripts by the same basic operation. To prevent that, we must introduce new variable names. When a computation refers to a variable twice with distinct subscripts, we rename one of the occurrences by attaching an m. (We arrange things such that the so renamed variables are moving through the systolic array, while the variables that keep the old names are stationary.)

When introducing new variables, we must make sure that they are initialized before they are read. This requires the introduction of additional operations.

With our system, we have to perform these adjustments by hand. Recently techniques for their mechanization have been developed (Quinton and van Dongen, 1989; Rajopadhye, 1989).

In the final program for pyramid initialization, the one that we submit to the systolic design method, paired target variables denote a multiple assignment (Gries, 1978) of the right-hand side to both components of the pair:

Computations:

$$\text{copy-node}(i, j) :: \text{nodem}_{i,j,l-1} := \text{node}_{i,j,l-1}$$
$$\text{sub-comp}(i, j) :: (c_{i,j,l-1}\ cm_{i,\,j,\,l-1}) := \text{node}_{i,j,l-1} + \text{nodem}_{i,j+1,l-1}$$
$$\text{comp}(i, j) :: (z_{i,j,l-1}, zm_{i,j,l-1}) := c_{i,j,l-1} + cm_{i+1,j,l-1}$$
$$\text{sub-divide}(i, j) :: (a_{i,j,l-1}, am_{i,j,l-1}) := z_{i,j,l-1} + zm_{i,j-2,l-1}$$
$$\text{divide}(i, j) :: \text{node}_{i,j,l} := (a_{i,j,l-1} + am_{i-2,j,l-1}) / 16$$

Basic operation:

$$
\begin{aligned}
i : j : k :: &\text{ if } k = 0 && \wedge j \text{ odd} \rightarrow \text{copy-node}(i, j) \\
&[\!]\ k = 1 && \wedge j \text{ even} \rightarrow \text{sub-comp}(i, j) \\
&[\!]\ k = 2 \wedge i \text{ even} \wedge j \text{ even} \rightarrow \text{comp}(i, j) \\
&[\!]\ k = 3 \wedge i \text{ even} \wedge j \text{ even} \rightarrow \text{sub-divide}(i, j) \\
&[\!]\ k = 4 \wedge i \text{ even} \wedge j \text{ even} \rightarrow \text{divide}(i, j) \\
&[\!] \text{ else} \rightarrow \text{skip} \\
&\text{fi}
\end{aligned}
$$

Loops:

$$
\begin{aligned}
&\text{for } k \text{ from 0 to 4 do} \\
&\quad \text{for } i \text{ from 0 to } 2^{h-l+1} - 1 \text{ do} \\
&\quad\quad \text{for } j \text{ from 0 to } 2^{h-l+1} - 1 \text{ do} \\
&\quad\quad\quad i : j : k
\end{aligned}
$$

8.8 Independence

The infusion of parallelism into the program exploits mutual independences of the program's operations. In the imperative method, we must specify these independences (Huang and Lengauer, 1987). In the functional method, one specifies the dependences instead (Quinton and Van Dongen, 1989). The usual independence criterion for systolic design is the absence of shared variable accesses. This accounts for the stream processing and the lack of shared memory in systolic arrays (Huang and Lengauer, 1987).

The arguments of the basic operation are i, j and k. We must exclude any two basic operations with the same pair i and j. In the layout that we have in mind (section 8.6), they will be mapped to the same processor and can therefore not be applied in parallel or an inconsistency of *step* and *place* results (section 8.2.2). For varying i, j and fixed k, all operations are mutually independent. For varying i, j and varying k, there is some independence, but declaring it does not alter the step function (we tried). Consequently, we declare:

$$i_0 \neq i_1 \text{ V } j_0 \neq j_1 \Longrightarrow i_0 : j_0 : k \text{ ind } i_1 : j_1 : k$$

8.9 The systolic array

8.9.1 For a fixed level

We are considering level l ($0<l<h$). With the previous program and independence declaration, our method generates the following temporal distribution:[1]

$$\text{step}(i : j : k) = k$$

We can choose a spatial distribution. The processor layout that we had in mind all along is place$(i : j : k) = (i, j)$ but, as mentioned in section 8.7.2, we scale the processor layout of level l by a factor of 2^{l-1}:

$$\text{place}(i : j : k) = (i, j) \cdot 2^{l-1}$$

If the determinant of the linear coefficients for the loop indices i, j and k is not zero, functions *step* and *place* are consistent (Huang and Lengauer, 1987):

$$\begin{vmatrix} 0 & 0 & 1 \\ 2^{l-1} & 0 & 0 \\ 0 & 2^{l-1} & 0 \end{vmatrix} = 2^{2 \cdot (l-1)} \neq 0$$

The data flows computed from *step* and *place* are:

$$
\begin{aligned}
\text{flow}(\text{node}_{i,j,l}) &= (0, 0) \\
\text{flow}(\text{node}_{i,j,l-1}) &= (0, 0) \\
\text{flow}(\text{nodem}_{i,j,l-1}) &= (0, -1) \cdot 2^{l-1} \\[4pt]
\text{flow}(c_{i,j,l-1}) &= (0, 0) \\
\text{flow}(cm_{i,j,l-1}) &= (-1, 0) \cdot 2^{l-1} \\[4pt]
\text{flow}(z_{i,j,l-1}) &= (0, 0) \\
\text{flow}(zm_{i,j,l-1}) &= (0, 2) \cdot 2^{l-1} \\[4pt]
\text{flow}(a_{i,j,l-1}) &= (0, 0) \\
\text{flow}(am_{i,j,l-1}) &= (2, 0) \cdot 2^{l-1}
\end{aligned}
$$

---

[1] Our present implementation returns *step* only for a fixed size, but mechanical techniques of generalization can reveal the general definition (Lengauer *et al.*, 1991)

Figures 8.6 and 8.7 sketch the array and its execution. In Fig. 8.6, all internal and input connections of the depicted array segment are shown; the output connections follow by repetition. Arrows that are partly dashed indicate channel connections between non-neighbours.

By linking the borders of the array, following the internal connection pattern, to form a torus (i.e., left with right and top with bottom), we are justified in disregarding border conditions in the specification of the problem (section 8.5) and development of the systolic array. Experiments have shown that this trick does not corrupt the processing of the border areas of the image (Hong and Rosenfeld, 1984).

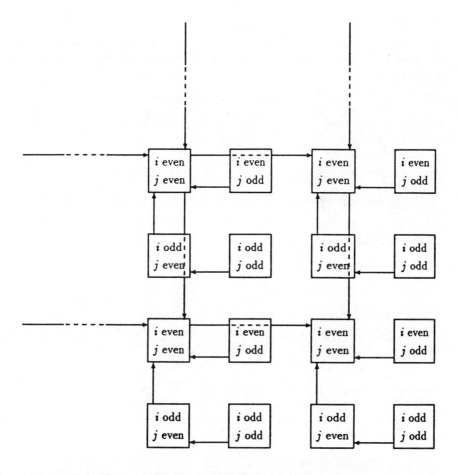

Figure 8.6 The systolic array. All internal and input connections of the depicted array segment are shown; the output connections follow by repetition. Arrows that are partly dashed indicate channel connections between non-neighbours.

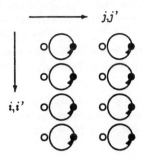

Step 0: *copy-node*

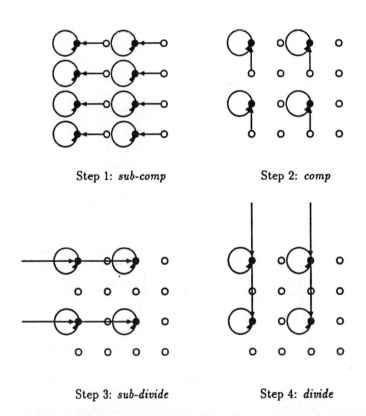

Step 1: *sub-comp*   Step 2: *comp*

Step 3: *sub-divide*   Step 4: *divide*

Figure 8.7 The five execution steps of the systolic array. All input communications are shown. Circular arrows indicate stationary input. Fat dots indicate active, circles inactive processors.

8.9.2 Composition of levels

This section contains an informal description that has not been derived with our method.

Levels are composed in sequence. Their systolic arrays are superimposed. The highest level of the pyramid stored at the processor (i, j) is given by:

$$u(i, j) = \min\{p(i), p(j)\} \text{ where } p(x) = \begin{cases} h - 1 & \text{if } x = 0 \\ \max\{n \mid n \in \mathbf{N}, 2^n \leq x\} & \text{if } x > 0 \end{cases}$$

The set of nodes held by the processor is:

$$\{\text{node}_{i/2^l, j/2^l, j} \mid 0 \leq i, j < 2^h, 0 \leq l \leq u(i, j)\}$$

We need not install separate channels for every level, even though, at first sight, the scaling factor seems to require it. The dormant processors that lie between two neighbouring active processors at level l can be used for routing. This means that the communication time increases for increasing level numbers.

8.10 Conclusions

8.10.1 On the systolic array

This is the first systolic array for pyramidal algorithms that we are aware of; some ideas of the layout and style of transformations originate in an earlier attempt at systolizing pyramid initialization (Lengauer *et al.*, 1990). The gain in execution speed is substantial: a quadratic dependence on the size of the image of the sequential execution has been eliminated – the length of the systolic execution is independent of the size of the image! But there remains a linear dependence on the height of the pyramid. For a fixed-size image, there is also an inverse linear dependence on the number of regions to be detected (with an additional increase in communication as activity in the array becomes sparser).

We do expect that the array, as specified, will become a practical possibility in hardware or software in the not too distant future.

Hardware: The processors required need to be able to hold some floating point numbers, perform logical, integer and floating point operations and connect their input to their output channels when they become dormant. And they need to be available in numbers of $2^h \times 2^h$.

Software: Present programmable processor networks do not fit the requirements of this systolic array. Either they offer close to the number but not the sophistication that is required of the processors, e.g., programmable gate arrays like the Computational Array Logic (Gray and

Kean, 1989; Kean and Gray, 1990; Xilinx, 1991; Altera, 1991), or they offer too few processors that are too powerful, e.g., transputer networks (Graham and King, 1990). We expect this gap to be filled; two suitable architectures are under development: Mosaic (Seitz, 1990) and the Rewrite Rule Machine (Aida *et al.*, 1990). For the use of transputers, one can partition the array, i.e., map several array cells to the same transputer – of course, at an expense of execution speed (a dependence on the image size is reintroduced). We have also derived a solution that accommodates the present restriction of only four channels per transputer.

Adapting the algorithm for a rectangular, not a square image is a minor modification, as long as one sticks to 4 × 4 neighbourhoods of sons.

Let us briefly review our decision to deviate from the traditional specification by imposing a scaling of the levels (section 8.7.9). Our main reason was to avoid communications between levels by making the variables that are the subject of an inter-level communication stationary. (An array that is not scaled requires additional, complex channel connections for interphase communications.) The price we pay is an increase in the distance of intra-level communications as the level number increases and the activity in the systolic array becomes sparser. However, the non-scaled array exhibits a similar increase in the distance of inter-level communications. One pleasing property of our solution is its symmetry, which makes a partitioning of the array very easy: intra-level communications up to a level that depends on the width of the partitions become local to one processor.

8.10.2 On the method

Even though a mechanical method was used, the derivation of this systolic array still involved a significant amount of preparation. The source program had to be tailored for the mechanical method. Still, the use of the method was invaluable. It made our development quicker and more precise (by use of an implementation of the method), and it gave us immediate faith in the correctness of the systolic array.

It would be wrong to claim that our transformations of the source program were motivated merely syntactically (i.e., to satisfy the requirements of the method). Many aim at a specific – not just any – systolic array. These transformations required some understanding of the range of systolic solutions. If this understanding does not exist *a priori*, the use of the method helps us acquire it by deriving less desirable solutions first. Carrying out this search in the comparatively simple setting of sequential programs is a significant advantage.

In our choice of transformations, we have given the benefit of parallelism higher priority than the cost of communication. In a setting (in hardware or software) where communication is a lot more expensive than computation, some of our transformations are better omitted (e.g., section 8.7.9).

We selected a particular processor layout at the start of the development (section 8.6) and simplified the independence declaration, knowing that it would serve this processor layout (section 8.8). Systolic design methods are even more useful for searching the space of all processor layouts based on a general independence criterion (for example, our treatment of Gauss-Jordan elimination - Huang and Lengauer, 1989).

The example of image segmentation becomes much more substantial when one considers the subsequent phases of the algorithm (Lengauer and Xue, 1991). The fact that the second author developed a variety of systolic arrays for this problem in a relatively short time – a couple of weeks – without previous experience in systolic design or image processing leads us to believe that the use of present-day systolic design methods may be feasible in real-world applications.

Acknowledgements

Thanks to D. Rogers and J. W. Sanders for discussions and comments.

Xue and Lengauer are supported by the Science and Engineering Research Council, Grant no. GR/G55457. Xue is also supported by a University of Edinburgh Postgraduate Fellowship.

References

Aida, H., Goguen, J. A., and Meseguer, J., 1990, Architectural design of the rewrite rule ensemble, in *Proc. Int. Workshop on VLSI for Artificial Intelligence and Neural Networks*, (eds J. Delgado-Frias and W. R. Moore). Also: Tech. Rep. SRI-CSL-90-17,

Altera Corporation, 1991, *Data Book*, Altera Corporation.

Benaini, A., and Robert, Y., 1990, Spacetime-minimal systolic architectures for gaussian elimination and the algebraic path problem, in *Application Specific Array Processors*, (eds S. Y. Kung and E. E. Swartzlander), IEEE Computer Society Press, 746–57.

Banâtre, J.-P., Coutant, A., and Le Métayer, D., 1988, A parallel machine for multiset transformation and its programming style, *Future Generation Computer Systems*, 4(2), September, 133–44.

Banâtre, J.-P., and Le Métayer, D., 1990, The gamma model and its discipline of programming, *Science of Computer Programming*, 15(1), November, 55–77.

Burt, P. J., Hong, T. H., and Rosenfeld, A., 1981, Segmentation and estimation of image region properties through cooperative hierarchical computation, *IEEE Trans. on Systems, Man and Cybernetics*, SMC-11(12), Dec., 802–9.

Chandy, K. M., and Misra, J., 1988, *Parallel Program Design*, Addison-Wesley, Reading.

Chen, M. C., 1986, A design methodology for synthesizing parallel algorithms and Architectures, *J. Parallel and Distributed Computing* **3**(4), Dec., 461–91.

Clauss, P., Mongenet, C., and Perrin, G. R., 1990, Calculus of space-optimal mappings of systolic algorithms on processor arrays, in *Application Specific Array Processors*, (eds S. Y. Kung and E. E. Swartzlander), IEEE Computer Society Press, 5–18.

Dijkstra, E. W., 1976, *A Discipline of Programming*, Series in Automatic Computation, Prentice-Hall, Englewood Cliffs.

van Dongen, V., 1989, Quasi-regular arrays: definition and design methodology, in *Proc. Int. Conf. on Systolic Array Processors*, Prentice-Hall, Englewood Cliffs, 126–35.

Fortes, J. A. B., Fu, K.-S., and Wah, B. W., 1988, Systematic design approaches for algorithmically specified systolic arrays, in *Computer Architecture – Concepts and Systems*, (ed. V. M. Milutinović), North-Holland, New York,, Chap. 11.

Graham I., and King, T., 1990, *The Transputer Handbook*, Prentice-Hall.

Gray, J. P., and Kean, T. A., 1989, Configurable hardware: a new paradigm for computation, in *Advanced Research in VLSI*, (ed. C. L. Seitz), MIT Press.

Gries, D., 1978, The multiple assignment statement, *IEEE Trans. on Software Engineering*, **SE-4**(2), Mar., 89–93.

Grosky, W. I., and Jain, R., 1986, A pyramid-based approach to segmentation applied to region matching, *IEEE Trans. on Pattern Analysis and Machine Intelligence*, **PAMI-8**(5), Sept., 639–50.

Hong, T. H., Narayanan, K. A., Peleg, S., and Rosenfeld, A., 1982, Image smoothing and segmentation by multiresolution pixel linking: further experiments and extensions, *IEEE Trans. on Systems, Man and Cybernetics*, **SMC-12**(5), May, 611–22.

Hong, T. H. and Rosenfeld, A., 1984, Compact region extraction using weighted pixel linking in a pyramid, *IEEE Trans. Pattern Analysis and Machine Intelligence*, **PAMI-6**(2), Mar., 222–9.

Huang, C.-H. and Lengauer, C., 1987, The derivation of systolic implementations of programs, *Acta Informatica*, **24**(6), Nov., 595–632.

Huang, C.-H., and Lengauer, C., 1989, An incremental mechanical development of systolic solutions to the algebraic path problem, *Acta Informatica*, **27**(2), Nov., 97–124.

Karp, R. M., Miller, R. E., and Winograd, S., 1967, The organization of computations for uniform recurrence equations, *J. ACM,* **14**(3), July, 563–90.

Kean T. A., and Gray, J. P., 1989, Configurable hardware: two case studies of micro-grain computation, *J. VLSI Signal Processing*, **2**(1), Sept., 9–16.

Kung, S.-Y., Lo, S.-C., and Lewis, P. S., 1987, Optimal systolic design for the transitive closure and shortest path problems, *IEEE Trans. on Computers*, **C-36**(5), May, 603–14.

Lamport, L., 1974, The parallel execution of DO loops, *Comm. ACM*, **17**(2), Feb., 83–93.

Lengauer, C., Barnett M., and Hudson, D. G., 1991, Towards systolizing compilation, *Distributed Computing*, **5**(1), 7–24.

Lengauer, C., Sabata B., and Arman, F., 1990, A mechanically derived systolic implementation of pyramid initialization, in *Proc. Workshop on Hardware Specification, Verification and Synthesis: Mathematical Aspects*, (eds G. Brown and M. Leeser), *Lecture Notes in Computer Science* **408**, Springer-Verlag, New York, 90–105.

Lengauer C., and Xue, J., 1991, A systolic array for pyramidal algorithms, *J. VLSI Signal Processing*, **3**(3), 239–59.

Quinton, P., 1984, Automatic synthesis of systolic arrays from uniform recurrent equations, in *Proc. 11th Ann. Int. Symp. on Computer Architecture*, IEEE Computer Society Press, New York, 208–14.

Quinton, P., and van Dongen, V., 1989, The mapping of linear recurrence equations on regular arrays, *J. VLSI Signal Processing*, **1**(2), Oct., 95–113.

Rajopadhye, S. V., 1989, Synthesizing systolic arrays with control signals from recurrence equations, *Distributed Computing*, **3**, 88–105.

Rajopadhye, S. V., 1990, Algebraic transformations in systolic array synthesis: a case study, in *Formal VLSI Specification and Synthesis (VLSI Design Methods-I)*, (ed. L. J. M. Claesen), North-Holland, Amsterdam, 361–70.

Rajopadhye, S. V., and Fujimoto, R. M., Synthesizing systolic arrays from recurrence equations, *Parallel Computing*, **14**(2), June, 163–89.

Rao, S. K. and Kailath, T., 1988, Regular iterative algorithms and their implementations on processor arrays, *Proc. IEEE*, **76**(2), Mar., 259–82.

Robert, Y., and Trystram, D., 1987, An orthogonal systolic array for the algebraic path problem, *Computing*, **39**(3), 187–99.

Rote, G., 1985, A systolic array algorithm for the algebraic path problem (shortest paths; matrix inversion)', *J. Computing*, **34**(3), 191–219.

Scheiman, C. J., and Cappello, P. R., 1990, A processor-time minimal systolic array for transitive closure, in *Application Specific Array Processors*, (eds S. Y. Kung and E. E. Swartzlander), IEEE Computer Society Press, 19–30.

Seitz, C. E., 1990, Multicomputers, in *Developments in Concurrency and Communication*, (ed. C. A. R. Hoare), Addison-Wesley, Reading, Chap. 5, 131–200.

Wong, Y., and Delosme, J. M., 1985, Optimal systolic implementations of n-dimensional recurrences, in *Proc. IEEE Int. Conf. on Computer Design (ICCD 85)*, IEEE Press, 618–21. Also: Tech. Report 8810, Department of Computer Science, Yale University, New Haven, April 1988.

Wong, Y., and Delosme, J.-M., 1988, Broadcast removal in systolic algorithms, *Proc. Int. Conf. on Systolic Arrays*, (eds K. Bromley, S.-Y. Kung and E. Swartzlander), IEEE Computer Society, New York, 403–12.

Xilinx Inc., 1991, *The programmable gate array data book*, Xilinx, Inc.

Yaacoby, Y., and Cappello, P. R., 1989, Scheduling a system of nonsingular affine recurrence equations onto a processor array, *J. VLSI Signal Processing*, **1**(2), Oct., 115–25.

9

Systolic Algorithm Design Environments (SADEs)

G. M. Megson and D. Comish

9.1 Introduction

What is design? Design is simply the process of creating describing and then selecting a form which must fulfil some function. More precisely in this text we are interested in engineering design – an iterative process defined by brief periods of insight and creativity followed by longer more tedious periods of refinement, selection, and modification until a product meets a set of constraints. In systolic design this means producing a number of prototype designs and choosing the best in terms of cell count, cell complexity, numbers of input-output connections, time complexity and so on. Systolic design is also about **algorithmic engineering** (McWhirter, 1989). That is, we take a source algorithm and perform a number of transformations to produce (or engineer) an equivalent but different algorithm which exhibits improved properties. In the current context such properties are algorithms that exploit massive parallelism, have regular connection structures, exploit bit-serial computations (Kung, 1982), or are easily mapped onto programmable architectures (Kung, 1984; 1988; Ibarra and John, 1990). To get from the raw input algorithm to the final output algorithm requires the application of engineering design principles and the formulation of constraints (or objective functions) which allow designs to be ranked in order of preference. Historically the AT and AT^2 measures based on VLSI complexity models (Savage, 1981; Brent and Kung, 1979) have been employed but in general the selection of constraints is a highly subjective issue and depends substantially on the design objectives. The theme in this chapter is the development of environments for systolic algorithm design and the kind of computer aided design (CAD) tools which are required to support the design process. In particular we shall consider the DTAGS transformation kernel which forms part of a systolic algorithm design environment (SADE) currently under development at Newcastle (Megson and Comish, 1991).

Our starting point is to decide what kind of operations users want in a systolic modelling system. In a complete system the user requires facilities which allow rapid modelling and prototyping of designs (see other papers in this volume and references for examples). The term modelling is used because, although synthesis techniques are based on a formal model of the design process, more heuristic methods that rely on the designer's intuition are also required. This latter point is especially true when the designer is operating at the limits of the current techniques – for example where computation domains are unbounded, synthesis of control signals (tags) (Lengauer et al., 1991) is necessary, or when non-constant/nonlinear dependencies are involved (Andonov et al., 1991). The core (or kernel) of any design environment is a computational procedure that removes the tedious, arduous, and error prone parts of the design process from the users allowing them to concentrate fully on the task of design. In a broader sense the environment needs to provide basic infrastructure facilities such as array generation, interactive features to allow design manipulation, and data base facilities to build a repository of common design objects (for use as building blocks in more complex designs).

9.2 Basic concepts

In DTAGS we adopt the synthesis procedure developed extensively by Quinton and van Dongen (1989) and based on the mapping of uniform recurrence equations (UREs) into Euclidean lattice space by means of a data dependency graph (DG) representation. For simplicity an algorithm is regarded as a nested for-loop program where statements in the loop body are assignments. The method can be extended to deal with conditional statements using CUREs (Rajopadhye, 1989) but this only complicates the discussion and will not be considered further. For n loops the dimension of the lattice space is n with axis j representing the jth loop index $j=1(1)n$. Index I_j has a range $U_j - L_j + 1$ where U_j and L_j are the upper and lower bounds of the index variable. In general the bounds may be nonlinear expressions made up of constants and the loop-indices I_k for $k=1(1)j-1$. The iteration space or domain, D, where computation takes place is defined by a set of hyperplanes (or directed half-spaces) with the form

$$a_1x_1 + a_2x_2 + \cdots + a_nx_n + a_{n+1} = 0 \qquad (9.1)$$

where x_i is an instance of index I_i. A particular point in the space is represented by an n element vector

$$p = (x_1, x_2, \cdots, x_n) \qquad (9.2)$$

thus an alternative version of (9.1) is

$$Hp + d = 0 \qquad (9.3)$$

where H is the n element outward normal vector of the hyperplane such that $Hp+d \leq 0$ for points corresponding to instances of the loop indices inside and on the boundary of D. The set of vertices of D correspond to the 2^n possible combinations of the lower and upper bounds of the nested loops. The set of hyperplanes enclosing the domain form a convex polytope and are easily determined by finding the n-dimensional convex hull of the given vertices (Chand and Kapur, 1970). Observe that conditional iterations (such as repeat and while constructs) are not permitted in this strict definition because they lead to potentially unbounded domains. However, systolic algorithms for semi-infinite or infinite domains can be designed using DTAGS provided we partition D into finite sized blocks prior to application of the design technique (Megson *et al.*, 1992). Finally, D is assumed to be contained inside the infinite region defined by positive axes of the lattice space. If D does not satisfy this condition a simple geometric translation is required to transform the problem into a standard form.

Individual assignments in the loop body are assumed to be of the form

> **indexed__variable :=**
> > **function__name(indexed__variable, . . . , indexed__variable)**

where an indexed variable has the form

> *indexed__variable = name*
> *[index__expression, index__expression, . . . , index__expression]*

in principle the number of index__variables in a function is unbounded but in practice it is useful to impose a small constant upper limit (say $k>0$) so that the input-output requirement of the final array cells is bounded. Similarly the number of **indexed__expressions** in an **indexed__variable** is bounded by n and the expressions themselves are restricted to be affine functions of the loop indices. Each variable can then be represented by a matrix-vector pair of the form

$$q = Ap + b \qquad\qquad (9.4)$$

where each row of A corresponds to an index-expression. When a variable has less than n index__expressions associated with it A is rank deficient – a situation that arises generally when the original algorithm is fully indexed to produce a canonical form (Quinton and van Dongen, 1989; Cappello and Steiglitz, 1984). A data dependency is defined by the difference between corresponding index__expressions in an indexed variable on the left of a statement and an indexed variable on the right of a statement. For example, if q_1 and q_2 are instances of (9.4) for variables on the left- and right-hand sides of a statement respectively, the direction vector $d = q_1 - q_2$ is defined showing the direction of data movement (the vector $-d$ shows a data dependency). A data dependency graph (DG) is constructed by considering each statement in turn and connecting all the points inside D for which a dependency exists. In general the DG is a multi-graph where different connections between the same points (or nodes) carry different variables. To preserve this distinction each connection is allocated a logical **colour**. Similarly each point in D corresponds to a particular instance of the loop-variables. If we assume that the left-hand side indexed_variable has $A=I$ and $b=0$ in (9.4) then each statement in the loop body is mapped to the same point p defining the computation at each node of the DG for the instance p of the loop variables. When only a single statement is mapped to each node the **function__name** can be interpreted as a logical shape defining the type of operation to be computed. The former can always be guaranteed by the process of tupling (Gachet *et al.*, 1986). In general if A is not a diagonal matrix a non-uniform data dependency is defined which describes some form of non-local data access. Non-uniform UREs are massaged into the correct form using a combination of pipelining and routing techniques (Fortes and Moldovan, 1984). The former is applicable when A is rank deficient. Any of the non-null vectors belonging to the kernel of A can be used as pipelining vectors. Such vectors are easily generated by finding a basis for the null space of A (Noble, 1969). The latter is generally applicable but is used mainly when no pipelining vectors can be found. Routing replaces non-uniform dependency by an equivalent linear combination of uniform direction vectors which is literally a routing path between two points in iteration space and demands conditional control at DG nodes to change direction. The required linear combination can be constructed from a selection of vectors from the basis of the lattice space or from the affine basis vectors of each facet of D. The standard synthesis method cannot be applied when the index_expressions involved are run-time dependent because of the resulting non-constant dependencies (e.g. the Knapsack problem (Andonov *et al.*, 1991).

Systolic designs are characterized by pairs of timing and allocation functions $(t(p), a(p))$ which determine the time and place that the shapes associated with point p in D are to be executed. A timing function imposes a schedule of computation on D and for linear schedules the optimal function can be obtained by solution of a linear programming (LP) problem. For example let

$$t(p) = \lambda^T p + \alpha \qquad (9.5)$$

where λ is an n element vector and α is a scalar. The LP is derived from relations between the vertices, rays and dependencies of D (Rajopadhye and Fujimoto, 1990). The rays of the domain can be generated in a number of ways – the simplest technique is to embed D into a convex cone with an apex at the origin of the lattice space. The set of half lines passing through the origin and at least one point of D define a set of rays. Indeed the extremal rays define the smallest convex cone into which the polytope can be embedded. Alternatively we can use the affine basis of orthonormal vectors describing the facets of D (these are available directly from the computation of D if the convex hull algorithm in (Swart, 1985) is adopted). The LP when solved determines λ and α in (9.5) and hence a schedule for the algorithm. In particular the solution space of the LP is itself a convex polytope T (Chvatal, 1980). The vertices of T define a set of possible timing functions and we normally choose the one that minimizes the time to evaluate all the computations in D. It should be clear that changing the dependencies modifies T and hence the possible timing schedules.

An allocation is of the form

$$a(p) = Mp \qquad (9.6)$$

where M is an $n \times n$ matrix chosen to remove one of the axes of the lattice space and hence project the n-dimensional DG into $n-1$ dimensional space (more complex projections can be derived by rotating a general line of projection onto one of the axes before performing the projection). The projected DG is a systolic array for the algorithm. When the points in D all contain the same shape single function cells result in the projected DG. In general D contains a collection of different shapes and it is possible to allocate different shapes to the same projected node (or cell). The matrix M is selected so that for two points p and q projected onto the same cell in the array $t(p) \neq t(q)$; this ensures that two shapes are not active at the same time in the same cell.

The design of systolic arrays can be seen as a two stage process. First the original computation is mapped into a uniform DG embedded into a convex polytope. Second, a search of the $(t(p), a(p))$ pairs is conducted and each pair evaluated according to a predefined list of design objectives (such as minimizing the number of different shapes mapped to the same cell, or the number of different coloured links between cells). It is apparent that considerable insight and creativity is required to produce a mapping of the starting algorithm into the DG representation. Once a representation is available a period of tedious searching is required to locate the best design. It is not surprising that the latter stage can be automated. What is less obvious is that substantial CAD support can be provided during the mapping phase.

9.3 SADE and DTAGS

Figure 9.1 gives the global view of a prototype SADE under development at Newcastle. The structure of the system has resulted from a detailed analysis of user requirements based on design experience and facilities offered by existing prototype packages. In addition it adds some new features such as modularity which permit the on-going extension of the environment and intermediate design representations that permit the

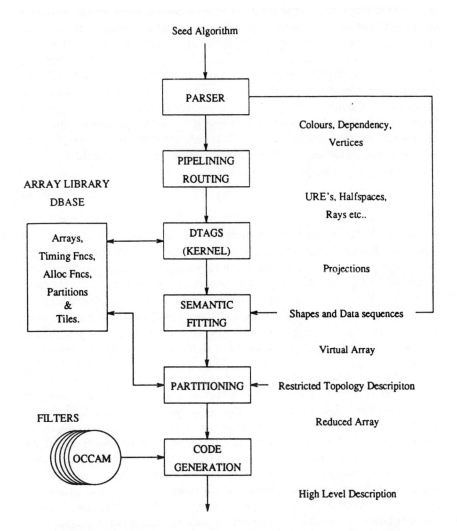

Figure 9.1 Systolic algorithm design environment (SADE).

abstract level of algorithmic specification to be selected by the user. The system is graphical, interactive, and menu driven and has been implemented in C on a SUN-4 workstation using X-windows and XGKS graphics.

The process of deriving a systolic array from a high level specification can be summarized as follows

1. Transform the high level specification into an Affine Recurrence Equation (ARE), and then to a URE to remove non-local connections.

If the latter step is omitted a valid design may still be obtained but it will not necessarily be a purely systolic array.

2. Apply the synthesis procedure described in section 9.2 to produce an abstract description of the systolic algorithm that describes the topology of the array, the data flow between cells, and the internal cell functions (i.e. a virtual systolic array)

3. Generate a parallel program to realize the virtual systolic array on the available architecture or apply a silicon compiler to produce a special purpose circuit (or ASIC).

Each of the above steps corresponds to two of the solid boxes in Fig. 9.1, and decomposes logically into pre-processing, synthesis, and post-processing stages. The remaining features of the SADE provide infrastructure facilities and a collection of re-usable data structures (a design bundle) that can be used at high levels of abstraction to upgrade the system with more powerful routines as the synthesis process develops.

Language parser This section accepts a high level description of the source (or seed) algorithm in an imperative form and generates an internal form more appropriate for manipulation by the rest of the system. In particular a compacted syntax tree of the input program is generated and used to produce the vertices of the domain D, the matrix-vector pairs for each of the variables referenced are also generated and stamped with colour and shape information. If at any stage a non-linear, or run time dependent, index-expression is encountered the process is aborted with appropriate diagnostics.

Pipeline and routing In this step the vertices are used to produce the directed half-spaces describing D. In addition the rays required in the solution of the LP problem can be generated (or if no rays are produced they will be generated automatically by a call to the LP solver). Finally, each matrix-vector pair is examined for non-uniformity and where applicable the basis of the associated kernel produced. The designer is allowed to select the pipelining or routing vectors required (or use the defaults generated automatically) and the design description is updated accordingly.

The design of timing allocation graphs (DTAGS) kernel This is the main transformation section which allows the manual or automatic generation of sets of timing and allocation functions. The former by solution of the LP to produce the vertices of the polytope T, and in the latter the construction of a projection matrix based on pre-defined directions (e.g. along the axes of the lattice space). The system is interactive so that the designer can select and view the domain polytope, projected DGs, or mask a selection of colours. The latter being useful when the behaviour of particular variable (such as a result variable) is important in the design.

Timing functions are simulated by running snapshots of DG node activation. For projected DGs a design file is created with colour, shape, and scheduling information.

Semantic filter In this section input and output data sequences are added to the design description; the code associated with shapes can also be extracted from the syntax tree of the input algorithm. At this stage a virtual description of the algorithm is complete so that the real network operation can be simulated and actual data flow snapshots produced.

Partitioning If the final design is targeted at a particular type of parallel architecture, in which resources are limited, further transformations of the final network may be required. For example, to map a number of cells onto the same processing element. The partitioning section identifies suitable mappings of the virtual array onto the real topology using the concepts of tiling (Darte, 1991) and load balancing (de Lange, 1991).

Code generation The virtual description of the algorithm is now converted into an executable program by selecting an appropriate code-conversion filter. For example Occam (Inmos) LINDA (Carriero, 1989), or VHDL (Lipsett *et al.*, 1989) code descriptions could be generated. The generated code is compiled using a standard compiler for the appropriate language and then executed or in the case of VHDL a circuit layout produced.

The above is the description of the ideal system – our SADE is not fully complete. The first three stages described above have been developed to a prototype level. Some stand-alone experimental code is available for the last three but has not been fully integrated into the system. The input language is PASCAL (ISO level 0) but we enforce certain style rules in order to simplify the data extraction process, consequently it is better to think of the input as a pseudo code description (in a subset of PASCAL) which simplifies the specification of a problem. For example no statements are allowed outside loops and must be of the form given in section 9.2. However unlike other CAD tools we do not require the use of pragmas embedded into programs to direct the design process – this is supplied by the designer who can override the normal default options at any point. Consequently all input programs can be tested sequentially for correctness before using the tool. For code generation we have established mechanisms for producing Occam and LINDA code (with the latter intended only for simulation purposes). The technique is easily extended to other languages by formulation of an appropriate YACC/LEX description of the associated grammar. Finally, at each stage of the design process the designer can extract existing structures such as timing functions, allocation matrices, or whole designs from the library Database. Indeed the package supports multiple versions of designs to allow a number of different design options to be explored simultaneously or to permit the

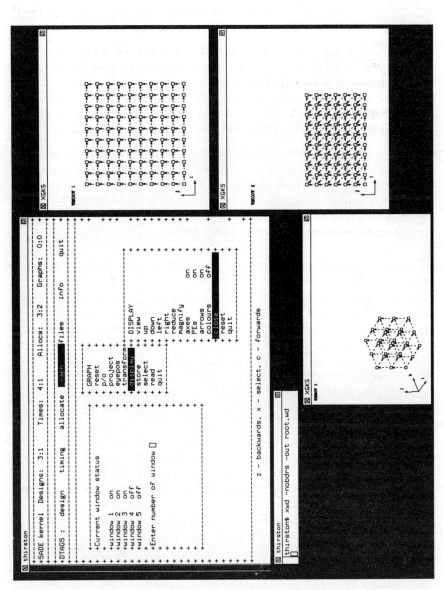

Figure 9.2 SADE interface.

designer to switch between one of a set of algorithms (for example in composite array specification). In the latter case more complex designs that require the composition of a number of different arrays are possible and we are currently developing a high level interface to simplify the process.

parser input:

```
program test(input,output);
var
  i, j, k : integer;
  a : array[1..10, 1..10, 1..10] of integer;

function test(a,b,c : integer) :integer;
  begin
    a := b+c;
  end;


begin

  for i:=1 to 10 do
    for j := 1 to 10 do
      for k := 1 to 10 do
        aa[i,j, k] := test(a[i,j-1, k], a[1,1], a[i-1, j, k+1]);

end.
```

parser output:

ERROR - variable not found

```
3
8
```

1	1	1
10	1	1
1	10	1
10	10	1
1	1	10
10	1	10
1	10	10
10	10	10

1	0	0	0	0
0	1	0	0	0
0	0	1	0	0
0	0	0	1	0
1	1	0	0	-706

1	0	0	0	0
0	1	0	0	-1
0	0	1	0	0
0	0	0	1	0
1	0	0	1	6

0	0	0	0	1
0	0	0	0	1
0	0	0	0	0
0	0	0	1	0
1	0	0	1	6

1	0	0	0	-1
0	1	0	0	1
0	0	1	0	1
0	0	0	1	0
1	0	0	1	6

Figure 9.3 SADE input for test program.

A detailed description of the SADE is beyond the scope of this paper, however we can illustrate the design method. Section 9.4 considers two examples for which manual construction of the arrays is more involved. The rest of this section demonstrates the high level interface to SADE for standard design examples as shown in Figs. 9.3 to 9.7. The format of each example is the same, a PASCAL program, the parser output, and the input to DTAGS (produced by the pipeline and router) is given. In the package Index_variables are represented by $(n+2) \times (n+2)$ matrices with the following form

$$\begin{bmatrix} A & 0 & b \\ 0 & 1 & 0 \\ state & colour & \end{bmatrix}$$

where *colour* is the number associated with a variable (derived from the syntax tree) and state is an $n+1$ element vector with the form

$$\begin{bmatrix} statno, & lvalue, & 0, & \cdots, & 0, & shape \end{bmatrix}$$

where *stat number* is the number of the assignment statement in the current nesting level, *lvalue* is 1 or 0 depending upon whether the variable

```
program test(input,output);

(* non-linear dependency *)

var
  a : array[1..10] of integer;
  i,j : integer;

function junk(a : integer) : integer;
  begin
  end;

begin

  for i:= 1 to 10 do
    for j := 1 to 10 do
      a[i] := junk(a[i*j]);

end.
```

```
2
4

1    1
10   1
1    10
10   10

1   0   0   0
0   0   0   0
0   0   1   0
1   1   0   3

0   0   0   0
0   0   0   0
0   0   1   0
1   0   1   3

ERROR - nonlinear dependency found
```

parser input   **parser output**

Figure 9.4 SADE input for non-linear dependency example.

```
program matv(input,output);

(* matrix vector product *)

const
  n = 10;
type
  matrix = array[1..n, 1..n] of real;
  vector = array[1..n] of real;
var
  i, j, k : integer;
  a     : matrix;
  x, y    : vector;

  function ips(a,b,c : integer) :integer;

    (* inner product cell *)

    begin
      ips := a + b*c;
    end;

begin

  for i := 1 to n do
    for j := 1 to n do
      y[i] := ips(y[i], a[i,j], x[j]);

end.
```

parser input

```
2
4
1   1
10  1
1   10
10  10
1   0   0   0
0   0   0   0
0   0   1   0
1   1   0   8
1   0   0   0
0   0   0   0
0   0   1   0
1   0   1   8
1   0   0   0
0   1   0   0
0   0   1   0
1   0   1   6
0   1   0   0
0   0   0   0
0   0   1   0
1   0   1   7
```

parser output

```
2
1   10
1   10
4
1   1
10  1
1   10
10  10
4
-1   0    1
 0   1  -10
 1   0  -10
 0  -1    1
0
```

DTAGS input

```
4
1   0   0   0
0   1   0   0
0   0   1   0
1   1   0   8

1   0   0   0
0   1   0   1
0   0   1   0
1   0   1   8

1   0   0   0
0   1   0   0
0   0   1   0
1   0   1   6

1   0   0   1
0   1   0   0
0   0   1   0
1   0   1   7
```

Figure 9.5 SADE input for matrix vector product.

is on the left or right of the assignment, and *shape* is a number denoting the **function_name**.

Figure 9.3 is a simple test program; the PASCAL code uses 'aa' which is not declared causing the design process to be aborted. The program name is not a valid variable (in our case) so **test** can be used as a function name. The parser attempts to generate as much data as possible, giving a value of three for the space dimension and eight vertices as shown. The indexed__variables are then listed, and belong to statement number 1. The first matrix belongs to the left hand side of the assignment the others on the right, and the -706 value is an error value to show that the colour is invalid. The right-hand variables are all associated with

```
program conv(input,output);

(* convolution problem *)

const
  n = 10;
  k = 4;
type
  vector = array[1..n] of real;
var
  i, j : integer;
  x, y, w : vector;

  function ips(a,b,c : integer) :integer;

    (* inner product cell *)
    begin
      ips := a + b*c;
    end;

begin

  for i := 1 to n do
    for j := 1 to n-k+1 do
      y[i] := ips(y[i-1], w[j], x[i+j-1]);

end.
```

parser output:

```
2
4

1   1
10  1
1   7
10  7

1  0  0  0
0  0  0  0
0  0  1  0
1  1  0  7

1  0  0  0
0  0  0  0
0  0  1  0
1  0  1  7

0  1  0  0
0  0  0  0
0  0  1  0
1  0  1  8

1  1  0  -1
0  0  0  0
0  0  1  0
1  0  1  6
```

DTAGS input:

```
2
1   10
1   7

4
1   1
10  1
1   7
10  7

4
-1  0   1
 0  1  -7
 1  0  -10
 0 -1   1

0

4
1  0  0  0
0  1  0  0
0  0  1  0
1  1  0  7

1  0  0  0
0  1  0  1
0  0  1  0
1  0  1  7

1  0  0  1
0  1  0  0
0  0  1  0
1  0  1  8

1  0  0  -1
0  1  0   1
0  0  1   0
1  0  1   6
```

| parser input | parser output | DTAGS input |

Figure 9.6 SADE input for convolution problem.

testing the first function in the program. In Fig. 9.4, the index__expression on the right of the assignment is nonlinear causing an error, with the corresponding matrix having both a null A and b part.

Figure 9.5 is a more meaningful example, the matrix vector product. The A parts of the matrices in the middle column show that the variables in the assignment have been fully indexed (by adding zero rows) to produce rank deficient and hence non-uniform dependencies. Smallest and largest points are added after the dimensions (i.e. (1, 1) and (10, 10)) to simplify the generation of the whole domain in the graphics section, and the half-spaces for D (a square) are added after the vertices. The number of rays is zero (i.e. they were not generated) and the indexed__variables have been pipelined (i.e the matrices A are diagonal and the b vector is non-null). Figure 9.6 is the SADE input for the well known convolution problem – this is the same as the matrix-vector problem except that a non-uniformity exists in the initial specification (the expression $i+j-1$) and the inner loop contains an expression for the upper bound. Again the middle column shows the parser output with fully indexed variable matrices while the third column shows the DTAGS input. The polytope D is a rectangle and the A and b parts of the variable matrices are uniform. Finally Fig. 9.7 shows the specification of the dense matrix product problem. The problem is 3-dimensional and produces eight vertices. The polytope D is a cube described by the six half-spaces in the third column. Uniformization of the variable matrices in column two produces the final input to DTAGS. The DGs for the last three examples are shown in Fig. 9.2, subsequent projections produce the well known arrays (Kung, 1980, 1982; Cappello and Steiglitz, 1984).

9.4 Examples

One of the disappointing features of current literature on systolic synthesis is the tendency to concentrate on only one or two simple examples such as those above. Indeed these designs are so simple that the case for a sophisticated design tool is difficult to make. Clearly the test of any real system is the ability to cope with more complex examples that lie at the limits of a designer's ability – it is at exactly this level that a tool provides real insight into algorithm design and becomes useful. To illustrate the graphical features of DTAGS we will derive some systolic algorithms for two different applications. The first is Aitken's method, an algorithm for determining the roots of transcendental equations, the second is the problem of bit multiplication. The former is somewhat esoteric (although finding roots of equations is an important application) but poses problems of infinite domains and difficulties in visualizing arrays; it also covers a wide class of algorithms that can be formulated as table generating problems (Megson and Evans, 1992). The latter is a well-studied problem parser input:

```
program test(input,output);

(* matrix-product *)

const
  n = 3;
type
  matrix = array[1..n, 1..n] of real;
var
  i, j, k : integer;
  a, b, c : matrix;

  function ips(a,b,c : integer) :integer;

    (* inner product cell *)

    begin
     ips := a + b*c;
    end;

begin

  for i := 1 to n do
    for j := 1 to n do
      for k := 1 to n do
        c[i,j] := ips(c[i,j], a[i,k], b[k,j]);

end.
```

parser output:

```
3
8

1 1 1
3 1 1
1 3 1
3 3 1
1 1 3
3 1 3
1 3 3
3 3 3

1 0 0 0 0
0 1 0 0 0
0 0 0 0 0
0 0 0 1 0
1 1 0 0 8

1 0 0 0 0
0 1 0 0 0
0 0 0 0 0
0 0 0 1 0
1 0 0 1 8

1 0 0 0
0 0 1 0 0
0 0 0 0 0
0 0 0 1 0
1 0 0 1 6

0 0 1 0 0
0 1 0 0 0
0 0 0 0 0
0 0 0 1 0
1 0 0 1 7
```

DTAGS input:

```
3
1 3
1 3
1 3

8
1 1 1
3 1 1
1 3 1
3 3 1
1 1 3
3 1 3
1 3 3
3 3 3

6
-1  0  0  1
 0  0  1 -3
 1  0  0 -3
 0  0 -1  1
 0  1  0 -3
 0 -1  0  1

0

4
1 0 0 0 0
0 1 0 0 0
0 0 1 0 0
0 0 0 1 0
1 1 0 0 8

1 0 0 0 0
0 1 0 0 0
0 0 1 0 1
0 0 0 1 0
1 0 0 1 8

1 0 0 0 0
0 1 0 0 1
0 0 1 0 0
0 0 0 1 0
1 0 0 1 6

1 0 0 0 1
0 1 0 0 0
0 0 1 0 0
0 0 0 1 0
1 0 0 1 7
```

Figure 9.7 SADE input for matrix product.

that requires a semi-infinite domain for pipelining of successive multiplications and has great relevance to the designers of fast VLSI circuits (McCanny and McWhirter, 1982).

9.4.1 Aitken's method

Consider the root finding problem first. We want to compute the roots of $K \geqslant 1$ polynomials of the form

$$f_k(z) = 1 + a_{1,k}z + a_{2,k}z^2 + \cdots \tag{9.7}$$

for $k=1(1)K$. Aitken's method solves a single equation of (9.7) by computing a doubly infinite table of Hankel Determinants (Householder, 1970) using the recurrence

$$H_{i,j-1,k} \, H_{i,j+1,k} = H_{i+1,j,k} H_{i-1,j,k} - H_{i,j,k}^2 \tag{9.8}$$

where it is known that $H_{i,0,k} = 1$ and $H_{i,1,k} = c_{v,k}$ where

$$h_k(z) = g_k(z) \, / \, f_k(z) = 1 + c_{1,k}z + c_{2,k}z^2 + \cdots \tag{9.9}$$

$$g_k(z) = 1 + b_{1,k}z + b_{2,k}z^2 + \cdots$$

so that the first two columns and first row of the table are given for each k. The significance of the table is that for $j > 0$ the ratio $H_{i,j,k} \, / \, H_{i+1,j,k}$ has a limit that satisfies

$$\lim_{i \to \infty} H_{i,j,k} \, / \, H_{i+1,j,k} \to r_{1,k} r_{2,k} \cdots r_{j,k} \tag{9.10}$$

where the $r_{j,k}$ are the zeroes of $f_k(z)$. Now if $f_k(z)$ has any other zeroes they are strictly greater in modulus. Thus if we know the limits of column j and $j+1$ the appropriate root can be found by a simple ratio.

Now, it is certainly possible to write a PASCAL program to generate the tables of Hankel Determinants for the K polynomials, but the program contains conditional iterations and is not suitable for direct input to the SADE. Furthermore the polytope D is unbounded preventing the derivation of a timing schedule by solution of an LP problem, and constrains projections to those that are simultaneously parallel to all the infinite directions, otherwise arrays are of unbounded size. To cope with the latter problem we may try (rather naively) to bound the number of columns so that the table is semi-infinite in the i direction (9.10). It follows that only one projection is possible in the direction of the i-axis. Unfortunately bounding the columns in this way is not really admissable unless the bound is very large, because the problem in (9.7) is changed to a polynomial of fixed degree. An alternative solution is to block partition the table, apply the synthesis procedure to the design of an array for a single block, and to use the array in a multi-pass mode to compute an arbitrary number of blocks. For example, suppose we define a block r, s of table k as $B_{r,s,k}$ where the block contains the elements $H_{m(r-1)+i,\,n(s-1)+j,\,k}$ for $i=1(1)m$,

$j=1(1)n$, $k=1(1)K$, and m, $n>0$ are arbitrary block parameters. Observe that when $m\rightarrow\infty$ the partitioning is equivalent to computing the first n roots of each polynomial and it may be thought that a projection in the infinite i direction will produce a fixed sized systolic array (n being an arbitrary parameter). Unfortunately the columns of the table have different rates of convergence and it is possible for the sth block of columns to require more rows than the $(s-1)$th block. Replicating the last element in a converged column is not practical because it is the ratio in (9.10) that has converged, not necessarily the column elements themselves.

The above considerations lead to the idea of rectangular blocks and the evaluation of the blocks using the nonlinear timing schedule

$$T(B_{r, s, k}) = s + \frac{(r+s-2)(r+s-1)}{2} \qquad (9.11)$$

which is a well-known diagonal counting method and is independent of k. In fact rectangular blocks also present difficulties because the rule (9.8) prohibits the computation of all the block elements unless a triangular portion of the additional elements is included. We require trapezoidal shaped blocks with the form $H_{m(r-1)+i, n(s-1)+j, k}$ for $j=1(1)n$, $i=1(1)m+n-1$, $k=1(1)K$, and m, $n>0$. Now the size of each block is bounded, by the choice of m and n, and a PASCAL program to compute a single block which obeys our style restrictions is shown in Fig. 9.8. The pre-processing stage will not detect any non-uniformities but a non-local connection is implied by the $j-1$ index_expression. The manual application of routing techniques can be used to produce a two-stage routing path. The path is non-unique and the design exercise can be repeated for each possibility – for simplicity and conciseness we will only examine one possibility. Figure 9.9(a) shows the 3-D DG produced by DTAGS. Once a timing function is known various projections of the graph into 2-D will produce a range of possible arrays (when $K=1$ arrays for a single table are produced). Generating and solving the LP problem gives the optimal timing schedule

$$t((i, j, k)) = j-1 \qquad (9.12)$$

which shows firstly that the fastest way to compute the block is a column at a time, and secondly that each of the K tables can be constructed simultaneously. For an experienced designer such features are apparent from the problem specification. Less obvious is the fact that only projections in directions that do not lie in the plane defined by (9.12) are permitted. It follows that the dimensions of arrays are dependent upon m and K. The former can be chosen arbitrarily but the latter is dependent on the number of problem instances being solved. A further problem (which is apparent if the arrays are projected) is that the simultaneous

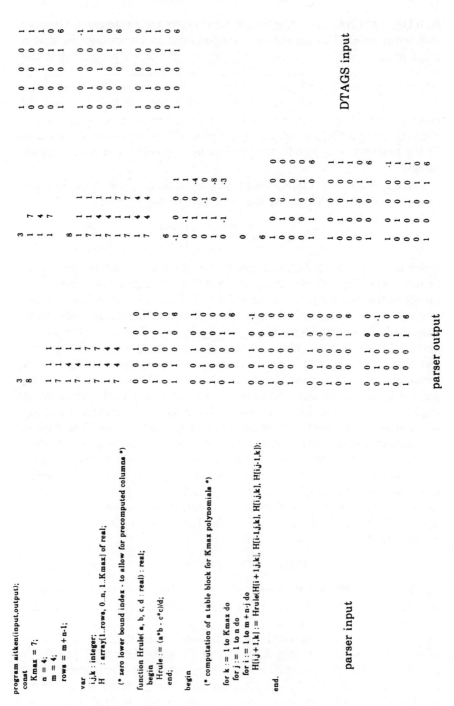

Figure 9.8 SADE input for Aitken's method.

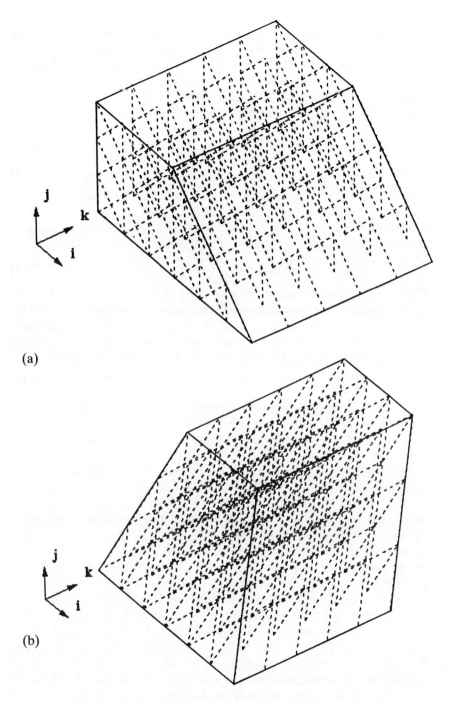

Figure 9.9 Data dependency graphs for Aitken's method.

computation of K tables requires the preloading of boundary values. These boundary values are produced from the last two columns of the previous left block and the mth row of the previous block in the same column – hence the nonlinear block schedule to guarantee that the required values are always available. Also observe that the triangular parts of blocks are re-computed but this is unavoidable.

To overcome some of the above difficulties we need to pipeline the K polynomials so that the computation of different tables can be overlapped, one way to achieve this is to replace (9.8) by the equivalent recurrence

$$H_{i,\,j+1,\,k} = (H_{i+1,\,j,\,k-1}H_{i-1,\,j,\,k-1} - H^2_{i,\,j,\,k-1}) \, / \, H_{i,\,j-1,\,k-2} \qquad (9.13)$$

and change the PASCAL program input to the SADE. However this is equivalent to applying a transformation to the existing domain D to produce the DG in Fig. 9.9(b). Solving the associated LP produces a new polytope for which the optimal timing function is

$$t((i, j, k)) = j + k - 1 \qquad (9.14)$$

Equation (9.14) still requires that blocks are computed a column at a time but in addition the computation of the block for polynomial k begins before the same block for polynomial $k+1$. That is the problem instances are pipelined. Alternatively we can choose any of the feasible timing functions offered by the LP polytope. In particular the timing function

$$t((i, j, k) = i+2j+k-1 \qquad (9.15)$$

describing a wavefront method is possible. The former projections in the direction $(\pm 1, 0, 0)$ are perpendicular to the time direction and are prohibited. Likewise, projections in the $(\pm 1, \pm 2, \pm 1)$ are prevented in the latter case.

Figure 9.10 shows some projections obtained from DTAGS for the pipelined case together with their directions of projection. Figures 10(b, c, f) show that K problems can be solved simultaneously by using K independent copies of a 1-D array that evaluates just a single table. Figure 10(c) is to be preferred because it employs only unidirectional data flow and requires a number of cells proportional to n. Figures 10(d, e, f) show hybrid projections which produce pipelined designs with the number of cells dependent on the problem size K. Figure 10(d) requires $m+n-1$ rows and $n+k-1$ columns of cells. Figure 10(e) uses $m+2n-2$ rows and $k+n-1$ columns, and Fig. 10(g) n rows and $m+n+k-2$ columns. In contrast Fig. 10(a) employs completely non-stationary data flow (i.e. no preloading) and requires $n(m+n-1)$ cells, which is independent of K. In addition all the data is input and output on the boundaries of the array. All the other designs require some preloading at the start or unloading at the end of computation, which in any real implementation would require extra control mechanisms. We will not discuss the details of the array operation

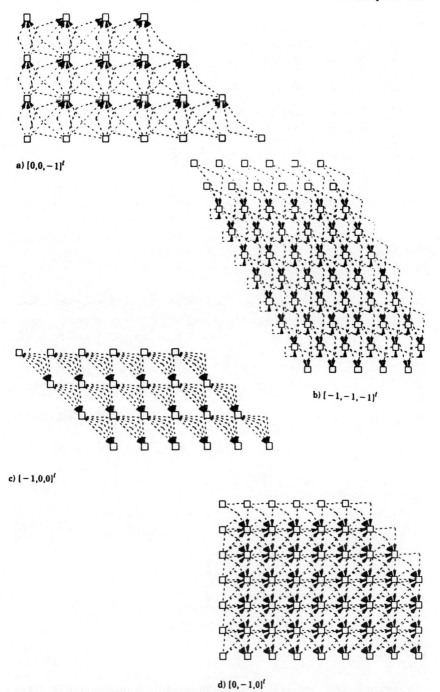

a) $[0,0,-1]^t$

b) $[-1,-1,-1]^t$

c) $[-1,0,0]^t$

d) $[0,-1,0]^t$

Figure 9.10(a), (b), (c), (d) 2D arrays derived from projections of 3D dependencies.

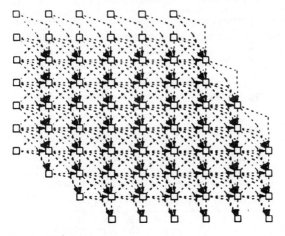

e) [−1, −1, 0]ᵗ

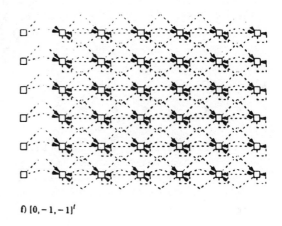

f) [0, −1, −1]ᵗ

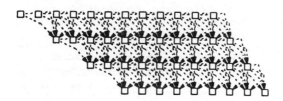

g) [−1, 0, −1]ᵗ

Figure 9.10(e), (f), (g) 2D arrays derived from projections of 3D dependencies.

here (the interested reader is referred to (Megson *et al.*, 1992) – the more enthusiastic reader is encouraged to try and construct the above projections by hand!).

9.4.2 Bit multiplication

The multiplication of two positive n bit numbers a and b can be stated as follows:

$$s_k = \sum_{i=0}^{n-1} a_i.b_i + carries \qquad (9.16)$$

where a_i, b_i for $i=0(1)n-1$ are bits of the two operands, and s_k for $k=0(1)2n-1$ is the sum (with the smallest index being the lowest significant bit). The carries result from a carry of a partial sum on the previous stage of the calculation. The method can be extended in a straightforward manner to perform multiplication of signed and two's complement numbers using the method discussed in (McCanny and McWhirter, 1982) and will not be considered further.

The design of VLSI circuits for bit multiplication is an important topic in digital design. In particular the decision to build bit serial or bit parallel devices can often be a contentious issue. Bit serial designs generally require less circuit area and fewer chip pins when compared to bit parallel equivalents. Consequently a bit serial device will be able to deal with larger numbers of bits and hence greater accuracy (for fixed point numbers) than a bit parallel device in the same circuit area. However, greater accuracy is offset by increased circuit latency and throughput which reduces the performance of the device. Other concerns also include power consumption, the introduction of latches to retain state between steps in a serial algorithm, and the clocking and control of circuits. The final design of a multiplier is often a trade-off between competing constraints such as power, area, throughput (especially in real-time situations), and bit parallel versus bit serial computations. The purpose of this section is to demonstrate how SADE and DTAGS can be used to generate and evaluate different bit multiplier designs. In particular we consider the automatic generation of the designs described by McCanny and McWhirter (1982, 1986) using a high level PASCAL specification.

Figure 9.11 shows a PASCAL program and the derivation of the DTAGS input. We have omitted the function bodies to save space although they are not required by the SADE unless code generation is to be performed. For completeness the computations are

$$s_{i,j} = s_{i-1,j-1} \oplus (a_i . b_j) \oplus c_{i-1,j} \qquad (9.17)$$

$$c_{i,j} = (s_{i-1,j-1} . (a_i . b_j)) + (s_{i-1,j-1} . c_{i-1,j}) + (c_{i-1,j}) . (a_i . b_j)) \qquad (9.18)$$

To generate the variable matrices from the fully indexed version output by

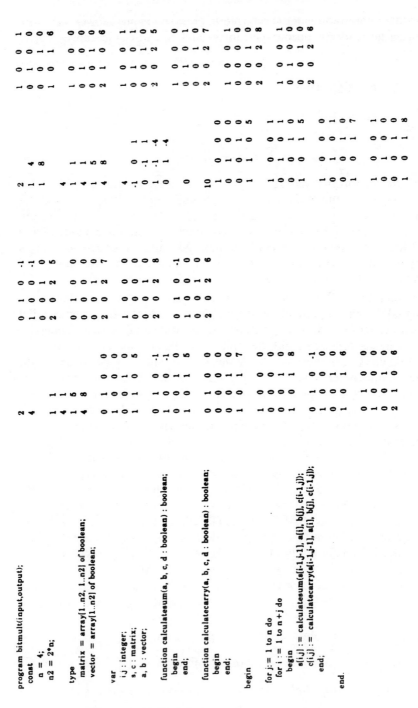

Figure 9.11 SADE input for *n* bit multiplication.

the parser, the a_i and b_j terms have to be pipelined so that (9.17) and (9.18) are re-written as the equivalent system

$$s_{i,\,j} = s_{i-1,\,j-1} \oplus (A_{i,\,j} \cdot B_{i,\,j}) \oplus c_{i-1,\,j} \qquad (9.19)$$

$$c_{i,\,i} = (s_{i-1,\,j-1} \cdot (A_{i,\,j} \cdot B_{i,\,j})) + (s_{i-1,\,j-1} \cdot c_{i-1,\,j}) + (c_{i-1,\,j}) \cdot \\ (A_{i,\,j} \cdot B_{i,\,j})) \qquad (9.20)$$

where

$$A_{i,\,j} = \begin{cases} a_i & \text{otherwise} \\ A_{i,\,j-1} & \text{indomain} \end{cases} \qquad (9.21)$$

$$B_{i,\,j} = \begin{cases} b_j & \text{otherwise} \\ B_{i-1,\,j} & \text{indomain} \end{cases} \qquad (9.22)$$

The loops of the program define a trapezoidal shaped domain D as shown in Fig. 9.12. Solving the LP problem produces the optimal timing function

$$t((i, j,k)) = i+j-1 \qquad (9.23)$$

and Fig. 9.13 summarizes the activation of the DG nodes and the movement of data. Studying this picture indicates three (useful) allocation or projection directions and the associated $(t(p), a(p))$ pairs produce the linear arrays shown in Fig. 9.14(a–c). A single processing element performs the computation

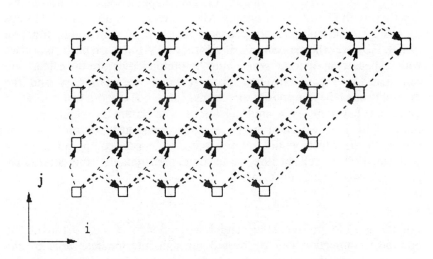

Figure 9.12 Data flow graph for n bit multiplication.

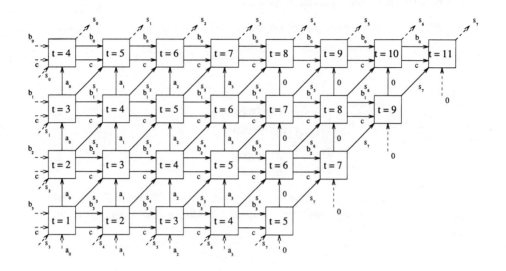

Figure 9.13 Timing snapshots for n bit multiplication.

$$s = s' \oplus (a.b) \oplus c' \tag{9.24}$$

$$c = s' \cdot (a.b) + s' c' + c' \cdot (a.b) \tag{9.25}$$

which may be derived by projecting the two shapes associated with the two functions in the PASCAL program. All the designs require $O(3n-1)$ steps for a single n bit multiplication, because they use the same timing function (9.23). However the arrays in Figs. 9.14(a) and 9.14(b) are both stationary with respect to an operand which must be preloaded before the calculation can start. In Fig. 9.14(c) the product terms are stationary and the multiplicands flow in opposite directions. Consequently the result must be unloaded between each multiplication. The latter problem may be removed by a projection in the $(1, -1)^t$ direction but this is prohibited by use of (9.23) which would require more than one computation to be performed in a cell at the same time. Fortunately, the alternative (non-optimal) timing function

$$t((i, j, k)) = i+2j-2 \tag{9.26}$$

can be used to produce the semi-systolic design in Fig. 9.14(d). The non-local connection can be routed through intermediate cells by the addition of suitable latches and a simple re-timing of the circuit. A similar array is shown in Fig. 9.14(e) using the optimal timing function and a

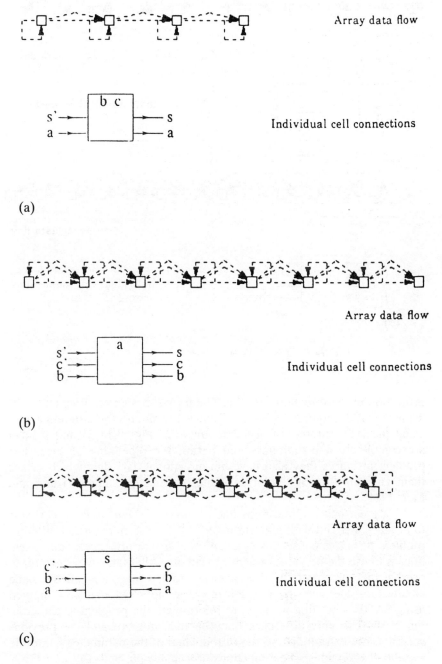

Figure 9.14(a), (b), (c) Bit serial multiplier arrays.

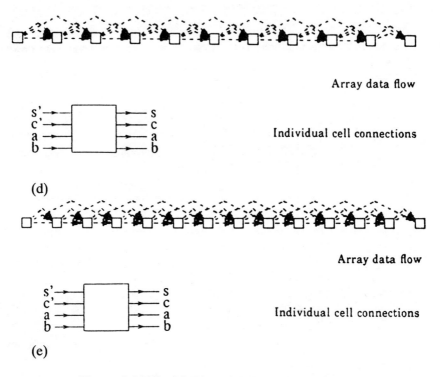

Array data flow

Individual cell connections

(d)

Array data flow

Individual cell connections

(e)

Figure 9.14(d), (e) Bit serial multiplier arrays.

projection in the direction $(2, -1)^t$. The former design requires $O(4n-2)$ while the latter requires $O(3n-1)$. Table 9.1 compares the different arrays using the AT^2 criteria. Notice that arrays in Figs 9.14(d) and 9.14(e) are completely non-stationary and permit the pipelining of successive problem instances they also have uni-directional data flow which makes them amenable to fault tolerant manufacturing techniques (Kung and Lam 1984).

For a great many applications one of the over-riding goals of design is to produce a circuit with high throughput (i.e. performing many different problem instances consecutively). One way to perform many multiplications is to use the previous designs repeatedly. Alternatively we can try to overlap the computations of successive problem instances on the same architecture. Designs which exploit this latter approach may be examined using SADE – but first we need to reformulate the problem as shown in Fig. 9.15. The only difference between this program and the previous version is the extra loop and the introduction of the parameter k into the variable expressions. The functions *CalculateSum* and *CalculateCarry* evaluate the recurrences

$$s_{i,j,k} = s_{i-1,j-1,k} \oplus (a_{i,k} \cdot b_{j,k}) \oplus c_{i-1,j,k} \qquad (9.27)$$

$$c_{i,j,k} = (s_{i-1,j-1,k} \cdot (a_{i,k}, b_{j,k})) + (s_{i-1,j-1,k} \cdot c_{i-1,j,k}) + \\ (c_{i-1,j,k} \cdot (a_{i,k} \cdot b_{j,k})) \qquad (9.28)$$

In the general case the number of problem instances is unbounded and $m \rightarrow \infty$ which would produce an unbounded domain. But for design purposes we can limit m to some constant value – provided we remember not to use any projections that produce an array with an area dependent on m. Figure 9.16 shows the 3-D DG for the new problem. Solving the associated LP problem produces the timing function

$$t((i, j, k)) = i + j - 1 \qquad (9.29)$$

which is the same as (9.23) and implies that each of the m instances could be computed in parallel using m copies of a 1-D array as shown in Fig. 9.17(a). For an array which is independent of m the only projection is along the k axis. The resulting array is shown in Fig. 9.17(b) and not surprisingly is a copy of the original DG in Fig. 9.14. Unfortunately with the current timing function this projection is not allowed because it is orthogonal to the time direction (the normal of the plane defined by (9.29)) forcing two simultaneously active DG nodes to be mapped onto the same cell. Fortunately the non-optimal timing function

$$t((i, j, k)) = i + j + k - 2 \qquad (9.30)$$

can be used instead. The effect of this function is to stagger the start up of the different problem instances allowing the desired projection.

9.5 Design principles

Given that primitive SADEs exist and will continue to improve in sophistication, what role is left for the designer? From our examples above it is readily appreciated that systolic design is similar to a systematic search of the solution space defined by $(t(p), a(p))$ pairs. In principle there is no reason why such a search cannot be conducted automatically and so the existence of a systolic compiler is a real possibility. However, the solution space for even quite simple problems can be extremely large and a full search demands an enormous amount of computer time. This is because the underlying algorithms for determining the domain polytope and the timing schedule are combinatorial in nature and expensive in computation time, especially when a number of polytopes (i.e. for different seed algorithms or transformed data dependencies) are possible. Some of these difficulties may be overcome by applying faster computer architectures to accelerate computation or using approximate/heuristic based algorithms to simplify the computational work. For example, trying projections along the axes of the lattice space or in the direction normal to the timing hyperplanes usually characterizes most possibilities. Indeed one of the key

Table 9.1 Comparison of bit serial and bit parallel multiplier arrays

Type	Figure / array	Timing function	Allocation direction	Number of cells (A)	Computation time (T)	AT^2	Pipelined time (T_P)	Pipelined AT_P^2
Bit serial	14(a)	$i+j-1$	$[-1,0]^t$	n	$3n-1$	$O(9n^3)$	$3n-1$	$O(9n^3)$
	14(b)	$i+j-1$	$[0,-1]^t$	$2n$	$3n-1$	$O(18n^3)$	$3n-1$	$O(18n^3)$
	14(c)	$i+j-1$	$[-1,-1]^t$	$2n$	$3n-1$	$O(18n^3)$	$3n-1$	$O(18n^3)$
	14(d)	$i+2j-2$	$[1,-1]^t$	$3n-1$	$4n-2$	$O(48n^3)$	n	$O(3n^3)$
	14(e)	$i-j-1$	$[2,-1]^t$	$4n-2$	$3n-1$	$O(36n^3)$	$n-1$	$O(4n^3)$
Bit parallel	5	$i+j+k-2$	$[0,0,1]^t$	$O(\ \ )$	$3n-1$	$O(\ \ )$	1	$O(\ \ )$

DTAGS input

parser output

parser input

```
program bitmult2(input,output);
  const
    m = 7;
    n = 4;
    n2 = 2*n;

  type
    matrix = array[1..n2, 1..n2] of boolean;
    vector = array[1..n2] of boolean;

  var
    i,j,k : integer;
    a, c : matrix;
    a, b : vector;

  function calculatesum(a, b, c, d : boolean) : boolean;
    begin
    end;

  function calculatecarry(a, b, c, d : boolean) : boolean;
    begin
    end;

  begin

    for k := 1 to m do
      for j := 1 to n do
        for i := 1 to n+j do
          begin
            a[i,j,k] := calculatesum(a[i-1,j-1,k], a[i,k], b[j,k], c[i-1,j,k]);
            c[i,j,k] := calculatecarry(a[i-1,j-1,k], a[i,k], b[j,k], c[i-1,j,k]);
          end;

    end.
```

Figure 9.15 SADE input for *m* pipelined *n* bit multiplications.

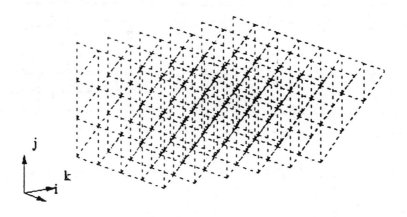

Figure 9.16 Data dependency graph for m pipelined n bit
multiplications.

skills in systolic design is the use of intuition and experience (i.e. the 'art'
in systolic design) to prune the solution space and limit computation time
to an acceptable limit. What we mean by an acceptable limit is subjective
and in general is influenced substantially by the market pressure for a
product. For our purposes we demand that our design system is interactive
and so heuristics and design experience play an important role.

There are a number of places in the synthesis process that allow the
designer to influence the design process. First and foremost is the
formulation of the initial input algorithm and the uniformization of the
data dependencies. Now although we have not emphasized the fact in our
discussions, systolic synthesis is based on the idea of representing
algorithms as recurrence equations. Recurrence equations correspond
quite neatly with the idea of indexed_variables and loops in standard
(imperative) programming languages. Consequently we would expect
better results from our SADE if we provide an initial specification which
has a regular and recurrent form. In particular the size and structure of the
index_expressions influence the complexity of the algorithm data dependencies. Dependencies can be manipulated by suitable choices of pipelining
and routing vectors. Usually the choice of vectors is non-unique and the
designer can select appropriate vectors to bring out particular features of
a design which match the goals of the design exercise. A particular set of
variable matrices determine data dependencies which in turn influence the
final solution polytope of timing schedules. Once possible schedules are

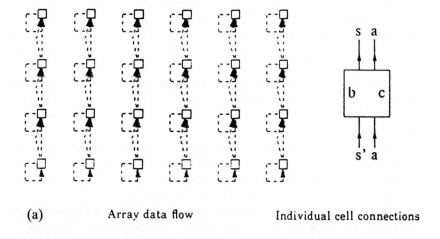

(a)   Array data flow   Individual cell connections

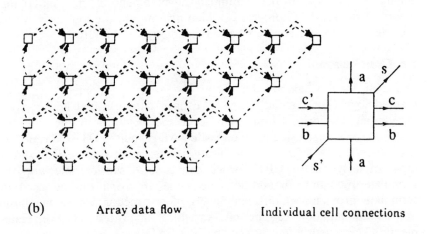

(b)   Array data flow   Individual cell connections

Figure 9.17 Bit parallel multiplier arrays.

known the designer can opt for the optimal schedule or choose one more appropriate for the design objective. For example each timing function prohibits certain sets of allocations – i.e. the directions parallel to the timing hyperplanes. Consequently the designer may choose a non-optimal schedule so that a projection prohibited by the optimal timing function can be employed. For instance to make data non-stationary and thus avoid loading or unloading of data at the initial or final stages of a computation, or to produce uni-directional data flow for fault tolerance. Another point worth stating is the following. Because more than one timing polytope is possible and each one has an optimal schedule. The globally optimal timing schedule will be the one that produces the best overall computation time – this function is difficult to find and requires identification and formulation of the best algorithm representation. Indeed, to give our package a unified and underlying mathematical framework only linear timing schedules are allowed – it is known that some nonlinear schedules can produce better results (see Chapter 3).

Finally a few words about the philosophy behind the Newcastle SADE. We envisage our tool not as a compiler, but more as a CAD tool for source-to-source transformation. The starting source is the PASCAL description; the end source a suitable high level parallel language or description language (in the case of circuits). Our view is that the SADE should be used in a similar manner to the way that control engineers use computer aided control system design packages. Provided a designer has an intuitive understanding of the synthesis process there should be nothing to prevent use of the environment. From a computer science and engineering viewpoint the continued development of the underlying theory of the synthesis process is a high priority and we look forward to the addition of more complex design techniques in the future.

9.6 Conclusions

Our aim in this chapter has been to promote automatic synthesis methodologies for systolic design. We have demonstrated how systolic arrays can be derived from high level specifications in the form of PASCAL programs using the Newcastle SADE and the DTAGS transformation kernel. A high level specification is far more flexible than direct input of a system of UREs which can require considerable work to formulate by hand. In addition the same approach can be used to formulate problems at different levels of abstraction where the basic unit of computation can be bit, variable, or procedural level statements. Consequently it is hoped that the SADE will promote the more widespread use of systolic techniques. Indeed one of the great advantages of our approach is that the designer requires only an intuitive knowledge of the design process as expressed in section 9.2. The technical and messy details of the underlying synthesis procedures such as pipelining and routing, or the construction of projections are hidden away from the user. All a designer has to do is write the initial program and select various alternatives.

At the start of this chapter we stated that systolic modelling was about algorithmic engineering. Our SADE is only the first step towards a comprehensive algorithmic engineering environment. In particular the DTAGS kernel deals only with single designs described by a single polytope. Such designs may be regarded as the building blocks for more complex design by domain composition techniques. Our work is now focused on the provision of a high level interface which supports the construction of composite and parameterized domains for more complex algorithms for which systolic solutions are known (e.g. the Kalman filter). The modular structure of the SADE makes the incorporation of these new facilities simple and straightforward. Perhaps such tools will form the next generation of systolic synthesis methods.

Acknowledgement

This work is supported by SERC grant GR/F80494.

References

Andonov, R., Aleksandrov, V., and Benaini, A., 1991, A linear systolic array for the knapsack problem, Technical Report No. 12, May 1991, Center for Informatics and Computer Technology, Bulgarian Academy of Sciences.

Brent, R. P., and Kung, H. T., 1979, The area-time complexity of binary multiplication, Technical Report CMU-CS-79-05, Dept Computer Science, CMU, USA.

Cappello, P. R., and Steiglitz, K., 1984, Unifying VLSI design with linear transformations of space-time, *Advances in Computing Research*, **2**, 23–65.

Carriero, N., and Gelernter, D., 1989, Linda in Context, *Comm. ACM*, **32**(4), 444–60.

Chand, D. R., and Kapur, S. S., 1970, An algorithm for convex polytopes, *J.ACM*, **17**, 78–86.

Chvatal, V., 1980, *Linear Programming*, W.H. Freeman and Co.

Darte, A., 1991, Regular partitioning for synthesizing fixed-sized systolic arrays, *Integration, The VLSI Journal*, **12**, 293–304.

Fortes, J. A. B., and Moldovan, D. I., 1984, Data broadcasting in linearly scheduled array processors, in *Proc. 2nd Ann. Symp. on Computer Architecture*, IEEE Press, Silver Springs, 224–31.

Gachet, P., Joinnault, B., and Quinton, P., 1986, Synthesizing systolic arrays using DIASTOL, in *Int. Workshop on Systolic Arrays* (eds Moore, McCabe, Uruquart), Adam Hilger, 25–6.

Householder, A. S., 1970, *The Numerical Treatment of a Single Non-linear Equation*, McGraw-Hill.

Ibarra, O. H., and Sohn, S. M., 1990, On mapping systolic algorithms onto the Hypercube, *IEEE J. Parallel and Distributed Computing*, **1** (1), 48–64.

Inmos, 1984, *Occam Programming Manual*, Int. Series in Computer Science, (ed. C.A.R Hoare), Prentice Hall.

Kung, H. T., 1982, Why systolic architecture?, *Computer*, **15**(1), 37–45.

Kung, H. T., 1984, Systolic algorithms for the CMU WARP processor, Report CMU-CS-84-158, Carnegie Mellon University.

Kung, H. T., and Leiserson, C. E., 1980, Systolic arrays for VLSI, *Introduction to VLSI Systems*, Addison-Wesley, Reading, Ch. 8.

Kung, H. T., and Lam, M. S., 1984, Wafer-scale integration and two-level pipelined implementation of systolic arrays, *J. of Parallel and Distributed Computing*, **1**, 32–63.

Kung, S. Y., 1988, *VLSI Array Processors*, Prentice-Hall.

de Lange, A. J. J., 1991, Design and implementation of highly parallel pipelined systems, PhD thesis, Delft University of Technology, Jan.

Lenguaer, C., Barnett, M., and Hudson, D. G., 1991, Towards systolizing compilation, *Distributed Computing*, **5**, 7–24.

Lipsett, R., Schaefer, C., and Usseus, C., 1989, *VHDL: Hardware description and design*, Kluwer Academic Publishers.

McCanny, J. V., and McWhirter, J. V., 1982, Completely iterative, pipelined multiplier array suitable for VLSI, *IEE Pt G*, **129**(2), 40–46.

McCanny, J. V., and McWhirter, J. G., 1986, The derivation and utilisation of bit level systolic array architectures, in *Int. Workshop on Systolic Arrays* (eds Moore, McCabe, and Uruquart), Adam-Hilger, 47–59.

McWhirter, J. G., 1989, Algorithmic engineering – an emerging discipline, *Advanced Algorithms and Architectures for Signal processing IV*, **1152**, 2–15.

Megson, G. M., 1991, Systolic array techniques II: a practical approach, in *Proc. Jt. ICL/Newcastle Int. seminar on Parallel Computing*, University of Newcastle upon Tyne, (ed. B.R. Randell), ppVIII, 19–34.

Megson, G. M., Brudaru, O., and Comish, D., 1992, Systolic algorithms for Aitken root finding method, *Parallel Computing*, **18**, 415–29.

Megson, G. M., and Comish, D., 1991, Systolic Algorithm Design Environments, in *2nd Int. Specialist Seminar on Parallel Digital Processors, Conf. Pub. No. 334*, 100–104.

Megson, G. M., and Evans, D. J., 1992, VLSI systolic arrays for table based algorithms, in *Advances in Parallel Computing Vol II*, JAI Press Ltd, 187–290.

Noble, B., 1969, *Applied Linear Algebra*, Prentice-Hall, 122–32.

Quinton, P., and van Dongen, V., 1989, The mapping of linear recurrence equations on regular arrays, *J. VLSI Signal Processing*, **1**, 95–113.

Rajopadhye, S. V., 1989, Synthesizing systolic arrays with control signals from recurrence equations, *Distributed Computing*, **3**, 88–105.

Rajopadhye, S. V., and Fujimoto R. M., 1990, Automating systolic array design, *Integration, The VLSI Journal*, **9**, 225–42.

Savage, J. E., 1981, Area-time trade-offs for matrix multiplication and related problems in VLSI models, *J. Computer and System Sciences*, **22**, 230–42.

Swart, G., 1985, Finding the convex hull facet by facet, *J. of Algorithms*, **6**, 17–48.

10

From Architecture to Algorithm – A Formal Approach

Nam Ling and Magdy A. Bayoumi

10.1 Introduction

In the past decade, the demand for high-speed computation in many arithmetic and digital signal processing (DSP) applications has increased dramatically. The availability and advances in low cost, high speed, high density very large scale integration (VLSI) technology has provided a new dimension in implementing architectures, particularly the evolution of algorithm-based application-specific architectures. One major class of such architectures is systolic arrays (Kung, 1978; Kung, 1988), which serve as an efficient means in realizing many algorithms in modern signal and image processing applications. As a result, the increasing demand in high-speed computation in the areas of DSP and image processing, and the rise in emphasis on system reliability, systolic arrays have become more complex in terms of cell structure, interconnection topology, and data flow (Ling and Bayoumi, 1989). Complete, precise, and formal description of architectures has undoubtedly become vital for unambiguous and complete communications among designers and implementers, as well as for formal verification of correctness. Design correctness has also become increasingly significant as errors in design may result in a strenuous debugging process, or even in the repetition of a costly manufacturing process. Although simulation has been used widely as the technique for checking hardware and architectural designs, it does not guarantee the conformance of designs to specifications. All these give the need for formal specification and verification: a mathematical, instead of an experimental, approach for describing and reasoning of architectures. In fact, experts predicted that commercial CAD tools will offer some formal verification techniques within three to five years (D&T, 1989). The influx of research in applying high-order and temporal logic to hardware designs further supports such evidence. The popularity of hardware description languages such as VHDL, Verilog, and even Occam, is certainly an intermediate step towards the need of fully formal systems for hardware design.

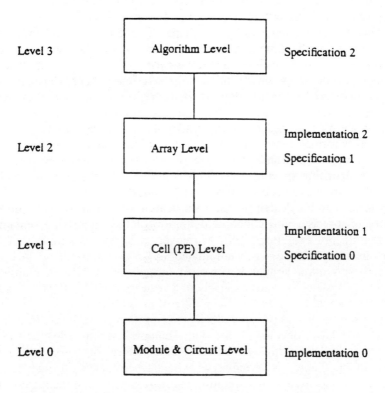

Figure 10.1 Different architectural levels of a systolic array.

A systolic array is a network of processors which rhythmically compute and pass data through the system, (Kung, 1978). A systolic array can be abstracted at different architectural levels (Kung, 1988) as shown in Fig. 10.1. The **algorithm level** (level 3) defines the algorithm/mathematical expression to be realized. The **array level** (level 2) defines the interconnection between different cells (PEs) and their functional capabilities. The **PE or cell level** (level 1) defines the hardware modules (e.g. adders, multipliers, registers) for the PEs and their interfaces. The **module and circuit level** (level 0) defines the internal circuitry of individual modules. A further **geometric or layout level** can be defined which specifies the photolithography mask features of the circuitry for VLSI fabrication. At each of the abstraction levels the architecture is hierarchically specified to decrease the complexity of the description. At, and only at, the array level an architecture depicts the properties of a systolic array (synchrony, modularity and regularity, spatial and temporal locality, and pipelinability) as well as features such as repeatability and parallel processing ability. This chapter is concerned with describing systolic architectures and transforming given array level systolic architecture designs to specified algorithms in a formal way. In other words, the chapter introduces a novel formalism and several mathematical techniques to show whether given systolic architectures satisfy their respective algorithm level specifications. Although several mapping techniques have already been developed to produce correct-by-construction arrays from given algorithms, these techniques can only be applied to a limited class of algorithms. In fact, many systolic arrays reported are designed by *ad hoc* or systematic, but not necessarily formal, techniques. Hence, formal techniques are necessary to serve as tools to guarantee the correctness of systolic design with respect to their algorithm specifications. This is in line with the current trend of formal techniques to reduce design and debugging time.

A formalism for description and verification of architectures requires a complete, precise, and coherent definition of the underlying semantics (Camurati and Prinetto, 1988). Moreover, it is very desirable that the formalism stays simple, easily automated for CAD, and be able to be easily unified with other similar lower level formalisms to form a multilevel reasoning system for various levels of hardware (IEEE, 1990). A good formalism should also exploit the nature of target architectures to provide elegant notations and possibly efficient verification procedures. In view of these, we have developed Systolic Temporal Arithmetic (STA) for specifying and verifying systolic array architectural designs at the array level. In this chapter, we briefly review the STA formalism, present several verification techniques by exploiting the attributes of systolic arrays, and describe a suitable Prolog-based verifier that we developed to automate the verifications. Several examples are also provided in this paper. Our verifier is designed with the following goals in mind: ease of encoding and manipulating the steps of execution; ease of debugging the codes; and fast execution time. Besides this, since Prolog is also applicable for lower level module and circuit verification, (e.g. Maruyama and Fujita, 1985; Fujita *et al.*, 1983), this allows the forming of a multilevel formal verification system.

10.2 Formal approaches to systolic design: related work

In line with the trend of formal verification, many techniques and verifiers have been developed for the specification and verification of circuit and module hardware (Camurati and Prinetto, 1988). However, work on specification with functional verification of systolic arrays at the array architectural level is still rare. One of the most significant contributions for proving techniques for systolic arrays is the mathematical model of systolic networks due to Melhem and Rheinboldt (1984). Data items are represented by data sequences and the cell computations are modelled by a system of difference equations involving operations on these data sequences. The input/output of the network are obtained by solving this system of difference equations. The correctness of the network is verified by the correct input/output description obtained. Melhem further develops a simulation language called SCE based on this model. Kuo, Levy, and Musicus (1984) formulate space-time-data equations to describe the motion of data elements and waves in an array; using this approach, the correctness of a systolic architecture implementing a desired algorithm can be proved. Jover *et al.* (1986) use equivalence transformations to convert an algorithm to an array. Verification is performed by reversing the transformation path to obtain an algorithm equivalent to the original one. Johnsson and Cohen (1981) propose a mathematical formalism that treats data and control in the same manner. Topology, pipelining, and other similar properties can be determined from the expressions, and can hence be used to provide analysis to computation networks such as systolic arrays.

Hennessey (1986) describes systolic arrays by a language called CCS (Calculus for Communicating Systems), due to Milner (1980, 1983), which is very similar to INMOS Occam (Wilson, 1983). He applies syntactic transformations for verification. Such a set of transformations can be used to transform specification descriptions to implementation descriptions, or vice versa. Chen and Mead (1982; Chen, 1983) embody the idea that each processing element implements a set of functions and that the behaviour of a whole network is a set of recursive equations obtained by analysing the interconnection of the processing elements. Inductive techniques for program verifications are used to show the correctness of systolic algorithms. Rajopadhye and Panangaden (1985) express the processing element as a function on a stream of data; they also use program verification techniques to verify the correctness of systolic arrays, each of which is a connection of these processing elements.

Other related work is due to Kung and Leiserson (1978), Lev-Ari (1983), Kung and Lin (1983), Tiden (1984), Probst and Li (1988), Sistla's (1983) uses of model logic, Jover and Kailath's (1984) Lines of Computation (LOCs) concept, Ossefort (1982) and Foster's (1981) program verification techniques, Purushothaman and Subrahmanyan's (1989) mechanical certification and the use of Boyer-Moore theorem prover, and a few others.

Provided above is a review on the techniques for systolic array design, verification and specification notations developed which can be used for verifications. However, many authors have applied formal notations for specifying systolic arrays and used them for synthesis purposes (Moldovan, 1983; 1984; Quinton, 1984; Cappello and Steiglitz, 1983; 1984; Rao, 1985; Kung, 1985; Clauss *et al.*, 1990; Bu *et al.*, 1990; Moreno and Lang, 1990; and many others).

10.3 Systolic temporal arithmetic (STA): a formalism for systolic design

Systolic temporal arithmetic (STA) is a special purpose formalism developed to exploit the unique attributes of systolic arrays to provide constructs to simplify description and verification of systolic array architecture. Moreover, it is developed with multi-abstraction level reasoning in mind. The constructs and operators involved are similar to interval temporal logic (Moszkowski, 1985) so that coherent multilevel reasoning for systolic arrays can be developed. Three abstraction mechanisms (Eveking, 1985; Melham, 1988) are applied to interval temporal logic to produce STA: **carrier abstraction** in which the hardware modules and circuits in the implementation of the cells are abstracted; **value and operation abstraction** in which values of data and variables are expressed in terms of real numbers instead of bit values 0 and 1 and arithmetic operations are used instead of logical operations; and **systolic feature abstraction** so that unique attributes such as synchrony, regularity, repeatability, modularity, spatial and temporal locality, pipelinability, and parallel processing ability can be represented. In this section, a brief overview of a simplified STA is given. More detailed description of our STA formalism is given in (Ling, 1989; Ling and Bayoumi, 1990).

10.3.1 STA time model

To exploit the highly synchronized and localized nature of systolic arrays, a linear, discrete time model is adopted and time points are finite sequences of cycles $c_1, c_2, \ldots, c_n$ as shown in Fig. 10.2. All cycles are of the same fixed duration. Changes of system state can only take place at the clock transitions (the boundary between c_i and c_{i+1}, for all i) and the system remains stable within each cycle; no changes are allowed within a *cycle*. The cycle is therefore the smallest indivisible time unit for systolic array description. In such a time frame, the 'next' concept for temporal operators refers to the next 'cycle'. The first occurrence of the cycle c_1 (i.e. systolic array begins its operation) begins at time equal to 0.

10.3.2 STA syntax and semantics

The sentences in STA are formed according to the context-free syntax described in Appendix A using the Backus-Naur Form (BNF). The brief presentation of the semantics is given in Appendix B. We highlight some of the important features here. In STA there is a distinction between normal and temporal variables and constants. A **normal variable** is a letter written in lower case italic font, with or without a subscript, each of which can have a value ranging over any real numbers. **Normal constants** are actual real numbers; a quantity with an unknown value is designated by '__'. Each normal variable/constant is used to denote a value in only one

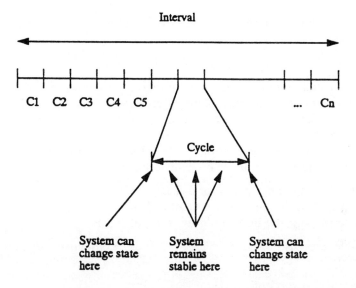

Figure 10.2 The model of time for STA.

cycle. One important feature of STA is the use of **temporal variables**. Each has a value which is a sequential temporal connection of real numbers from the first to the last cycle of operation. A temporal variable, denoted by a letter written in lower case Roman font, with or without a subscript, is expressed canonically by a sequential connection of normal variables, normal constants, and/or normal arithmetic expressions from the first to the last cycle (syntactic category < temp. var. expr. >). For convenience, temporal variables can also be expressed in terms of other temporal variables. Using temporal variables enables us to describe dynamic arithmetic values and operations effectively. The *AND* operator ∧ and temporal operators such as henceforth ⟦⟧, next ○, transport next O^i, etc., borrowed from ITL, are used to provide temporal connection of arithmetic entities to indicate arithmetic operations and values at different times. For example, ○ indicates the value in the next cycle, O^2 indicates the value in the next next cycle, and so on, and ⟦⟧ indicates the value that remains the same from that cycle onward. Take, for instance, a temporal variable u, where

$$u = u_0 \wedge \bigcirc u_1 \wedge \bigcirc {}^2 u_2 \wedge O^3 \llbracket u_k$$

indicates that u is u_0 in the present cycle, u_1 in the next cycle, u_2 in the next next cycle, and u_k thereafter. Variables that have values in only one cycle are written in italic font.

A few other symbols require some explanation. First, to simplify the writing of some temporal variables, the symbol $\bigwedge\limits_{\alpha=a}^{b}$ is created and is defined as

$$\bigwedge\limits_{\alpha=a}^{b} u_\alpha \equiv_{\mathrm{def}} u_a \wedge u_{a+1} \wedge \cdots \wedge u_b;$$

Also, an underscore '＿' is used to denote an unknown value in the cycle. The priorities of the operators are implied in the BNF syntax description. Conventional mathematical operators have their priorities as in conventional mathematics.

Several **identifiers** are introduced in STA to identify subjects with respect to subjects. The list of predefined identifiers is given below:

In(I_i, B_i): the input port I_i of cell B_i
Out(O_i, B_i): the output port O_i of cell B_i
Mem(M_i, B_i): the memory location M_i of cell B_i

Predicates are also used in STA; a list of predefined predicates is given below:

Sys(S): S is a systolic array
Cell(B_i): B_i is a cell (PE)
Ip(B_i): B_i is an inner-product cell (performs multiplication and addition)
Conn(X, Y): X and Y are directly connected (by wires) (same as Conn(Y, X))
Val(X, m): the value of the data on/in the port/memory location X is m

The last predicate is the **value predicate,** which is commonly used to indicate data items on input/output/memory of a cell/array. Besides these predicates, users can define additional predicates if needed.

10.3.3 STA axioms, rules, and theorems

STA temporal variables are operated by a few axioms, rules, and theorems developed for STA.

Axiom 1
Let 'op' be a binary arithmetic, logical, or relational operator operating on two temporal variables, then quantities of the same cycle are 'op' with each other; that is

$$(u_0 \wedge \bigcirc u_1 \wedge \cdots \wedge \bigcirc^{k-1} u_{k-1} \wedge \bigcirc{}^k[] u_k) \text{ op } (v_0 \wedge \bigcirc v_1 \wedge \cdots$$
$$\wedge \bigcirc{}^{m-1} v_{m-1} \wedge \bigcirc{}^m[] v_m)$$
$$= (u_0 \text{ op } v_0) \wedge \bigcirc (u_1 \text{ op } v_1) \wedge \bigcirc^2 (u_2 \text{ op } v_2) \wedge \cdots$$
$$\wedge \bigcirc{}^{m-1}(u_{m-1} \text{ op } v_{m-1}) \wedge \bigcirc{}^m(u_m \text{ op } v_m) \wedge \bigcirc^{m+1}(u_{m+1} \text{ op } v_m) \cdots$$
$$\wedge \bigcirc{}^k[](u_k \text{ op } v_m) \quad (\text{if } k \geqslant m)$$

or $(u_0 \text{ op } v_0) \wedge \bigcirc (u_1 \text{ op } v_1) \wedge \bigcirc^2 (u_2 \text{ op } v_2) \wedge \cdots \wedge \bigcirc^{k-1}(u_{k-1} \text{ op } v_{k-1}) \wedge$
$\bigcirc^k (u_k \text{ op } v_k) \wedge \bigcirc^{k+1}(u_k \text{ op } v_{k+1}) \cdots \wedge \bigcirc^m \Box (u_k \text{ op } v_m)$ (if k ≤ m)

Axiom 2
Let 'op' be a binary arithmetic or logical operator, then

$$x \text{ op } \_\_ = \_\_ \text{ op } x = \_\_$$

That is, if one operand of 'op' is unknown, then the result is unknown.

Axiom 3
Quantities that appeared in time < 0 are purely mathematical results; they have no practical meaning and can be ignored.

Axiom 4
Two temporal quantities are equal if and only if their quantities are equal in each cycle:

$$(u_0 \wedge \bigcirc u_1 \wedge \cdots \wedge \bigcirc^{k-1} u_{k-1} \bigcirc^k \Box u_k) = (v_0 \wedge \bigcirc v_1 \wedge \cdots$$
$$\wedge \bigcirc^{m-1} v_{m-1} \wedge \bigcirc^m \Box v_m)$$

iff $u_0 = v_0, u_1 = v_1, \ldots, u_m = v_m, u_{m+1} = v_m, \ldots,$
$$u_k = v_m \text{ (if k } \geq \text{ m)}$$
or $u_0 = v_0, u_1 = v_1, \ldots, u_k = v_k, u_k = v_{k+1}, \ldots,$
$$u_k = v_m \text{ (if k } \leq \text{ m)}$$

The validity of these axioms can be seen trivially using common sense reasoning and arithmetic. The above axioms express a temporal variable as

$$u_0 \wedge \bigcirc u_1 \wedge \cdots \wedge \bigcirc^{k-1} u_{k-1} \wedge \bigcirc^k \Box u_k$$

which is the most general form for expressing temporal variables. Any other form is a special case of this form. Some rules concerning temporal operators that are also useful for systolic array reasoning are stated below:

$\bigcirc \bigcirc$ rule:

$$\bigcirc (u_0 \wedge \bigcirc u_1 \wedge \bigcirc^2 u_2 \ldots.) = \bigcirc u_0 \wedge \bigcirc \bigcirc u_1 \wedge \bigcirc \bigcirc^2 u_2 \cdots$$

$\Box$ rules:

$$\Box x = x \wedge \bigcirc \Box x$$

$\bigcirc$ rule:

$$\bigcirc^k x = \bigcirc \bigcirc^{k-1} x \qquad \bigcirc^p \bigcirc^q x = \bigcirc^{p+q} x$$

These rules follows directly from temporal logic (Abadi and Manna 1986; Hailpern 1980). As an example of using these rules, we can have

$$\bigcirc (u_0 \wedge \bigcirc u_1 \wedge \cdots \wedge \bigcirc{}^{k-1}u_{k-1} \wedge \bigcirc{}^{k}\Box u_k) =$$
$$\bigcirc u_0 \wedge \bigcirc{}^{2}u_1 \wedge \cdots \wedge \bigcirc{}^{k}u_{k-1} \wedge \bigcirc{}^{k+1}\Box u_k$$

as the result of $\bigcirc\,\bigcirc$ rule and $\bigcirc$ rule. Two theorems, which are particularly useful in the reasoning of bi-directional systolic arrays, are developed as follows:

Theorem T1

Let u_1, u_i, u_{i+1}, etc., denote temporal variables, then the STA difference equation

$$u_i = \_ \wedge \bigcirc u_{i+1} \qquad \text{for } i = 0, 1, \ldots, k-1 \qquad (10.1)$$

has solution

$$u_t = \bigwedge_{r=0}^{k-t-1} \bigcirc{}^{r}\_ \wedge \bigcirc{}^{k-t}u_k \qquad \text{for } t = 0, 1, \ldots, k \qquad (10.2)$$

Theorem T2

Let u_i, v_i, etc., denote temporal variables, then the STA difference equation

$$v_{i+1} = (\_ \wedge \bigcirc v_i) + u_i \qquad \text{for } i = 1, 2, \ldots, k \qquad (10.3)$$

has solution

$$v_t = (\bigwedge_{r=0}^{t-2} \bigcirc{}^{r}\_ \wedge \bigcirc{}^{t-1}v_1) + \sum_{j=1}^{t-1} (\bigcirc{}^{j-2}\_ \wedge \bigcirc{}^{j-1}u_{t-j})$$
$$\text{for } t = 2, 3, \ldots, k+1 \qquad (10.4)$$

Theorem 1 can be proved by successive substitution and Theorem 2 can be proved by induction (detailed proofs, Ling (1989)). Axioms, rules, and theorems are useful for simplifications, deductions, and often provide convenient and natural short-cuts in proofs and reasonings for many systolic arrays.

Each sentence in STA is written in a declarative manner, in the form of 'Quantification. Predicate(subjects)', which can be mapped to a truth value. Examples are given in the next section.

10.4 Specification of systolic design: a formal approach

Mathematical (formal) specification of an architecture serves as an unambiguous tool in describing the structure and the behaviour of its design. Such descriptions also serve as given facts and goals in the formal verification process. In this section, formal specification of a systolic array based on STA is described. It is a mathematical description of its design structure and its intended behaviour at the array architectural level. The specification is written in declarative STA sentences. A validity symbol $\models$ is added to a sentence if it is true in all cycles. In our presentation, a two-dimensional systolic array for matrix-matrix multiplication

(Kung, 1985), as shown in Fig. 3a, is used as an example to briefly illustrate the framework. The array is used to multiply matrix A (elements $a_{11}, a_{12}, \ldots, a_{1n}, a_{21}, a_{22}, \ldots, a_{nn}$) and the matrix **B** (elements $b_{11}, b_{12}, \ldots, b_{1n}, b_{21}, b_{22}, \ldots, b_{nn}$) to produce the resulting product matrix **Y** (elements $y_{11}, y_{12}, \ldots, y_{1n}, y_{21}, y_{22}, \ldots, y_{nn}$), where y_{ij} is defined by $y_{ij} = \sum_{k=1}^{n} a_{ik} * b_{kj}$. Matrix elements are input in a skewed manner as shown. The contents of cell memories y_{ij} are initialized as 0s. At the end of the computations, the values of the elements of the resulting matrix are the values stored in the cell memories as shown. Computations and data flow are pipelined in two directions.

Our complete STA-based specification framework for systolic array has a structure specification and a behaviour specification, as discussed in detail below.

10.4.1 Structure specification

Component type specification

Here the type of cells (PEs) and modules used to build the array are specified. Typical specification uses the predicate 'Ip', indicating that the subject is an inner-product cell (i.e. perform multiplication and accumulation). The type of cells used in the array of Fig. 10.3(a) are collectively specified as

$$\vDash \forall\, 1 \leqslant i \leqslant n.\ \forall\, 1 \leqslant j \leqslant n.\ Ip(Y_{ij}) \tag{10.5}$$

Structural connectivity specification

Here the structural manner in which the cells are connected to form the entire systolic network is specified. Predicates of the form

$$\text{Conn}(\text{Out}(\text{port1, cell1}), \text{In}(\text{port2, cell2}))$$

are typically used to indicate the output port1 of cell1 is connected to the input port2 of cell2.

For example, for the array of Fig.10.3(a), the local connections in the horizontal direction can be collectively specified as

$$\vDash \forall\, 1 \leqslant i \leqslant n.\ \forall 1 \leqslant j < n.\ \text{Conn}(\text{Out}(O_\alpha, Y_{ij}), \text{In}(I_\alpha, Y_{i,j+1})) \tag{10.6}$$

where the predicate $\text{Conn}(\text{Out}(O_\alpha, Y_{ij}), \text{In}(I_\alpha, Y_{i,j+1}))$ indicates that the output O_α of cell Y_{ij} is connected to input I_α of cell $Y_{i,j+1}$. Similarly, the local connections in the vertical directions are

$$\vDash \forall 1 \leqslant j \leqslant n.\ \forall 1 \leqslant i < n\ \text{Conn}(\text{Out}(O_\beta, Y_{ij}), \text{In}(I_\beta, Y_{i+1,j})) \tag{10.7}$$

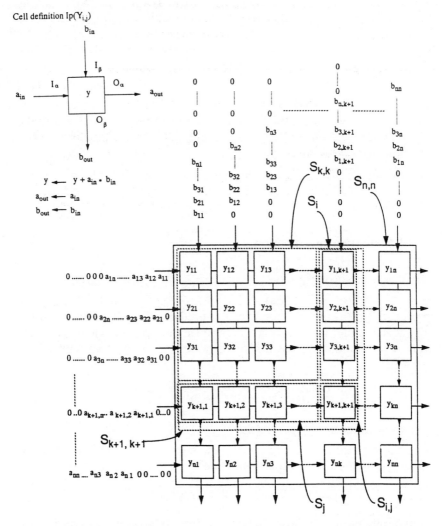

Figure 10.3(a) A 2D systolic array for matrix-matrix multiplication and its cell definition.

10.4.2 Behaviour specification

Component function specification

Here the function of each cell (PE) used in composing the array is specified. These functions are specified using implications. As an example, the function of the cells used in the array of Fig. 10.3(a) (see informal cell definition in Fig. 10.3(a)) is specified as

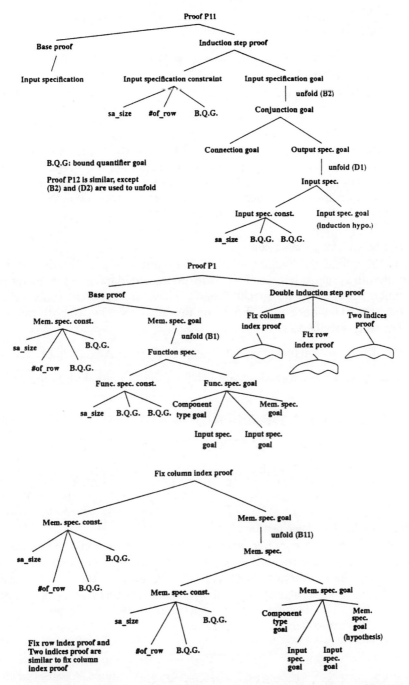

Figure 10.3(b) Proof tree and sub-proof trees showing the verification process for the 2D matrix-matrix multiplication systolic array.

$$\models \forall\ Y_{ij}\quad Ip(Y_{ij})\ \wedge Val(In(I_\alpha,\ Y_{ij}),\ a_{in})\ \wedge Val(In(I_\beta,\ Y_{ij}),\ b_{in})\ \wedge$$
$$Val(Mem(M,\ Y_{ij}),\ y)$$

$$\rightarrow Val(Mem(M,\ Y_{ij}),\_\wedge \bigcirc (y+a_{in}*b_{in}))$$
$$\wedge Val(Out(O_\alpha,\ Y_{ij}),\_\wedge \bigcirc a_{in})$$
$$\wedge Val(Out(O_\beta,\ Y_{ij}),\_\wedge \bigcirc b_{in}) \tag{10.8}$$

The antecedent of each implication is the conjunction of several predicates representing the cell type and the inputs and/or memory contents of this cell. The consequent of each implication is a value predicate or the conjunction of several value predicates representing the outputs and/or memory contents of this cell as a result of the computation being performed on the cell. Notice that outputs are always a cycle delay from the inputs, reflected by the next operator '$\bigcirc$'.

Input behaviour specification
Here the intended dynamic pattern of the input data at each input of the systolic array must be specified. The preloaded data in each memory location should also be specified here. These are specified using value predicates. The horizontal inputs to the array of Fig. 10.3(a) can be collectively specified as

$$\forall\ 1 \leqslant i \leqslant n.\ Val(In(I_\alpha,\ Y_{i1}),\ \bigwedge_{r=0}^{i-2} \bigcirc {}^r 0 \wedge \bigwedge_{r=1}^{n} \bigcirc {}^{i+r-2}a_{ir} \wedge \bigcirc {}^{i+n-1}[\ ]\ 0) \tag{10.9}$$

Temporal variable expressions are usually used to express the input data in these value predicates. The above expression is equivalent to

$$Val(InI_\alpha,\ Y_{11}),\ a_{11} \wedge \bigcirc a_{12} \wedge \cdots \wedge \bigcirc {}^{n-1}a_{1n} \wedge \bigcirc {}^n[\ ]\ 0) \qquad\text{and}$$

$$Val(In(I_\alpha,\ Y_{21}),\ 0 \wedge \bigcirc a_{21} \wedge \bigcirc {}^2 a_{22} \wedge \cdots \wedge \bigcirc {}^n a_{2n} \wedge \bigcirc {}^{n+1}[\ ]\ 0)\ \text{and} \ldots$$

Similarly, the vertical inputs are specified as

$$\forall\ 1 \leqslant j \leqslant n.\ Val(In(I_\beta,\ Y_{1j}),\ \bigwedge_{r=0}^{i-2} \bigcirc {}^r 0 \wedge \bigwedge_{r=1}^{n} \bigcirc^{j+r-2}b_{rj} \wedge \bigcirc^{j+n-1}[\ ]\ 0) \tag{10.10}$$

Output behaviour specification
Here the intended dynamic pattern of the array outputs (or memory contents if these are treated as outputs) are specified. Temporal variables expressing the output results should take the form of the mathematical specification at the algorithm level with some expected array operation cycle delays. The memory content (as output) of the cells in the array of Fig. 10.3(a) are collectively specified as

$$\forall\ 1 \leqslant i \leqslant n \ \forall\ 1 \leqslant j \leqslant n$$

$$Val\ (Mem(M,\ Y_{ij}),\ \bigwedge_{r=0}^{i+j-2} \bigcirc^r 0 \wedge \bigwedge_{r=1}^{n-1} \bigcirc {}^{i+j+r-2}(\sum_{m=1}^{r} a_{im}*b_{mj}) \wedge$$
$$\bigcirc^{i+j+n-2}[\ ]\ (\sum_{m=1}^{n} a_{im}*b_{mj})) \tag{10.11}$$

That is, the content of the memory location for cell Y_{ij} is 0 for the first $i+j-1$ cycles; then it takes the values $a_{i1}*b_{1j}$, $a_{i1}*b_{1j}+a_{i2}*b_{2j}$, ... in the cycles thereafter. From cycle $i+j+n-2$ onwards, the memory content of cell Y_{ij} remains as $\sum_{m=1}^{n} a_{im}*b_{mj}$, which is the value of the element i, j of the resultant matrix.

Specifications (10.5), (10.6), and (10.7) above provide a complete physical description of the design at the array level while specifications (10.8), (10.9), (10.10), and (10.11) give a complete functional description of the array. The preciseness of the description is followed from the precise semantics of STA used (Appendix B).

10.5 Verification of systolic design: a formal approach

In this section we present several formal techniques for proving the correctness of array designs based on STA. These strategies are adopted to exploit the attributes of systolic arrays to produce fast proofs and for possible automation. A formal verification of a systolic array at the array architectural level is a mathematical process for checking whether the array level architecture realizes the algorithm level specification. The verification process comprises the proving of the correctness of the following implication:

$$< Structural\ spec.> \wedge < Component\ function\ spec.>$$
$$\wedge <Input\ spec.> \rightarrow < Output\ spec.> \qquad (10.12)$$

That is, the correctness of the array means that if the array is built according to the structural specification, if the array inputs satisfy the input specification (includes initial conditions), and each array component and connection operates in faithfulness to its functional specification, then the array outputs are guaranteed to satisfy the output specification. Since the output specification constitutes the algorithm level mathematical specification with appropriate array operation cycle delays, proving the correctness of this implication will mean that the array realizes the algorithm level specification.

10.5.1 Verification by symbolic simulation

Symbolic simulation is a straightforward strategy when we apply it to exploit the locality nature of systolic arrays. This can be described by using the following loop procedure:

derive the outputs of the cells nearest to the array inputs;

while (output of array not arrived) do
   begin
            apply these outputs to be the inputs to the next level of cells
            and derive their outputs

end;

If the output of array = output specification of the array

then the correctness of the array is verified

else the array is incorrect with respect to the algorithm level specification.

Output derivation at each step is accomplished by using the structural and behavioural specifications (except output behaviour specification) as premises, together with the axioms and rules of STA. The final output of the array will arrive in the form with value predicates and temporal variables. If this is equal to the intended output specification, the correctness of implication (10.12) will be verified, and the array is thus correct with respect to the algorithm.

As a brief example, consider the 2-D systolic array of Fig. 10.3(a). To prove that the array is correct with respect to the matrix-matrix multiplication algorithm, we first derive the outputs and memory content of cell y_{11} from the structural, cell functional, and input behaviour specifications. The data on the input I_α to cell y_{21}, the data on the input I_β to cell y_{12}, as well as the output of cell y_{11} then serve as the inputs to cells y_{12} and y_{21}, for which the outputs and the memory contents can be derived. In a similar manner, we can derive the outputs and the memory contents of cells y_{13}, y_{22}, and y_{31}. This derivation proceeds like a wavefront until the outputs and the memory contents of all the cells are derived. The results can then be compared to the output specification to see if the array is correct. As a matter of fact, this technique can also be performed in a backward chaining manner (which is more appropriate for our Prolog verifier), starting from cell y_{nn} as our goal, and treating each previous cell and its input/output as a subgoal to be proved, and each subgoal is treated as a goal for which further subgoals have to be proved. The procedure repeats until the goals are matched by facts (e.g. input specifications), in which case the proof is complete. The procedure of symbolic simulation generally takes an enormous time if the array is large, or if the data flow is complex.

10.5.2 Verification by induction

Most hardware systems have irregular structures and as such the concept of induction cannot be applied to verify their correctness. However, due to the repeatability, regularity, and locality nature of systolic arrays, we found that induction techniques are very suitable for the formal verification of their designs. The principle exploits these properties to construct a proof that an array of any size is correct. The strategy is especially efficient for large arrays or arrays of a parameterized size, since the number of steps in the procedure does not depend on the number of cells in general (i.e. unlike symbolic simulation). Although applying induction

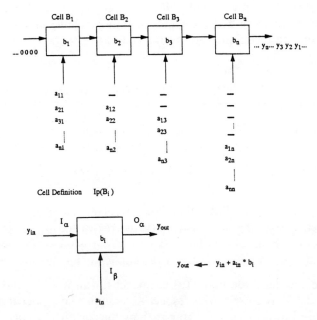

Figure 10.4(a) A 1D systolic array for matrix-vector multiplication and its cell definition.

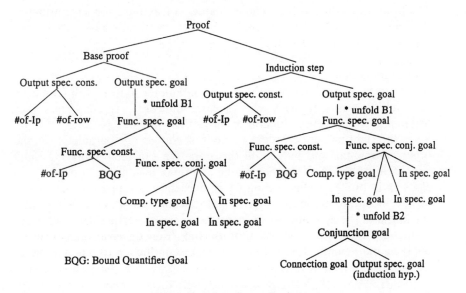

Proof tree showing the verification process

Figure 10.4(b) A proof tree showing the verification process for the 1D matrix-vector multiplication systolic array.

to proving 1-D array is not difficult, applying it to 2-D arrays and automating the proof with logic programming techniques is not as trivial. Four induction techniques are introduced in this section.

Regular mathematical induction

The regular mathematical induction procedure is stated as follows:
Let $P(n)$ be the statement of the form

$$< Structural\ spec.> \wedge < Component\ function\ spec.> \wedge$$
$$< Input\ spec.> \rightarrow <Output\ spec.>$$

for a systolic array of size n (can be n cells, n rows, etc.). There are three steps to proofs.

1. Basis of Induction. Show that $P(n_0)$ is correct ($n_0 < n$).
2. Inductive Hypothesis. Assume $P(k)$ is correct for any k ($k \geqslant n_0$).
3. Inductive Step. Show that $P(k+1)$ is correct on the basis of the inductive hypothesis. That is, $P(k)$ implies $P(k+1)$.

Then we can conclude that $P(n)$ is correct for all $n \geqslant n_0$; and hence the array of size n is correct with respect to its upper level specification. This can be used to prove a 1-D array such as that of Fig. 10.4(a).

Structured induction

The proof procedure is the same as mathematical induction except that in the inductive hypothesis, we assume $P(k)$ is correct for **all** k, $n> k \geqslant n_0$. This is a stronger induction.

Double induction

If $P(n)$ to be proved has more than one parameter to deal with (common for multidimensional array with several indices i, j, etc.), this is a technique of applying induction to more than just one parameter. If we know the right induction order, we can first choose one parameter, fix the other parameters and induce on this one. We can then apply the same approach to the other parameters one at a time, in some right order, until $P(k+1)$ is proved. This technique is necessary for proving many 2-D arrays, including the matrix-matrix multiplication example shown in later sections and the appendices. In these cases, after selecting the right order to prove a 2-D array, we can perform induction on each dimension by applying mathematical, structured, or reverse induction to one parameter at a time.

Reverse induction

This is similar to the mathematical induction except that the proof is proceeded backward. Our base case consists of proving $P(N)$, where N is a very large number. The induction step consists of proving $P(k-1)$

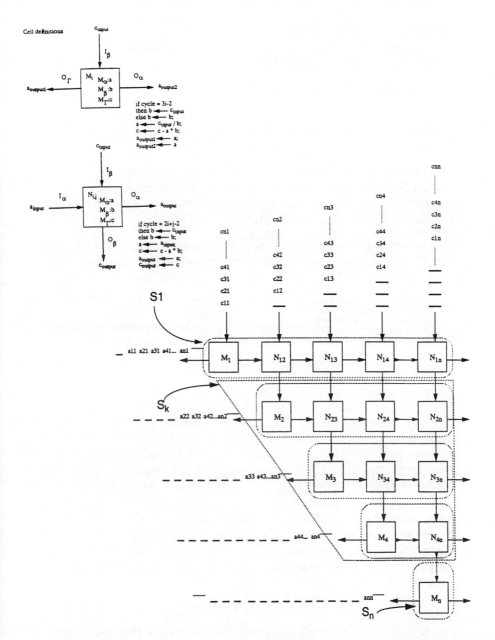

Figure 10.5(a) A triangular systolic array for LU decomposition and its cell definition.

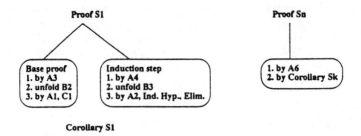

Corollary S1

T1 & T2 & T3 ==> S1 & Sk & Sn
Sk ==> G1 & G2 & G3

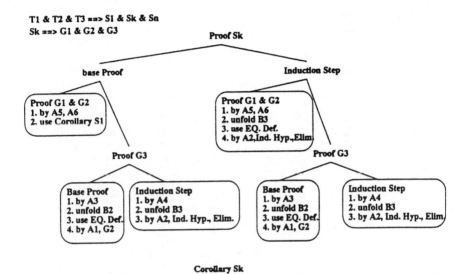

Corollary Sk

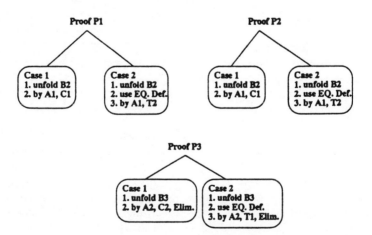

Figure 10.5(b) Sub-proof trees showing the verification process for the triangular LU decomposition systolic array.

assuming $P(k)$. Then we have a proof for $P(n)$ for $n \leqslant N$. Such proof is sufficient in some cases. For example, suppose we apply double induction on two parameters. We can apply regular induction on one parameter, and reverse induction on the second parameter if the second parameter can be bounded in terms of the first one. In this chapter, we apply reverse induction in providing our sub-proof for the sub-array S_k in the LU decomposition example of Fig. 10.5(a). This technique is useful here because the sub-array is a trapezoid, forming a part of the triangular array as shown in Fig. 10.5(a), with the longest row closest to the inputs. In this case we can prove the longest row first and use it as the base for induction.

Induction techniques introduced here greatly simplify the steps involved in verifying large arrays or arrays of any parameterized size. A logic programming based verifier was developed to automate these induction techniques using backward chaining and is discussed in section 10.6. In sections 10.7 and 10.8, we briefly illustrate how different induction techniques can be utilized to verify a 2-D array for matrix-matrix multiplication and a triangular array for LU decomposition.

10.5.3 Verification by solving STA difference equations

This technique is developed to verify arrays with dataflow in several complex directions, where induction techniques could be too difficult or impossible. Recalling that using difference equations to model cell computations were earlier proposed by Melhem and Rheinboldt (1984), we modify this model to be suitable for our STA formalism. The strategy exploits the regularity, locality, and repeatability nature of systolic arrays. It can be applied to arrays of any parameterized size. The disadvantages of this strategy are first, for simple arrays and dataflows it takes more time to verify the array as compared to using the other two strategies, and second, it depends on our ability to solve the systems of difference equations involved. Fortunately, in the cases of many systolic arrays, the STA difference equations take some standard forms for which we have developed the solutions (Theorems T1 and T2). The procedure for systolic array verification by solving STA difference equations is stated as follows:

1. **STA difference equations generation:** For a typical interior cell i in the array, express each of its output behaviours in terms of its inputs, using temporal variables. This can be obtained from the functional specification of the cell. From here we form the system of STA difference equations describing the input/output (I/O) relation of each typical cell.
2. **Array I/O relation derivation:** This is done by solving the system of STA difference equations obtained from step 1. The results are the STA

equations expressing each output of the array in terms of the array inputs. Theorems 1 and 2 can be used to provide standard solutions to many difference equations concerning systolic arrays.

3. **Output behaviour derivation:** Substitute each input temporal variable in the output expressions of step 2 by the corresponding data variables and constants in each cycle (obtained from the array input behaviour specification) and manipulate the expressions using STA axioms and rules to obtain the output behaviour of the array.

4. **Output comparison:** Compare the output derived from step 3 with the output specification of the array:

If the output of step 3 is equal to the output specification of the array

then the correctness of the array is verified;

else the array is incorrect with respect to the algorithm level specification.

An example of applying the technique to verify a bi-directional systolic array for 1-D convolution is given in section 10.9.

10.6 VSTA: a Prolog-based formal verifier for systolic design

In this section, we provide a brief discussion on automating the proof techniques discussed. In line with the trend of formal verification of hardware, several automated tools have been developed to implement formal verification of hardware designs (e.g. Barrow, 1984; German and Wang, 1985; Gordon, 1986; Hunt, 1987; Shostak, 1983; Probst and Li, 1988; Purushothaman and Subrahmanyan, 1989). Prolog, being the most popular logic programming language, has served as a powerful tool for proving the correctness of hardware (e.g. Clocksin, 1987; Bosco et al., 1988; Maruyama and Fujita, 1985; Fujita et al., 1983). To automate our proof techniques for systolic arrays, we developed a verifier called VSTA, implemented in Prolog. Prolog is adopted for automating the STA formalism and the corresponding verification techniques for systolic arrays due to the following factors; its usefulness and similarity to STA in representing bodies of facts in predicate forms (hence efficiency in encoding, understanding, and debugging); its power in symbolic manipulation (Prolog's pattern matching automatic backtracking mechanisms are very useful for implementing logical inferences); its ability to complete a proof within a reasonable amount of time; its implementation minimizes the unnecessary lower abstraction layers; its popularity and its wide acceptance for lower level module and circuit specifications and verifications. This allows the formation of a multilevel reasoning system.

In our verifier, temporal variables are encoded using list structure. Slight dissimilarity between Prolog and STA is bridged by a few operator definitions in Prolog. The backwards analysis of the systolic array is possible because of the description of the structures in terms of relations. The search-based computation in Prolog mimics 'don't know' nondeterminism. The nondeterministic nature of hypothetical reasoning about array structure can be captured by the logic programming method. The representation of STA axioms, rules, and theorems are expressions in Prolog. They can be decomposed and built up by Prolog predicates. These are represented as abstract objects in VSTA. Such meta-linguistic abstraction can be manipulated easily by our verifier (which is a meta-interpreter). The verifier is further described in the form of a proof tree later in this section.

Formal specification of a systolic design is input to the verifier in three different forms (clauses). If both the antecedents and consequent exist in a logic implication, the resulting clause is an 'inference rule'. Component function specification falls into this category. If a clause has only the consequent part, the clause is a 'fact'. Structural specification and input behaviour specification fall into this category. On the other side, if a clause has only the antecedent part, the clause is a 'question'. The output specification to be proved is provided by the user as a question to the verifier. The input to our verifier thus consists of declaring constrained facts (quantified predicate-type specifications), defining inference rules (implication-type specifications), and asking questions (a yes/no question on output specification). Our Prolog-based verifier is a man-machine interactive tool using backward chaining and rewriting to perform a proof of the goal. When temporal variables are evaluated, normalization techniques are applied. The output specification is formulated as a yes/no question input to the verifier and is treated as the goal to be proved. Our verifier takes care of different kinds of goals. Backwards proof takes place by matching a goal with the consequent of a rule; the antecedents become the subgoals. This unfolding process (replacing the consequent part by the corresponding antecedents) repeats until a sufficient number of facts are matched, in which case the proof of that goal is completed. Since the STA specification involves some bound quantifier (e.g. $\forall\, 1 \leq i \leq n$), a fact (or the antecedents of a rule) may have constraints. If the constraints are satisfied, the fact is valid and thus it can be used in the deduction step.

10.6.1 Automation of symbolic simulation by VSTA

Formal verification by symbolic simulation can be automated in VSTA in the backward way. The output specification to be proved is formed as a goal. Using valid facts (structural specification) and inference rules (functional specification of cells), backward chaining can take place by matching the goal with the consequent of a rule. The antecedents (inputs to the cells nearest to the array outputs) become the subgoals to be proved. Each of these subgoals can then be matched with the consequent of a rule and further subgoals (next level of inputs) can be established. Such an unfolding process repeats until the subgoals are matched with valid facts (input specification). At this point the goal is proved. Although easy to implement, symbolic simulation can be time consuming if the array to be proved is large. In such cases induction and other size independent techniques are preferred.

10.6.2 Automation of induction by VSTA

VSTA uses backward chaining to implement induction. The goal of proving $P(n)$ is set as a yes/no question and is divided into two, proving two subgoals: proving $P(n_0)$ (or $P(N)$) and $P(k+1)$ (or $P(k-1)$), assumed $P(k)$. Each subgoal is then treated as goal with the corresponding antecedents treated as subgoals to be proved. This process is done recursively, matching goals against consequents, setting up antecedents as subgoals, and backtracking in case of failure. If all the subgoals can be satisfied or validated, the goal is proved and the answer to the yes/no question will be yes. An example of this is depicted as a proof tree shown in Fig. 10.4(b) for verifying a 1-D systolic array for matrix-vector multiplication. At certain points in the tree, the subgoals are simply the constrained facts (i.e. structural and input specifications themselves), and are therefore satisfied, or auxiliary predicates, which are validated. These are shown as leaf nodes in the tree. Implication specifications such as the component functional specifications can be used as rules of inference to help set up subgoals. Our verifier allows the user control over backtracking and selects appropriate rules to improve efficiency. The fact that Prolog representation is close to our STA notation in representing bodies of facts in predicate forms makes user control and debugging easy.

Referring to the proof tree of Fig. 10.4(b), the root of the proof tree is our goal (i.e. output specification). Proof of this goal consists of proving the base and the induction step (the two branches from the root). The base proof is a constrained goal consisting of constraints (left branch) and a goal body. The constraints (the size of the base case) is a conjunction of subgoals which checks the number of the inner product cells and the number of input cycles. These subgoals are satisfied due to the structural specification and the input specification applied to the base case. The goal body of the base proof (its right branch) is the output 'Val' specification part of $P(n_0)$. This value predicate is the output specification in STA for the array of size n_0. The verifier matches this predicate with a consequent in the implication of the component function specification ((B1) in the figure). This implication is treated as an inference rule and the verifier then unfolds this functional specification, replacing the consequent with the corresponding antecedents (with proper substitution) as subgoals to be proved. This is called the functional specification goal, which is again a constrained goal. The constraint subgoal is similarly satisfied by the quantification aspect of the component type specification. The goal body of the constrained goal is a conjunction goal of four elements: one component type goal and three input specification goals. These four elements are constrained facts given in the specifications, and are therefore satisfied. Hence the base proof is completed. The induction step proof (proof of $P(k+1)$) is done in the same manner except that in one of the input specification goals we have another unfold. This unfold is due to the fact that the input to the level of cells forming the array of size $k+1$ depends on the output of the array of size k. This is done by unfolding the function of an interconnection ($\models \forall X \forall -Y.$ (Conn(X, Y) $\wedge$ Val(X, x) $\rightarrow$ Val(Y, x)), which is simply to transmit signals from one end to another without alteration. This is given as (B2) in the figure. This function specification is applied to the interconnections which connect the array of size k to cells to form the array of size $k+1$. The antecedents of this implication requires the proof of the existence of appropriate interconnections (connection goal on its left branch) and correct output value from the array of size k (output specification goal for size k on the right branch). The connection goal is satisfied by structural connectivity specifications while the output specification goal is validated by the inductive hypothesis (correctness of $P(k)$). In summary, the proof tree shows the decomposition of the proof procedure down to the leaf level. Each formula at the leaf level is either a constrained fact or a goal that can be validated by auxiliary predicates. Since all the leaf goals are satisfied (constrained facts) or valid (auxiliary predicates), the proof is completed. Our Prolog verifier uses depth-first search in the proof process. Pruning the proof to improve efficiency is also performed whenever appropriate.

10.7 Correctness of a 2D systolic design: a formal approach

In this section, we briefly describe how the correctness of a 2-dimensional systolic array design can be formally verified using our approach. The 2D systolic array for matrix-matrix multiplication of Fig. 10.3(a) is used as our example. A formal description of the array is briefly described in section 10.4. Appendix C shows the specification of the matrix-matrix multiplication array design that is input to our verifier for STA (VSTA). In this section, we briefly describe a formal approach to prove the correctness of such design. A sample session of an automated proof provided by our Prolog-based verifier VSTA is given in Appendix 10.D.

Given the specifications, $P(n)$ is now set to proving the output specification (10.11) of section 10.4:

$$P(n) = \forall \, 1 \leq i \leq n \quad \forall \, 1 \leq j \leq n$$

$$\text{Val} \, (\text{Mem}(M, Y_{ij}), \bigwedge_{r=0}^{i+j-2} \bigcirc^r 0 \wedge \bigwedge_{r=1}^{n-1} \bigcirc^{i+j+r-2}$$

$$(\sum_{m=1}^{r} a_{im}*b_{mj}) \wedge \bigcirc^{i+j+n-2} [] \, (\sum_{m=1}^{n} a_{im}*b_{mj}))$$

Noticing that the computation wavefront is in the diagonal direction, we first show that the result of a, say, 2×2 array (base) is correct with respect to its output specification. This can be done by symbolic simulation and implemented by using rewriting rules on the verifier (section 10.6.1). We can then assume that the intermediate $k\times k$ size array is correct. This will allow us to formulate the memory contents of all cells in the $k\times k$ array $S_{k,k}$, as

$$P(k) = \forall\ 1 \leq i \leq k\ \ \ \forall\ 1 \leq j \leq k$$

$$\text{Val (Mem(M, } Y_{ij}), \bigwedge_{r=0}^{i+j-2} \bigcirc^r 0 \wedge \bigwedge_{r=1}^{n-1} \bigcirc^{i+j+r-2} (\sum_{m=1}^{r} a_{im}*b_{mj})$$

$$\wedge \bigcirc^{i+j+n-2} \square\ (\sum_{m=1}^{n} a_{im}*b_{mj}))$$

and output of cells Y_{k1}, Y_{k2}, ..., Y_{kk}, Y_{1k}, Y_{2k}, ..., Y_{kk}, in STA, as

$$\forall\ 1 \leq i \leq k.\ \text{Val(Out}(O_\alpha, Y_{ik}), \bigwedge_{r=0}^{i-2+k} \bigcirc^r 0 \wedge \bigwedge_{r=1}^{n} \bigcirc^{i+r-2+k} a_{ir} \wedge \bigcirc^{i+n-1+k} \square\ 0)$$

$$\forall\ 1 \leq j \leq k.\ \text{Val(Out}(O_\beta, Y_{kj}), \bigwedge_{r=0}^{j-2+k} \bigcirc^r 0 \wedge \bigwedge_{r=1}^{n} \bigcirc^{j+r-2+k} b_{rj} \wedge \bigcirc^{j+n-1+k} \square\ 0)$$

At this point we need to apply double induction on two parameters i and j to prove $P(k+1)$ (i.e. $(k+1) \times (k+1)$ array $S_{k+1,k+1}$). Referring to Fig. 3(a), a correct induction order can be as follows. Based on the assumption of the sub-array $S_{k,k}$ being correct, the outputs O_α of $S_{k,k}$ (i.e. O_α output of cells Y_{ik}, $1 \leq i \leq k$), can be determined (as shown above) and become the inputs to sub-array S_i. With all its inputs defined, we can apply regular mathematical induction (fix index j at $k+1$ and induce on i) to prove the 1-D sub-array S_i, and from which we can determine the O_β output of S_i (i.e. O_β output of cell $Y_{k,k+1}$). Similarly, we can prove sub-array S_j (fix index i at $k+1$ and induce on j) and determine the output O_α of S_j (i.e. O_α of cell $Y_{k+1,k}$). The proof of a 1-D array (such as S_i and S_j) are similar to the proof described in Fig. 10.4(b). With its two outputs known the correctness of $S_{i,j}$ can be easily determined using (10.8) by simple rewriting. Hence the correctness of $S_{k+1,k+1}$ is proved. Therefore $P(k+1)$:

$$\forall\ 1 \leq i \leq k+1\ \forall\ 1 \leq j \leq k+1.$$

$$\text{Val (Mem(M, } Y_{ij}), \bigwedge_{r=0}^{i+j-2} \bigcirc^r 0 \wedge \bigwedge_{r=1}^{n-1} \bigcirc^{i+j+r-2}(\sum_{m=1}^{r} a_{im}*b_{mj}) \wedge$$

$$\bigcirc^{i+j+n-2} \square\ (\sum_{m=1}^{n} a_{im}*b_{mj}))$$

is proved. We can therefore conclude that $P(n)$ is correct and the correctness of the array of size n is thus proved. Our verifier conducts the same proof in the reverse order, as briefly presented in Appendix 10.D and the proof tree of Fig. 10.3(b).

The proof tree of the entire 2D array consists of several sub-proof trees to implement the proof discussed. This is briefly given in Fig. 10.3(b). Two sub-proofs (P11 and P12) are proved before the main proof (P1) is dealt with. The subproof (P11) shows the intermediate values at the input ports of y cells in the horizontal positions. The subproof P11 is done by mathematical induction which consists of a base proof and an induction step proof. Each proof uses input specifications, structure specifications and other rules in the nodes of the proof tree. Subproof P12 (not shown in Fig. 10.3(b)) is similar to P11 except that it shows the intermediate values of ports in the vertical positions. The main proof (P1) is pursued by double induction on both the horizontal direction and the vertical direction. The base case is proved by an unfolding using specification (10.8) while the induction proof consists of three cases (fix column index, fix row index, and extend both indices). Each of the fixed index cases (S_i, S_j sub-array) is done by unfolding using different specifications, and can be proved by using the 1-D array inductive proof technique, similar to that of Fig. 10.4(b). The case of extending both indices (sub-array $S_{i,\,j}$) can be proved by simple rewriting (simple deduction), since only one cell is involved. Appendices 10.C and 10.D show a simplified sample session of the specifications of the matrix-matrix multiplication example that is input to our Prolog-based verifier and the corresponding proof output.

10.8 Correctness of a triangular systolic design: a formal approach

Compared to the 2-D array of the previous section, a triangular array has more complicated data flow and topology that demands a different formal strategy for proof of correctness. In this section we briefly discuss a proof of correctness of a triangular systolic array for LU decomposition as shown in Fig. 10.5(a). The LU decomposition problem and its corresponding systolic array architectures are described in books such as (Kung, 1988).

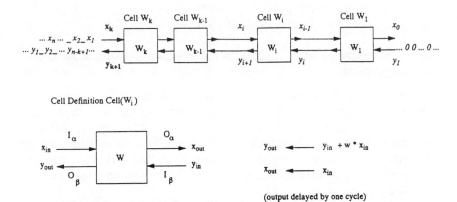

Figure 10.6 A bi-directional systolic array for 1D convolution and its cell definition.

Figure 10.5(a) shows one such array for decomposing a matrix **C** into a lower triangular matrix **A** and an upper triangular matrix **B**. Proving the correctness of the array is more complicated than that of a 2-D array. The structural and behavioural extension in the i direction going from a size k array to a size k+1 array is different from those in the j direction. As such, a regular double induction technique cannot be applied here in a straight-forward manner. Besides topology, the data flow is also less homogeneous compared to that of the 2-D matrix multiplication array. Moreover, the array consists of two different types of cells, namely, N_{ij} and M_i. A more detailed STA specification and proof of this systolic array using STA is described in Appendix 10.E. In this section we simply provide an outline of our proof.

To prove the correctness of the LU decomposition array of Fig. 10.5(a), we decompose the array into three subarrays S_1, S_k, and S_n, as shown in Fig. 10.5(a). We need to prove these three different sub-arrays. S_1 is considered as a separate case due to different inputs, and S_n is another separate case since it does not consist of cells N_{ij} and the corresponding data flow. The 1-D array S_1 can be proved easily by regular mathematical induction given the inputs, the structural, and the cell functional specifica-tions. Based on the correctness of S_1 we can confirm the outputs from this S_1 sub-array, and hence the inputs to the sub-array S_k. With the correct inputs and the given specifications, reverse induction is now used to prove the array S_k, because this array is trapezoidal, forming a part of the triangular array as shown in Fig. 10.5(a), with the longest row closest to the inputs. We should therefore prove this longest row first and use it as the base for reverse induction. Finally the sub-array S_n can be proved by trivial rewriting (simple deduction) technique since only one cell is involved. This completes the proof. An abstract proof tree (consists of several sub-proof trees) for the LU decomposition example is given in Fig. 10.5(b), and a more formal description in Appendix 10.E.

10.9 Correctness of a bidirectional systolic design: a formal approach

In this section the technique of solving STA difference equations is illustrated to provide a proof for a systolic array design with data flow in two directly opposite directions. In some of these cases, induction techniques could be difficult. A 1-D bi-directional systolic array for 1-D convolution as shown in Fig. 10.6 is used as our example. Given weights w_1, w_2, . . . , w_k and inputs x_1, x_2, . . . , x_n, 1-D convolution computes y_1, y_2, ..., y_{n-k+1} defined by $y_m = \sum_{i=0}^{k-1} w_{i+1} * x_{m+i}$. A bidirectional systolic array for this problem and its cell definition suggested by Kung (1982) is given in Fig. 10.6. All y_m are initialized to zeros and all w_i are preloaded into the cells. x and y move systolically in opposite directions and consecutive elements of x (y too) are separated by one cycle time. y_1 enters the network when x_1 has arrived at cell W_1. Computations are pipelined and the results y_m start to appear at the output of cell W_k $2*k-1$ cycles after the first input, followed by a new output every two cycles. The last result will appear $2*n-1$ cycles after the first input, giving the total computation time of $2*n$ cycles. The input specifications are expressed as

$$Val(In(I_\alpha, W_k), \bigwedge_{r=0 \text{ by } 2}^{2*n-2} (\bigcirc {}^r x_{\frac{r+2}{2}} \wedge \bigcirc {}^{r+1}\_) \wedge \bigcirc {}^{2*n} [\ ] \_)$$

$$Val(In(I_\beta, W_1), \bigwedge_{r=0}^{k-2} \bigcirc {}^r\_ \wedge \bigcirc {}^{k-1} (\bigwedge_{r=0 \text{ by } 2}^{2*(n-k)} (\bigcirc {}^r 0 \wedge \bigcirc {}^{r+1}\_)) \wedge \bigcirc {}^{2*n-k+1} [\ ]\_)$$

$$\forall 1 \leqslant i \leqslant k. \ Val(Mem(M, W_i), [\ ] w_i)$$

The output specification is

$$Val \ (Out(O_\beta, W_k), \sum_{r=0}^{2*k-2} \bigcirc {}^r\_ \wedge \bigcirc {}^{2*k-1} (\bigwedge_{r=0 \text{ by } 2}^{2*(n-k)} (\bigcirc {}^r y_{\frac{r}{2}+1} \wedge$$

$$\bigcirc {}^{r+1}\_)) \wedge \bigcirc {}^{2*n+1} [\ ]\_)$$

where $y_m = \sum_{i=0}^{k-1} w_{i+1} * x_{m+i}$

The construct of the form '$\bigwedge_{\alpha=a \text{ by } 2}^{b}$' is used to capture successive similar variables or quantities, each separated from the other by one cycle time,

$$\bigwedge_{\alpha=a \text{ by } 2}^{b} (u_\alpha \wedge v_\alpha) \equiv _{def} u_a \wedge v_a \wedge u_{a+2} \wedge v_{a+2} \wedge u_{a+4} \wedge v_{a+4} \wedge \cdots \wedge u_b \wedge v_b$$

We omit the rest of the specifications of the array here and concentrate only on briefly presenting the proof of correctness of the array. Readers can easily work out the rest of the specifications. Also, in presenting the proof, instead of showing STA predicate type representations, we present the manipulation of STA equations to illustrate the technique.

Let cell 1 denote the rightmost cell and cell k denote the leftmost cell of the systolic network; let temporal variables x_i, x_{i-1}, y_i, y_{i+1}, and w_i denote the sequences of values on input/output/memory I_α, O_α, I_β, O_β, and M respectively, of cell i. Temporal variables x_k, x_0, y_{k+1}, and y_1 thus denote the sequence of values on array inputs/outputs as shown in Fig. 10.6. The verification is given by the following steps:

1. STA difference equations generation
The input/output relationship for the cells are first obtained from the functional specification (see also cell definition of Fig. 10.6) and expressed using STA difference equations as

$$x_{i-1} = \_ \wedge \bigcirc x_i \quad \text{for } i = 1, 2, \ldots, k \tag{10.13}$$

$$y_{i+1} = \_\bigwedge \bigcirc (y_i + w_i * x_i) \qquad \text{for } i = 1, 2, \ldots, k \tag{10.14}$$

2. Array I/O relation derivation

Applying STA Theorem 1, the solution of (10.13) is:

$$x_i = \bigwedge_{r=0}^{k-i-1} \bigcirc {}^r \_\bigwedge \bigcirc {}^{k-i}x_k \qquad \text{for } i = 0, 1, \ldots, k \tag{10.15}$$

Substitute the value of x_i given by (10.15) into (10.14) and manipulate using STA axioms and rules, and the fact that $w_i = []w_i$, gives

$$y_{i+1} = (\_\bigwedge \bigcirc y_i) + (\bigwedge_{r=0}^{k-i} \bigcirc {}^r \_\bigwedge \bigcirc {}^{k-i+1}(w_i * x_k))$$
$$\text{for } i = 1, 2, \ldots, k \tag{10.16}$$

which is of the form specified in STA Theorem 2. Hence by Theorem 2 the solution is

$$y_t = \bigwedge_{r=0}^{t-2} \bigcirc {}^r \_\bigwedge \bigcirc {}^{t-1}y_1 + \sum_{j=1}^{t-1} (\bigcirc {}^{j-2} \_\bigwedge \bigcirc {}^{j-1} (\bigwedge_{r=0}^{k-t+j} \bigcirc {}^r \_\bigwedge \bigcirc {}^{k-t+j+1}(w_{t-j} * x_k)))$$

for $t = 2, 3, \ldots, k+1$. Hence for $t = k + 1$ we can manipulate STA axioms and rules to arrive at

$$y_{k+1} = \bigwedge_{r=0}^{k-1} \bigcirc {}^r \_\bigwedge \bigcirc {}^k y_1 + \sum_{j=1}^{k} (\bigwedge_{r=0}^{2*j-2} \bigcirc {}^r \_\bigwedge \bigcirc {}^{2*j-1} (w_{k-j+1} * x_k)) \tag{10.17}$$

(10.17) gives the array I/O relation.

3. Output behaviour derivation

We substitute each input temporal variables x_k, y_1, and w_{k-j+1} in the I/O relation (10.17) by the corresponding normal variables and constants (using the input specifications) to obtain the output behaviour of the array. After simplification using STA axioms and rules we have

$$y_{k+1} = \bigwedge_{r=0}^{2*k-2} \bigcirc {}^r \_\bigwedge \bigcirc {}^{2*k-1}(\bigwedge_{\substack{r=0 \\ \text{by } 2}}^{2*(n-k)} (\bigcirc {}^r (\sum_{j=1}^{k} (w_j * x_{j+\frac{r}{2}}))\bigwedge$$
$$\bigcirc {}^{r+1}\_))\bigwedge \bigcirc {}^{2*n+1}[] \_$$

This is now expressed in predicate form as

$$\text{Val}(\text{Out}(O_\beta, W_k), \bigwedge_{r=0}^{2*k-2} \bigcirc {}^r \_\bigwedge \bigcirc {}^{2*k-1}(\bigwedge_{\substack{r=0 \\ \text{by } 2}}^{2*(n-k)}$$
$$(\bigcirc {}^r (\sum_{j=0}^{k-1} (w_{j+1} * x_{\frac{r}{2}+1+j}))\bigwedge \bigcirc {}^{r+1}\_))\bigwedge \bigcirc {}^{2*n+1}[]\_)$$

which is equal to the output specification. The correctness of the array is thus verified.

10.10 Conclusion

In this chapter, we have presented a novel formalism, named Systolic

Temporal Arithmetic (STA), for formal specification and verification of systolic arrays at the array architecture level. We have also developed several verification techniques to exploit systolic attributes to provide efficient proofs of correctness for systolic designs. Finally, we have implemented our techniques on a Prolog-based verifier, named VSTA, to automate our verification procedures. The execution of the proofs are performed in SICStus Prolog on our Sun workstations. A sample session of the automated formal proof of correctness for a matrix-multiplication systolic design listed in Appendix 10.D takes a total elapsed time of less than five minutes, and an execution time of less than 30 seconds, if excluding time of interaction. Such a verifier can also be integrated as part of a design tool to ensure the correctness of systolic designs.

Acknowledgements

The first author wishes to acknowledge the funding from National Science Foundation under Grant No. MIP–9010385. He would also like to acknowledge the IBM Faculty Research Grant and the Arthur Vining Davis Junior Faculty Fellowship awarded by Santa Clara University.

Appendix 10.A: Syntax of STA

The sentences in STA are formed according to the syntax described in this section. The Backus-Naur Form (BNF) (Marcotty and Ledgard, 1986) is adopted to specify the context-free syntax of STA. The meta-symbols used are:

::=	meaning 'is defined as', same as $\equiv _{def}$.
|	meaning 'or', used to separate alternatives.
< >	angle brackets used to surround category names.
[ ]	square brackets used to enclose optional items.
{ }	braces used to indicate repetition of enclosed items, an arbitrary number (including null) of times.
( )	large parenthesis used to group elements of a syntactical unit. (Not to be confused with a regular-sized parenthesis '( )', which can be part of an STA sentence).

Using the above meta-symbols, the context-free syntax of STA is presented as follows:

<specification> ::= <structural spec.> <behaviour spec.>
<structural spec.> ::= {⊨ [<quantification>] <predicate> }
<behaviour spec.> ::= <functtional spec.> <input/output spec.>
<functional spec.> ::= {⊨ [<quantification>] <implication> }
<input/output spec.> ::= { [<quantification>] <value predicate>}
<spec. sentence> ::=   (⊨ [<quantification>] <predicate>) |

$$\Big(\vDash [\text{<quantification>}] \text{<implication>}\Big) \mid$$

$$\Big([\text{<quantification>}] \text{<value predicate>}\Big)$$

<implication> ::=　　<pred. or value pred.> {∧ <pred. or value pred.> }

　　　　　　　　　→ <value predicate> {∧ <value predicate> }

<quantification> ::=　{[<quantifier>] [<integer> | <lower roman letter>]

　　　　　　　　　[<relational operator>] <lower roman letter>

　　　　　　　　　[<relational operator>]

　　　　　　　　　[<integer>|<lower roman letter>]}

<pred. or value pred.> ::= <predicate> | <value predicate>

<predicate> ::= <name> (<subj. or iden.> [,<subj. or iden.>])

<subj. or iden.> ::= <subject> | <identifier>

<value predicate> ::= Val (<identifier> , <general data>)

<name> ::= <upper letter> {<lower roman letter>}

<quantifier> ::= ∃ | ∀

<identifier> ::= <identifier name> (<subject>, <subject>)

<identifier name> ::= Row | Col | In | Out | Mem | Term

<subject> ::= <upper letter> [<unsigned integer>]$_{[\text{<index>}]}$

<temporal equation> ::= <general data> = <general data>

<general data> ::=　　<temporal variable> | <temp. var. expr.> |

　　　　　　　　　<temporal constant> | <temporal arith. expr.> |

　　　　　　　　　<temp. temp. expr.> | <temp. temp. arith. expr.>

<temp. temp. arith. expr.> ::=<temp. temp. term> | $\Big($<add. op.>

　　　　　　　　　<temp. temp. term>$\Big) \mid \Big($<temp.

　　　　　　　　　temp. arith. expr.> <add. op.>

　　　　　　　　　<temp. temp. term>$\Big)$

<temp. temp. term> ::=　<temp. temp. factor> |

　　　　　　　　　$\Big($<temp. temp. term> <mul. op.>

　　　　　　　　　<temp. temp. factor>$\Big)$

<temp. temp. factor> ::= <temporal data> | (<temp. temp. expr.>)|

　　　　　　　　　(<temp. temp. arith. expr.>)

<temp. temp. expr.> ::= <normal data> { ∧○$^{[\text{<ind.>}]}$ <normal data>}

　　　　　　　　　∧○$^{[\text{<ind.>}]}$<temporal data>

<temporal data> ::= <temporal factor>

<temporal arith. expr.> ::= <temporal term> |

　　　　　　　　　$\Big($<add. op.> <temporal term>$\Big) \mid$

$$\Big(\text{<temporal arith. expr.>} \ \text{<add. op.>}$$
$$\text{<temporal term>}\Big)$$

<temporal term> ::= <temporal factor> $\Big|\Big($<temporal term>
<mul. op.> <temporal factor>$\Big)$

<temporal factor> ::=<temporal variable> | (<temp. var. expr.>) |
(<temporal constant>) | (<temporal arith.
expr.>)

<temporal variable> ::=<lower roman letter>$_{[\text{<index>}]}$

<temp. var. expr.> ::= $\Big($<normal data> $\{\wedge\bigcirc^{[\text{<ind.>}]}$ <normal data> $\}$
$\wedge\ \bigcirc^{[\text{<ind.>}]}$ [] <normal data>$\Big)$ | $\Big($[]<normal
data>$\Big)$

<temporal constant> ::= $\Big($<normal constant>
$\{\wedge\ \bigcirc^{[\text{<ind.>}]}$ <normal constant> $\}$
$\wedge\ \bigcirc^{[\text{<ind.>}]}$ [] <normal constant>$\Big)$ |
$\Big($[]<normal constant>$\Big)$

<normal data> ::= <normal variable> | <normal constant> |
(<normal arith. expr.>)

<normal arith. expr.> ::= <normal term> | $\Big($<sign> <normal
term>$\Big)$ |
$\Big($<normal arith. expr.> <add op.>
<normal term>$\Big)$

<normal term> ::= <normal factor> |
$\Big($<normal term> <mul. op.> <normal factor>$\Big)$

<normal factor> ::=<normal variable> | <unsigned normal
constant> |
(<normal arith. expr.>)

<normal variable> ::= <lower italic letter>$_{[\text{<index>}]}$

<normal constant> ::= <number> | <unknown>

<unsigned normal constant> ::= <unsigned number> | <unknown>

<index> ::= <ind.> [, <ind.>]

<ind.> ::= $\Big($[{<lower roman letter> | <greek letter>}]
[<number>]$\Big)$ |
$\Big($[<number>] [{<lower roman letter> | <greek
letter>}]$\Big)$ |
<index arith. expr.>

<index arith. expr.> ::= <ind. term> | $\Big($<sign> <ind. term>$\Big)$ |
$\Big($<index arith. expr.> <add op.> <ind.

$$\text{term}>\Big)$$

\<ind. term\> ::= \<ind. factor\> | $\Big($\<ind. term\> \<mul. op.\> \<ind. factor\>$\Big)$

\<ind. factor\> ::= \<lower roman letter\> | \<greek letter\> | \<unsigned number\> | (\<index arith. expr.\>)

\<temporal operator\> ::= $[]$ | $\bigcirc^{[<\text{ind.}>]}$ | ; | *del*

\<add. op.\> ::= + | −

\<mul. op.\> ::= * | / | div | mod

\<arithmetic operator\> ::= + | | * | /

\<logical operator\> ::= − | $\wedge$ | $\vee$ | $\oplus$ | $\rightarrow$

\<relational operator\> ::= = | $\neq$ | > | $\geq$ | < | $\leq$

\<number\> ::= $\Big($\<integer\> [.\<unsigned integer\>]$\Big)$ | \<number\>$^{[<\text{number}>]}$

\<unsigned number\> ::= (\<unsigned integer\> [.\<unsigned integer\>]) | \<unsigned number\>$^{[<\text{number}>]}$

\<integer\> ::= [\<sign\>] \<unsigned integer\>

\<unsigned integer\> ::= \<digit\> {\<digit\>}

\<boolean\> ::= *true* | *false*

\<sign\> ::= \<blank\> | + | −

\<greek letter\> ::= $\alpha|\beta|\gamma|\delta|\varepsilon|\zeta|\eta|\theta|\iota|\varkappa|\lambda|\mu|\perp|x_i|o|\pi|\rho|\sigma|\tau|\upsilon|\phi|\chi|\psi|\omega$

\<upper letter\> ::= A|B|C|D|E|F|G|H|I|J|K|L|M|N|O|P|Q|R|S| T|U|V|W|X|Y|Z

\<lower italic letter\> ::= a|b|c|d|e|f|g|h|i|j|k|l|m|n|o|p|q|r|s|t|u|v|w|x|y|z

\<lower roman letter\> ::= a|b|c|d|e|f|g|h|i|j|k|l|m|n|o|p|q|r|s|t|u|v|w|x|y|z

\<digit\> ::= 0|1|2|3|4|5|6|7|8|9

\<unknown\> ::= _

\<blank\> ::=

Appendix 10.B: A brief presentation of the semantics of STA

A sentence in STA can be mapped to either a truth value, or a real number, or a temporal sequence of real numbers (e.g. temporal variables and constants), depending on the domain and the situation to which it is applied. We can make this statement more precise by stating the existence of cycles $c_1, c_2, \ldots, c_n$ and a meaning function M that maps sentences and cycles to data values in data domain D. For example, if x is a numerical variable,

$$M_{c_i}<x> = 4$$

signifies that the value of x in cycle c_i is 4.

The value of a sentence u on an interval or subinterval $I = c_1, c_2, \ldots, c_n$ is defined as the value of u in the initial cycle of I:

$$M_{c_1, c_2, \ldots, c_n}<u> \equiv {}_{\text{def}} M_{c_1}<u>$$

All sentences used in the reasoning of a systolic array are by default defined over the interval specified for the array.

The semantics of arithmetic operators, relational operators, logical operators, quantifiers, functions, and predicates are well established and defined in conventional mathematics, propositional, and predicate logics for static environments. We shall now extend these semantics for dynamic environments, and very briefly describe them here. Let u and v be sentences, arithmetic operands, or logical operands, etc., in STA.

1. **Logical operations.** The semantics for logical operations on logical operands over an interval are:

$$M_{c1, c2, \ldots, cn} <\text{log\_opl } u> \equiv_{def} \text{log\_opl } M_{c1, c2, \ldots, cn} <u>$$
$$M_{c1, c2, \ldots, cn} <u \text{ log\_op2 } v> \equiv_{def} M_{c1, c2, \ldots, cn} <u> \text{ log\_op2}$$
$$M_{c1, c2, \ldots, cn} <v>$$

where log_opl $= \neg$ and log_op2 $= \wedge, \vee, \oplus,$ or $\rightarrow$. Hence

$$M_{c1, c2, \ldots, cn} <\neg u> \equiv_{def} \neg M_{c1, c2, \ldots, cn} <u>$$
$$M_{c1, c2, \ldots, cn} <u \wedge v> \equiv_{def} M_{c1, c2, \ldots, cn} <u> \wedge M_{c1, c2, \ldots, cn} <v>$$
$$M_{c1, c2, \ldots, cn} <u \rightarrow v> \equiv_{def} M_{c1, c2, \ldots, cn} <u> \rightarrow M_{c1, c2, \ldots, cn} <v>$$

For example,

$$M_{c1, c2, \ldots, cn} <\neg u> = true \text{ iff } M_{c1, c2, \ldots, cn} <u> = false \text{ (i.e. } M_{c_i}<u> = false)$$
$$M_{c1, c2, \ldots, cn} <u \wedge v> = true \text{ iff } M_{c1, c2, \ldots, cn} <u> = M_{c1, c2, \ldots, cn} <v>$$
$$= true$$
$$\text{(i.e. } M_{c_i} <u> = true \wedge M_{c_i} <v> = true)$$

2. **Arithmetic operations.** The semantics for arithmetic operations on arithmetic operands over an interval are:

$$M_{c1, c2, \ldots, cn} <\text{arith\_opl } u> \equiv_{def} \text{arith\_opl } M_{c1, c2, \ldots, cn} <u>$$
$$M_{c1, c2, \ldots, cn} <u \text{ arith\_op2 } v> \equiv_{def} M_{c1, c2, \ldots, cn} <u> \text{ arith\_op2}$$
$$M_{c1, c2, \ldots, cn} <v>$$

where arith_op1 $= +$ or $-$ and arith_op2 $= +, -, *, /,$ div, or mod. Hence

$$M_{c1, c2, \ldots, cn} <u+v> \equiv_{def} M_{c1, c2, \ldots, cn} <u> + M_{c1, c2, \ldots, cn} <v>$$
$$M_{c1, c2, \ldots, cn} <u*v> \equiv_{def} M_{c1, c2, \ldots, cn} <u> * M_{c1, c2, \ldots, cn} <v>$$

For instance,

$$M_{c1, c2, \ldots, cn} <u+v> = 10 \text{ iff } M_{c1, c2, \ldots, cn} <u> + M_{c1, c2, \ldots, cn} <v> = 10$$
$$\text{(i.e. } M_{c_i} <u> + M_{c_i} <v> = 10)$$
$$M_{c_i} <u*v> = 20 \text{ iff } M_{c_i} <u> * M_{c_i} <v> = 20$$

3. **Relational operations.** The semantics for relational operations over an interval are:

$$M_{c1, c2, \ldots, cn} <u \; rel\_op \; v> \equiv_{def} M_{c1, c2, \ldots, cn} <u> \; rel\_op.$$
$$M_{c1, c2, \ldots, cn} <v>$$

Hence

$$M_{c1, c2, \ldots, cn} <u=v> \equiv_{def} (M_{c1, c2, \ldots, cn} <u> = M_{c1, c2, \ldots, cn} <v>)$$
$$M_{c1, c2, \ldots, cn} <u \geqslant v> \equiv_{def} (M_{c1, c2, \ldots, cn} <u> \geqslant M_{c1, c2, \ldots, cn} <v>)$$

4. **Quantifiers.** The semantics of quantifiers over an interval are defined as follows:

$$M_{c1, c2, \ldots, cn} <\forall \; i. \; u> \equiv_{def} M_{c1', \ldots, cn'} <u> \text{ for any } \alpha$$
$$M_{c1, c2, \ldots, cn} <\exists \; i. \; u> \equiv_{def} M_{c1', \ldots, cn'} <u> \text{ for some } \alpha$$

where $c_1', \ldots, c_n' = (c_1, c_2, \ldots, c_n) [i/\alpha]$. Here '/' denotes a substitution, i is a variable and function constant α maps variables to values in data domain.

5. **Predicates.** The meaning of a predicate $p(y_1, y_2, \ldots, y_k)$ given by

$$M<p> \; \varepsilon \; (D^k \rightarrow \{true. \; false\})$$

where '$\rightarrow$' denotes a mapping, can be extended to take into account of dynamic behaviour over time as

$$M_{c1, c2, \ldots, cn} <p(x_1, x_2, \ldots, x_k)> \equiv_{def}$$
$$M <p(M_{c1, c2, \ldots, cn} <x_1> , M_{c1, c2, \ldots, cn} <x_2> , \ldots, M_{c1, c2, \ldots, cn} <x_k>)>$$

Higher level constructs used to capture collective arithmetic operations can be similarly defined based on the above semantics. The semantics for temporal operators in STA are defined below. Unlike temporal logic, temporal operators in STA mainly operate on arithmetic entities instead of logical entities. Their semantics are given as follows:

6. **Temporal operations.** Their semantics are:

$$M_{c1, c2, \ldots, cn} <u> \equiv_{def} M_{c1} <u>$$
$$M_{c1, c2, \ldots, cn} <[] \; u> \equiv_{def} \forall 1 \leqslant i \leqslant n. \; M_{ci} <u>$$
$$M_{c1, c2, \ldots, cn} <\bigcirc u> \equiv_{def} M_{c2} <u> \text{ (provided } n \geqslant 2)$$
$$M_{c1, c2, \ldots, cn} <\bigcirc {}^i u> \equiv_{def} M_{ci+1} <u> \text{ (provided } n \geqslant i + 1)$$

Hence for example

$$M_{c1, c2, \ldots, cn} <\bigcirc (u*v)> = 20 \text{ iff } M_{c2} < u*v> = 20 \text{ (provided } n \geqslant 2)$$
$$M_{c1, c2, \ldots, cn} <[] \; 0> \text{ means } M_{c1}<0> \text{ and } M_{c2}<0> \ldots \text{ and } M_{cn}<0>$$

More explanation of the STA semantics are provided in section 10.3.2. Each STA construct is simply the combination of the operations, quantifications, etc., discussed so far in this section; hence its semantics is simply the combination of one or more of the already defined semantics.

Appendix 10.C: Specification of matrix-matrix multiplication systolic array input to VSTA

```
%%% STA temporal variable operator definitions

%%% temporal variable external representation
%%%   tv:List:L is a temporal variable of length L. List is a list
%%%   of the first L normal variables in the temporal variable
:- op(600, xfy, :).


%%% next operator:
%%%   N o T is a temporal variable obtained by normal vari-
able N and
%%%   temporal variable T
:- op(610, xfy, o).


%%% temporal variable substitution:
%%%   X $ Y is a temporal variable obtained by substitut-
ing the i th
%%%   normal variable of Y for the i th normal variable of X, where
%%%   i is the position of the first unknow normal variable in X.
%%%   That is, the difference between temporal variable X $ Y and
%%%   temporal variable X is only at the i th normal variable.
:- op(615, xfy, $).


%%% temporal variable concatenation:
%%%   X ^ Y is a temporal variable obtained by concatenat-
ing temporal
%%%   variables X and Y
:- op(620, yfx, ^).


%%% temporal variable multiplication:
%%% X ** Y is the temporal product of temporal vari-
ables X and Y
:- op(630, yfx, **).


%%% temporal variable addition:
%%% X ++ Y is the temporal sum of temporal variables X and Y
:- op(640, yfx, ++).


%%% temporal variable assignment:
%%% V := T assigns the temporal variable T a name V
:- op(650, xfx, :=).


%%% bound universal quantifier:
%%% forall 1 ¡= I ¡= N suchthat A
:- op(610, fx, forall).
```

```
:- op(600, yfx, ¡=).
:- op(600, yfx, ¡).
```

%%% implication:
%%% Hyps implies Concl
```
:- op(630, xfx, implies).
```

%%% such that
%%% WFFa suchthat WFFb
```
:- op(620, xfx, suchthat).
```

%%% concatenation
%%% conc Idx-LB-UB-Parm-Term
```
:- op(550, fx, conc).
```


%%% summation
%%% sum Idx-LB-UB-Parm-Term
```
:- op(550, fx, sum).
```

%%% accumulation
%%% acc Idx-LB-UB-Parm-Term
```
:- op(550, fx, acc).
```


%%% Structure Specifications

%%% Specification A1
```
(sa`size(N), forall 1 ¡= I ¡= N, forall 1 ¡= J ¡= N) suchthat
  ip(y:(I, J)).
```

%%% Specification A2
```
(sa`size(N), forall 1 ¡= I ¡= N, forall 1 ¡= J ¡ N) suchthat
  conn(out(o:alpha, y:(I, J)), in(i:alpha, y:(I, J+1))).
```

%%% Specification A3
```
(sa`size(N), forall 1 ¡= J ¡= N, forall 1 ¡= I ¡ N) suchthat
  conn(out(o:beta, y:(I, J)), in(i:beta, y:(I+1, J))).
```


%%% Behavior Specifications

%%% Specification B1
```
( ( sa`size(N),
    forall 1 ¡= I ¡= N,
    forall 1 ¡= J ¡= N) suchthat
  ( ip(y:(I, J)),
    val(in(i:alpha, y:(I, J)), Ain),
    val(in(i:beta, y:(I, J)),  Bin),
    val(mem(m:alpha, y:(I, J)),  Y) ) )
  implies
    val(mem(m:alpha, y:(I, J)), f(Ain, Bin, Y)).
```

%%% Specification B13
```
( ( sa`size(N),
```

nof row(NofR),
forall 1 ¡= I ¡ N,
forall 1 ¡= J ¡ N) suchthat
(ip(y:(I, J)),
  val(in(i:alpha, y:(I, J)), tv:[0]:I-2+J ⌃
                   conc R-1-NofR-I-(a:[I, R]) ⌃
                   tv:[0]:1),
  val(in(i:beta, y:(I, J)), tv:[0]:J-2+I ⌃
                   conc R-1-NofR-J-(b:[R, J]) ⌃
                   tv:[0]:1),
  val(mem(m:alpha, y:(I, J)),
    tv:[0]:I+J-1 ⌃
    conc R-1-NofR-(I+J+R)-(sum M-1-R-(I+J)-
      (a:[I, M] * b:[M, J])) ⌃
    tv:[0]:1)))
implies
  val(mem(m:alpha, y:(I+1, J+1)),
    tv:[0]:(I+1)+(J+1)-1 ⌃
    conc R-1-NofR-((I+1)+(J+1)+R)-(sum M-1-R-((I+1)+(J+1))-
      (a:[I+1, M] * b:[M, J+1])) ⌃
    tv:[0]:1).

%%% Specification B11
((sa·size(N),
  nof row(NofR),
  forall 1 ¡= I ¡ N,
  forall 1 ¡= J ¡= N) suchthat
(ip(y:(I, J)),
  val(in(i:alpha, y:(I, J)), tv:[0]:I-2+J ⌃
                   conc R-1-NofR-I-(a:[I, R]) ⌃
                   tv:[0]:1),
  val(in(i:beta, y:(I, J)), tv:[0]:J-2+I ⌃

                   conc R-1-NofR-J-(b:[R, J]) ⌃
                   tv:[0]:1),
  val(mem(m:alpha, y:(I, J)),
    tv:[0]:I+J-1 ⌃
    conc R-1-NofR-(I+J+R)-(sum M-1-R-(I+J)-
      (a:[I, M] * b:[M, J])) ⌃
    tv:[0]:1)))
implies
  val(mem(m:alpha, y:(I+1, J)),
    tv:[0]:(I+1)+J-1 ⌃
    conc R-1-NofR-((I+1)+J+R)-(sum M-1-R-((I+1)+J)-
      (a:[I+1, M] * b:[M, J])) ⌃
    tv:[0]:1).

%%% Specification B12
((sa·size(N),
  nof row(NofR),
  forall 1 ¡= I ¡= N,
  forall 1 ¡= J ¡ N) suchthat
(ip(y:(I, J)),
  val(in(i:alpha, y:(I, J)), tv:[0]:I-2+J ⌃
                   conc R-1-NofR-I-(a:[I, R]) ⌃
                   tv:[0]:1),
  val(in(i:beta, y:(I, J)), tv:[0]:J-2+I ⌃

```
                        conc R-1-NofR-J-(b:[R, J])  ˙
                        tv:[0]:1 ),
    val(mem(m:alpha, y:(I, J)),
       tv:[0]:I+J-1  ˙
       conc R-1-NofR-(I+J+R)-(sum M-1-R-(I+J)-
          (a:[I, M] * b:[M, J]))  ˙
       tv:[0]:1 ) ) )
  implies
    val(mem(m:alpha, y:(I, J+1)),
       tv:[0]:I+(J+1)-1  ˙
       conc R-1-NofR-(I+(J+1)+R)-(sum M-1-R-(I+(J+1))-
          (a:[I, M] * b:[M, J+1]))  ˙
       tv:[0]:1 ).
```

%%% Specification D1
(sa˙size(N), forall 1 ¡= I ¡= N, forall 1 ¡= J ¡= N) suchthat
  val(in(i:alpha, y:(I, J)), Ain) implies
  val(out(o:alpha, y:(I, J)), 0 o Ain).

%%% Specification D2
(sa˙size(N), forall 1 ¡= I ¡= N, forall 1 ¡= J ¡= N) suchthat
  val(in(i:beta, y:(I, J)), Bin) implies
  val(out(o:beta, y:(I, J)), 0 o Bin).

%%% Specification B2
(conn(X, Y),
  val(X, Xval)) implies
  val(Y, Xval).

%%% Specification C1
(sa˙size(N), nof row(NofR), forall 1 ¡= I ¡= N) suchthat
  val(in(i:alpha, y:(I, 1)), tv:[0]:I-2+1 ˙
                        conc R-1-NofR-I-(a:[I, R]) ˙
                        tv:[0]:1).

%%% Specification C2
(sa˙size(N), nof row(NofR), forall 1 ¡= J ¡= N) suchthat
  val(in(i:beta, y:(1, J)), tv:[0]:J-2+1 ˙
                        conc R-1-NofR-J-(b:[R, J]) ˙
                        tv:[0]:1).

%%% Specification C3
(sa˙size(N), forall 1 ¡= I ¡= N, forall 1 ¡= J ¡= N) suchthat
  val(mem(m:alpha, y:(I, J)), tv:[0]:1).

%%% Specification P11
(sa˙size(N), nof row(NofR), forall 1 ¡= I ¡= N) suchthat
  val(in(i:alpha, y:(I, N)), tv:[0]:I-2+N ˙

  conc R-1-NofR-I-(a:[I, R]) ˙
  tv:[0]:1).

%%% Specification P12
(sa˙size(N), nof row(NofR), forall 1 ¡= J ¡= N) suchthat
  val(in(i:beta, y:(N, J)), tv:[0]:J-2+N ˙
    conc R-1-NofR-J-(b:[R, J]) ˙
    tv:[0]:1).

%%% Specification P1
(sa`size(N), nof`row(NofR),
  forall 1 ¡= I ¡= N, forall 1 ¡= J ¡= N) suchthat
    val(mem(m:alpha, y:(I, J)),
  tv:[0]:I+J-1 ˉ
  conc R-1-(NofR)-(I+J+R)-(sum M-1-R-(I+J)-
    (a:[I, M] * b:[M, J])) ˉ
  tv:[0]:1).

Appendix 10.D: VSTA proof output for matrix-matrix multiplication systolic array

The complete proof output from VSTA is quite lengthy. A highly simplified sample is presented here.

Script started
scusun% sp
SICStus 0.6 #17: Sat Nov 17 00:34:35 PST 1990
Copyright (C) 1987, Swedish Institute of Computer Science.
All rights reserved.
— ?- [sta2].
–consulting /users1/tshih/sta/sta2.pl...ˉ
......
yes
— ?- prove.
****
*** Starting Sub Proof1 ***
****
%%%%%%%%%%%%%%%%
%%% Base Case %%%
%%%%%%%%%%%%%%%%
%%% Try Help predicate:
sa`size(1),nof`row(`177),forall 1¡=`185¡=1
  SUCH THAT
val(in(i:alpha,y:(`185,1)),tv:[0]:`185-2+1ˆconc `233-1-`177-`185-(a:[
`185,`233])ˆtv:[0]:1)

*** Help predicate succeeds
%%%%%%%%%%%%%%%%%%%%
%%% Base Case Done %%%
%%%%%%%%%%%%%%%%%%%%
%%%%%%%%%%%%%%%%%%%%
%%% Induction Step %%%
%%%%%%%%%%%%%%%%%%%%
%%% Try Constrained goal:
sa`size(k+1),nof`row(`674),forall 1¡=`682¡=k+1
  SUCH THAT
val(in(i:alpha,y:(`682,k+1)),tv:[0]:`682-2+(k+1)ˆconc `730-1-`674
-`682-(a:[`682,`730])ˆtv:[0]:1)

%%% Try Conjunction goal:
sa`size(k+1)

nof`row(`674)

forall 1¡=`682¡=k+1

%%% Try Help predicate:
sa˙size(k+1)

*** Help predicate succeeds
%%% Try Conjunction goal:
nof˙row(˙674)

forall 1ᵢ=˙682ᵢ=k+1

%%% Try Help predicate:
nof˙row(4)

*** Help predicate succeeds
%%% Try Help predicate:
forall 1ᵢ=˙682ᵢ=k+1

*** Help predicate succeeds
*** Conjunction goal succeeds
*** Conjunction goal succeeds
%%% Try Value predicate:
val(in(i:alpha,y:(˙682,k+1)),tv:[0]:˙682-2+(k+1)˙conc ˙730-1-4-
˙682-(a:[˙682,˙730])˙tv:[0]:1)
*** Value predicate fails
%%% Try Valid fact:
val(in(i:alpha,y:(˙682,k+1)),tv:[0]:˙682-2+(k+1)˙conc ˙730-1-4-
˙682-(a:[˙682,˙730])˙tv:[0]:1)
......
*** Valid fact fails
%%% Try Unfolding:
val(in(i:alpha,y:(˙682,k+1)),tv:[0]:˙682-2+(k+1)˙conc ˙730-1-4-
˙682-(a:[˙682,˙730])˙tv:[0]:1)

*** Rule:
(sa˙size(˙2733),forall 1ᵢ=˙2744ᵢ=˙2733,forall 1ᵢ=˙2752ᵢ=˙2733)
suchtha t(ip(y:(˙2744,˙2752)),val(in(i:alpha,y:(˙2744,˙2752)),
˙2769),val(in(i:beta,y:(˙2744,˙2752)),˙2787),val(mem(m:alpha,
y:(˙2744,˙2752)),˙2802))
  IMPLIES
val(mem(m:alpha,y:(˙2744,˙2752)),f(˙2769,˙2787,˙2802))
Fire this rule? (yes./no.) no.
......
*** Rule:
conn(˙2730,˙2731),val(˙2730,˙2734)
  IMPLIES
val(˙2731,˙2734)
Fire this rule? (yes./no.) yes.

%%% Try Conjunction goal:
conn(˙2730,in(i:alpha,y:(˙682,k+1)))

val(˙2730,tv:[0]:˙682-2+(k+1)˙conc ˙730-1-4-˙682-(a:[˙682,˙730])
˙tv:[0]:1)
......
*** Unfolding succeeds
*** Constrained goal succeeds
%%%%%%%%%%%%%%%%%%%%%%%%%%%
%%% Induction Step Done %%%

```
%%%%%%%%%%%%%%%%%%%%%%%%%%%%
%%%%%%%%%%%%%%%%
%%% Q.E.D. %%%
%%%%%%%%%%%%%%%%
*****************************
*** Starting Sub Proof2 ***
*****************************
%%%%%%%%%%%%%%%%%%%%
%%% Base Case %%%
%%%%%%%%%%%%%%%%%%%
..........
```

Similarly, P12 is done by mathematical induction
....

```
%%%%%%%%%%%%%%%%%%%%%%%%%%%%
%%% Induction Step Done %%%
%%%%%%%%%%%%%%%%%%%%%%%%%%%%
%%%%%%%%%%%%%%%%
%%% Q.E.D. %%%
%%%%%%%%%%%%%%
*****************************
*** Starting Main Proof ***
*****************************
%%%%%%%%%%%%%%%%%%%%
%%% Base Case %%%
%%%%%%%%%%%%%%%%%%%
%%% Try Constrained goal:
sa˙size(˙11578),nof˙row(˙11583),forall 1ᵢ=1ᵢ=˙11578,forall
1ᵢ=1ᵢ=˙11578
  SUCH THAT
val(mem(m:alpha,y:(1,1)),tv:[0]:1+1-1^conc ˙11650-1-˙11583-
(1+1+˙1165 0)-(sum ˙11670-1-˙11650-(1+1)-(a:[1,˙11670]*b:
[˙11670,1]))^tv:[0]:1)
%%% Try Conjunction goal:
sa˙size(˙11578)
......
*** Constrained goal succeeds
*** Unfolding succeeds
*** Constrained goal succeeds
%%%%%%%%%%%%%%%%%%%%%%
%%% Base Case Done %%%
%%%%%%%%%%%%%%%%%%%%%%%%%%
%%%%%%%%%%%%%%%%%%%%%%%%%%
%%% Induction Step %%%
%%%%%%%%%%%%%%%%%%%%%%%%%%
%%% Try Constrained goal:
sa˙size(˙19683),nof˙row(˙19688),forall 1ᵢ=k+1ᵢ=˙19683,forall
1ᵢ=kᵢ=˙19683
  SUCH THAT
val(mem(m:alpha,y:(k+1,k)),tv:[0]:k+1+k-1^conc ˙19755-1-˙19688
-(k+1+k+˙19755)-(sum              ˙19775-1-˙19755-(k+1+k)-
(a:[k+1,˙19775]*b:
[˙19775,k]))^tv:[0]:1)
......
```

```
*** Constrained goal succeeds
%%%%%%%%%%%%%%%%%%%%%%%%%
%%% Induction Step Done %%%
%%%%%%%%%%%%%%%%%%%%%%%%%%%%
%%%%%%%%%%%%%%%%%%%%%%%%
%%% Induction Step %%%
%%%%%%%%%%%%%%%%%%%%%%
..........
```

The proof fixing another index is done in the same mannar.
....

```
%%%%%%%%%%%%%%%%%%%%%%%%%%
%%% Induction Step Done %%%
%%%%%%%%%%%%%%%%%%%%%%%%%%%%%
%%%%%%%%%%%%%%%%%%%%%%%%%
%%% Induction Step %%%
%%%%%%%%%%%%%%%%%%%%%%%%%
```

....
The proof inducts on both index is done in tha same mannar
....

```
%%%%%%%%%%%%%%%%%%%%%%%%%%%%
%%% Induction Step Done %%%
%%%%%%%%%%%%%%%%%%%%%%%%%%%%%%%
%%%%%%%%%%%%%%%%
%%% Q.E.D. %%%
%%%%%%%%%%%%%%
yes
— ?- halt.
- End of SICStus execution, user time 26.780 "
scusun%
script done
```

Appendix 10.E: Formal specification and verification of LU decomposition systolic array

The matrix to be decomposed (matrix C) is fed into the array from the top. Specification C1 and C2 gives the symbolic temporal value of the input matrix. Matrix C is decomposed into matrix A (the lower matrix) and matrix B (the upper matrix) after $3n-2$ cycles where n is the width (or height) of the input matrix. Matrix A is output from the terminal O_γ of the M cells (specified in specification P1) while matrix B is stored in registers M_β of cell M's and N's (indicated by specification P2 and P3). Specifications A1 and A2 declare type of cells in the array. Specifications A3 to A6 describe the connection between cells. Behaviour specification B1 indicates the temporal value is passed from a terminal to another. Specification B2 says if the input to the cell M_i on terminal port I_β is c_{input}, the register contents M_α, M_β, and M_γ and output terminals O_α and O_γ have their values indicated. Note that $V(M_\alpha)$ represents the content of register α of the cell M_i. Specification B3 is similar to specification B2 excepts cell $N_{i,j}$ is described.

According to the algorithm of LU decomposition, the LU Decomposition Equality Definitions are derived. They are used in the STA verifier as domain specific heuristics. Intermediate axioms T1, T2, and T3 are also given since proving P1, P2, and P3 needs these three axioms. Thus, T1, T2, and T3 are proved first and stored in the axiom database before proof P1, P2, or P3 is proceeded. The specification of LU decomposition systolic array is shown in this section. The next section shows the proof of specification T1, T2, T3, P1, P2, and P3,

Note that the abbreviation

$$\bigwedge_{n=1}^{k} a_n$$

denotes $a_1 \wedge a_2 \wedge a_3 \wedge \ldots \wedge a_k$ which is a sequence consists of k normal variables. The projection operator provides a mapping from the temporal value domain to the normal value domain. For instance, TV $\downarrow_i$ maps a temporal variable TV to its ith normal variable. For simplicity, the next operators 'o' are omitted in the examples.

I. Specification of LU decomposition systolic array

Structure specifications

Specification (A1) $\forall 1 \leq i \leq N$, $Ip_M(M_i)$

Specification (A2) $\forall 1 \leq i \leq N-1$, $\forall i+1 \leq j \leq N$, $Ip_N(N_{i,j})$

Specification (A3) $\forall 1 \leq i \leq N-1$,
$\text{Conn}(\text{Out}(O_\alpha, M_i), \text{In}(I_\alpha, N_{i,i+1}))$

Specification (A4) $\forall 1 \leq i \leq N-2$, $\forall i+1 \leq j \leq N-1$,
$\text{Conn}(\text{Out}(O_\alpha, N_{i,j}), \text{In}(I_\alpha, N_{i,j+1}))$

Specification (A5) $\forall 1 \leq i \leq N-2$, $\forall i+2 \leq j \leq N$,
$\text{Conn}(\text{Out}(O_\beta, N_{i,j}), \text{In}(I_\beta, N_{i+1,j}))$

Specification (A6) $\forall 1 \leq i \leq N-1$,
$\text{Conn}(\text{Out}(O_\beta, N_{i,i+1}), \text{In}(I_\beta, M_{i+1}))$

Behaviour specifications

Specification (B1) $\text{Conn}(X, Y)$, $\text{Val}(X, x) \rightarrow \text{Val}(Y, x)$

Specification (B2)
$\forall 1 \leq i \leq N$, $Ip_M(M_i)$, Val(In(I_β, M_i), c_{input}), $\rightarrow$
Val(Mem(M_β, M_i), $\bigwedge_{r=1}^{3i-2}$ - $\wedge []c_{input} \downarrow_{3i-2}$),
Val(Mem(M_α, M_i), - $\wedge c_{input}$ / V(M_β)),
Val(Mem(M_γ, M_i), - $\wedge c_{input}$ - V(M_α) * V(M_β)),
Val(Out(O_γ, M_i), V(M_α)),
Val(Out(O_α, M_i), V(M_α))

Specification (B3)
$\forall 1 \leq i \leq N\text{-}1$, $\forall i+1 \leq j \leq N$, $Ip_N(N_{i,j})$,
Val(In(I_α, $N_{i,j}$), a_{input}), Val(In(I_β, $N_{i,j}$), c_{input}), $\rightarrow$
Val(Mem(M_β, $N_{i,j}$), $\bigwedge_{r=1}^{2i+j-2}$ - $\wedge []c_{input} \downarrow_{2i+j-2}$),
Val(Mem(M_α, $N_{i,j}$), - $\wedge a_{input}$),
Val(Mem(M_γ, $N_{i,j}$), - $\wedge c_{input}$ - V(M_α) * V(M_β)),
Val(Out(O_α, $N_{i,j}$), V(M_α)),
Val(Out(O_β, $N_{i,j}$), V(M_γ))

Input specifications

Specification (C1) Val(In(I_β, M_1), $\bigwedge_{r=1}^{N} c_{r,1} \wedge []_-$)

Specification (C2) $\forall 2 \leq j \leq N$,
Val(In(I_β, $N_{1,j}$), $\bigwedge_{r=1}^{j-1}$ - $\wedge \bigwedge_{r=1}^{N} c_{r,j} \wedge []_-$)

Output specifications

Specification (P1) $\forall 1 \leq i \leq N$,
Val(Out(O_γ, M_i), $\bigwedge_{r=1}^{3i-2}$ - $\wedge \bigwedge_{r=i}^{N}$ FA(r, i, i) $\wedge []_-$)

Specification (P2) $\forall 1 \leq i \leq N$,
Val(Mem(M_β, M_i), $\bigwedge_{r=1}^{3i-2}$ - $\wedge []$FB(i, i, i))

Specification (P3) $\forall 1 \leq i \leq N\text{-}1$, $\forall i+1 \leq j \leq N$,
Val(Mem(M_β, $N_{i,j}$), $\bigwedge_{r=1}^{2i+j-2}$ - $\wedge []$FB(i, j, i))

LU Decomposition equality definitions

FC(i, j, 0) = $c_{i,j}$

FC(i, j, k) =
FC(i, j, k-1) - FA(i, j, k) * FB(i, j, k) where k > 0

$FB(1, j, 1) = c_{1,j}$
FB(i, j, k) = FC(i, j, k-1) where i = k and i > 1
FB(i, j, k) = FB(i-1, j, k) where i ≠ k and i > 1

FA(i, 1, k) = FC(i, 1, k-1) / FB(i, 1, k)
FA(i, j, k) =
FC(i, j, k-1) / FB(i, j, k) where j = k and j > 1
FA(i, j, k) = FA(i, j-1, k) where j ≠ k and j > 1

Intermediate axioms

Specification (T1) ∀2 $\leq$ i $\leq$ N-1, ∀i+1 $\leq$ j $\leq$ N,
Val(In(I_β, $N_{i,j}$)), $\bigwedge_{r=1}^{2i+j-3}$ - ∧$\bigwedge_{r=i}^{N}$ FC(r, j, i-1) ∧〔_)

Specification (T2) ∀2 $\leq$ i $\leq$ N,
Val(In(I_β, M_i)), $\bigwedge_{r=1}^{3i-3}$ - ∧$\bigwedge_{r=i}^{N}$ FC(r, i, i-1) ∧〔_)

Specification (T3) ∀1 $\leq$ i $\leq$ N-1, ∀i+1 $\leq$ j $\leq$ N,
Val(In(I_α, $N_{i,j}$)), $\bigwedge_{r=1}^{2i+j-3}$ - ∧$\bigwedge_{r=i}^{N}$ FA(r, i, i) ∧〔_)

II. Proofs of LU decomposition systolic array

II.1 Proof T1, T2, T3

Due to the architecture and data flow of the array, T1, T2, and T3 are difficult to prove. To prove T1, one needs to prove T3 first. To prove T2, one needs to prove T1 and T3. And to prove T3, one needs to prove T1 and T2. Since specifications T1, T2, and T3 mutually depend on each other, special heuristics need to be applied to the proof of T1, T2, and T3 to avoid vicious circle. Our solution is to transform specification T1 & T2 & T3 to their semantic identical forms S1 & Sk & Sn.

Axiom (S1) from specification (T3)
∀2 $\leq$ j $\leq$ N,
Val(In(I_α, $N_{1,j}$)), $\bigwedge_{r=1}^{j-1}$ - ∧$\bigwedge_{r=1}^{N}$ FA(r, 1, 1) ∧〔_)

Axiom (Sk) from specification (T1, T2, and T3)
∀2 $\leq$ i $\leq$ N-1, ∀i+1 $\leq$ j $\leq$ N,
Val(In(I_β, $N_{i,j}$)), $\bigwedge_{r=1}^{2i+j-3}$ - ∧$\bigwedge_{r=i}^{N}$ FC(r, j, i-1) ∧〔_) &

$Val(In(I_\beta, M_i), \bigwedge_{r=1}^{3i-3} - \wedge\bigwedge_{r=i}^{N} FC(r, i, i-1) \wedge []_-)$ &
$Val(In(I_\alpha, N_{i,j}), \bigwedge_{r=1}^{2i+j-3} - \wedge\bigwedge_{r=i}^{N} FA(r, i, i) \wedge []_-)$

Axiom (Sn) from specification (T2)
$Val(In(I_\beta, M_N), \bigwedge_{r=1}^{3N-3} - \wedge FC(r, N, N-1) \wedge []_-)$

Axiom S1 is proved by induction on the number of N cells. Based on the proof, corollary S1 is also derived:

Corollary (S1) $\forall 2 \leq j \leq N,$
$Val(Out(O_\beta, N_{1,j}), \bigwedge_{r=1}^{j+1} - \wedge\bigwedge_{r=2}^{N} FC(r, j, 1) \wedge []_-)$

Axiom Sk is proved by reverse induction on the length of rows of the array. The base case and the induction step both invoke another level of simple induction. The output of axiom Sk (corollary Sk) is used to prove axiom Sn which is done by unfolding and rewriting.

Base case: $i = 2 \ \forall 3 \leq j \leq N,$
$Val(In(I_\beta, N_{2,j}), \bigwedge_{r=1}^{j+1} - \wedge\bigwedge_{r=2}^{N} FC(r, j, 1) \wedge []_-)$ &
$Val(In(I_\beta, M_2), \bigwedge_{r=1}^{3} - \wedge\bigwedge_{r=2}^{N} FC(r, 2, 1) \wedge []_-)$ &
$Val(In(I_\alpha, N_{2,j}), \bigwedge_{r=1}^{j+1} - \wedge\bigwedge_{r=2}^{N} FA(r, 2, 2) \wedge []_-)$

let these three value predicates be G1, G2, and G3 in their order respectively,

by (A6), i = 1, $Conn(Out(O_\beta, N_{1,2}), In(I_\beta, M_2))$

(G2) becomes
$Val(Out(O_\beta, N_{1,2}), \bigwedge_{r=1}^{3} - \wedge\bigwedge_{r=2}^{N} FC(r, 2, 1) \wedge []_-)$

by (A5), i = 1, $\forall 3 \leq j \leq N,$
$Conn(Out(O_\beta, N_{1,j}), In(I_\beta, N_{2,j}))$

(G1) becomes
$Val(Out(O_\beta, N_{1,j}), \bigwedge_{r=1}^{j+1} - \wedge\bigwedge_{r=2}^{N} FC(r, j, 1) \wedge []_-)$

combining (G1) and (G2), we have
$\forall 2 \leq j \leq N,$
$Val(Out(O_\beta, N_{1,j}), \bigwedge_{r=1}^{j+1} - \wedge\bigwedge_{r=2}^{N} FC(r, j, 1) \wedge []_-)$

by (Corollary S1), we have [].

To prove G3, we do a mathematical induction on the length of the row. Finally, the base case of proof Sk is done.

Induction step:

Hypothesis: $i = k$, $\forall k+1 \leq j \leq N$,

$\text{Val}(\text{In}(I_\beta, N_{k,j}), \bigwedge_{r=1}^{2k+j-3} - \wedge \bigwedge_{r=k}^{N} \text{FC}(r, j, k-1) \wedge \square_-)$ &

$\text{Val}(\text{In}(I_\beta, M_k), \bigwedge_{r=1}^{3k-3} - \wedge \bigwedge_{r=k}^{N} \text{FC}(r, k, k-1) \wedge \square_-)$ &

$\text{Val}(\text{In}(I_\alpha, N_{k,j}), \bigwedge_{r=1}^{2k+j-3} - \wedge \bigwedge_{r=k}^{N} \text{FA}(r, k, k) \wedge \square_-)$

let these three value predicates be H1, H2, and H3 in their order respectively.

Goal: $i = k+1$, $\forall k+2 \leq j \leq N$,

$\text{Val}(\text{In}(I_\beta, N_{k+1,j}), \bigwedge_{r=1}^{2k+j-1} - \wedge \bigwedge_{r=k+1}^{N} \text{FC}(r, j, k) \wedge \square_-)$
&

$\text{Val}(\text{In}(I_\beta, M_{k+1}), \bigwedge_{r=1}^{3k} - \wedge \bigwedge_{r=k+1}^{N} \text{FC}(r, k+1, k) \wedge \square_-)$
&

$\text{Val}(\text{In}(I_\alpha, N_{k+1,j}), \bigwedge_{r=1}^{2k+j-1} - \wedge \bigwedge_{r=k+1}^{N} \text{FA}(r, k+1, k+1)$
$\wedge \square_-)$

let these three value predicates be G1, G2, and G3 in their order respectively. Using A5, A6, and combining G1 and G2, G1 and G2 are proved similar to the base case discussed, except that A2, H1 and H3 are used. Mathematical induction is used again to prove goal G3. Thus, the induction step of proof Sk is done.

Corollary (Sk)

$\text{Val}(\text{Out}(O_\beta, N_{N-1,N}), \bigwedge_{r=1}^{3N-3} - \wedge \text{FC}(r, N, N-1) \wedge \square_-)$

Finally, axiom Sn is proved by using A6 and corollary Sk. Thus, the proof of S1 & Sk & Sn is complete.

II.2 Proof P1, P2, P3
Proof P1 is done by case analysis.

$\forall 1 \leq i \leq N$,
$\text{Val}(\text{Out}(O_\gamma, M_i), \bigwedge_{r=1}^{3i-2} - \wedge \bigwedge_{r=i}^{N} \text{FA}(r, i, i) \wedge \square_-)$

case 1: $i = 1$
$\text{Val}(\text{Out}(O_\gamma, M_1), \bigwedge_{r=1}^{1} - \wedge \bigwedge_{r=1}^{N} \text{FA}(r, 1, 1) \wedge \square_-)$

by (B2)(4)

$V(M_\alpha)$
$= \bigwedge_{r=1}^{1} - \wedge \bigwedge_{r=1}^{N} \text{FA}(r, 1, 1) \wedge \square_-$
$= - \wedge \bigwedge_{r=1}^{N} \text{FA}(r, 1, 1) \wedge \square_-$
$= - \wedge \text{FA}(1, 1, 1) \wedge \text{FA}(2, 1, 1) \wedge ... \wedge \text{FA}(N, 1, 1) \wedge \square_-$

since

$$V(M_\alpha)$$
$$= {}_- \wedge c_{input} \: / \: V(M_\beta)$$
$$= {}_- \wedge c_{input} \: / \: \bigwedge_{r=1}^{3-2} {}_- \wedge \Box c_{input} \downarrow_{3-2}$$
$$= {}_- \wedge c_{input} \: / \: {}_- \wedge \Box c_{input} \downarrow_1$$
$$= {}_- \wedge (c_{input} \: / \: \Box c_{input} \downarrow_1)$$

by (C1), $c_{input} = \bigwedge_{r=1}^{N} c_{r,1} \wedge \Box_-$

$$V(M_\alpha)$$
$$= {}_- \wedge (\bigwedge_{r=1}^{N} c_{r,1} \wedge \Box_- \: / \: \Box c_{1,1})$$
$$= {}_- \wedge c_{1,1} \: / \: c_{1,1} \wedge c_{2,1} \: / \: c_{1,1} \wedge c_{3,1} \: / \: c_{1,1} \wedge ...$$
$$\wedge c_{N,1} \: / \: c_{1,1} \wedge \Box_-$$
$$\doteq {}_- \wedge FA(1, 1, 1) \wedge FA(2, 1, 1) \wedge ... \wedge FA(N, 1, 1) \wedge \Box_-$$

the new goal becomes

$$Ip_M(M_1), \: Val(In(I_\beta, M_1), \bigwedge_{r=1}^{N} c_{r,1} \wedge \Box_-)$$

by (A1) $Val(In(I_\beta, M_1), \bigwedge_{r=1}^{N} c_{r,1} \wedge \Box_-)$

by (C1), we have $\Box$

case 2: $\forall 2 \leq i \leq N$,
$$Val(Out(O_\gamma, M_i), \bigwedge_{r=1}^{3i-2} {}_- \wedge \bigwedge_{r=i}^{N} FA(r, i, i) \wedge \Box_-)$$

by (B2)(4) $V(M_\alpha) = \bigwedge_{r=1}^{3i-2} {}_- \wedge \bigwedge_{r=i}^{N} FA(r, i, i) \wedge \Box_-$

since

$$V(M_\alpha)$$
$$= {}_- \wedge c_{input} \: / \: V(M_\beta)$$
$$= {}_- \wedge c_{input} \: / \: \bigwedge_{r=1}^{3i-2} {}_- \wedge \Box c_{input} \downarrow_{3i-2}$$

by (T2), $c_{input} = \bigwedge_{r=1}^{3i-3} {}_- \wedge \bigwedge_{r=i}^{N} FC(r, i, i-1) \wedge \Box_-$

$$V(M_\alpha)$$
$$= \bigwedge_{r=1}^{3i-2} {}_- \wedge \bigwedge_{r=i}^{N} FC(r, i, i-1) \wedge \Box_- \: /$$
$$\bigwedge_{r=1}^{3i-2} {}_- \wedge \Box c_{input} \downarrow_{3i-2}$$
$$= \bigwedge_{r=1}^{3i-2} {}_- \wedge \bigwedge_{r=i}^{N} (FC(r, i, i-1)/FC(i, i, i-1)) \wedge \Box_-$$
$$\doteq \bigwedge_{r=1}^{3i-2} {}_- \wedge \bigwedge_{r=i}^{N} FA(r, i, i) \wedge \Box_-$$

so,

$$\bigwedge_{r=i}^{N} FA(r, i, i) \doteq \bigwedge_{r=i}^{N} (FC(r, i, i-1)/FC(i, i, i-1))$$

by LU Decomposition Equality Definitions,

$FA(r, i, i) = FC(r, i, i\text{-}1) \; / \; FB(r, i, i)$
$= FC(r, i, i\text{-}1) \; / \; FC(i, i, i\text{-}1)$

the new goal becomes

$Ip_M(M_i),$
$Val(In(I_\beta, M_i), \bigwedge_{r=1}^{3i-3} - \wedge\bigwedge_{r=i}^{N} FC(r, i, i\text{-}1) \wedge [\!]_-),$

by (A1),

$Val(In(I_\beta, M_i), \bigwedge_{r=1}^{3i-3} - \wedge\bigwedge_{r=i}^{N} FC(r, i, i\text{-}1) \wedge [\!]_-),$

by (T2), we have $[\!]$

Q.E.D.

Proof P2 and Proof P3 are also proved by case analysis which are similar to proof P1.

References

Abadi, M., and Manna, Z., 1986, A timely resolution, Report No. STAN-CS–86–1106, Stanford University, April.

Barrow, H. G., 1984, VERIFY: A program for proving correctness of digital hardware design, *Art. Intell.*, **24**, 437–91.

Bosco, P. G., Cecchi, C., and Moiso, C., 1988, Exploiting the full power of logic plus functional programming, *Proc. of the 5th Int. Logic Programming Conf.*, August.

Bu, J., Deprettere, E. F., and Thiele, L., 1990, Systolic array implementation of nested loop programs, *Proc. of the Int. Conf. on Application Specific Arrays Processors*, Princeton, New Jersey, Sept.

Camurati, P., and Prinetto, P., 1988, Formal verification of hardware correctness: introduction and survey of current research, *IEEE Computer Magazine*, July.

Cappello, P. R., and Steiglitz, K., 1983, Unifying VLSI array design with geometric tranformations, *Proc. of the 1983 Int. Conf. on Parallel Processing*, Aug.

Cappello, P. R., and Steiglitz, K., 1984, Unifying VLSI array design with linear transformations of space-time, *Advances in Computing Research*, **2**.

Chen, M. C., 1983, Space-time algorithms: semantics and methodology, PhD thesis, California Institute of Technology, Pasadena, CA, May.

Chen, M. C., and Mead, C. A., 1982, Concurrent algorithms as space-time recursion equations, *USC Workshop on VLSI and Modern Signal Processing*.

Clauss, P., Mongenet, C., and Perrin, G. R., 1990, Calculus of space-optimal mappings of systolic algorithms on processor arrays, *Proc. of the Int. Conf. on Application Specific Array Processors*, Princeton, New Jersey, Sept.

Clocksin, W. F., 1987, Logic programming and digital circuit analysis, *J. of Logic Programming*, **4**, 59–82.

A D&T Roundtable, 1989, Formal verification: is it practical for real-world design? *IEEE Design & Test of Computers*, Dec.

Eveking, H., 1985, The application of CHDLs to the abstract specification of hardware, *CHDL '85: IFIP 7th Int. Conf. on Comp. Hardware Description Lang. and their Applications*, Aug.

Foster, M. J., 1981, Syntax directed verification of circuit functions, *VLSI Systems and Computations* (eds H. T. Kung, B. Sproull, and G. Steele), Computer Science Press, Rockville, MD.

Fujita, M., Tanaka, H., and Moto-Oka, T., 1983, Verification with Prolog and temporal logic, *CHDL '83: IFIP 6th Int. Symp. on Comp. Hardware Description Lang. and their Applications*, May.

German, S. M., and Wang, Y., 1985, Formal verification of parameterized hardware designs, *Proc. of Int. Conf. on Computer Design*, 549–52.

Gordon, M., 1986, Why higher-order logic is a good formalism for specifying and verifying hardware, in *Formal Aspects of VLSI Design* (eds G. Milne and P. A. Subrahmanyan), Amsterdam, The Netherlands: North Holland, 153–77.

Hailpern, B. T., 1980, Verifying concurrent processes using temporal logic, Tech. Report. No. 195, Stanford University, April.

Hennessey, M., 1986, Proving systolic system correct, *ACM Trans. on Prog. Lang. and Syst.*, July.

Hunt, W. A., 1987, The mechanical verification of a microprocessor design, in *From HDL Descriptions to Guaranteed Correct Designs* (ed. D. Borrione), Amsterdam, The Netherlands: North Holland, 89–129.

IEEE, 1990, CAS workshop on future directions of circuits, systems, and signal processing: computer-aided design, *IEEE Circuits and Systems Society Newsletter*, **1**(3), 12–14, Sept.

Johnsson, L., and Cohen, D., 1981, A mathematical approach to modelling the flow of data and control in computational networks, in *VLSI Systems and Computations* (eds H. T. Kung *et al.*), Computer Science Press, Inc., 213–25.

Jover, J. M., and Kailath, T., 1984, Design framework for systolic-type arrays, *Proc. of the 1984 IEEE Int. Conf. on Acoustics, Speech, and Signal Processing*, San Diego, Mar.

Jover, J. M., Kailath, T., Lev-Ari, H., and Rao, S. K., 1986, On the analysis of synchronous computing arrays, *1986 IEEE Workshop on VLSI Signal Processing II*, IEEE Press.

Kung, H. T., and Leiserson, C. E., 1978, Systolic arrays (for VLSI), *Sparse Matrix Symp.*, SIAM.

Kung, H. T., 1982, Why systolic architectures? *IEEE Computer Magazine*, Jan.

Kung, H. T., and Lin, W. T., An algebra for VLSI algorithm design, *Proc. of the Conf. on Elliptic Problem Solvers*, Monterey, CA, Jan.

Kung, S. Y., 1985, VLSI Array Processors, *IEEE ASSP Mag.*, July.

Kung, S. Y., 1988, *VLSI Array Processors*, Prentice-Hall, Englewood Cliffs, New Jersey.

Kuo, C. J., Levy, B. C., and Musicus, B. R., 1984, The specification and verification of systolic wave algorithms, *1984 IEEE Workshop on VLSI Signal Processing I*, IEEE Press.

Lev-Ari, H., 1983, Modular computing networks: a new methodology for analysis and design of parallel algorithms/architectures, *Integrated Systems Inc.*, Report No. 29, Palo Alto, CA, Dec.

Ling, N., 1989, Systolic temporal arithmetic: a new formalism for specification, verification, and synthesis of systolic arrays, PhD dissertation, University of Southwestern Louisiana, Summer.

Ling, N., and Bayoumi, M. A., 1989, Systematic algorithm mapping for multi-dimensional systolic arrays, *Journal of Parallel and Distributed Computing*, 7(2), 368–82, Oct.

Ling, N., and Bayoumi, M. A., 1990, Systolic temporal arithmetic: a new formalism for specification and verification of systolic arrays, *IEEE Trans. on Computer-Aided Design*, 9(8), 804–20, August.

Ling, N., Lin, F., Shih, T. and Davis, R., 1991, Automatic formal verification of systolic array designs, *Proc. of the Int. Conf. on Applications-Specific Array Processors*, Costa Brava, Spain, Sept. 2–4.

Marcotty, M., and Ledgard, H. F., 1986, *Programming Language Landscape*, Science Research Associates, Inc.

Maruyama, F., and Fujita, M., 1985, Hardware verification, *IEEE Computer Mag.*, 22–32, Feb.

Melhem, R. G., and Rheinboldt, W. C., 1984, A mathematical model for the verification of systolic networks, *SIAM J. of Comput.*, 13(3), Aug.

Melham, T. F., 1988, Abstraction mechanisms for hardware verification, *VLSI Specification, Verification and Synthesis* (eds G. M. Birtwistle and P. A. Subrahmanyan), Kluwer Academic Publishers.

Milner, R., 1980, A calculus of communicating systems, *Lecture Notes in Computer Science*, **92**, Springer-Verlag, New York.

Milner, R., 1983, Calculi for synchrony and asynchrony, *Theor. Comput. Sci.*, **25**.

Moldovan, D. I., 1983, On the design of algorithms for VLSI systolic arrays, *Proc. of the IEEE,* **71**(1), Jan.

Moldovan, D. I., 1984, ADVIS: a software package for the design of systolic arrays, *Proc. of the IEEE Int. Conf. on Computer Design.*

Moreno, J. H., and Lang, T., 1990, A graph-based approach to map matrix algorithms onto local-access processor arrays, *Proc. of the Int. Conf. on Application Specific Array Processors*, Princeton, NJ, Sept.

Moszkowski, B., 1985, A temporal logic for multilevel reasoning about hardware, *IEEE Computer Mag.*, Feb.

Ossefort, M., 1982, Correctness proofs of communicating processes – three illustrative examples from the literature, TR-LCS–8201, Dept. of Computer Science, University of Texas, Austin, TX, Jan.

Probst, D. K., and Li, H. F., Abstract specification of synchronous data types for VLSI and proving the correctness of systolic network implementations, *IEEE Trans, on Computers*, **37**(6), June.

Purushothaman, S., and Subrahmanyan, P. A., 1989, Mechanical certification of systolic algorithms, *J. of Automated Reasoning*, Mar.

Quinton, P., 1984, Automatic synthesis of systolic arrays from uniform recurrent equations, *Proc. of the 11th Annual Symp. on Computer Architecture.*

Rajopadhye, S. V., and Panangaden, P., 1985, Verification of systolic arrays: a stream functional approach, UUCS–85–001, University of Utah, Salt Lake City, UT, Mar.

Rao, S. K., 1985, *Regular iterative algorithms and their implementation on processor arrays,* PhD dissertation, Stanford University, Stanford, CA.

Shostak, R. E., 1983, Verification of VLSI Designs, in *Proc. of Third Caltech Conf. on VLSI*, 185–206.

Sistla, A. P., 1983, *Theoretical issues in the design and verification of distributed systems*, PhD dissertation, Harvard University, Cambridge, MA, 1983.

Tiden, E., 1984, Verification of systolic arrays – a case study, *Technical Report TRITA-NA–8403,* Dept. of Numerical Analysis and Computer Science, The Royal Institute of Technology (Sweden).

Wilson, P., 1983, Occam architecture cases system design, *Computer Design*, Nov.

Epilogue

What lies in the future for systolic design? It is now clear that the systolic design is an established paradigm and that the days of *ad hoc* design are numbered. However it is somewhat disconcerting to find that a great many designers still persist with the 'seat-of-the-pants' method. In the past this could be understood, if not readily justified, by the weakness of the available synthesis techniques and the lack of awareness of them by the research community. Today such excuses are no longer valid, usable CAD tools based on a well defined mathematical theory of design are emerging. It can be expected that the widespread use of systolic design techniques will be prompted by the increasing availability of these tools. Designers will no longer require an intimate knowledge of the synthesis procedure in order to proceed with a design exercise. Indeed we can expect that *ad hoc* designers will find it increasingly difficult to compete with designers using CAD tools – this will be especially true at the leading edge of the subject where multi-phase and composite algorithms are of significant interest and new synthesis methods are likely to emerge as a result of the more comprehensive testing made possible by automatic generation methods.

The current state of systolic CAD tools is similar to that of geometric modelling tools only a few years ago. In particular an observation by David Hilbert (Hilbert and Cohn-Vossen, 1952) seems quite appropriate here

> On the one hand, the tendency toward abstraction seeks to crystallize the logical relations inherent in the maze of material that is being studied, and to correlate the material in a systematic and orderly manner. On the other hand, the tendency toward intuitive understanding fosters a more immediate grasp of objects one studies, a live rapport with them, so to speak, which stresses the concrete meaning of their relations.

In the current context design objects are domain polytopes and data dependency graphs and the goal of systolic synthesis is to crystallize and unify the different *ad hoc* designs into a mathematical framework. At the same time one cannot deny the natural affinity of humankind for intuitive understanding of geometric forms. Indeed it is the exploitation of this fact that makes synthesis techniques attractive. The above remark is particularly pertinent when one considers the constantly improving performance of modern workstations and their capabilities for improving visualization of algorithm structures using geometric forms.

Although synthesis techniques have come a long way in the last decade there is still some way to go. Researchers are actively pursuing the extension of synthesis methods to more general data flow dependencies as well as the synthesis of control flow signals. Nonlinear scheduling and allocation function are also a subject of active development. It is interesting to view current techniques as forming the first principles of an engineering design methodology. Perhaps the future will see the development of robust and reliable algorithm engineering techniques based on building blocks or parameterized domains constructed using current synthesis methods and 'glued' together with higher level methodologies. The provision of these additional techniques together with a powerful visualization mechanism in the form of a design environment is a significant and worthwhile endeavour.

Reference

Hilbert, D., and Cohn-Vossen, S., 1952, *Geometry and the Imagination*, Chelsea, New York.

Index

abstract processor array 136
Aitken's method 220
algebraic path problem 179
algebraic transformations 78
algorithm level 243
algorithmic engineering 205
allocation matrix (assignment) 3,
    138, 209, 229
anti-delay 81
application specific 242
array
– compiler 134
– level 243
– realization 141
– VLSI 145
atomic operations 193
axioms 248

band matrix *see* matrix 191
bi-directional array 268
bit-level
– design 143
– DG 138
– implementation 84
– multiplication 227
blocks 143
– building 162, 172
– matching 174
Boyer-Moore 245
broadcast 137, 163
buffering 121, 144

CAD tool 161, 205, 238, 242
CCS 245
cellular automata (CA) 34, 101

– 1-way 48
– 2-way 51
– simulation of 51
– structural 160
chains 83
channels 115
clock 99
– local 100
– skew 77
closed curves *see* retiming
closed form expression 31
clustering theorem 87
code generation 212
commutation 190
component type specification 251
computation diagram *see*
    network 38
conditional statements 206
constraint
– equations 9, 19, 205
– linear 55
– symmetric 27
constrained scheduling 57
contour 86
control bits 24, 206
convolution 142, 146, 174, 268
cut set 86
cylindrical wrapping 64

DAG *see* also graph 53
data
– conflict 24
– distribution 9
– streams 138
de-convolution 5

delays
– constant 100
– constraints on 122
– duality of 83
– edges 136
– global, local 140
– non-unit 121
– unit hypothesis 100
dependence graph (DG) 133, 206
– generation of 136
– local 135
– n-dimensional 161
dependencies 2, 207
– functional 120
– run-time 208
– violation of 57
dependency method 3
design environments 205
design methodology 10
digital signal processing (DSP) 242
discrete Fourier transform 5
discrete time 99

EDIF-200 161
end 102
enumeration procedure 25
– in polynomial time 26
envelope 108, 111

feedback 14
fence symbol 37
filter
– FIR 5
– recursive 90
finite-state machine 35
fixing the level 187
flow function 182
formal tools 118, 244
fundamental assumption 18

Gauss-Jordan elimination 146
generalised trail 94
geometric (or layout) level 243
granularity 141

graph
– acyclic 34
– algorithms 14, 26, 58, 72
– directed 35
graphical method 86
guarded command 181

heterogenous arrays 77
hexagonally shaped 70, 79
homogenous arrays 77
hyperplanes 206

immersion 102
increasing independence 191
index expression 207
indexed variable 207
indexing function 4
induction
– double
– regular
– reverse 258
– structured
infix combinators 81
initiation function 40
integer programming problem 3
isomorphic 39
iterative computation 7

kernel 211

labelling function 37
lag function 42
language parser 211
latency 160
length 102
linear function 182
linear programming 208
LISP 173
longest path 54, 59, 72
loop elimination 189
lower dimensional arrays 23
LSGP, LPGS 143
LU-decomposition 58, 146, 267

machine independent 54
mapping 31, 135
matrix
– banded 152
– computation 47
– inversion 6
– multiplication 2, 6, 13, 54, 77,
    93, 146, 174, 250
– vector 146
maximum parallelism 54
meshes cylindrically connected 70
metric space topology 99
modules 115, 243

netlists 161, 172
networks
– algorithm 34
– computation 38
– equivalence 39
– implementation 41
– neural 101
– simulation 46
– specification 117
non-stationary data 230
normal
– constant 246
– variable 246
NP-complete (scheduling) 57
null space 208

objective function 11, 205
odd-even transposition see sorting
operator abstraction 246
optimal
– array 133
– criteria 144
– design 26
– parallelism 180
– time 185, 230
optimization 9, 11, 55, 147

parameter
– general 15
– method 4, 7

parametric design 29
parameterized expression 79
partitioning 31, 143, 212
pattern function 182
performance objective see
    optimization
Petri nets 144
pipelining 17, 77, 208, 243
– two-level 142
place function 181
polynomial multiplication 5
polytope (convex) 207
pragmas 212
prediction element 86
prefix combinators 81
processor
– availability 140
– location 55
processor time
– lower bound 59
– minimal (scheduling) 57
– upper bound 61
projection
– (allocation, assignment) 185
– multi- 140
– optimal 169
pyramid 182

rational approximation 112
rays 208
recurrence
– equation 2
– feedback 14
– n-dimensional 15
– non-linear 206
– non-uniform 4
– uniform 2, 53, 138, 206
relational composition 78, 83
replication 18
retiming 82, 101
– approximation of 114
– clocks 99
– computable 109
– lemma 42

– linear 99, 105
– relations 103, 129
– theorems 84
– topology of 109
routing 208
rules 248

sampling predicates 127
scaling 187
schedule 138
– linear 139
– vector 3
search space 11, 182, 191, 209, 236
semantic
– adaptation 180
– filtering 212
semi-systolic 43
shared variable 192
shift invariant 136
signal flow graph 136
signal processing algorithms 160
silicon compiler 133, 155
simulation tools 146, 151
single assignment 135
single valued function 2
sinks (sources) 115
skew (de-skew) 84
slowdown 88
sorting 35
space-time diagram 35, 135
spacing *see* data distribution
span factor 183
spatial distribution 181, 243
special purpose computers 133
start 102
(non-) stationary data 230
step function 181
– feature extraction 246
– temporal arithmetic 244
stream transformer 121
structural connectivity specification
    251
subscript access function 4
symbolic simulation 263

synchronization 118
– maps 100
synchronous
– concurrent algorithm 99, 122,
    123, 124
syntactic adaptation 180
synthesis 163
systematic enumeration 11
systolic
– conversion 42
– modelling system 206
– theorem 44

target description 181
temporal
– distribution 181
– localization 136, 243
– variable 247
throughput 87, 161
time less circuits 82
time-minimal schedule 53
time step 55
timing function 224
topological 82
– equivalence 35
– transformation 34
transitive closure 135, 146
trellis network 47
triangular shaped array 79, 267
tuple 78
tuple comparison 6

unidirectional
– array 35
– dataflow 238
unrolling 35
user-programmable gate array 157

value
– abstraction 246
– functions 119
– predicate 248
velocity 9
verification 180, 242, 244

– by difference equations 261
– by induction 256
– by symbolic simulation 255
– in prolog 262
vertices 208
VHDL 242

VLSI 161, 242
Von-Neumann 1

wavefront array 133
wrap-around 69